W9-BRY-158

A HISTORY OF THE
ARABIAN PENINSULA

Fahd Abdullah al-Semmari is the Editor-in-Chief of the literary periodical *Al Darah Quarterly*, and Secretary-General of the King Abdul Aziz Foundation. He has a PhD in Modern History from the University of California

Salma K. Jayyusi received her PhD from the University of London (SOAS), and has published several books of her own writing, as well as introducing numerous Arab writers to the English-speaking world for the first time. In 2005 she was awarded the Edward Said Award for Arab American literature. Her previous publications include *Beyond the Dunes: An Anthology of Modern Saudi Literature* (I.B.Tauris).

A HISTORY OF THE ARABIAN PENINSULA

EDITED BY

Fahd al-Semmari

TRANSLATED BY

Salma K. Jayyusi

In association with the

KING ABDUL AZIZ FOUNDATION

Published in 2010 by I.B.Tauris & Co. Ltd, in association with
the King Abdul Aziz Foundation for Research and Archives

6 Salem Road, London W2 4BU
175 Fifth Avenue, New York NY 10010
www.ibtauris.com

Distributed in the United States and Canada Exclusively by Palgrave Macmillan
175 Fifth Avenue, New York NY 10010

ISBN: 978 1 84511 688 0

A full CIP record for this book is available from the British Library

Typeset in Times by Ellipsis Books Limited, Glasgow
Printed and bound in Great Britain by
CPI Antony Rowe, Chippenham, Wiltshire

Contents

Preface

Fahd al-Semmari

Studies of Arabian peninsula history have proliferated greatly over the last two decades. This growth reflects the increased interest in this part of the world from researchers and centres of academic and policy studies.

The Arabian peninsula was the cradle of many civilizations, and is the heartland of all Muslims throughout the world. Many studies and books have already been published on this theme, and Arabia continues to command the attention of academia.

But because of the language in which they are written, many sources for Arabian history are not yet generally available: most Arabic sources are still a closed book for researchers in the East and the West. For this reason, the King Abdul Aziz Foundation (Darat Almalik Abdulaziz) created this project for translating selected studies, published in Arabic, into English, thus expanding readers' horizons, to the benefit of the subject.

This book is a collection of selected articles and research studies on several aspects of Arabian peninsula history, originally published in Arabic in *Al Darah* Quarterly. They have been translated into English by Professor Salma Jayyusi. The articles are based mostly on unpublished and published materials in Arabic, largely local manuscripts, documents and books. They explore subjects such as the origins of Saudi history, industry in Arabia during the Umayyad period, the migrations of Banū Hanifa, Najd during the sixteenth, seventeenth and eighteenth centuries, the reform movement of Sheikh Muḥammad ibn ʿAbd al-Wahhāb, the town of Ad-Dirʿīyah, King Abdul Aziz, Arab travellers' accounts, Riyadh city architecture and Soviet diplomacy in Arabia in the 1920s. They thus cover a variety of fields such as the economy, literature, religion, travel accounts, politics, society and architecture.

The purpose of preparing this book is to make available, in the English language, several Arabic studies based on local and Arabic sources to those researchers whose interest is Arabian history. This, we hope, will provide new perspectives and new findings for the history of the Arabian peninsula and generate more studies and analyses of its many aspects to enrich future scholarship.

Chapter 1

Migrations of the Banū Ḥanīfa To Other Islamic Regions During the Umayyad Period

ʿAbd Allāh Ibrāhīm al-ʿAskar

1.1. *Introduction*

Any study of this subject faces many difficulties, and in particular a scarcity of contemporary sources. The few sources available do not deal fully with Yamama and the inhabitants of Banū Ḥanīfa. Yamama's towns and villages are still covered with sand; little of their remains can be seen, which may at least help to explain its more obscure historical mysteries. No serious excavations have as yet been carried out, other than some in the Kharj area. These revealed the presence of three architectural periods, with no connection between them, as each represents an independent period of settlement, ending around the end of the fifth/eleventh century.[1] This is all the more difficult to believe given the historical information that describes the thriving economic life in the Yamama area up to the middle of the eighth/fourteenth century.[2]

Bearing these circumstances in mind, I have relied completely on the historical and literary sources, collecting and organizing scattered data to extract a picture of the waves of migration of the Banū Ḥanīfa into various Islamic territories during the Umayyad period. Despite these efforts, many points remain unclear, so I have tried to explain them by referring to the available information about other territories, clans and tribes, especially those of Bakr ibn Wāʾil, Rabīʿa, or neighbouring tribes unrelated by lineage to Banū Ḥanīfa, such as Bāhila or Banū Numayr. Still, whatever is written about the subject will remain inadequate, because the sources are scarce, incomplete, and often ambiguous and contradictory.

By way of introduction to the subject I deal briefly with the most ancient Arab migrations and then offer a quick overview of pre-Islamic Arab migrations. Then follows a simplified description of Arab migrations in the Islamic era, which constitutes the first part of this chapter. The second part deals with the Banū Ḥanīfa in the early period of Islam, and then examines the conditions of tribes in the Umayyad period in relation to their locations. The third part deals with the reasons for the tribe's migration to various other Islamic regions or cities (*amṣār*) along with a historical analysis; the fourth traces these migrations from a historical–geographical perspective, discussing migrations to Basra and Kufa in Iraq, to the Islamic East, to Syrian territories, and finally to Egypt, North Africa and al-Andalus (Islamic Spain).

Perhaps the earliest record of our subject in history outside the Arabian peninsula is of Banū Ḥanīfa's migration to Babylon.[3] The Babylonians (sometimes referred to as Akkadians), the Chaldeans and the Assyrians would migrate to Mesopotamia in periods of dearth.[4] The Semites settled in Iraq after expelling the Sumerians from that region and inheriting their civilization. The Babylonians were the first descendants of the Semites. With the Egyptians, they share the honour of laying the foundations of the cultural heritage of the Middle East.

The earliest Arab migration to Egypt goes back to the end of the pre-dynastic age – about 3500 BCE.[5] Pharaonic Egypt used the name 'Amo' or 'Shaso' to describe the Arabs from the peninsula.[6] According to one modern historian, these migrations led to the formation of relations between the two parties on both military and economic levels. The migrants also carried their gods and languages with them to Egypt. Proof of this relationship can be seen in the later Ptolemaic age, which was almost contemporaneous with the early Arabian states and the city-states that flourished in the north and south of the Arabian peninsula. The aspects of that connection were nearly parallel with various cultural aspects, as both parties were especially interested in trade, sea and land transport.[7]

1.2. *Arab Migrations before Islam*

There is no need to point out that the last Arab migration from the peninsula to the Syrian territories and Egypt before Islam involved some branches of the Khuzāʿa tribe.[8] There are references in western sources to the effect that, before Islam, a number of Arabs lived in Alexandria. The historian Sharp states that Arabs formed an important part of the army of the Sasanian Khusraw II Parvī, which conquered Egypt in 618 or 619.[9] In his *Conquest of Egypt*, Ibn ʿAbd al-Ḥakam states that ʿAmr ibn al-ʿĀṣ had help from peninsular Arabs living in Alexandria when he invaded Egypt. Those Arabs could speak Coptic as well. He adds that a number of Arabs were among the Roman soldiers during the Muslim siege of the fortress of Babylon.[10] Al-Maqrīzī speaks extensively of the peninsular Arab migration to Egypt, quoting al-Masʿūdī, who believed that large numbers of Arabs migrated to Egypt before Islam. The same observation was made by Butler, but requires further verification before being accepted.[11]

1.3. *Arab Migrations after Islam*

No social issues were more closely related to the Muslim conquests than Arab migration and Arab genealogy. This triangle forms an accumulation of closely interrelated data. None of these three areas can be studied without knowledge of the others. In the light of modern scholarship, it is no longer possible to ignore the importance of Arab migrations to the conquered regions, whether in number or in influence. That importance stems also from their influence on the direction of the conquests themselves, and from Arab tribal conflicts, which, in turn, led to the emergence of Arab genealogy as we know it today.

In his discussions of Arab migration, P. K. Zhuze says that Islam is not merely a religious idea, but an economic, social and political system that allows its followers to move about in the conquered areas.[12] I might add that the migrations and conquests led to an interest in genealogy, and to changes in tribal alliances from those based on genealogy to new ones based on religious, economic or social circumstances. Philip Hitti believed that the Arab migrations that accompanied the conquests were the greatest event in Islamic history. He pointed out that Arab historians did not ignore the economic aspect in their study of the conquests. The same theory is held by Caetani and Baker. In Abū Tammām's *Ḥamāsa* we find a line of poetry which supports those theories:[13]

> It was not in search of paradise that you migrated, but rather, I think, you were summoned by bread and dates.

We take a rather neutral stand on this matter, and stress that religion was the main force that sent the Arabs to explore new areas outside their original homeland. We consider that Arab migration in the form of invading armies was the motive for these successive migrations over many long years, whether from the arid desert or from agricultural and mining settlements to the neighbouring fertile crescent, to the Syrian or Nile regions, and others mentioned above.[14]

We must also note that some Islamic conquests took on the characteristics of migrations, and that the Arab soldiers in the Muslim army were known as 'migrants' (*muhājirūn*).[15] One may also think that the Arabs would not have undertaken those extensive migrations were it not for the advent of Islam. At the same time, it was Islam that provided the Arabs, especially those living under unfavourable conditions as a result of the political, economic and social situation, with a chance to prosper through migration and fighting for the cause of God, and consequently improving their living conditions.[16]

The study of tribes, their genealogies and their alliances, their places of living and migration, and their contributions to various fields of civilization, is a purely Arab discipline, and it developed both before Islam and after, along with other Arab-Islamic disciplines, as a result of its close relation with religious studies, which attracted much interest at the time. The relationship between Arab migrations and genealogy retains its social and economic significance when one considers any matter related to the Islamic conquests. In order to discuss the migration of Banū Ḥanīfa beyond their homelands to other regions, inside or outside the peninsula, it is necessary to review their political history, and also their economic and social history, in the Islamic age.

2.1. *The Banū Ḥanīfa in the Early Islamic Age*

It seems that the history of Banū Ḥanīfa before Islam was closely related to the history of the mother tribe of Rabīʿa, not only in Yamama but wherever Rabīʿa subdivisions were found before they migrated from Tihama to Yamama and Najd. Banū Ḥanīfa's relations with all subdivisions of Rabīʿa were strengthened after the battle of Qadda,[17] as Banū Ḥanīfa provided the necessary military and economic support for their success in that battle. Banū Ḥanīfa continued to seek the support of some of Rabīʿa's subdivisions as required, and assumed the name of Rabīʿa, especially when they were obliged to hide their real tribal identity during the Rāshidī and Umayyad periods. After the battle of Qadda, the Taghlib became hostile towards Banū Ḥanīfa, an attitude that persisted to later in the early Islamic period.[18] Yet Banū Ḥanīfa, in their long history before Islam, had kept out of the tribal disputes which were customary among the Arab tribes of the peninsula, especially the Bedouins. We have clear indications that they refrained from indulging in tribal fights, even when one of the parties involved was one of their cousins from the subdivisions of Bakr ibn Wāʾil or Rabīʿa. Perhaps the reason was that the tribe had settled in agricultural and mining areas, away from Bedouin life. In fact, one may safely say that Banū Ḥanīfa had not experienced Bedouin life for several decades before the rise of Islam.[19]

Banū Ḥanīfa formed the majority of Yamama's population. It was even said that they equalled in number the entire tribe of Bakr ibn Wāʾil and all its subdivisions.[20] They enjoyed economic and political control of most of Yamama, and were able to establish political and economic relations with their neighbours in Yemen, Hijaz, Iraq, the Syrian territories and Persia. The economic power of Banū Ḥanīfa and the rich resources of Yamama could easily be turned into political and military power. This formed a formidable force in resisting Islam. Although a small number of the Banū Ḥanīfa embraced Islam in its early days, the majority followed Musaylima ibn Ḥabīb al-Ḥanafī, who claimed to be the prophet and political leader of Banū Ḥanīfa and Yamama. This led Abū Bakr (11–13/632–64), the first Rāshidī caliph, to launch military campaigns against Yamama. Although the fighters in Musaylima's camp showed great courage and enthusiasm in defending their tribes and villages, the Muslim army, led by Khālid ibn al-Walīd, was able to inflict a resounding defeat on Banū Ḥanīfa. The Yamama groves witnessed a terrible massacre, and came to be known as 'the Garden of Death'.

Were the Banū Ḥanīfa completely uprooted as a result of these battles? The question is a valid one in the light of some reports to the effect that the caliph Abū Bakr wrote to Khālid ibn al-Walīd ordering him to root out Banū Ḥanīfa, leaving no man alive who had reached puberty. There are also references to letters sent by some dignitaries in Madinah asking Khālid to kill all the men of Banū Ḥanīfa.[21] There is no doubt that the killing of Banū Ḥanīfa was extensive, and that entire villages were completely wiped out, their inhabitants killed, captured or deported. There are indications of this in expressions which refer to villages that suffered military raids after the famous battle of ʿAqrabāʾ (12/633), such as 'They were uprooted by Khālid in the wars of apostasy', or 'emptied of its inhabitants because they were killed'. Perhaps Khālid ibn al-Walīd was literally applying the order issued by Abū Bakr against the apostates.[22]

There is also no doubt that a sizeable number of Banū Ḥanīfa's men were captured, enslaved and moved with their masters to the Hijaz. Even when the caliph ʿUmar ibn al-Khaṭṭāb (13–23/634–44) decided to ransom the Arab slaves, he assigned for the slaves from Banū Ḥanīfa a ransom smaller than that for slaves from other tribes. Although this measure was aimed at liberating the Arab slaves, with special consideration for the difficult economic situation of Banū Ḥanīfa, it was also considered a mark of shame, which compounded others incurred by that tribe as a result of their apostasy and defeat in war and the enslavement of a large number of their men, women and children. A further mark of shame was added when Banū Ḥanīfa were prevented from participating in the honour of the Islamic conquests. Even when, later, the apostates were allowed to join the Islamic armies, the sources name few from Banū Ḥanīfa who took part in the conquests.

A review of the tribe's former situation may provide possible answers to some queries about Banū Ḥanīfa. The prevailing opinion that they were not mentioned in connection with the Islamic conquests or migrations to other countries may be due to the belief that they had been completely eradicated. Let me suggest some points in support of this view. One is that the Banū Ḥanīfa did not share in the conquests because they were exhausted and scattered, with no financial resources to cover the costs of participation in battle. A second possibility is that they did take part in the battles, especially in Iraq, but under the names of other tribes to whom they were related by genealogy, neighbourhood or alliance. That is, they used the names of related tribes to avoid the name of Ḥanīfa, the tribe of Musaylima, disgraced as a result of the apostasy. Both possibilities are tenable, as there is nothing in the Arabic sources to support one theory over the other, yet we tend to accept the second, for the simple reason that it is difficult to believe that Banū Ḥanīfa tribesmen would refrain from jihād (holy war). Moreover, adopting the genealogy of other tribes was neither difficult nor prohibited. Therefore, in the absence of any decisive evidence, the second theory is generally accepted.

2.2. *Banū Ḥanīfa in the Umayyad Age*

To study the Banū Ḥanīfa in the Umayyad age is also to study the political history of Yamama, since a tribe's attachment to its land is usually so strong that each becomes an image of the other. The political history of the tribe (Banū Ḥanīfa) or the land (Yamama) provides a key to some historical problems we may face when exploring the tribe's affairs: its political, social and economic situation, its migrations and its motives for leaving the original homeland.

After Damascus became the Islamic capital, Yamama, like other parts of the Arabian peninsula, was not among the priorities of the new administration. In fact, Yamama came under the administration of Madinah or Basra. This was undoubtedly due to the power of the governor and his position in either town.[23] As a result of Umayyad policy in administering the provinces, governors were constantly changed, due to political and administrative disputes between the central government and opposition in the provinces. Consequently, the caliph changed his governors, either because of their incompetence, or simply to please the opposition. Moreover, governors could be changed for failing to realize certain of the caliph's personal interests that might antagonize the population and lead them to mutiny or rebellion.[24]

During the second civil war (62–71/681–90) the history of Yamama and its people became a history of the Khārijīs (dissenters). Najda ibn ʿĀmir al-Ḥanafī, one of the Khārijī leaders and founder of the Najdiyya faction, succeeded easily in removing the Umayyad governors from Yamama. It seems that Najda did not face much difficulty because the Khārijī leaders Abū Ṭālūt (from Bakr ibn Wāʾil), Abū Fudayk and ʿAṭiyya ibn al-Aswad al-Yashkuri had paved the way for him by declaring a revolt in Yamama which was joined by many of its inhabitants. Najda and his successor Abū Fudayk were able to establish an independent government in Yamama, and then in Bahrain, which lasted ten years. Najda assumed the title of Commander of the Faithful (Amīr al-Muʾminīn, the caliphal title), which openly challenged the Umayyad caliph in Damascus. During the first five years of his reign, Najda was able to expand his power; he then moved his official seat from Yamama to Bahrain, a step which Banū Ḥanīfa never forgave. The leaders of his government advocated firm sectarianism and took a severe stand against the central government in Damascus. They also challenged other neighbouring political powers, such as the Zubayrīs. This behaviour recalls their predecessors' action in challenging the Islamic government in Madinah. Would they face the same consequences? The caliph ʿAbd al-Malik ibn Marwān (65–86/685–705), the second founder of the Umayyad state, was able to keep a tight hold over the various regions of the Arabian peninsula, including Yamama. The Khārijīs were subjected to the sword or dispersed.[25] Most were from Banū Ḥanīfa. This was yet another mark of shame attached to them as a result of the apostasy and its aftermath.

From this review of the political history of the land and the tribe, it seems clear that there were political, economic and probably sectarian factors that brought frequent sedition and conflict to the area. Consequently, a number of Banū Ḥanīfa migrated to other Islamic regions; this is the subject of the following sections.

3.1. *Reasons for Banū Ḥanīfa's Migration to Other Islamic Territories*

The reasons that lead individuals or groups to migrate are the same in every time and place. They have changed little since men became mobile and looked for new homes. The Banū Ḥanīfa were exposed to many factors – political, economic and social – at various times; those factors led many of them to leave their homes in Yamama for other places outside the Arabian peninsula. The waves of migration varied in size, reason and timing from one period to another. It is unfortunate that the Arabic sources give no details about these migrations; in fact, most are silent on the matter. But fragmentary information found in books on history, literature and languages, creeds and factions may help to paint a picture, albeit a faint one, of the Banū Ḥanīfa's migration from their original homeland in Yamama to neighbouring regions conquered by Islam. It seems to this writer that some of the reasons behind those migrations go back to the Rāshidī period, and some to the Umayyad. Perhaps what happened in the Rāshidī period continued to be effective in the following ages, and over a long period. Here follows an outline of those reasons.

3.1.1. *Ardour for Jihād*

Islam urged its followers to spread its call and to fight for it. This required participation in the armies of conquest and migration to the conquered regions. Although the sources do not provide information about Banū Ḥanīfa's participation in the armies or their migration to other Islamic towns, we know of some of their number who took part in wars or migration. For example, Thumāma ibn Āthāl al-Ḥanafī joined the Islamic armies at an early stage. He left his home in Yamama before the battle of ʿAqrabāʾ (12/633) and joined the Islamic army in Bahrain. The same may be said of a number of people from Yamama who joined the victorious Islamic armies in Iraq and participated in its conquest. Some were army commanders, and some assumed high administrative or religious positions, like Abū Maryam al-Ḥanafī and Khulayd ibn ʿAbd Allāh. The desire to atone for the apostasy perhaps led some Banū Ḥanīfa to seek martyrdom through participating in the conquests. Therefore it is not unlikely that members of the tribe joined the Islamic army in Iraq, especially when the need arose for more fighters. The young men of the apostate tribes were sent by the caliph ʿUmar ibn al-Khaṭṭāb to reinforce the Islamic front.[26]

3.1.2. *Political and Military Results of the Wars of Apostasy*
The situation that prevailed after the wars of apostasy (*ridda*) forced the defeated young men of Banū Ḥanīfa to try to join the armies that marched to conquer Iraq or Syria. The Islamic administration in Madinah felt that if these men stayed in their own regions some might start another rebellion, so it made it easy for them to join the armies of conquest. In fact, depriving the apostates, young and old, of the honour of participating in the conquests was a sort of punishment for them, and a disparagement of their honour and gallantry, in a society that considered warfare a sign of manhood and chivalry. In addition, the income of the Banū Ḥanīfa dropped severely as a result of the extensive destruction that followed the wars, and the confiscation of agricultural and residential property aggravated the difficult living conditions of the tribe, and led some tribesmen to look for new sources of livelihood. Migration to join in the conquests or to look for work in the conquered areas was one available solution.[27]

3.1.3. *The Economic Factor*
In addition to the importance of the economic factors noted above, which pushed some of the Banū Ḥanīfa to migrate, there is no doubt that good living conditions in the conquered areas motivated the tribe's migration to Iraq and other territories during both the Rāshidī and the Umayyad periods. After the battle of Dhāt al-Salāsil (8/629), Khālid ibn al-Walīd addressed the Arabs in his army thus: 'Do you not see that food is as plentiful as sand! By God, if we did not need to fight for His cause and His mission, and if it were only for sustenance, our motive would have been to fight for this countryside so as to deserve better, and leave hunger and scarcity to those who want them and who felt too burdened to join you.'[28] On another occasion, the caliph ʿUmar (ibn al-Khaṭṭāb) addressed the armies headed for Syria: 'Go forth to holy war against a people who

have enjoyed the arts of living; perhaps God will grant you your share of what they have, so you may live like those who have lived well.[29] This is similar to a remark by Abū Bakr, who, when he had finished with the apostasy wars, wrote to 'the people of Makkah, Ṫāʾif, Yemen, and all the Arabs in Najd and the Hijaz, urging them to go on jihād, and arousing their desire for Roman spoils. People hurried to the call, out of calculation and greed, and came to Madinah from every corner of the land.'[30]

3.1.4. *Sedition in Yamama*

The frequent political and tribal uprisings in Yamama led many Banū Ḥanīfa tribesmen to leave their homelands for places where they could find security. Reports tell of the movement led by Najda ibn ʿĀmir al-Ḥanafī, the Khārijī wars led by Abū Hamza al-Khārijī, and the many Ḥanafīs who were forced to join them, which led to great loss of life. In the battle of Qudayd (130/747) between the Khārijīs and the Madinahns, the latter lost about 2,000 men. How many men from Yamama were killed? We believe that many more lives were lost in the rebellions, which continued for much of the Umayyad period.[31]

3.1.5. *Lack of Security in Yamama*

The lack of security and the feeling that people's lives and property were not safe led many to emigrate. Al-Iṣfahānī relates that Mālik ibn al-Raib al-Tamīmī and his followers used to terrorize the road between al-Falj and al-Qaṣīm in Najd.[32] Abū al-Nashnāsh al-Tamīmī led a large gang that raided trade caravans on their way from Syria to the Hijaz.[33] Another gang, no less dangerous, was headed by al-Samharī ibn Bishr al-ʿAklī, and specialized in attacking the Makkah–Kufa road, which passed through Madinah, and thus threatened the trade caravans.[34]

In his *al-Maḥāsin wa-al-aḍdād*, [pseudo]al-Jāḥiẓ tells of an exciting character who used to perpetrate sedition and disorder. Jahdar ibn Mālik al-ʿAkli used to raid Yamama, its provinces, markets and roads.[35] He was so scornful of security that he would raid the camel market and snatch a she-camel from the hands of its owner who was trying to sell it.[36] That led Ibrāhīm ibn al-ʿArabī, then governor of Yamama, to put him in prison.[37] It is not difficult to believe such stories, as security was almost non-existent in Yamama under the Umayyads, except for brief periods. Al-Ṭabarī reports that looting and plundering (especially the robbing of commodity stores and slaves) and the spreading of disorder were increasingly visible.[38] That these remarks were made by a serious historian leads one to trust those reports.

3.1.6. *Political Disorder*

The political situation in Yamama was not stable. The people of Yamama were not happy with the administrative policy in their region; nor were they content to carry out orders issued from Damascus, Madinah or Basra. Yamama was subject to violent disturbances after the murder of the Umayyad caliph al-Walīd ibn Yazīd (127/744). In 126/743 the Banū Ḥanīfa did not recognize the governor appointed over them, ʿAlī ibn al-Muhājir ibn ʿAbd Allāh al-Kilābī, and peace in their territories was disturbed. Raids, looting and plunder increased among tribes and settlers alike. These disturbances continued until the arrival of al-Muthannā ibn Yazīd ibn ʿUmar ibn Hubayra, who was appointed governor of Yamama by his father.[39] But he could do nothing to stop the destabilization, both political and in terms of security, which prevailed throughout the area.

Political disturbances were not new to Yamama. We know that Banū Ḥanīfa always longed for independence from the central authority. Thus they were ready, spontaneously and emotionally, to join any rebellion or incipient revolt against the central authority. This led some observers to call them 'Khārijīs', although few of them embraced the Khārijī creed. The followers of Najda ibn ʿĀmir al-Ḥanafī were barely 3,000 in Yamama.[40] But even this number does not really indicate that the Banū Ḥanīfa embraced Khārijī beliefs, because the historical sources tell us that many who followed the Khārijīs and participated in the wars were not really true believers, or approved the policy of the Khārijī leaders, but feared the terror meted out by those leaders against those who did not follow them. The savage fanaticism of the Khārijīs planted fear in the hearts of the population, which gave some historians the impression that the Khārijīs enjoyed their sympathy, while the truth was quite different.[41]

3.1.7. *Chronic Terror*

Chronic and continuous terror plagued social life in Yamama. Many people were killed in the successive disturbances, civil wars and rebellions. The confiscation of property, the destruction of the local economy, the pressure on the populace for political and doctrinal reasons, made people easy prey to fear and poverty. In many cases they became homeless and without refuge. This constant instability caused a halt in the natural growth of the population, or at the least stunted its natural increase, because of constant migration to areas outside Yamama.[42]

3.1.8. *Spread of Diseases and Epidemics*

Diseases, epidemics and plagues, such as the plague that swept the entire Middle East in the second/eighth century, were widespread, as was jaundice, which spread quickly in southern Iraq and which probably affected neighbouring regions, both administratively and demographically, such as Yamama and Bahrain.[43] There was also the 'Jāf' plague in 69/688 that killed many people in southern Iraq and in the Arabian peninsula.[44] This led people from Yamama to think of leaving their towns and villages.

3.1.9. *The Effect of Floods on Trade and Agriculture*

We have no reliable information about the destruction of agricultural products by floods in Yamama, or the destruction of earthwork dams and irrigation wells and channels. But we do have information about floods in the Hijaz in 80/699.[45] By analogy, we may assume that something similar might have happened in other parts of the Arabian peninsula. Similar to the effect of floods on agricultural production was that of drought; both may have forced sections of the population to leave their homeland for other regions.

3.1.10. *Agrarian Reforms outside Yamama and the Migration of Farmers*

The Umayyads paid special attention to agriculture and the reclamation of fallow land, and to irrigation systems in Iraq and Syria. But Yamama did not enjoy similar attention. New agricultural methods were introduced in Iraq, but not in all Umayyad territories. Encouraged by these measures, some Banū Ḥanīfa who were expert farmers seized this opportunity to leave their own farms and join the reclaimed farms in Iraq, where they could apply the new methods and enjoy financial rewards. Ibn Khurdādhbih states that Maslama ibn ʿAbd al-Malik undertook large agricultural and water reforms in Iraq. Iraq's governor, al-Ḥajjāj, initiated a million-dirham loan with no interest for farmers in Iraq in order to alleviate the economic crisis there.[46] Such measures must have led to the migration of some farmers and skilled labourers from agricultural villages in Yamama to other regions. The decay of agricultural villages in Yamama and the accompanying lower wages were reasons behind the migration of farm owners and labourers to wherever they could find material incentives.[47]

Information about the Umayyad period, though scant, shows that changes introduced by the government to agricultural lands were rather slow. The Umayyad caliphs kept the conquered lands in the hands of skilled workers. They also granted land to their followers, and themselves acquired large lots. Part of these were unclaimed property, let by their new owners, partly or wholly, to poor farmers for large sums of money. This practice called for trained Arab hands, expert in farming. But where would those hands come from, as Banū Ḥanīfa's farmers had already left their lands? The first Umayyad caliph was obliged to send 4,000 farm labourers to work the lands he held in Yamama, because he could not find enough local men for the job.[48]

When the Umayyad caliph Yazīd II (101–105/720–24) adopted a programme to increase state revenue, he confiscated former state-owned lands that had been granted to some farmers and put them under the treasury's supervision. This measure caused violent protest, which forced the caliph not only to abandon the programme but also to grant new lots from state-owned lands to important government officials.[49] This led to the expansion of agricultural land, thus creating a further need for skilled farm labourers to work on these properties.

3.1.11. *Rising Prices and the Cruelty of Some Tax Collectors*

The cruelty of some alms-tax (*zakāt*) and land-tax (*kharāj*) collectors probably lay behind the complaint presented by the poet al-Rāʿī al-Numayrī to the caliph ʿAbd al-Malik ibn Marwān. This exemplifies the reality suffered by the farmers, the populace and the livestock owners, who had to pay *zakāt*, as well as other taxes, to the Umayyad administration. Some poor farmers were compelled to abandon their farms and migrate to Iraq to work on state-owned and private lands.[50] Something similar happened in Iraq, as the policy of raising taxes and imposing various kinds of taxes on farmers obliged many farm labourers and farm owners to migrate from villages to towns in search of cheap labour. This, in turn, caused a decrease in land tax revenues, which led the government in Iraq to force those farmers to return to their villages, under very harsh conditions. However, such measures were not applied in the case of migrants from Yamama to Iraqi or other towns, as they proved difficult to administer.

The rise in taxes was accompanied by a similar rise in the prices of some basic commodities, such as wheat and dates. Prices are usually negatively affected by a lack of security. During the caliphate of Yazīd ibn Muʿāwiya in Damascus, a measure of wheat cost one dirham, but it was more expensive and rare in the Arabian peninsula.[51] Price rises during periods of wars and rebellions were greater than at other times. Disturbances prevailed in Yamama throughout the Umayyad period; in general, the prices of basic commodities did not decrease significantly except during the short caliphate of ʿUmar ibn ʿAbd al-ʿAzīz (99–101/717–20).[52]

3.1.12. *The Search for Religious Knowledge*

The list presented by Ibn Saʿd in his *Ṭabaqāt* points to the existence of a number of the Prophet's Companions who were from Banū Ḥanīfa and who settled in Yamama and spread religious learning throughout the land. Among them were Mujāʿa ibn Marāra, Thumāma ibn Āthāl, ʿAlī ibn Shaybān and Ṭalq ibn ʿAlī. It is known that the presence of this group was the starting point for religious education in Yamama,[53] where learning spread, especially *ḥadīth* and *fiqh* (the sayings of the Prophet and principles of jurisprudence). But some of the Companions from Banū Ḥanīfa were not satisfied with the learning to be found in their homeland, and migrated to Basra to seek further knowledge. Among these were Hanzala ibn Judhaym ibn Ḥanīfa and Ahmar ibn Jaziyy. They were the first to migrate for the sake of religious learning; other groups of scholars and students followed them, and found their way to Basra, Kufa, Khurasan and other centres of learning, during the Rāshidī and Umayyad periods.

In the Umayyad period the hubs of religious knowledge in Yamama still did not satisfy the Banū Ḥanīfa, or others living in Yamama, so they travelled to Basra and Kufa in Iraq, in particular. Among them were Shaqīq ibn Thawr al-Sadūsī, Thumāma ibn Āthāl al-Qushayrī, Ḥakīm ibn Muʿāwiya al-Qushayrī, Yazīd ibn ʿAbd al-Rahmān ibn Udhayna al-Suhaymī, ʿAbd al-Rahmān ibn ʿAlī ibn Shaybān al-Ḥanafī, Sulaymān ibn Rabīʿa al-Bāhilī (the first from Yamama to assume the position of *qāḍī* in Kufa) and Muḥārib ibn Dithār al-Sadūsī (who became a judge in both Kufa and Yemen).

This early group was followed by scholars from Banū Ḥanīfa who settled in Kufa, Basra, or some towns in Khurasan. During the Umayyad period they were seekers of religious learning; in the Abbasid period they became scholars specializing in certain branches of that learning. This shows that migration in search of religious learning or occupation in its (various) disciplines found a suitable climate during the Umayyad period, and that centres of religious learning in the Islamic territories attracted a number of (scholars from) Banū Ḥanīfa.[54]

This picture makes it difficult to believe that only a few Banū Ḥanīfa migrated from their homeland, instead remaining in their own territory and merging with its population. We have shown that many factors made it impossible for Banū Ḥanīfa, especially the town-dwellers, to subsist under the difficult conditions. Migration was a possible solution. But why do the Arabic sources say little about the migrations of Banū Ḥanīfa? In the following pages we will attempt to answer this question.

3.2. *Historical Analysis of Banū Ḥanīfa Migrations*

It is difficult to follow the migrations of Banū Ḥanīfa in the Umayyad period or in the previous period. In our earlier discussion there were possibly some pointers towards explaining this matter. But it is better to begin with a historical analysis of the factors that underlie this question. These include the following:

(1) The Banū Ḥanīfa were a settled tribe which for some time had taken significant steps towards urbanization. They had been cut off from Bedouin life and had become settled in towns, villages and the countryside, and had become accustomed to practising trade, agriculture, mining and some crafts. Their traditional tribal ties had therefore weakened. Hence when, in the Islamic period, they migrated to Islamic towns, they did not do so as a tribal unit, as did Tamīm, Asad, ʿAbd al-Qays and al-Azd. A modern writer believes that involvement with town life and its economic and social aspects would lead to a situation similar to what happened to Banū Ḥanīfa: they mixed with other migrating tribes, especially those that were related to them or were their neighbours before the migration.[55]

Charles Pellat also noted this point when he stated that 'the Umayyad age was characterized by petty conspiracies, personal rivalries, and conflicts among men and tribes. Yet, the individual became more aware of his individuality, and began to disentangle himself from tribal ties, in order to merge in a larger and more flexible social class. Political, economic, or even religious concerns might encourage him to move from one social class to another.'[56] If this analysis is correct, it would explain the difficulties faced when trying to trace the migrations of Banū Ḥanīfa. It seems that Pellat's analysis applies mostly to tribes with an urban background. As is well known, the Banū Ḥanīfa are characterized by having sedentary roots, far removed from Bedouin life. This caused them to be described as city-dwellers, with a lack of concern for the tribe and, moreover, an increased sense of individuality.

The weakness of the Banū Ḥanīfa tribe led a number of their members to emigrate and settle in towns in the eastern Arabian peninsula and beyond. It seems that they joined in the social and economic activities prevailing in their new environment, and formed relationships with members outside their own tribes. Moreover, the Islamic faith called for brotherhood and equality, which weakened tribal fanaticism and, in turn, helped a number of Banū Ḥanīfa to assume new loyalties.[57] This further explains the difficulty facing anyone attempting to identify Ḥanīfa migrants.

But what made Banū Ḥanīfa resort to strategies such as merging with other tribes and assuming new loyalties? In the absence of clear sources, we can only resort to analysis and to historical analogy. The following are some suggested reasons:

(a) The high ratio of females to males, since many men from Banū Ḥanīfa were killed in the wars and battles waged in the region from the early days of Islam until the end of the Umayyad period. The decreasing number of men called for tribal support, and perhaps gave rise to the need for entering into new tribes, which in turn could lead to concealing one's true genealogy for political or economic reasons.[58]

(b) The captivity of a large number of Banū Ḥanīfa women as a result of the Yamama truce, and their marriage to men outside their tribe, which undermined the tribe's natural rate of increase.[59]

(c) The shame attached to the Banū Ḥanīfa as a result of their apostasy and their joining of movements perceived as being against Islam. People continued to blame Banū Ḥanīfa because of their apostasy, their defeat in the battle of ʿAqrabāʾ, and their killing of Companions. This was noted by a poet from the tribe, who said that the Banū Ḥanīfa were not the only ones who rebelled against Islam. Nevertheless, shame and disgrace continued to be attached to them; this led some tribesmen to hide their true genealogy and claim kinship with other clans or tribes.[60]

(2) Some tribesmen wanted to take part in the Islamic conquests, but could not do so because they were banned by the caliphate. This obliged them to claim kinship with other clans or tribes. They might trace their genealogy to Bakr ibn Wāʾil, or even further back, to their ancestor Rabīʿa. They might have been listed in the register of payment (*dīwān al-ʿaṭāʾ*) under various names, but we cannot be sure of this, since our

information about the Rāshidī register of payment is very scant. Moreover, the genealogists do not say whether they have gleaned any of their information from that register. We also cannot be sure whether that register covered all tribes or only those who participated in military service during the early Islamic period; and, naturally, Banū Ḥanīfa were not among them.[61]

But the question persists: did the fighters and emigrants from Banū Ḥanīfa continue to conceal their lineage, even after ʿUmar ibn al-Khaṭṭāb allowed the former apostates among them to join the Islamic armies? Moreover, he proscribed the enslavement of Arabs and ordered that those who had been enslaved be freed. The state treasury paid for their liberation. But there is an anecdote in the sources which states that the amount paid to free members of Banū Ḥanīfa was less than that paid for members of other Arab tribes.[62] If we consider that the Banū Ḥanīfa's concealment of their lineage was felt by them to be necessary in order to avoid the shame attached to them by their apostasy, ʿUmar's measures may be seen as a further insult, which led them to continue to hide their genealogy.

The decisive factor may have been that, with the passage of time, it was no longer possible to go back to the old, original tribal names. The Banū Ḥanīfa migrants merged into new groups and were known by new names. The tribes became intermixed, as did their original homelands, as a result of the extensive migration of many clans and tribes. Neighbouring or related tribes, or weak ones who had lost their power, could no longer protect themselves if they were to return to their former names. What happened to Banū Ḥanīfa happened to other tribes as well. This was not a new phenomenon in the history of the Arabs.[63]

4.1. *Banū Ḥanīfa's Migration to the Islamic Territories*

The preceding survey shows that Banū Ḥanīfa, like other Arab tribes, found in Islam a strong incentive to move into the conquered lands and settle there, either by joining the Muslim armies in the early conquests, or by migrating later on. The Rāshidī period witnessed constant activity in conquests and migration alike.[64] In the Umayyad period migration to territories outside Yamama continued, for the reasons previously discussed. The Ḥanīfa tribesmen's knowledge of the regions to which they migrated was not born in the Umayyad period; they knew those regions in the Rāshidī period and even in pre-Islamic times. As a trading people they had strong links with their neighbours, both political and economic; moreover, their close relatives from Bakr ibn Wāʾil used to frequent these areas, which, according to al-Hamadhānī, 'extended from Yamama to Bahrain, to the Kāẓima coast [Kuwait] to the sea, and to the peripheries of Iraq and Ubulla'.[65] If this is so, then Iraq should have been first among the areas to which Banū Ḥanīfa emigrants headed. They may have adopted the names of Bakr ibn Wāʾil clans to conceal (the fact of) their migration.

It is not unlikely that migrations from Yamama accelerated at various times in the Umayyad period, and even in the Abbasid period, due to political or sectarian reasons. To say this demands a degree of caution, as there are some who believe that most migrations took place along with the early Islamic conquests in Iraq and Syria and continued until the first civil war.[66] At the same time, we cannot dismiss certain terms with political or administrative significance or with implications as regards migration without studying them in detail. Such terms, which we find in writings pertaining to the Umayyad and Abbasid periods, add to our knowledge of Arabian migrations.[67]

Among the terms that may describe migration is *al-rawādif*, meaning the waves that went to Iraq. Others are *ahl al-Qādisiyya* and *ahl al-ayyām*, used for administrative categories or those dealing with payment, but also describing waves of Arab migration. Most of our knowledge about *rawādif*, for instance, comes from their position on the register of payment. We know that they were divided into groups – the first and second *rawādif* – and that the difference between them was in the amount of payment. That difference definitely shows that they came to the Islamic regions during successive periods. What is true of migrations to Iraq may also be true of those to Syria, Egypt and North Africa. However, F. Donner is of the opinion that after the early Islamic conquests Syria was not a goal for migrations of tribes from the Arabian peninsula except on a small scale.[68] But proving this opinion requires some effort, because, as we shall see, the migration of tribes from the Arabian peninsula to Syria and other territories continued, perhaps, up to the fourth/tenth century.[69]

4.2. *The Migration of Banū Ḥanīfa to Iraq*

Tribes from the Arabian peninsula moved into Iraq and settled in new places created by them or in towns and agricultural villages that were already inhabited. Perhaps the first indication of the numbers that entered Iraq at the beginning of the Islamic conquests from the tribes of Rabīʿa and Muḍar was the 8,000 men, the reinforcements sent by Abū Bakr to Khālid ibn al-Walīd when he reached Ubulla, on the periphery of Iraq. It is not unlikely that some men of Banū Ḥanīfa were among those of Rabīʿa, since we have no details about tribes that came under the names of Rabīʿa and Muḍar.[70] It seems that the battle of the Bridge (13/634) shocked the Islamic state, and led the government to enlist tribesmen to fight in the war.[71] Groups (whose numbers cannot be estimated) came to Madinah from various parts of the peninsula, among them tribes from Najd and Yamama.[72]

The various tribes of Rabīʿa and Bakr ibn Wāʾil settled in the villages and towns of Iraq; these amounted to some 14,000 men, according to al-Ṭabarī.[73] Al-Wāqidī says that Saʿd ibn Abī Waqqāṣ settled Arabian tribes in Kufa. He names some of these, then says, 'and he also settled some of "mixed" ancestry'. The term 'mixed' may indicate individuals who did not constitute an independent tribe or clan. Perhaps some of these, who settled in Kufa or other Iraqi towns, were from Banū Ḥḍanīfa, as will become clear in what follows.

4.2.1. *Banū Ḥanīfa in Basra*

In the time of the caliph ʿAlī ibn Abī Ṭālib, the number of Arabs on the rolls of the register of payment was 60,000.[74] Their number increased to 80,000 during the governorship of Ziyād ibn Abī Sufyān (Ziyād ibn Abīhi; appointed 45/665), and their dependants counted 120,000.[75] These are only the numbers of those registered; if we add those not registered, the total might reach half a million.[76] But how can we calculate the number of Banū Ḥanīfa among the population of Basra? This is difficult; but we must remember that Yamama was annexed to Basra in the caliphate of Muʿāwiya I ibn Abī Sufyān (41–60/661–80), which made Banū Ḥanīfa, the majority of the population of Yamama, head towards Basra for both migration and jihād.[77]

The conjoining of Yamama with Basra was a purely administrative measure taken by Muʿāwiya with respect to the tribesmen of Yamama, who were obliged to fight in the Basra army. This measure seems to have had no connection with financial affairs. Since the days of the Rāshidī caliphs, Yamama used to send land-tax revenue to Madinah.[78] This became a tradition until the caliphate of ʿAbd al-Malik ibn Marwān. It seems that this measure was adopted when Muʿāwiya separated unclaimed estates in Yamama from the treasury and turned them into the caliph's own private property.[79]

We can also see the relationship between Basra and Yamama from the measures taken by Ziyād and his son ʿUbayd Allāh. The former modified Arab genealogies in Basra, integrating some Arabian tribes into others unrelated to them. He even integrated some Persian units into Arabian clans, as when he combined the Banū ʿAmm from Ahwaz with the Arabian Banū Tamīm.[80] Similarly, he combined the Hijazi Ḥamīs tribe with Tamīm,[81] and the Asāwira, Sayābija and ẓuṭṭ with the Persians.[82] He also joined Banūna and ʿĀisha,[83] Nājiya[84] and the Omani Wisāma to the inhabitants of al-ʿliya.[85]

ʿUbayd Allāh ibn Ziyād brought 2,000 of the Turks he had captured on his campaigns in Central Asia and settled them in Basra, put them on regular payment, assigned them provisions, and used them to subject some mutinous Arabs in Yamama. The Arabs called these Turks 'Bukhārīs';[86] some settled in Yamama, then migrated to Iraq. It is not improbable that they formed some sort of alliance with members of Banū Ḥanīfa. Such measures could not have been taken had there not been some Arabian tribes of small numbers and little political weight. Perhaps Banū Ḥanīfa in Basra were among those tribes designated as 'mixed people', a prevalent term at the time. This is how the Umayyad state dealt with migrants from Banū Ḥanīfa. It was common to join them with Muslim minorities from Persia, based on previous relations between the two parties. Al-Balādhurī refers to this when he cites a report that a group of Persians migrated from Yamama to Basra, where they built a mosque called 'al-Ḥāmira'. In Basra they were considered part of Banū Ḥanīfa because of their long residence in Yamama prior to emigrating.[87]

This matter was noted by a modern writer who found that five tribes were linked with Banū Ḥanīfa in Basra during the Umayyad period. It is not unlikely that those tribes were not even related to Banū Ḥanīfa by genealogy.[88] On the other hand, thirty tribes claimed to be related to Bakr ibn Wāʾil. These numbers were mentioned by several historians, but we cannot ascertain the precise names of these tribes. This leads one to assume that some Ḥanīfa tribesmen may have been included among those tribes, and especially among Yashkur, to whom, according to al-Ṭabarī, four tribes were attached, although al-Balādhurī states that there were six tribes.[89] In any case, we cannot say that Banū Ḥanīfa had their own settlements in Basra; this supports our previous suggestion that Banū Ḥanīfa migrants to Basra in the Umayyad period lived within the settlements of other tribes, and therefore did not attract the attention of the historians.[90]

We have other historical evidence. The poet Wahb ibn Abjar al-ʿIjlī, describing the battle of Jafra (69/688) between the Zubayrīs and the Umayyads, mentions some tribes related to Banū Ḥanīfa, and ultimately to Bakr ibn Wāʾil; these were Lujaym, Ibn Masmaʿ, Ḥanīfa and ʿIjl. This shows that Banū Ḥanīfa's migration to and settlement in Basra increased constantly during the Umayyad period. Al-Farazdaq's poetry makes many references to the large numbers of Banū Ḥanīfa in Basra in the Umayyad period. This is not surprising when we recall that Basra was one of the towns that received successive migrations beginning in the early years of the Rāshidī period. During the caliphate of ʿAlī ibn Abī Ṭālib, the chieftain of Rabīʿa, the mother tribe of Ḥanīfa, was Hurayth ibn Jābir al-Ḥanafī.[91] The chieftain was almost always from Banū Ḥanīfa or Bakr ibn Wāʾil, as in the case of al-Hudayn ibn al-Mundhir al-Dhuhlī, from Bakr ibn Wāʾil, who was succeeded by Khālid ibn Muʿammar.[92] We also find that four famous military commanders from Banū Ḥanīfa led armies in the conquests of areas connected to Basra: Amīr ibn Ahmar al-Yashkurī (conquest of Qūhistān and Ṭalaqān), Khulayd ibn ʿAbd Allāh (conquest of Herat), Abū Maryam al-Ḥanafī (conquest of Māhurmuz) and Manjūf ibn Thawr al-Sadūsī (conquest of Mahrajān-Qadhaf and Yathbān).

4.2.2. *Banū Ḥanīfa in Kufa*

Kufa was the second Iraqi destination of migrants and fighters from Banū Ḥanīfa. It seems that their settlement in Kufa was later than that in Basra. Al-Balādhurī notes that Banū Ḥanīfa had special relations with the governor of Kufa at the time, ʿUbayd Allāh ibn Ziyād, and we can conclude that their number was not large.[93] In the civil war between Muṣʿab ibn al-Zubayr and al-Mukhtār al-Thaqafī (67/686), the latter was killed by two brothers from Banū Ḥanīfa, Ṭurfa and Ṭirāf, sons of ʿAbd Allāh ibn Dajāja al-Ḥanafī.[94]

The population of Kufa in the Umayyad period was over half a million, half of them from Rabīʿa tribe alone.[95] It is difficult to estimate the percentage of Banū Ḥanīfa among the population of Rabīʿa. Some sources mention that villages around Kufa were settled by Arabs. Moreover, the Umayyads built a number of garrisons in the vicinity of Kufa for security purposes, especially to deal with the Khārijīs. We have already seen that some of the latter were from Banū Ḥanīfa or neighbouring tribes from Yamama. This means that a number of Banū Ḥanīfa emigrated from Yamama to Kufa and its surrounding areas in order to join their Khārijī relatives, and probably settled in Kufa or neighbouring areas.

The geographic distribution of the garrisons denotes the locations of the Khārijīs in Kufa and its peripheries, extending from Madāʾin, al-Anbār, Jūkhī and Rādhān up to Jalawlāʾ. The Arabic sources tell us that Banū Ḥanīfa spread over a large area of Kufa and neighbouring areas, but not as extensively as in Basra.[96] We do not think that the geographic area of the garrisons covered more than the geographic and administrative limits of Kufa's bordering areas, which had been the same since the Rāshidī period.[97] We also learn from another account in al-Ṭabarī that major Arab expansion in the Kufa area did not take place until after the death of the caliph ʿUmar I. Whatever the case, Arabs spread over numerous Kufan areas during the Umayyad period. Those migrations were called *rawādif*.[98]

To attempt to understand the demographic situation of Kufa in the

Umayyad period, one encounters the problem of the 'quarters' and 'fifths', the residential areas settled by the Arabian tribes from the time of the city's foundation until the governorate of Ziyād ibn Abīhi. There is no mention of an area belonging to Banū Ḥanīfa. But al-Sariyy mentions a number of areas in Kufa bearing no tribal names, but with place names instead, because, as he says, they were inhabited by 'mixed people'.[99] We already know that this term described a number of small tribes that did not have a common ancestry. It is not unlikely that Banū Ḥanīfa lived in such quarters.

4.3. *Migration of Banū Ḥanīfa to the Islamic East*

One of the most important results of the battle of Nihāwand was the spread of the Arabs throughout the Iranian plateau. Before this battle the Arabs lived securely in conquered towns such as Māsabadhām, Madāʾin, Ahwaz, Ramhurmuz, Tustar and Jundishapur. Arab settlement in those towns was due to their proximity to Basra. Moreover, the Khārijīs chose some of those areas as a field for their activities. The Arabs had seven administrative centres there, inhabited by their governors, their relatives and their tribes.

The Muslim Arabs were not unfamiliar with Persia. Al-Ṭabarī relates that some tribes of Bakr ibn Wāʾil used to live in Kirman, and were called 'Bakr Ābān'. The Banū Ḥanẓala lived in the village of al-Rumayla, in the Ahwaz area, and in Jundishapur. Those migrations and settlements took place before Islam.[100] Those same areas witnessed migrations by Banū Ḥanīfa during the Rāshidī and Umayyad periods. These varied from one time to another, perhaps due to administrative modifications and the division of military responsibilities in the caliphate of ʿUthmān ibn ʿAffān (23–35/644–56), which put Qarqīsiya and Mosul under the governor of Damascus and made them part of the Jazīra (roughly, upper Mesopotamia), while Rayy and Azarbaijan were placed under the governor of Kufa.[101] This writer believes that Azarbaijan, Rayy and Ardabil did not witness extensive migration and large-scale settlement by Banū Ḥanīfa during the Rāshidī period; most of their migrations were during the Umayyad period, since ʿAlī ibn Abī Ṭālib was the first caliph to settle Arabs in those regions. In his time the payment register did not contain many names from Banū Ḥanīfa, because of their sympathy with the Khārijīs and the fact that few supported ʿAlī; thus it seems unlikely that they migrated to those areas during the Rāshidī period, and more likely that they did so in the Umayyad period. Perhaps most migrants were workers and farmers who found in the cultivated land an opportunity for work and residence. The histories tell us that some Arabs bought large farms from their Persian owners.[102]

A close look at the historical and literary reports of the Rāshidī and Umayyad periods shows clearly that there were many migrants and settlers from Banū Ḥanīfa in the regions around Basra. Here is a list of those areas:[103]

Town	*Historical Notes*
Nihāwand	30,000 Arabs from different tribes took part in its conquest
Ahwaz	Inhabited by a large number of Khārijīs
Ramhurmuz	Conquered and governed by Abū Maryam al-Ḥanafī, delegated by Abū Māsā al-Ashʿarī, governor of Basra
Surraq	In the Ahwaz area, governed by Abū Maryam al-Ḥanafī, appointed by ʿUmar I
Ardashīrkhura, Ṣābūr-i Nūh, Tasā, Darābjird, Sij istan, Kirman, Marv	Governed by Amīr ibn Aḥmar, mostly populated by Bakr ibn Wāʾil tribes, according to al-Ṫabarī[104]
Abarshahr	Governed by Khulayd ibnʿAbd Allāh, appointed by Ziyād ibn Abīhi
Tustar	Conquered by Khālid ibn Muʿammar and Manjūf ibn Thawr al-Sadūsī
Qum, Ṫukhāristān, Jurjan, Herat	Conquered by Khulayd ibn ʿAbd Allāh
Iṣtakhar, Qūhistān	Conquered by Amīr ibn Ahmar al-Yashkurī
Isfahan	Some Ḥanīfa tribesmen migrated there

It is clear from this list that Ḥanīfa tribesmen, or their relatives either from tribes of Bakr ibn Wāʾil or from their neighbours in Yamama, assumed high military and administrative positions. Consequently, this means that they encouraged their relatives to emigrate and settle in those towns. Abū ʿUbayda states in this connection that Amīr ibn Ahmar al-Yashkuri conquered Qūhistān and that it is 'the country of Bakr ibn Wāʾil to the present day'.[105]

There is a clear historical reference to the fact that Khurasan was heavily populated by Banū Ḥanīfa when it became attached to the administration of Basra in the Umayyad period. A political–administrative problem broke out in 51/671 on the death of Khurasan's governor Amīr ibn Ahmar al-Yashkurī, who was supported by Bakr ibn Wāʾil. Muḍar and Rabīʿa contested the governorship, which was won by Anas ibn Abī Anas. However, Ziyād, the governor of Basra, did not like this, so he deposed Anas and appointed Khulayd ibn ʿAbd Allāh al-Ḥanafī. This measure pleased the majority of the population from Banū Ḥanīfa and the other tribes of Bakr ibn Wāʾil. The deposed governor composed a poem describing the incident and satirizing Banū Ḥanīfa in Khurasan, describing them as farmers who knew nothing about administration and were not fit to govern. He said that they were slaves first and last, which was a clear reference to the shame that continued to attach to them from the time of the battle of ʿAqrabāʾ (see above).[106]

Al-Madāʾinī mentions the tribes that were in Khurasan at the time of the revolt of Qutayba ibn Muslim al-Bāhilī against the Umayyad caliph Sulaymān ibn ʿAbd al-Malik. He states: 'In Khurasan . . . there were 9,000 fighters from the people of Basra, 7,000 from Bakr, 10,000 from Tamīm, 4,000 from ʿAbd al-Qays, 10,000 from al-Azd, 7,000 from the Kūfans, and 7,000 *mawālī* [manumitted slaves].'[107] This is a unique reference, according to Nājī Hasan, as it gives the numbers of tribes and clans living in Khurasan in the Umayyad period. We have no doubt that Banū Ḥanīfa represented the majority of the 7,000 men ascribed to Bakr ibn Wāʾil. (Naturally, this number does not include women and children.) Our suggestion is supported by a speech by the governor Qutayba ibn Muslim al-Bāhilī addressing the tribes of Bakr ibn Wāʾil when he decided to withdraw his allegiance to Sulaymān ibn ʿAbd al-Malik in 86/705:

'O men of Bakr ibn Wāʾil! O people of arrogance, lies and avarice! Which of your two days do you celebrate: your day of war, or your day of peace! O followers of Musaylima!' He then reminded them that he had brought to them their families and relatives. This indicates that a number of Ḥanīfa migrations to Khurasan took place during the Umayyad period.[108]

The Arabs also settled in Karaj (in Fars). Some were from ʿIjl and their followers from other Arabian tribes who joined with them and who clearly lived with them. It seems not unlikely that some members of Banū Ḥanīfa migrated to Karak with ʿIjl, as we find indications of strong relations between ʿIjl and Ḥanīfa, who were neighbours in Yamama before migrating to the east.[109]

4.4. *Migration of Banū Ḥanīfa to Syria*

There was Arabian settlement in Syria before Islam, which seems to have facilitated the process of new settlement there. It is worth noting that the new migrants settled in coastal towns and villages.[110] The flow of migrants continued until late in the Umayyad period. Syria was the destination of a large number of Arabian tribes. A modern writer, however, believes that migration to Syria ended after the completion of the conquests, except for some minor cases.[111]

Perhaps the first reference to the existence of Banū Ḥanīfa in Syria before the rise of the Umayyads is Naṣr ibn Muzāḥim's statement that 'the chieftain of Khathʿam and its followers was Hamal ibn ʿAbd Allāh al-Ḥanafīʾ, at the time of their march to the battle of Ṣiffīn (37/657).[112] We understand from this that a commander from Banū Ḥanīfa headed a company in the army of Muʿāwiya. Hamal ibn ʿAbd Allāh could not have reached this position had there not been a good number of his tribe among his troops. Moreover, Naṣr says Khathʿam and followers; some narrators often mentioned one tribe and ignored others.

Some historical reports say that Syria also witnessed later waves of migration. In 124/741 the Umayyad caliph Hishām ibn ʿAbd al-Malik (105–25/724–43) recruited a number of Arab tribes as the 'Andalusian vanguard'. Some were from Rabīʿa, and it was said that some Khārijīs were among them.[113] These may have been from Yamama, and related to

Rabīʿa, but ultimately from Banū Ḥanīfa (see above). The Umayyad administration made the acceptance of new migrants from Yamama to Syrian areas conditional upon their rejection of the Najdi Khārijīs. When the Banū Numayr of Yamama migrated to Syria, their poet al-Rāʿī al-Numayrī preceded them, was given an audience with ʿAbd al-Malik ibn Marwān, and declared in a famous poem his repudiation of both ʿAbd Allāh ibn al-Zubayr and the Khārijīs of Yamama.[114] Al-Yaʿqūbī says that a number of Syrian towns and villages were settled by Banū Ḥanīfa or people from Yamama. Among them were al-Ghāṭa (near Damascus), populated mostly by Rabīʿa, and ʿArqa, inhabited by Banū Ḥanīfa. In Jinīn in Palestine there were many people from Bakr, who usually include Banū Ḥanīfa.[115]

The Jazīra, the region to the north-east of Syria, was of special importance, particularly in the Umayyad era. It includes Bālis, Qāṣirīn, Ruhā (Edessa), Ḥarrān, Raʾs Kayfā, Sumaysāṭ, Mārdīn, Sinjār, Raqqa, Qinnasrīn and Qarqīsiya.[116] Muʿāwiya ibn Abī Sufyān settled tribes from Rabīʿa in the Jazīra, especially in Sinjār. Some changes took place in the Arab settlements in the Jazīra at the time of the first civil war, after the murder of the caliph ʿUthmān ibn ʿAffān, when a group from Yamama settled in Ḥarran.[117] The final image of the Jazīra's inhabitants was described by Ibn Hawqal, who noted that there were tribes and 'mixed people' from Rabīʿa, Qushayr, ʿAqīl and Banū Numayr. It is possible that some members of Banū Ḥanīfa found their way to the Jazīra, along with the tribes named by Ibn Hawqal who had formerly lived in Yamama.[118]

4.5. *Migration of Banū Ḥanīfa to Egypt, Africa and al-Andalus*

The Muslim conquest of Egypt was organized on a tribal basis. Each tribe formed an independent contingent, carrying its own banner. But there were tribes only a few of whose members witnessed the conquest, as they were not numerous enough to form an independent contingent. ʿAmr ibn al-ʿĀṣ placed them under a special banner, and they were called 'the banner bearers' (*ahl al-rāya*). This title was later relied upon in matters concerning residences (*khiṭaṭ*) and registers of payment (*dīwān*).[119] But the history books do not mention the names of 'the banner bearers', so the matter is left to speculation.

The tribes of ʿAnaza, Banū Ḥanīfa, Banū Numayr and others from Rabīʿa migrated to Egypt at various times following the Islamic conquest, and continued to do so intermittently until the time of the Abbasid caliph al-Mutawakkil (232–47/847–61). Ibn ʿAbd al-Hakam states that in Egypt there was a cluster of about twenty houses belonging to ʿAnaza.[120] It seems that migration from Yamama to Egypt, especially in the Umayyad period but also later in the Abbasid, was by individuals or groups joining their relatives or tribes who had gone before them. Al-Yaʿqūbī states that Banū Ḥanīfa's extensive migration to Egypt in the third/ninth century, and their settlement in the region of al-ʿAlāqī, famous for its mines,[121] took place because some of their relatives had migrated to that region earlier. This point is scarcely noticed by modern writers, who usually focus on sources of livelihood which attracted new migrants. Ibn Hawqal reports that Banū Ḥanīfa had about 1,000 men capable of going to war. If we add their family members the number of Banū Ḥanīfa in Egypt at that time might reach 5,000. Al-Maqrīzī adds that Rabīʿa tribes built up some villages in Nubia, such as al-Nammās, and that they went all the way to Sawākin (Suakin, a Sudanese port on the Red Sea coast).[122]

A number of Rabīʿa tribes settled in Ifrīqiya (eastern North Africa) and al-Andalus. Perhaps the first reference to these tribes comes from Ibn al-Qūtiyya, who states that the army sent by Hishām ibn ʿAbd al-Malik to al-Andalus in 124/741 included some members of Rabīʿa tribes. He adds that Khārijīs from Yamama, the Jazīra and Mosul were among those tribes. It is possible some Banū Ḥanīfa who had migrated from Yamama to North Africa and al-Andalus, after passing through Damascus and registering themselves on the rolls of payment, were referred to as 'the Khārijīs of Yamama, the Jazīra and Mosul', because it seems that, in the Umayyad period, the name 'Khārijī' had become attached to the Banū Ḥanīfa in particular, and to the people of Yamama in general.[123]

After leaving Yamama, the Bāhila tribe settled in Jaen, Toledo and Guadalajara. Numayr settled in Granada and al-Barājīl. Qushayr settled in Jaen, and Bakr ibn Wāʾil in Guadana.[124] Arab migrations continued; many individuals or families left as a result of suffering some harm. We know that between 124 and 126/741 and 743 major disturbances took place in Yamama. There was no security, and the local authorities were unable to maintain the peace. There were numerous cases of murder, robbery and aggression. Those who suffered most were the farmers and miners, who were mostly from Banū Ḥanīfa and their neighbours of Bāhila, Numayr, Qushayr and other Bakr ibn Wāʾil tribes. They left for Syria and probably for al-Andalus. It is possible that some members of Banū Ḥanīfa merged with Numayr or Qushayr, or came under the name of Bakr ibn Wāʾil or Bāhila, in their migration to al-Andalus. It should be noted that the Umayyad government did not realize the situation of the mines in Yamama until about 128/745, when they began to form a special commission to supervise the mines.[125] But this came too late, as a large number of miners had already left.

These pages point to several conclusions, foremost among which is that the Arab migrations, including that of Banū Ḥanīfa, did not cease in the Umayyad period, as some historians have suggested. We also note that migrations of Banū Ḥanīfa from Yamama during the Umayyad period were due to religious, political, economic and sectarian reasons. These were largely the same reasons that led early migrants from Yamama to the eastern parts of the Arabian peninsula and Iraq during the Rāshidī period.

This chapter has shown that most of Banū Ḥanīfa's migrations were to Iraq, and especially to Basra and the towns attached to it. We have also seen that politics often interfered to change the destination of some waves of migration. Perhaps one of the most significant points addressed has been to try to find an answer to a long-standing question which has occupied historians of Yamama, namely, the course taken by Banū Ḥanīfa after the apostasy, and how they merged, or rather dissolved, into other tribes and clans related to them by genealogy or neighbourhood. This is the issue that has led the present writer to trace the migrations of Banū Ḥanīfa to other Islamic regions.

Notes:

1. ʿAbd al-ʿAzīz al-Ghazī believes that settlement began in Yamama early in the third millennium BCE, reaching its peak in the first millennium BCE, and beginning to decline in the fourth century CE. The old settlements came to

an end in the fifth/eleventh century. See ʿA. al-Ghazī, 'A Comparative Study of Pottery from a Site in the Kharj Valley, Central Arabia' (unpublished thesis, University of London, Institute of Archaeology, 1990), pp. 197–288.

2. Abū al-Fidā, *Kitāb taqwīm al-buldān* (ed. J. T. Reinaud and W. MacGuckin de Slane, Paris, 1840), p. 97.
3. Israel Wolfenson, *Tārīkh al-lughāt al-Sāmiyya* ([trans. of *History of Semitic Languages*] Cairo, 1929), p. 5.
4. Karl Brockelmann, *Tārīkh al-shuʿūb al-Islāmiyya* (trans. Nabīh Amīn Fāris and Munīr al-Baʿlabakī [of *History of the Islamic Peoples*], Beirut, 1968), p. 13.
5. ʿAbd Allāh al-Birrī, *al-Qabāʾl al-ʿArabiyya fī Miṣr fī al-qurūn al-thalātha alūlā* (Cairo, 1967), p. 7.
6. *Ibid*., p. 3.
7. Al-Birrī discusses the importance of trade to the Ptolemies and the Arabian states, and the influence of merchants on both parties (*ibid*., p. 24).
8. Muḥammad Kāmil Ḥusayn, *Adab Miṣr al-Islāmiyya* (Beirut, 1948), p. 16.
9. See Sharp's view in A. J. Butler, *Fatḥ al-ʿArab li-Miṣr* (trans. Muḥammad Farīd Abū Hadīd *[The Arab Conquest of Egypt]*, Cairo, 1933), p. 40. The participation of peninsular Arabs in Khusraw II's conquest of Egypt was not the first of its kind. Herodotus says that Cambyses used the help of some peninsular Arabs in his campaigns against Egypt. See Jawād ʿAlī, *al-Mufaṣṣal fītārīkh al-ʿArab qabl al-Islām* (Beirut, 1976), I, p. 621.
10. Ibn ʿAbd al-Ḥakam, *History of the Conquest of Egypt (Futūḥ Miṣr)* (ed. Charles C. Torrey, Leiden, 1920), pp. 59–62.
11. A discussion of the views of al-Masʿūdī, al-Maqrīzī and Butler is found in Ḥusayn, *Adab Miṣr*, p. 17 ff.
12. P. K. Zhuze, *Min tārīkh al-ḥarakāt al-fikriyya fī al-Islām* (Jerusalem, 1848), p. 17. Zhuze was greatly impressed by the studies of Wellhausen, Caetani, Laurence, Nöldeke, Barthold and Butler on Arabian migrations in the early Islamic era. The studies of those scholars emphasize economic factors and rather ignore religious matters, which is unacceptable in Islamic studies. See the view of Jawād ʿAlī on this question, *al-Mufaṣṣal* 44, p. 414ff.
13. Abū Tammām, *Dīwān al-Hamāsa* (ed. ʿAbd Allāh Uṣaylān, Riyadh, 1401/1982), II, p. 418. The line is by Ḥakīm ibn Qubayṣa.
14. See the discussion of some historians' views, especially those views of Philip Hitti, in his *Tārīkh al-ʿArab* (Beirut, 1958), I, pp. 195–6.
15. No historian has looked at these migrations as having been undertaken for religious reasons, because of the differences between the conquests and the

migrations. See Abū ʿUbayd al-Qāsim Ibn Sallām, *Kitāb al-Amwāl* (ed. Muḥammad Khalīl Harrās, Beirut, 1968), pp. 230–1.

16. Al-Birrī discusses the philosophy of the Arab migrations and their relation to the Islamic religion; see *Qabāʿil*, p. 42ff. For the view of Islam on jihād, see al-Ṭabarī, *Mukhtaṣar . . . Jāmiʿ al-bayān ʿan taʾwīl āy al-Qurʾān* (ed. M. al-Ṣābūnī and ʿAlī Aḥmad Rā, Beirut, 1963), I, p. 327.
17. There are those who hold the opposite view, namely, that the participation of Banū Ḥanīfa in the battle of Qadda, along with other branches of Rabīʿa, was a result of close relations developed many years before the battle. See Nizār al-Ḥadīthī, 'al-Yamama wa-riddat Musaylima' (unpublished MA thesis, Baghdad, 1971), p. 53. On the battle of Qadda, in which Bakr ibn Wāʾil, ʿAnaza and Ḍubayʿa defeated Taghlib, al-Numayr and Ghufayla, see Abū ʿUbayd Allāh al-Bakrī, *Muʿjam mā istaʿjam min asmāʾ al bilād wa-al-mawāḍiʿ* (ed. Muṣṭafā al-Saqqā, Cairo, 1945–51), I, p. 85. Abū Aḥmad al-ʿAskarī says that the battle of Qaḍḍa took place during the wars of Basūs (*Sharḥ mā yaqaʿu fīhi al-taṣḥīf wa-al-taḥrīf* [ed. ʿAbd al-ʿAzīz Aḥmad, Cairo, n.d.], p. 4); Ibn Qutayba says that it was the great battle between Bakr and Taghlib (*Maʿārif* [ed. Tharwat ʿUkāsha, Cairo, 2nd edn, 1969], p. 97).
18. Ibn Qutayba, *al-Shiʿr wa-al-shuʿarāʾ* (ed. Muḥammad Yūsuf Najm, Beirut, 1964), I, p. 925. See also Hishām ibn Muḥammad al-Kalbī, *Jamharat al-nasab* (ed. Nāji Hasan, Beirut, 1986), p. 490.
19. Banū Ḥanīfa refrained from joining tribal/military alliances, as in their non-participation in the Lahāzim alliance, which included most of Rabīʿa's subdivisions living in Yamama, and played a major role in some Arabian battles, such as those of Ṫalḥ and Balqāʾ. That alliance was headed by Abjar ibn Bujayr al-ʿIjlī. See Abū ʿUbayda, *Naqāʾiḍ Jarīr wa-al-Farazdaq* (ed. Anthony Ashley Bevan, Leiden, 1905); see also Abū al-Faraj al-Iṣfahānī, *Kitāb al-Aghānī* (ed. Muḥammad Abū al-Faḍl Ibrāhīm *et al.*, Cairo, 1923–9, 1970–4), XI, p. 296; Maḥmūd Shukrī al-Alūsī, *Bulūgh al-arab fī maʿrifat aḥwāl al-ʿArab* (ed. Muḥammad Bahjat al-Atharī, Cairo, 1342/1923), II, p. 69. Al-Isfahānī thinks that Banū Ḥanīfa were distanced from Bedouinism, and that their relations with others were described as civilized, even with their rivals (*Aghānī*, XI, p. 50).
20. Al-Jāḥiz, *Kitāb al-Hayawān* (ed. ʿAbd al-Salām Muḥammad Hārān, Cairo, 1968), IV, p. 380.
21. Ibn Sallām, *Kitāb al-Amwāl*, p. 59. On these reports see Muḥammad Hamid Allāh, *Majmūʿat al-wathāʾiq al-siyāsiyya lil-ʿahd al-nabawīwa-al-khilāfa al-rāshida* (Beirut, 1969), p. 296.

22. See Aḥmad ibn Yaḥyā al-Balādhurī, *Liber expugnationis regionum (Futūḥ al-buldān)* (ed. M. G. deGoeje, Leiden, 1866), p. 64.
23. Aḥmad Shalabī believed that the Umayyad state was interested in Yamama because of its connection with Persia and the Umayyads' fears that intellectual currents and the spirit of rebellion might penetrate the area, as well as because of its strategic position. He adds that Yamama was never ignored by the political leadership in Damascus. See his questionable analyses in *Mawsūʿat al-tārīkh al-Islāmī* (Cairo, 1974), VII, p. 420.
24. See, e.g., al-Ṫabarī, *tārīkh al-umam wa-al-mulūk* (Cairo, 1939), VI, p. 289, on the appointment of al-Shammākh as governor of Yamama by Ziyād ibn Abī Sufyān.
25. Khalīfa ibn Khayyāṫ al-ʿUṣfurī, *Kitāb al-tārīkh* (ed. Akram Ḍiyāʾ al-ʿUmarī, Riyadh, 1982), I, p. 393. Perhaps the reason for calling them 'Najdāt' was to set them apart from the people of Najd; see al-Maqrīzī, *al-Mawāʾiẓ wa-al-iʿtibār fī dhikr al-khiṫaṫ wa-al-āthār* (henceforth *Khiṫaṫ*) (Cairo, 1324–6/1906–17), I, p. 178. After the murder of Najda, the Yamama Khārijīs broke up into three groups: the Najdiyya, ʿAṫwiyya and Fudaikiyya. See Abū al-Hasan ʿAlī al-Ashʿarī, *Maqālāt al-Islāmiyyīn wa-ikhtilāf al-muṣallīn* (ed. M. M. ʿAbd al-Hamīd, Cairo, 1969–70), I, p. 176; ʿAbd al-Qāhir ibn Ṫāhir al-Baghdādi, *al-Farq bayna al-firaq* (ed. M. M. ʿAbd al-Hamīd, Cairo, 1964), p. 79.
26. Al-Balādhurī, *Futūḥ*, p. 91.
27. Following the *ridda* war, the caliph Abū Bakr issued an order preventing the apostates from joining the armies of conquest (see al-Ṫabarī, *Tārīkh*, III, p. 347), but later allowed them to do so (*ibid.*, IV, pp. 70–1). The confiscation of the tribe's property was a result of the truce between the Muslims and Banū Ḥanīfa (see Ḥamid Allāh, *Wathāʾiq*, p. 296).
28. Al-Ṫabarī, *Tārīkh*, IV, p. 9.
29. *Ibid.*, IV, p. 72.
30. Al-Balādhurī, *Futūḥ*, p. 128.
31. See ʿAbd Allāh al-Sayf, *al-Ḥayāt al-iqtiṣādiyya wa-al-ijtimāʿiyya fi Najd wa-al-Ḥijāz fī al-ʿaṣr al-Umawī* (Riyadh, 1403/1982), p. 73.
32. Al-Iṣfahānī, *Aghānī*, XXII, p. 287.
33. *Ibid.*, XX, p. 171.
34. *Ibid.*, XXI, pp. 230–8.
35. [Pseudo] al-Jāḥiẓ, *al-al-Maḥāsin wa-al-aḍdād* (ed. ʿĀṣim ʿAytānī, Beirut, 1996), p. 67.
36. Yāqāt al-Ḥamawī, *Muʿjam al-buldān* (Beirut, 1988), II, p. 161.
37. *Ibid.*, II, p. 478.

38. Al-Ṭabarī, *Tārīkh*, VI, p. 193.
39. Aḥmad ibn ʿAbd al-Wahhāb al-Nuwayrī, *Nihāyat al-arab fī funūn al-ʿArab* (ed. Muḥammad Abū al-Faḍl Ibrāhīm, Cairo, 1952), XIX, p. 144.
40. 'Izz al-Dīn Ibn al-Athīr, *al-Kāmil fī al-tārīkh* (ed. C.J. Tornberg, Leiden, 1851–76, repr. Beirut, 1965–67), IV, p. 201.
41. Al-Jāḥiẓ, *al-Bayān wa-al-tabyīn* (ed. ʿAbd al-Salām Muḥammad Hārūn, Cairo, 1975), p. 283.
42. Ibn al-Athīr, *Kāmil*, III, p. 352.
43. Caetani and Ashtor believed that the epidemics spread over large areas outside Iraq. See E. Ashtor, *al-Tārīkh al-iqtiṣadī wa-al-ijtimāʿī lil-sharqal-awsaṭ fī al-ʿuṣū al-wusṭā* (trans. ʿAbd al-Hādī ʿAbla [of *Economic and Social History of the Middle East in the Middle Ages*], Damascus, 1985), p. 220.
44. Leone Caetani, *Chronographia Islamica, ossia, riassunto cronologico della storia di tutti popoli musulmani* . . . (Paris, 1912), III, p. 102.
45. For example, the famous floods of 'al-Hijāf' and 'al-Makhbal'. See al-Ṭabarī, *Tārīkh*, VI, p. 55; Abū al-Walīd al-Azraqī, *Akhbār Mecca wa-mā jāʾa fīhā min āthār* (ed. R. S. Malhas, Beirut, 1969), pp. 395–7.
46. Ibn Khurdādhbih, *al-Masālik wa-al-mamālik* (ed. M. J. de Goeje, Leiden, 1889), p. 15. Abū Yūsuf and al-Māwardī say that digging wells, leasing them, and whatever (else) that benefits tax-payers as to lands and rivers was paid for by the state treasury; see Abū Yūsuf Yaʿqūb, *Kitāb al-Kharāj* (Cairo, 1302/1884–5), p. 131; ʿAlī ibn Muḥammad al-Māwardī, *al-Ahkām al-sulṭāniyya wa-al-wilāyāt al-dīniyya* (Cairo, 1973), p. 174.
47. Ashtor believed that the entire Middle East witnessed extensive migrations from agricultural villages to towns, and probably to other new areas, and that migration continued in different degrees from the first to fifth/seventh to eleventh centuries (*al-Tārīkh al-iqtiṣādī*, p. 219).
48. Ibn al-Athīr, *Kāmil*, III, p. 352.
49. Al-Balādhurī, *Futūḥ*, pp. 128, 151; Muḥammad ibn Yūsuf al-Kindī, *al-Wulāt wa-al-quḍāt* (ed. Rhuvon Guest, Beirut, 1908), p. 364. Ashtor discussed this point usefully and extensively; see *al-Tārīkh al-iqtiṣādī*, p. 50.
50. Ashtor, *al-Tārīkh al-iqtiṣādī*, p. 80ff. On the complaint of al-Rāʿī al-Numayrī against the *zakāt* collectors, see Abū Zayd al-Qurashī, *Jamharat ashʿār al-ʿArab* (Beirut, 1991), II, pp. 279–83.
51. See al-Sayf's discussion of a reference by Ibn Qutayba (in *al-Imāma wa-al-siyāsa* [Cairo, 1967], I, p. 177) and his conclusion that the price of wheat in the Hijaz was high during critical periods of high temperatures, *al-Ḥayat al-iqtiṣādiyya*, p. 128).

52. Abū Yūsuf Yaʿqūb, *Kitāb al-Kharāj*, p. 76.
53. Muḥammad Ibn Saʿd, *al-Ṭabaqāt al-kubrā* (ed. Iḥsān ʿAbbās, Beirut, 1976), V, p. 549ff. Ibn Saʿd's list, and that of the savants from Banū Ḥanīfa mentioned by Khalīfa ibn Khayyāṫ al-ʿUṣfurī (*Kitāb al-Ṭabaqāt* [ed. Akram Ḍiyāʾ al-ʿUmari, Baghdad, 1967], pp. 289–90), by Ibn Abī Ḥātim al-Rāzī (*Taqdimat al-maʿrifa li-Kitāb al-Jarḥ wa-al-taʿdīl* [Hyderabad, 1952], pp. 253–7), by Ibn ʿAsākir (*al-Tārīkh al-kabīr* [ed. ʿAbd al-Qādir Badrān, Damascus, 1329–32/1911–13], II, p. 69) and by Shams al-Dīn Muḥammad al-Dhahabī (*al-Kāshif fī maʿrifat man lahu riwāya fī al-kutub al-sitta* [ed. ʿIzzat ʿAlī ʿAṫiyya and M. M. Muwashshī, Cairo, 1972], I, p. 197) clearly show the level of cultural activity and intellectual and scholarly florescence in Yamama.
54. See the list of scholars from Banū Ḥanīfa who settled in Yamama and the Islamic territories in Ibn Ḥibbān al-Bustī, *Mashāhīr ʿulamāʾ al-amṣār wa-aʿlām fuqahāʾ al-aqṫār* (ed. Marzuq ʿAlī Ibrāhīm, Cairo, 1967), p. 148ff. See also Ibn Saʿd, *Ṫabaqāt*, V, p. 549ff.
55. Hamad al-Jāsir, 'Qabīlat Juhayna wa-furāʿuhā', *Majallat al-ʿArab* 12 (1967), p. 1139; and see al-Iṣfahānī, *Aghānī*, XI, p. 50, on the urbanization of Banū Ḥanīfa and their distance from Bedouinism.
56. Charles Pellat, *al-Jāhiẓ fī al-Bạsra wa-Baghdād wa-Samarrāʾ* (trans. Ibrāhīm al-Kīlānī [of *Le mileieu Basrien et la formation de Jāḥeẓ*], Damascus, 1985), p. 89.
57. Ṣaliḥ Aḥmad al-ʿAlī, *al-Tanẓīmāt al-ijtimāʿiyya wa-al-iqtiṣādiyya fī al-Baṣra fī al-qarn al-awwal al-Hijrī* (Beirut, 1969), p. 56.
58. Numerous and often contradictory stories about the enslavement of women and children in the Yamama surrender agreement make it difficult to estimate the number of women. But there is a reference to the effect that one-fifth of the Yamama captives sent to Madinah represented 500 people. See al-Ṫabarī, *Tārīkh*, III, p. 300.
59. *Ibid.*
60. See some of the stories mocking Banū Ḥanīfa, such as that from al-Asmaʿī quoted by al-Jāḥiẓ. It tells of a dignitary from Basra who had a dream and wanted Ibn Sīrīn (a famous interpreter of dreams) to interpret it for him. Such stories made the concealment of lineage acceptable to some Ḥanīfa tribesmen, to avoid the wave of ridicule (see al-Jāḥiẓ, *Hayawān*, IV, p. 368). The poet ʿAlī ibn Hawdha ibn ʿAlī al-Ḥanafī composed an apology for Banū Ḥanīfa, pointing out that they bore all the blame for the apostasy instead of other Arabian tribes (quoted by ʿAbd Allāh ibn Khamīs, *Tārīkh al-Yamāma* [Riyadh, 1407/1987–8], IV, p. 25).

61. Ibn Hibban al-Bustī says that the majority of Banū Ḥanīfa migrants in the Umayyad period were occupied with jihād, and that only a few were interested in learning (*Mashāhīr*, p. 201).
62. Ibn Sallām, *Amwāl*, p. 133.
63. For example, see the case of Juhayna and its branches (al-Jāsir, 'Qabīlat Juhayna'); see also Jawād ʿAlī, *Mufaṣṣal*, IV, p. 370ff.
64. Although the migrations of Banū Ḥanīfa in the Rāshidī period form an introduction to their continued migrations during the Umayyad period, tracing them falls outside the scope of this chapter.
65. Al-Hasan ibn Aḥmad al-Hamdānī, *Ṣifat jazīrat al-ʿArab* (ed. Muḥammad ibn ʿAlī al-Akwaʿ, Riyadh, 1974), p. 319. It is not unlikely that Banū Ḥanīfa merged with Rabīʿa, who used to raid the Sasanian territories; the Arabs called them 'the Rabīʿa lion'. See al-Ṭabarī, *Tārīkh*, IV, p. 87. Barthold believed that a number of Banū Ḥanīfa may have assumed prominent positions in the Sasanian court and administration (see 'Musaylima', *Bulletin de l'Académie des Sciences de la Union des Républiques Soviétiques Socialistes* 19 [Sept.–Nov. 1925], pp. 485–511).
66. For a discussion of these views, see F. Donner, *The Early Islamic Conquests* (Princeton, 1981), p. 231.
67. See *Ibid.*
68. *Ibid.*, p. 250.
69. Aḥmad ibn ʿAlī al-Qalqashandī, *Ṣubḥ al-aʿshā fī ṣināʿat al-inshāʾ* (ed. ʿAbd al-Laṭīf Ḥamza, Cairo, 1962), p. 339.
70. Al-Ṭabarī, *Tārīkh*, III, p. 347. Abū Bakr was of the opinion that those who had conquered Irāq should settle there and not migrate to newly conquered areas. This is apparent in his testament to his successor ʿUmar (Ibn al-Khaṭṭāb): 'Since God had made us victorious over the people of Syria, return those (men) from Iraq to Iraq. They are its people, and in charge of its affairs, and have the courage for it' (Ibn al-Athīr, *Kāmil*, II, p. 175).
71. This battle (against the Sasanian Persians) is also called the battle of al-Qurqus, al-Qusqus al-Nāṭif, or al-Mirwaḥa; see al-Ṭabarī, *Tārīkh*, III, p. 454.
72. Al-Balādhurī, *Futāḥ*, p. 242.
73. Al-Ṭabarī, *Tārīkh*, III, p. 86.
74. *Ibid.*, V, p. 79.
75. Al-Balādhurī, *Futāḥ*, p. 350.
76. Ṣāliḥ Aḥmad al-ʿAli, *Imtidād al-ʿArab fī ṣadr al-Islām* (Beirut, 2nd edn, 1983), p. 26.
77. Sibṭ ibn al-Jawzī, *Mirʾāt al-zamān* (Hyderabad, 1951), VIII. 1–2, p. 289.

78. Al-Iṣfahānī, *Aghānī*, IX, p. 34.
79. Abū Yūsuf Yaʿqūb, *Kitāb al-Kharāj*, p. 76.
80. Al-Iṣfahānī, *Aghānī*, III, p. 257.
81. Aḥmad ibn Abī Yaʿqūb al-Yaʿqūbī, *Kitāb al-Buldān* (Najaf, 1957), p. 75.
82. Al-Balādhurī, *Futāḥ*, p. 372.
83. Abū Jaʿfar ibn Ḥabīb al-Baghdādī, *Kitāb al-muḥabbar* (ed. Ilse Lichtenstadter, Beirut, n.d.), p. 168.
84. Al-Ṭabarī, *Tārīkh*, III, p. 315; al-Iṣfahānī, *Aghānī*, III, p. 257.
85. Al-Iṣfahānī, *Aghānī*, III, p. 257. (The 'Ahl al-ʿĀliya' refers to 'the inhabitants of the high district' of the Hijaz; see *EI2*, art. 'Basra'. The Asāwira were of Persian origin, the Sayābija from Sind, the Ẓuṭṭ from north-west India. -Ed.)
86. Ibn Qutayba, *ʿUyūn al-akhbār* (Cairo, 1925–30), I, p. 333.
87. Al-Balādhurī, *Futūḥ*, p. 372. Al-Ṭabarī says that before Islam there was a group of Persians in Yamama called 'Azadhbih', some of whom went with Khālid ibn al-Walīd to Iraq (*Tārīkh*, III, p. 347).
88. See the list prepared by Ṣ. al-ʿAlī, *Tanẓīmāt*, p. 322.
89. Al-Balādhurī, *Futūḥ*, p. 323.
90. Many expressions occur in the geographical literature, such as 'inhabited by some Arabs', or 'by many Arabs', or 'by a mixture of Arabs and non-Arabs'. See al-Yaʿqūbī, *Buldān*, pp. 86–7, 89–90.
91. Naṣr ibn Muzāḥim, *Waqʿat Ṣiffin* (ed. ʿAbd al-Salām Muḥammad Hārūn, Cairo, 1382/1962), p. 205.
92. Al-Ṭabarī, *Tārīkh*, V, p. 34.
93. Al-Balādhurī, *Ansāb*, IV. 1, p. 387.
94. Al-Ṭabarī, *Tārīkh*, VI, p. 108.
95. See Ṣ. al-ʿAlī's calculation of the population of Kufa, based on Sayf ibn ʿUmar and Bishr ibn ʿAbd al-Wahhāb al-Qurashī, *Imtidād*, p. 26ff.
96. See *ibid*. for a discussion of this matter.
97. Al-Ṭabarī, *Tārīkh*, IV, p. 49.
98. See *ibid*., IV, p. 45ff
99. *Ibid*., IV, p. 45.
100. *Ibid*., II, p. 57.
101. *Ibid*., IV, p. 246. The modifications introduced by ʿUthmān ibn ʿAffān to the previous order established by ʿUmar ibn al-Khaṭṭāb stipulated that Basra should be responsible for conquests in Persia, Kirman and Isfahan, and Kufa for those in Isfahan, Azarbaijan and Rayy. See al-Ṭabarī, *Tārīkh*, IV, p. 137; Ibn Khayyāṭ, *Tārīkh*, I, p. 148.
102. Al-Balādhurī, *Futūḥ*, p. 329. ʿAlī (ibn Abī Ṭālib) adopted a measure

requiring his opponents to emigrate. Ibn Muzāḥim says, '"Alī summoned the tribe of Bāhila and said to them, "O people of Bāhila, I bear witness before God that you hate me and I hate you. So take your property and go to Daylam".' They had refused to support him in the battle of Ṣiffīn, on which see *ibid.*, p. 130. It is known that Bāhila had emigrated from Yamama to Kufa; it is not unlikely that some of Banū Ḥanīfa who worked in industry, mining or agriculture were among them.

103. See the list and sources in Ṣ. al-ʿAlī, *Tanẓīmāt*, pp. 327–43.
104. Al-Ṭabarī, *Tārīkh*, V, p. 225.
105. *Ibid.*, V, p. 172.
106. *Ibid.*, V, pp. 225, 286.
107. See al-Madāʾinī's account in *ibid.*, VI, p. 512.
108. *Ibid.*, VI, pp. 509–10. On the settlement of Bakr ibn Wāʾil in Khurasan and their role in its political and economic history, see Nājī Ḥasan, *al-Qabāʾil al-ʿArabiyya fī al-mashriq khilāl al-ʿaṣr al-Umawī* (Baghdad, 1980), p. 163ff.
109. Al-Yaʿqūbī, *Buldān*, p. 42. On the alliance of Banū Ḥanīfa and ʿIjl, see al-Iṣfahānī, *Aghānī*, XI, p. 50.
110. Perhaps the nature and climate of the Syrian regions and the earlier Arabian migrations influenced settlement in towns. See al-Balādhurī, *Futūḥ*, p. 129, and the verses quoted.
111. Donner, *Conquests*, p. 250.
112. Ṣ. al-ʿAli, *Imtidād*, p. 7. (The battle of Ṣiffīn took place between ʿAlī ibn Abī Ṭālib and Muʿāwiya ibn Abī Sufyān; see the entry in *EI2*. -Ed.)
113. Muḥammad Ibn al-ʿAbbār, *Iʿtab al-kuttāb* (ed. M.S. al-Ashtar, Damascus, 1961), p. 356. On the 'vanguard' of the conquest of Spain, see Ḥusayn Muʾnis, *Fajr al-Andalus* (Cairo, 1959), p. 356.
114. Muḥammad ibn Yazīd al-Mubarrad, *al-Kāmil fī al-lugha wa-al-adab* (ed. Muḥammad Abū al Faḍl Ibrāhīm *et al.*, Cairo), III, p. 184.
115. Al-Yaʿqūbī, *Buldān*, pp. 87–8ff. On the migration of Bakr ibn Wāʾil to Palestine see al-Qalqashandī, *Ṣubḥ al-aʿshā*, I, p. 338.
116. On the Jazīra see al-Balādhurī, *Futūḥ*, pp. 124–76.
117. See *ibid.*
118. Ibn Ḥawqal, *Ṣūrat al-arḍ*, pp. 195–200.
119. Yāqūt, *Muʿjam*, IV, p. 219.
120. Ibn ʿAbd al-Ḥakam, *Futūḥ Miṣr*, p. 116.
121. Al-Yaʿqūbī, *Tārīkh*, p. 234.
122. Al-Birrī, *Qabāʾil*, p. 52. See also Ibn Ḥawqal, *Ṣūrat al-arḍ*, p. 141. On the building of villages, digging of wells, the arrival of migrations of Rabīʿa

tribes to Aswan and Sawākin, see al-Maqrīzī, *al-Bayān wa-al-iʿrab ʿammā bi-arḍ Miṣr min al-Aʿrāb* (ed. Ibrāhīm Ramzī, Cairo, 1916), p. 48.

123. ʿAbd al-Wāḥid Dhannūn Ṫāhā, *al-Fatḥ wa-al-istiqrār al-ʿArabī al-Islāmī fī shamāl Ifrīqiya wa-al-Andalus* (Baghdad, 1982), pp. 239–42.

124. Ibn Ḥazm, *Jamharat ansāb al-ʿArab* (ed. ʿAbd al-Salām Muḥammad Hārūn, Cairo, 1971), pp. 246, 290, 321. See also al-Maqqarī, *Nafḥ al-ṭīb min ghuṣn al-Andalus al-raṭīb* (ed. Iḥsān ʿAbbas, Beirūt, 1968), p. 292.

125. Al-Nuwayrī, *Nihāya*, XIX, p. 144. On the metals of Yamama, see al-Hamdānī, *Buldān*, p. 299.

Chapter 2

Industry in Najd and Hijaz in the Umayyad Period

ʿAbd Allāh Muḥammad as-Sayf

In the Umayyad period, the limited industries that were to be found in Najd and Hijaz could not satisfy the needs of society, especially following the influx of money and the rise in the populations' purchasing power, and the demand for complementary goods. In response, people decided to import the industries they needed from other regions. In this chapter, I shall examine the metal and tanning industries, as well as ironmongery, weaving, carpentry and papermaking, among other things.

Metallurgy was one of the most important industries in these lands, since gold and silver were abundant. One of the most significant mines was that of Bani Saleem,[1] where in the Umayyad period a large amount of gold was mined.[2] Its name came from the tribe in whose land it was situated; another name for it was Farran's mine, perhaps following the name of the tribe that, working in the metal industry, profited from it – these were Bani Farran bin Bala bin Saleem.[3] It seems that this mine was very valuable because of the amount of gold mined there, indicated by the appointment of a special manager: in 128/746 this was Kathir bin Abdullah.[4]

Other famous mines were the Qibaliyyeh mines, bestowed by the Prophet, with some other lands, on Bilal bin al-Harith al-Mazni.[5] These were highly productive mines, the whole area being rich with metals, for al-Baladhiri recounts that the Bani Hilal tribe sold Omar bin Abdul Aziz a piece of land there in which he discovered metal. When they learnt about his discovery they went to him and said, 'We sold you the land but not the metal,' to which he replied, 'Look what I have extracted from it and what I have spent on it.' He then demanded that they repay him his costs, thus reciprocating their accusations.[6] This text indicates that in the Umayyad age any investments in mining were the responsibility of its owners, who had to pay an alms tax on what was extracted from the mine to the value of a quarter of a tenth.[7]

Another famous gold mine was the mine of Hileet, situated in Hima Dariyyeh, named al-Najjadi because it belonged to a man called Najjad bin Musa bin Sa'ed bin Abi Waqqas. This mine was rich in gold.[8] Al-Bakri recounts that 'A richer mine was not known on earth, it was excavated at a time when gold was expensive in all regions and its impact was to make gold cheaper in Iraq and Hijaz.'[9] The Buhran mine is also considered one of the most famous, and lies on the Fara' side on the road from Makkah to Madinah.[10]

The sources mention other mines in Najd and Hijaz but we do not know if these were exploited during the Umayyad period or only afterwards. The mines at al-Ahsan,[11] al-hufayr, al-dabeeb and al-thaniyyeh were among those richly productive in gold.[12] As for silver, al-Hamadani mentions that silver was extracted from the Shamam mine in Yamama,[13] while al-Bakri mentions that the mine of Abriq Khutrub was abundant in silver: 'There was a silver mine in Abriq Khutrub that contained all you could desire of silver and was easy to extract.'[14] The sources also mention that whetstones, used to sharpen knives, were extracted from Mount Radwa and transported to other regions.[15] Another 'industrial' product was salt, which was dried in al-Hajir in the Najd area, considered one of the finest salts of the region.[16]

Another industry that could be found in Najd and Hijaz was ironmongery.[17] It included the production of metal household utensils, as well as the production of weapons, which, since the Jahiliyyeh period, were of great importance in the lives of the Arabs, and which increased in importance after the rise of the Islamic state and the accompanying need of the Muslims to support and consolidate their conquests. The Arabs were forced to import iron from India and Persia through Basra into Najd and Hijaz because of the scarcity of the metal.[18] Al-Kitani relates that the origins of the metal industry in the Arabian peninsula go back to the time when the Prophet conquered Khaybar, capturing thirty slaves who were ironmongers and artisans. He asked for God's blessing to be upon him and said: 'Leave them to live among the Muslims so that they can benefit from their industry and be strengthened in their fight against their enemies.' So they were allowed to remain, and those who learned a skill at their hands were called craftsmen or artisans, while their descendants were called slaves, who from that day on took refuge with and attached themselves to the great personages.[19]

Ironmongers were to be found in Makkah[20] as well as in Madinah.[21] The city of Hajar in Najd was famous for the quality of its ironmongery, in particular the quality of the spear tips produced there.[22] Ibn Manthour recounts Abu Hanifa's saying 'The iron of Hajar is first in good quality.'[23] Other sources mention Hanafi swords,[24] attributed most probably to the Bani Hanifa tribe that lived in al-Yamama in Najd. Swords were also manufactured in Jildan in Hijaz.[25]

Goldsmithing, learned from the Jews, had continued from the time they left the Hijaz. At-Tabari recounts that the Prophet took over the craftworks of the Ibn Qaynuqaʾ Jews after they were removed from Madinah.[26] Ibn Zubalah mentions that in the village of Zuhra, one of the villages of Madinah, there were 300 goldsmiths.[27] During the Umayyad period, the number of goldsmiths who worked in their shops increased,[28] while Ibn Saʾad mentions that Wardan was a goldsmith in Makkah.[29]

The most important craft the goldsmiths engaged in was the making of gold and silver jewellery: bracelets, anklets, rings and earrings with which women adorned themselves.[30] This trade took place especially following the flow of money to Hijaz and the rise of the standard of living there, with a corresponding rise in the demand for luxury goods. The goldsmiths also made gold casings for swords.[31]

Another industry for which the city of Taʾif in Hijaz was famous and which was important in the region was the tannery industry. Al-Hamdani says, 'It is the city of tanners in which the skins of Taʾif are tanned.'[32] The climate, favourable for tanning, combined with Taʾif's geographical location, made it easily accessible for merchants, and helped to establish this industry there. Additionally, in Hijaz,[33] there was an abundance of the animals traditionally used in the tanning industry, such as camels, cattle and sheep, as well as deer and buffalo that lived in the Sarawat Mountains. All this contributed to the prosperity and fame of the tanning industry of Ta'if, which expanded to include neighbouring areas.[34]

Another factor that helped this industry to flourish was the presence in Najd and Hijaz of the natural materials used in tanning, such as the leaves of the acacia (sant) tree.[35] These trees could be found in the region of Yamama in Najd,[36] and grew in the ʿAqiq valley near al-Madinah al Mun-awwara, and on the outskirts of Makkah al-Mukarrama.[37] The tools used by the tanners are not specifically mentioned in the sources, except by Ibn Sayyida who says the most important, such as the mahat used to polish and embellish the skins, was normally made from wood and occasionally from metal, and the mujlah was used to cleanse the dirt that stuck to the skins.[38]

The leather industry was so developed in Ta'if that its reputation spread far and wide and its products were exported to the other Islamic regions. This reputation seems to have continued until the late Islamic period, for al-Idrissy mentions merchants in Ta'if 'whose best products were of leather of a high and precious quality, such that soles made in Najd are taken as exemplary, which is well known'.[39] Ibn al-Mujawar also mentions that the people of Ta'if were involved in the tanning of skins, saying 'All their industry is in the tanning of skins, using that heavy high quality skins for which they are famous and which is suitable for khawarerem.'[40]

Tanning was not confined solely to Ta'if but could also be found in Makkah in the early Islamic period.[41] It seems that this carried on into the Umayyad period, for Ibn Sa'ad mentions that some inhabitants of Ta'if who settled in Makkah continued to work in tanning,[42] while Ibn al-Mujawar states that the tanning of skins was widespread in Makkah and in its neighbouring villages.[43] It seems that there were insufficient quantities of acacia trees in Makkah to satisfy the needs of the tanning industry, and it is for that reason that the leaves were brought in from the ʿAqiq valley, near Madinah.[44] Al-Azraqi mentions that the tanners in Makkah had their own shops, and that in the *ḥajj* season the trade in leather would flourish.[45]

Leather was of immense importance for the Kharrazin (leather craftsmen), of whom there were many in the cities of Ta'if and Makkah.[46]

They bought it from the tanners and out of it they made soles and slippers,[47] saddles, tents and troughs or basins, and leather containers used by the Bedouins of Najd and Hijaz to preserve water, oil, honey, ghee and yogurt;[48] the material was highly suitable for their nomadic existence. These containers were also used to preserve dates,[49] for only containers made from leather could resist the hot sun of that region. After tanning, skins could also be used to make leather rugs.[50] There are indications that some household slaves were skilled leatherworkers, and would undertake this activity when asked by their masters to do so.[51]

Another industry to be found in Najd and Hijaz during the Umayyad period was the textile industry. In the al-Washm region of Najd high-quality cloaks were woven and from here exported to other countries. The village of Tharmuda' was particularly famous for its cloaks.[52] The poet Hamid bin Thawr al-Hilali attributed cloak weaving to Tharmuda'. His son, witnessing that his father always returned sumptuously robed by the different princes he visited, tried to imitate him by going to Marwan bin al-Hakim, who, however, gave him nothing. Upon his return the father said:

> Muqbil al-Thukair commenting on the attribution of cloaks to Tharmuda' says, 'The attribution of cloak making to Tharmuda' is without doubt correct, for it was engaged in their production until quite a recent time. Washm was famous for its weaving of wool and other raw material until a period less than two hundred years ago, when, about a hundred years ago, it began to decline until it totally disappeared'.[53] It can be gleaned from Ibn Sa'ad''s tale that the Faqih Abdullah bin Aswad who lived in Yamama in the Umayyad period was a weaver of cloaks.[54]

The town of Mar a-Zhahran in Hijaz was also famous for its cloth weaving, so much so that the phrase 'a Zhahrani' dress was coined in reference to it.[55] The sources indicate the existence of some household weaving, but of a rudimentary type lacking in skill, mostly in the deserts of Najd and Hijaz.[56] From the account of Imam Malik it can be gleaned that girls in the Umayyad period were involved in weaving, and their products (of al-Rayt) displayed for sale in the markets;[57] these girls, it seems, were involved in this production at the behest of their masters who provided them with the necessary raw material.

However, the sources do not indicate how such workshops were formed, or what social, financial and economic problems they faced, nor do they comment on the availability of capital or the raw materials needed for production, or the work itself and how it was managed. An exception is al-Asfahani, who mentioned the tools that were used in the weaving of cloth such as the loom called *al-haf*.[58] The raw materials used seem to have been wool,[59] raw silk[60] and cotton.[61]

It is also apparent that most of those engaged in weaving were either slaves or dependants (mawali). Al-Asfahani mentions that Omar bin Abi Rabiʾah had seventy slaves engaged in weaving in Makkah.[62] Omar also seems to have benefited from his father's slaves who were engaged in all the different trades.[63] Ibn Saʾad relates that Maʾan bin ʿIssa, the dependant of al-Ashjaʾ, was involved in the manufacture of textiles in Madinah; he had some slaves who were experienced in weaving, and he bought them silk yarn to weave.[64] A man from the Bani Makhzum had a slave in Makkah who used a loom at home to weave cloth,[65] while some Arabs also engaged in this industry, as can be gleaned from Ubeid bin Sharih's poetry; for example, a paean of the people of Qahtan in the presence of Muʾawiyya bin Abi Sufyan, mentioned that some of the members of the Bani Numayr tribe, who lived in Najd, had engaged in the weaving of cloaks.[66]

Textile production was dependent on another craft, that of dyeing cloth. Dyers would dye cloth in their shops in return for specified sums that the owner of the cloth would pay. To dye the cloth, dyers would use natural dyes extracted from plants, such as safflower to dye cloth yellow (some sources say that the safflower produces a red dye); Ibn Saʾad stated that Urwah bin Zubayr would have his wrap dyed yellow at the dyers for one dinar.[67]

Dyers also used saffron for dyeing clothes. Al-Qasem bin Muḥammad, the son of Abu Bakr, would wear a wrap lightly dyed with saffron,[68] while al-Hussein bin Ali bin Abi Taleb wore a saffron-dyed shawl,[69] and Abdullah bin Omar wore cloth dyed with saffron as well as that dyed with red anemones.[70] Salem bin Abdullah's wife, Um Kalthum, wore yellow-dyed cloth,[71] while clothes were also dyed red.[72] The other colours used by the dyers were green and black.[73] Some people would dye their own and their children's clothes at home without using a dyer, and they too used safflower in dyeing.[74]

Carpentry was a craft held in high regard. Carpenters produced household goods such as chairs, doors, plates and drinking bowls. Craftsmen from Makkah had their own neighbourhood,[75] while the sources indicate that carpenters were also to be found in Madinah.[76] They practised their trade in shops as well as in their homes, and they also sold their products. Abu Na'im recounts that one of the dependants, a Persian, crafted drinking bowls in his home in Madinah.[77] Occasionally carpenters were hired to work in the homes of the wealthy, who bought wood for them and commissioned them to craft what they wanted.[78]

Weapons of war were also produced, including lances, arrows and bows,[79] from the trees that grew in Najd and Hijaz. Al-Hijri recounts that the Muzayna and Bilharith tribe made bows from the Ta'lub tree,[80] as well as from the wood of the Shuhat and Nashm trees.[81] The arrows of Bilad in Yamama and those of Yathrib in Hijaz were particularly famous in the period of al-Jahiliyyah,[82] and it seems that the production of weaponry continued in the Umayyad period, as witnessed by the mention of the Yathrib arrows that were so famous in this period that pilgrims stipulated that soldiers should be equipped with them.[83] The arrows were made from the wood of the pomegranate tree, and al-Asfahani mentions that the poet al'Arji would hone many arrows from the tree in his compound in al-ʿArj in Ta'if.[84] The poet Nasib also was good at sharpening and trimming arrows,[85] and the author of *tartib al-madarek* mentions that Uns bin Malik made arrows too,[86] while Kathir ʿAzzah was skilled in this craft too.[87]

Since some of the regions of Najd and Hijaz were agricultural lands, there must have been some industry based on agricultural produce, but the sources are not clear on this point. However, it does seem that cages were made out of palm branches; mats, various kinds of baskets, and plates out of palm leaves were also made.[88] Tents were fashioned from palm branches and leaves,[89] while the inhabitants benefited from the use of wood and palm branches in the construction of mosque and house ceilings, as well as doors and windows.[90]

Papermaking is considered one of the skills that were to be found in Hijaz during the Umayyad period. Paper was made from silk, hemp and cotton. A-Shihab al-Murjani says, 'The making of paper from silk, cotton and hemp was widespread. Yusef bin ʿAmr of Makkah invented paper making from cotton around 88 h. in Hijaz.'[91] It seems that the paper produced was not of good quality, as evidenced by the importation of paper from Egypt for use by the state in Hijaz in the period of ʿUmar bin Abdul Aziz.[92]

Another product was al-Ghaliyyeh, a kind of perfume made from musk, ambergris, aloes and fat. The first to make this was Abdullah bin Jaʾfar in Hijaz, and, on being scented with it, Muʾawiyyeh bin Sufyan named it al-Ghaliyyeh ('The precious'), after enquiring how it was made.[93]

The chiselling of stones for use in construction was undertaken in Makkah and Madinah. Al-Sammhudi mentions that Bani Haram in al-Madinah had a Romish slave who hewed and carved chiselled stones.[94] Al-Asfahani mentions that Saʾid al-Hadli would chisel the stones that he hewed out of the Abu Qubais Mountain in Makkah, making cooking pots from them as well.[95]

Notes:

1. Al-Harbi, *al-manasik* (Beirut, 1389), p. 333; al-Asfahani, *bilad al-ʿarab* (Riyadh, 1388), p. 403; at-Tabari, *tarikh al-rusul wasl-muluk* (Dar al-Ma'arif edition), VII, p. 348.
2. Al-Harbi, *al-manasik*, p. 335.
3. Al-Asfahani, *bilad al-ʿarab*, p. 402 n. 1; al-Bakri, *muʾjam ma ustuʾjam* (Cairo, 1945). Bani Saleem's mine is called the birthplace of gold. Exploitation of this mine continued until recent times when it became apparent that gold production did not offset the costs of production, and so work was stopped, and a small town was established there. See Hamad al-Jasir, *al-maʾadin al-qadimafi bilad alʾarab* (Riyadh, 1388), X and XI, p. 926.
4. At-Tabari, *tarikh al-rusul wal-muluk*, VII, p. 348; al-Asfahani, *al-aghani* (edition of al-hayʾah al-masriyyeh al-ʿameh), XXIII, pp. 227–8.
5. Malik, *al-mudawana* (Cairo, 1923), II, p. 289; Abu ʿUbeid, *al-amwal* (Cairo, 1396), p. 423; al-Baladhiri, *futuh al-buldan* (Beirut, 1957), p. 22; al-Bakri,

mu'jam ma ustu'jam, III, pp. 1047, 1051. al-Qibaliyyeh is a mountain range that extended midway from al-Mseijid and the city of Madinah in the south, to the edge of Mount Buwat in the north. This area was known as the qibaliyyeh because many of its valleys inclined in the direction of the qibla (the Kaaba) until they joined up with the valleys of Madinah. There is still evidence of mining today; see Hamad al-Jasir, *al-ma'adin alqadimafi bilad al-ʿarab*, p. 979.

6. Abu ʿUbeid, *al-amwal*, pp. 523–4; al-Baladhiri, *futuh al-buldan*, p. 22.
7. Abu ʿUbeid, *al-amwal*, p. 423; Malik, *al-mudawana*, II, p. 289; Muḥammad KurfʿAli, *al-Idara al-Islamiyyeh fi ʿiz al-ʿarab* (Cairo, 1934), p. 101.
8. Al-Bakri, *mu'jam ma ustu'jam*, III, p. 875.
9. *Ibid.*, p. 875.
10. *Ibid.*, p. 1021.
11. Al-Astahani, *bilad al-ʿarab*, p. 159; al-Hamadani, *sifat jazeerat al-ʿarab* (Riyadh, 1394), p. 299.
12. Al-Hamadani, *sifat jazeerat al-ʿarab*, p. 299. All these mines lie in Yamama.
13. *Ibid.*, p. 299.
14. Al-Bakri, *mu'jam ma ustu'jam*, III, p. 864. Abriq Khutrub lies near Huma dariyyeh.
15. Yaqut, *mu'jam al-buldan* (Leipzig edition), II, p. 790; Ibn Huqal, *surat al-ard* (Leiden, 1967), p. 33; as-Samhoudi, *wafa' al-wafa'*, IV, p. 1218.
16. Al-Hamadani, *sifat jazeerat al-ʿarab*, pp. 293, 301.
17. Al-Azraqi, *akhbar mecca* (Ghattanqah, 1275) p. 476. See also Ibn Bikar, *jamharat nasab qureish* (Cairo, 1381), I, p. 372, and Asfahani, *bilad al-ʿarab*, p. 30.
18. Al-Azdi, *tarikh al-mosul* (Cairo, 1387), p. 49, and al-ʿAli, *al-tanzimat al-ʿjtima'iyyeh wal iqtisadiyyeh fil basra* (Beirut, 1969), p. 247.
19. Al-kitani, *at-taratib al-idariyyeh*, II, p. 75. I have consulted the six volumes of as-Sahah but could not find this *ḥadīth*.
20. Ibn Bikar, *jamharat nasab qureish*, I; also Al-Azraqi, *akhbar mecca*, p. 476.
21. Al-Azdi, *tarikh al-mosul*, p. 49.
22. Ibn Manthour, *lisan al-ʿarab* (Cairo, 1307), V, p. 242.
23. *Ibid.*, p. 242.
24. Ibn Sa'ad, *at-tabaqat* (Leiden edition), VI, p. 185. See also al-ʿAli, *al-tanzimat*, p. 247.
25. Al-Asfahani, *bilad al-ʿarab*, p. 30.
26. At-Tabari, *tarikh al-rusul wal-muluk*, II, p. 481.
27. As-Samhoudi, *wafa' al-wafa'*, IV, p. 1230. See also al-Isami, *Samt an-nujum al-ʿawali* (Cairo, 1380), III, p. 94.

28. Malik, *al-mudawanah*, XI, pp. 391 and 491.
29. Ibn Sa'ad, *at-tabaqat*, V, p. 360.
30. Malik, *al-muwtta'* (Cairo, 1387), p. 116, XI, p. 392. See also Ibn Sa'ad, *at-tabaqat*, V, p. 189, at-Tabari, *tarikh al-rusul wal-muluk*, V, pp. 452, 463; al-Asfahani, *al-aghani*, XVII, pp. 45–6.
31. Ibn al-Jouzy, *sifat as-safwa* (Hyderabad, 1355), II, p. 61.
32. *Ibid.*, p. 260.
33. *Ibid.*, p. 260, See also al-Zubayr bin *Bikar, jamharat nasab quraysh*, p. 468, as well as ar-Rashid bin al-Zubayr, *azhakha'ir wat-tuhaf (Kuwait*, 1959), p. 11.
34. Ibn Sa'ad, *at-tabaqat*, V, p. 366, see also Ahmad Farouk, ʿdibaghat al-julud wa tijaratiha ʿind al-ʿarab fi mustahal al-islam', *majallat al-ʿarab*, VIII and IX (Riyadh), pp. 539–40.
35. Yaqut, *mu'jam al-buldan*, III, p. 123. See also Ibn al-Mujawer, *tarikh al-mustabser* (Leiden, 1951), p. 32.
36. Yaqut, *ibid.*, p. 123.
37. Ibn al-Mujawer, *tarikh al-mustabser*, p. 32.
38. Ibn Sayyida mentions a number of instruments used for different purposes in tanning such as al-minhaz, almabqar, al-masrad, al-miqrad and al-makhsaf. See *al-mukhasas*, IV, pp. 100–15. See also Ahmad Farouq, ʿdibaghat al-julud wa tijaratiha ʿind al-ʿarab fi mustahal al-islam', *majallat al-ʿarab*, p. 545.
39. Al-Idrissy, ʿnazhat al-mushtaq', annotated by Dr Ibrahim Shawqi, *majallat al-mujamma' al-ʿilmi, Iraq* 21 (1971), p. 26.
40. Ibn al-Mujawer, *tarikh al-mustabser*, p. 25.
41. Ibn Sa'ad, *at-tabaqat*, VIII, pp. 73, 206.
42. *Ibid.*, V, p. 366.
43. Ibn al-Mujawer, *tarikh al-mustabser*, p. 13.
44. *Ibid.*, p. 25.
45. Al-Azraqi, *akhbar mecca*, p. 474.
46. Al-Mus'ib al-Zubeiri, *nasab qureish* (Cairo, 1953), p. 178. Ibn Sa'ad, *at-tabaqat*, V, p. 230.
47. Ibn Sa'ad, *at-tabaqat*, p. 230.
48. Ibn Bikar, *jamharat nasab qureish*, I, p. 370. See also Ibn Qutaiba, *as-shi'ir washshuʿara'* (Cairo, 1966), I, p. 440; al-Asfahani, *al-aghani*, VIII, pp. 152–3, and Ahmad Farouq, *dibaghat al-julud*, p. 554.
49. Ibn Bikar, *jamharat nasab qureish*, p. 370.
50. Malik, *al-mudawanah*, I, p. 75.
51. Al-Baghdadi, *khazanat al-adab* (Cairo, 1347), I, p. 106.

52. Yaqut, *mu'jam al-buldan*, I, p. 922; Muqbil al-Thukair, *tarikh najd*, ma'had al-makhtutat, The Arab League, no. 1464 d., paper 170.
53. Muqbil al-Thukair, *ibid*, paper 170b.
54. Ibn Sa'ad, *at-tabaqat*, V, p. 404.
55. Yaqut, *mu'jam al-buldan*, III, p. 581. See also Ibn Balihid, *sahih al-akhbar* (Cairo, 1392), II, p. 139. Mar a-Zhahran is known now as Wadi Fatmeh, the biggest of Mecca's seven valleys, and the most abundant in water, and in the number of villages and population. See Mahdi as-Sahhaf, 'mawdi' mecca al-mukarramah wabi'atuha al-jugrafiyyeh', majallat kuliyyat al-adab, Baghdad University, no. 14, II (Baghdad, 1970), p. 904.
56. Malik, *al-mudawanah*, V, p. 380; Ibn Qutaiba, *as-shi'ir wa-shu'ara'*, I, p. 439; al-Asfahani, *al-aghani*, XVIII, p. 11.
57. Malik, *al-mudawanah*, IX, pp. 24, 131.
58. Al-Asfahani, *al-aghani*, V, p. 114. On al-haf see Ibn Manzhur, *lisan al-ʿarab*, X, p. 396.
59. Muqbil al-Thukair, *tarikh najd*, paper 170b.
60. Ibn Sa'ad, *at-tabaqat*, V, p. 324.
61. Ibn Kathir, *al-bidayah wal-nihayah* (Riyadh, 1966), VIII, p. 114.
62. Al-Asfahani, *al-aghani*, I, p. 78.
63. *Ibid.*, p. 65.
64. Ibn Sa'ad, *at-tabaqat*, V, p. 324.
65. Al-Asfahani, *al-aghani*, V, p. 114.
66. Ubeid bin Sharih, *akhbar Ubeid bin Sharih*, p. 75. Verse p. 251. From Ahmad Farouq, ʿdibaghat al-julud wa tijaratiha ʿind al-ʿarab fi mustahal al-islam', *majallat al-ʿarab*, p. 546.
67. Ibn Sa'ad, *at-tabaqat*, V, p. 134.
68. *Ibid.*, p. 140.
69. Al-Baladhiri, *ansab al-ashraf* (Jerusalem, 1938), IV, part 3, p. 22.
70. Ibn Sa'ad, *at-tabaqat*, IV, part 1, p. 127.
71. *Ibid.*, VIII, p. 364.
72. *Ibid.*, V, p. 161; Abu ʿUbayda, *naqa'id jarir wal-farazdaq* (Leiden, 1905), II, p. 526.
73. Malik, *al-mudawanah*, XI, p. 392; Ibn Qutaiba, *al-imamah wal-siyasah* (Cairo, 1387), I, p. 188.
74. Abu Na'im, *hiliyyat al-awliya'* (Cairo, 1932), VII, p. 319.
75. Al-Azraqi, *akhbar mecca*, p. 455; a-Jahiz, *al-mahasin wal-addad* (Cairo, 1924), p. 119.
76. Al-Asfahani, *al-aghani*, XVI, p. 149; XIX, p. 165; Abu Na'im, *hiliyyat al-awliya'*, III, p. 152. See also Ibn ʿAbed Rabbo, *al-ʿaqd al-farid* (Cairo,

n.d.), VI, p. 433; al-Qayrawani, *jam' al-jawahir fil-muluh wal-nawadir* (Cairo, 1953), p. 67.

77. Abu Na'im, *hiliyyat al-awliya'*, p. 152.
78. Al-Asfahani, *al-aghani*, XVI, p. 149.
79. Ibn Manzhur, *lisan al-'arab*, V, pp. 242–3.
80. Abu 'Ali al-Hijri, *at-ta'liqat wal-nawadir* (Dar al-kutub) (Indian edition), p. 479. Out of the Ta'lub tree are made the Arabian bows. Al-Asma'i says that that Ta'lub and Shuhat are mountain trees. See Ibn Manzhur, *lisan al-'arab*, I, p. 219.
81. 'Aram a-Silmi, *asma' jibal tuhamah* (Cairo, 1394), pp. 403, 408. The Shuhat tree has many twigs sprouting from the same branch, and grows in the Sarawat mountains. Bows are made from its wood, and its edible fruit is similar to grapes. See Ibn Manzhur, *lisan al-'arab*, XII, pp. 200–1. The Nashm tree is another mountain tree out of which bows are made, see Ibn Manzhur, *lisan al-'arab*, XVI, p. 54.
82. Al-Bakri, *mu'jam ma ustu'jam*, I, p. 271. Also Yaqut, *mu'jam al-buldan*, I, p. 707.
83. Al-Baladhiri, *ansab al-ashraf* (Ahlawart edition), p. 273.
84. Al-Asfahani, *al-aghani*, I, p. 403.
85. *Ibid.*, p. 333.
86. 'Ayyad, *tartib al-madarek* (Beirut, 1387), I, p. 108.
87. Al-Asfahani, *al-aghani*, IX, p. 29.
88. *Ibid.*, XIX, p. 150. The people of Madinah made baskets out of palm leaves at the dawn of Islam. See al-Khuza'i, *ad-dallalat al-sam'iyyeh* (Dar al-Kutub al-masriyyeh, no. 648, tarikh taymur), p. 669.
89. Al-Azraqi, *akhbar mecca*, p. 474.
90. As-Samhudi, *wafa' al-wafa'*, II, p. 204, 753.
91. As-Shihab al-Murjani, *wafiyyat al-aslaf*, p. 337. Cited from al-Kittani, *at-taratib alidariyyeh* (Beirut), II, p. 242.
92 Al-Baladhiri, *ansab al-ashraf*, manuscript of Dar al-kutub al-masriyyeh, no. 1103, VII, p. 158.
93. Ibn Rustuh, *al-a'laq an-nafisah* (Leiden, 1891), p. 198.
94. As-Samhudi, *wafa' al-wafa'*, p. 204.
95. Al-Asfahani, *al-aghani*, V, p. 65. Al-barm is a kind of cooking pot made from a brittle and supple kind of stone. Until recent times these were used instead of metal pots in parts of the Arabian peninsula. See Hamad al-Jasir, *al-ma'adin al-qadimafi bilad al-'arab*, p. 998.

Chapter 3

AD-DIRʿĪYAH: LANDMARKS AND RUINS

ʿAbd Allāh ibn Khamīs

In the depths of the Wādī Ḥanīfa, twenty kilometres north-west of Riyadh, seven mountain passes meet. Five of them (Sudayr, Ṣafār, Ghubayrāʾ, al-Ḥarīqa and al-Khasīf) begin from the west, while the other two (Qurā ʿUmrān and Qurā Quṣayr) begin from the east. In the open land where these passes end lies the town of ad-Dirʿīyah, located on both sides of the Wādī Ḥanīfa. Before the mid-ninth/fifteenth century this town did not exist. But after Māniʿ al-Muraydī, the thirteenth grandfather of King Fayṣal, came to his cousin, the master of Ḥajar and al-Jizʿa, having left Wādī Ḥanīfa and his home town of ad-Dirʿīyah in the Qaṭīf area (this is a long story), his cousin, Ibn Dirʿ, gave Māniʿ the lands of al-Mulaybīd and Ghaṣība. Māniʿ settled there and called the place ad-Dirʿīyah, after his original home in Qaṭīf. Over the centuries the place prospered and its population increased, until it became not only the chief city in the region but the capital of an empire dominating the area between Syria and Iraq in the north to Oman and Yemen in the south, and from the eastern to the western coasts, from the mid-twelfth/early thirteenth (late eighteenth/early nineteenth) centuries. Ad-Dirʿīyah was the home of the Salafiyya movement announced by Muḥammad ibn ʿAbd al-Wahhāb. The leaders of the Saudi dynasty patronized that movement, despite the many difficulties that faced them in its propagation, until they were finally graced by success.[1]

The movement that began at ad-Dirʿīyah attracted many supporters. It was brutally resisted by the powers who tried to suppress it; but it found an unprecedented response in the minds of the people. It encouraged Muslims to rise above myths and superstitions, the worship of the dead and glorification of leaders and notables, and instead restricted glorification and worship to God, to Whom, the movement's leaders claimed, it was due. In this they followed their predecessors of the original Islamic community. But the custodians of graves, and those who enjoyed powerful positions of authority, were often not pleased to see people dignified by their faith and proud of their humanity. They would rather have seen their people as puppets whom they could control as they wished and who would do their bidding; then they could subjugate them and rob them of their free will. Thus the enemies of the Salafiyya movement declared war on the movement from the first day, leading to bitter warfare in ad-Dirʿīyah. Following this, ad-Dirʿīyah was left a desolate ruin.[2]

To enumerate these events in detail would require many lengthy chapters, and this is not the place to expand on this theme. The title of this chapter refers to what is seen by visitors to ad-Dirʿīyah today, more than 160 years after these events, and in particular to the landmarks and ruins that bear witness to its bygone glory and its prosperous past. The main quarters of ad-Dirʿīyah were as follows:

(1) Al-Ṭurayf, the main quarter of the city, inhabited by the Āl Suʿūd, their ministers and their followers, and containing government buildings, forts and stables. To the east was the palace of the Āl Suʿūd and their fortress ('Salwa'). To the south-east was the treasury; to the north was the Great Mosque of Muḥammad ibn Suʿūd. North of the mosque was the house of the poet ʿUmar ibn Suʿūd. In the centre of this quarter was the house of Su'd ibn Suʿūd. To the west was the public bath, built in the characteristic style of the time. To the north-west stood the fortress overlooking Wādī Ḥanīfa which is now called al-Darīsha. In addition there were many more buildings, currently unnamed. This quarter was located on the south-west cliff of al-Darʿiyya, surrounded by a strong wall and overlooking all ad-Dirʿīyah's quarters. This surviving wall can be seen from a long way off, its impressive ruins hinting at its former glory and illustrious past.

(2) Al-Bujayrī, located on the eastern side of the valley, and the site of Ibn ʿAbd al-Wahhāb's mosque, *madrasa* and house. This is where the descending steps

to the valley begin, and is beside the marketplace and the site of commercial activity.

(3) Al-Surayha lies to the north of al-Bujayrī; it contained the houses of dignitaries such as Ṫawq, Āl Abī Nahya and others. Little remains of other quarters such as al-Ẓuwayhra, al-Naqīb, Malwī and al-Ḥuwayṫa, which lie on the eastern side of the valley, next to al-Bujayrī and al-Surayḥa, and which are now covered by date-palm plantations and new buildings.

(4) Al-Ẓahra (Ẓahrat Samḥān) faces al-Ṫurayf on the north, atop the opposite cliff. It has some houses belonging to poets and other notables.

(5) Al-Ṫarfiyya lies to the north of Ẓahrat Samḥān, and includes the quarter of Āl Suwaylim, an important family well known in Riyadh today, as well as other quarters.

(6) Ghuṣayba lies also to the north, on the same cliff. It is the quarter of Dughaythir, a famous family of Banū Ḥanīfa.

(7) Opposite these, on the western side of the valley, is the al-ʿAwda quarter. Above it, higher up the cliff, is the Ghiyāẓī palace, which belongs to Nāṣir ibn Suʿūd ibn ʿAbd al-ʿAzīz. Al-ʿAwda is one of the oldest quarters in ad-Dirʿīyah. There are also other famous sites in ad-Dirʿīyah whose ruins still remain.

(8) Al-Bulayda has an ancient palace and is overlooked by forts and towers. Al-Bulayda is the 'Dhāt al-Faḥḥāl' mentioned by the historian Ibn Ghannām when discussing popular superstitions in the area before the rise of Ibn ʿAbd al-Wahhāb. He states:

> In Bulaydat al-Fidā there is a male date-palm known as *faḥḥāl*, to which women and men come and sacrifice new-born camels and sheep. A woman comes to it if she is late in marrying and no (prospective) husband has proposed. She hugs the tree with a heart full of hope, and says to it, 'O male of all males! I want a husband before the year is over!' This is what is reported of these people, and no doubt the devil has inspired their actions.[3]

Al-Bulayda became the scene of fierce battles between the people of ad-Dirʿīyah and Ibrāhīm Pāshā's army, and became the graveyard of many warriors. Quraywa Pass is the main graveyard of ad-Dirʿīyah; in it lie many leaders of Āl Suʿūd, princes and notables, as well as Ibn ʿAbd al-Wahhāb and other dignitaries of his family. Ghubayrā' Pass, in its approach to Wādī Ḥanīfa, contains many archaeological sites; this may have been the quarter of the Banū Ghabrā', who were blessed by the Prophet; it is said that their date-palms used to bear fruit twice a year. There were also forts here, which became famous in ad-Dirʿīyah's wars, such as Samḥa, Maʿāniya, Lazzāz, al-Salmānī, Shadīd, Mushayrifa, Katla, al-Rafāyiʿ Samḥān and others. From the heights of ad-Dirʿīyah one can make out the encampments of Ibrāhīm Pāshā's army, and documentary evidence complements the picture, so that one can see how strategic arrangements were carried out, identify the main battle sites, fortresses, and so on.

Notes:

1. Agreement between Muḥammad ibn Saʿūd and Muḥammad ibn ʿAbd al-Wahhāb, concluded in 1157/1744.
2. The war in ad-Dirʿīyah and the capture of the town took place in 1233/1817.
3. Ḥusayn ibn Ghannām, *Tārīkh Najd* (old edition), p. 3; see also the edited edition (n.p., 1381/1961), p. 10.

Chapter 4

NAJD FROM THE TENTH/SIXTEENTH CENTURY UNTIL THE RISE OF SHEIKH MUḤAMMAD IBN ʿABD AL-WAHHĀB

ʿAbd Allāh al-Ṣāliḥ al-ʿUthaymīn

In a 1976 issue of *Al Darah*, we briefly discussed the relations between Najd and the powers surrounding it in the east and west. We noted that those powers enjoyed some political influence inside Najd, but that that influence was not strong enough to dominate the course of events in the region. The influence of the Sharīfs of Makkah failed to create a stable political atmosphere in other areas of the region, while wars between the various tribes of Najd continued. In this chapter we begin to discuss the internal conditions of Najd, dealing first with social and economic conditions.

Social and Economic Conditions

During the period under discussion, Najd was one of the least affected regions of the Arabian peninsula in terms of the intermixture of non-Arab inhabitants with the indigenous Arab population, since Najd was far from the areas most favourable to this, which were usually the coastal areas and holy places. As a result, the vast majority of the Najdi population belonged to Arab tribes of well-known genealogical descent. But despite the fact that these tribes were completely independent of one another with regard to nomenclature – which suggests the tribes' unity, distinction and segregation from each other, a prevalent phenomenon in tribal structure

– it sometimes happened that some elements or individuals of one tribe would join another for one reason or another, such as differences with the majority of their own tribe, which compelled them to leave their kinfolk and join another, stronger tribe in order to enjoy its protection and obtain a share in the spoils usually acquired by the strong. And as a rule, strong tribes welcomed newcomers, either out of gallantry or from the desire to increase their own strength (since those who join a tribe normally assume the name of the host tribe and are regarded as a part of it). This process of affiliation takes place, on the whole, before the phase of settlement and stability.

Other groups in Najdi society could claim Arab origins which they had lost or had been deprived of for various reasons, and others descended from non-Arab origins. This latter category comprises elements that came to Najd through various channels, such as slavery, or flight (people hoping to distance themselves from pressing circumstances under which they lived elsewhere), or who came to the Arabian peninsula to perform the *ḥajj* (ritual pilgrimage). The majority of these people no doubt settled in the larger cities of the Hijaz, where they came to constitute a large proportion of the inhabitants. But a smaller number settled in some Najdi towns, and usually worked in trade or in different crafts.

The Najdis' social outlook was a tribal one. The establishment of genuine Arab origin or descent was an important factor in deciding the status of an individual or a family. This outlook was present among both Bedouin nomads and settled people. It was most clearly manifested in matters like marriage or in the practice of certain trades and professions; a man descended from Arab origins does not marry someone who is not so descended, nor does he practise such trades as smithing or the like. Najdi society was divided into two categories: settled or sedentary people (*ḥaḍar*) and nomads (*badw*). But there was a transitional stage through which some of the population passed where it is difficult to identify those involved as belonging to either category, for they had neither severed their ties with the Bedouin life which they were about to abandon, nor familiarized themselves with the urban settled life into which they were about to move. There were many motives behind the abandonment of pastoral and nomadic life in exchange for a life of settlement. Some involved climatic factors; seasons of drought and famine might force Bedouins to seek refuge in urban areas simply for survival. But most of those who became refugees in hard times doubtless left the urban areas as soon as conditions improved through rainfall and growth of pasture, although others, who relished the sedentary life, stayed where they were. Trading contacts may also have played a part in the issue of settlement.

As might be expected, the settlement of Najdis took place around areas where water resources were available in sufficient quantity to enable them to practise agriculture, the most important element required for viable urban economic life at that time, such as the sides of well-known valleys and various oases. Geographical location – for example, the location of a particular place on a trade route – may also have been an important factor, but suitability for agriculture was generally the primary consideration. It is noticeable that Najdi towns varied in the way they developed and expanded. Some were initially single villages which gradually grew into large townships; this was the most common form of transformation. Others consisted of groups of population concentrations or small adjacent villages which grew and expanded until they linked up with one another and eventually became one city.

As for the evolution of the village itself, it too varied from one village to another. Sometimes the village evolved by means of one or a group of town-dwellers who purchased the land from its owner, as in the case of al-ʿUyayna;[1] by donation of the land by its owner to another party, as happened in al-Mujammaʿa and ad-Dirʿīyah;[2] or by taking the land by force from its owner and then starting to cultivate and settle that land, as in al-Bīr.[3] Sometimes, for one reason or another, a settled community would leave its home and settle in the ruins of a deserted village, and revive it, as in al-Tuwaym and Harmah. These formerly belonged to Banū ʿĀyid, who abandoned them, and were later revived by Āl Wāʾil, who had been forced to leave Ushayqir.[4] A village might also be established by the settlement of a family or sub-clan of a tribe around a water source, where cultivation begins along with building houses. However, the references in the sources to the rise of villages and towns in Najd in this period indicate that these were established by urban-dwellers.

As noted above, those people undergoing the transition from nomadism to urbanization led a life that was neither completely Bedouin nor entirely urban. Part of their time was devoted to pastoral life, another part to agriculture. During this period the importance of the *ḥimā* (protected reserve) was great, because of the inhabitants' partial reliance on grazing livestock. In fact, the importance of protected lands was carefully observed even after this stage, as is shown, for example, by the stand taken by the people of Jurma when they asked ʿAbd Allāh al-Shammārī to settle at the top of the valley so as not to interfere with their grazing land.[5]

When a town or village was settled by people not belonging to the same clan or tribe, troubles sometimes broke out, either for an economic reason, such as dispute about the use of water, or for a political reason, such as fear that one group might fall under the control of the other. Sometimes the inhabitants tried to resolve these problems, especially economic ones, by peaceful means. But their attempts were successful only for a limited period, and then met with trouble, ending in failure because of the political aspect. This happened with the people of Ushayqir, where Āl Wahba and Āl Wāʾil lived. They agreed that one group would make use of the water resources for one day, while the other would take its livestock to the pastureland for grazing; on the following day they would exchange these roles. But this peaceful arrangement did not last long; for Āl Wahba were afraid that Āl Wāʾil might come to dominate them because the latter's relatives came to them in growing numbers; so they decided to get rid of them. They evicted the Āl Wāʾil families from the village, while their menfolk were in the grazing land with their livestock, and did not allow them to enter the village except to take what belongings they could from their homes.[6]

Before continuing our discussion of some of the social and economic aspects among sedentarics and Bedouins in Najd, and their economic relations with each other, we should note the Bedouins' outlook towards the sedentaries from a social angle. The Bedouin was proud of himself and of his desert, in which he saw the proper place in which to preserve his personality and his tradition. In his opinion, heroic attributes were restricted to the people of the desert, who moved about freely from one place to another, whereas settled people lacked these noble traits. The Bedouin did not, however, look down upon the Najdi town-dweller because he himself was of a more noble Arab lineage; he, like others, knew well that most sedentaries were descended from pure Arab origins, and were his cousins. But he believed that the readiness to meet challenges posed by the desert decrease when an individual settles down and becomes protected by city walls. Thus an urban person, even if he outwardly appears to be a courageous horseman, is not equal to the Bedouin. This is seen in the following extract from the poet al-ʿAnqarī, on his having been forsaken by a Bedouin woman because he was a town-dweller:

> I see that you of the feathered lashes forsake us,
> saying that village horsemen are just ornamental![7]

Urban reactions to the Bedouins' social outlook were varied. Some made it clear that heroic qualities were equally abundant among both sedentaries and nomads, without any distinction. Others opined that the Bedouin is haughty and must be dealt with harshly and violently, so that he will conduct himself correctly. The first view is represented by al-ʿAnqarī, who said,

> You see that victory is not bestowed on nomads alone,
> but is evenly divided among all who are noble and successful.
> Both Bedouins and those who dwell in villages
> have gallantry bestowed on them by God.[8]

The mouthpiece of the second view was Ḥumaydān al-Shuwayʿir, who says:

> If you give to a Bedouin, he will master you,
> and say that you are afraid of him; so give him not.
> Given power, he will be unjust and mischievous;
> if dominated, he will behave well and pay his dues.[9]

Agriculture was the mainstay of economic life among the Najdi sedentaries; they respected it and devoted much attention to it. It was practised both by 'purebred' Arabs and by others; all relied on it, regardless of differences in social status and trends of thought. Most of the leaders under whom Najdi towns and villages developed patronized agriculture, and some scholars of the period also respected it. One prominent example was the historian and *faqīh* (jurist) Aḥmad al-Manqūr, who earned his living through agriculture.[10] Naturally, not all landowners cultivated their lands themselves. The overall situation determined matters. Sometimes the landowner cultivated the land himself; sometimes he hired people to do it for him. If he were wealthy enough to buy slaves, they would share in cultivating the land; or the owner might lease it to others to cultivate,[11] or make agreements with them for maintenance and development of the farm in return for a share of the produce.

Najd produced a variety of agricultural crops, vegetables and fruits. It seems that date-palms were the most important of these for all the inhabitants, because of their numerous benefits. For in addition to their extremely important and nutritional fruits, each and every part of the palm tree was utilized in daily life. When one realizes the great economic value of the palm, it is not surprising to hear Ḥumaydān al-Shuwayʿir say of them:

> You see bounty in the deeply rooted trunks
> which have braved the crushing years.
> They support your livestock and please your children,
> and increase your gifts in hard times.

He also urges people to defend them, saying:

> Fight, and strike hard, for love of the palms.
> Remember what Ḥātim says and nothing else:
> 'Your death by the sword is a source of pride for you
> and your death of painful disease is an infamy.'[12]

Najdi farmers faced numerous problems; but these differed from one place to another. The people of al-Kharj and al-Aflāj, for example, faced fewer obstacles than the inhabitants of other areas, because they could easily irrigate and had abundant water supplies. Other Najdi farmers had to cope with other difficulties, such as getting water from wells, which requires both animals and the manpower to supervise them, and the occasional drying up of wells because of irregular rainfall, as in Sudayr, which forced some of its people to leave in 1926.[13] There were other problems from which Najdi farmers sometimes suffered and which caused serious damage to their crops and harvests and worsened their economic condition. These included severe cold and heavy rain, sometimes accompanied by storms and hail; plagues of locusts; and attempts by enemies to destroy or plunder the crops. In 1122/1710, for example, cold destroyed the farms of Mulhim, while small locusts laid waste the crops in some parts of the country, and hail devastated the ears of grain.[14] In 1098/1687 winds felled a thousand palm trees in al-Qāra and al-Rawḍa.[15] In 1100/1680 the tribe of ʿAnaza cut down the palm trees of ʿAshīra;[16] and enemies plundered the millet of the people of Ushayqir in 1139/1736.[17]

In the geographical region and period of time that we are discussing, certain animals enjoyed special economic importance. Camels were of particular significance for settled people; farmers would use them to get water out of wells, and their tanned leather was used to make large buckets for this purpose. They also served traders, travellers and fighters. Their meat was a major source of food. Cows were also useful both in agriculture and in supplying people with milk and meat. The same applied to sheep, which were kept by town-dwellers for the benefits of their milk and meat. Horses were not as numerous among sedentary people as they were among the Bedouins, because of differences in social life between the two groups. Raids were fewer among the sedentaries than among the Bedouins; in such raids horses were of particular importance. Donkeys, on the other hand, were used for agricultural tasks, for carrying agricultural and other products to the markets, and for transport from one place to another.

This is a very brief account of agriculture – the most important economic element among Najd's urban population – and other relevant issues. The other vitally important side of Najdi life was trade. There were three types of trade at that time: local, regional and external. The first type was manifested in commercial transactions between the urban populations within each individual city. Agricultural products or locally manufactured articles were sometimes sold directly to the consumer, or sometimes through another party who took his share of the profit from either of the two other parties. Sometimes this middleman bought the commodity from the farmer or the manufacturer or imported it from outside the town and then sold it to the consumer. Regional trade, on the other hand, was carried out between two or more Najdi towns or between urban and desert inhabitants. Some towns were more productive than others; thus the surplus from one was exported to another in time of need. Both settled and nomadic populations needed each other. The Bedouin came to the town to buy what he needed, such as dates, grain, salt, clothes, vessels and weapons, and to sell what exceeded his needs with respect to camels, sheep, fats, leather and wool. In a few cases some urban dealers went to the places where Bedouins lived to buy what they needed and sell whatever commodities they might have which might be needed by the Bedouins.

Food prices fluctuated greatly in this period, depending on the quantity and availability of crops, whether the year was one of drought or of rainfall, or subject to the law of supply and demand. For example, a *ṣāʿ* (a cubic measure of varying magnitude) of wheat sold for three Muḥammadiyyas in 1096/1685, while three years later five *ṣāʿ* sold for one Muḥammadiyya.[18] In 1125/1712–13, 100 *waznas* (weight units) of dates were sold initially for one *aḥmar*, but when groups of ʿAnaza tribesmen came to buy what they needed of this crop, the price suddenly doubled.[19] In addition to normal on-the-spot sales there were other ways of selling. One was that a person paid a sum of money on condition that the latter provided him with a quantity of dates, wheat or something else at harvest time.[20] The most well-known currencies used by the Najdis at that time were the *aḥmar* ('red coin') and the Muḥammadiyya. Besides these two, there were less well-known currencies such as the *mushakhkhaṣ*, the *muṭabbaq*, the *ḥarf* and the *jadīda*.[21]

External trade was carried out between the people of Najd and the inhabitants of other regions. Najd did not produce all the requirements of its inhabitants; therefore, it was necessary to import commodities that were not available or of which the production fell short of people's needs, such as certain foodstuffs, clothing and weapons. Hence Najdi merchants left their country for other places to sell and to buy. On the other hand,

Najd was rich in some livestock, such as camels and horses. It had such a good supply of camels that it was called Umm al-Bill (*ibil*) 'mother of camels'. According to accounts written by certain western travellers who visited the area somewhat later, a man from the tribe of ʿAnaza who owned fewer than ten she-camels was considered poor. The average wealth of a household in the Qaḥṭān tribe was about sixty camels.[22] Whether the above estimate was correct or exaggerated, there is no doubt that Najd had many more camels than it needed, which continued to be the case until recently. Najdi horses were exported to various areas, including Basra, and were later taken from there to India.[23] Although Najdi merchants went to various regions adjacent to them, their trade relations with the eastern and north-eastern parts of the Arabian peninsula were apparently closer than with anywhere else. They used to import some of their needs from the eastern region or through its seaports.[24] Eastern cloaks were held in higher esteem than others by the people of Najd.[25]

Merchants who frequented the regions mentioned were often accompanied by people seeking work in agricultural, maritime or other fields. Some settled in those regions, extending as far as Baghdad, where they became so influential that Turkish pashas sought their help in their contests for power in that city.[26] However, trade caravans between Najd and other regions were sometimes endangered by attacks by tribesmen, because there was no political authority strong enough to maintain security in the area. It is true that caravans used to have a companion from each tribe through whose territory they expected to pass, thereby protecting themselves from attacks by the members of that tribe. But sometimes they encountered a group belonging to a tribe of which no member was accompanying them. This exposed the caravan to the danger of being pillaged, especially if the tribesmen were nomadic. Even settled urban people might attack trade caravans if there were hostile relations between them and the people of the caravan, as happened when the inhabitants of al-Bīr captured a caravan carrying clothing for the people of al-ʿUyayna in 1072/1660–1.[27]

In discussing the economic situation in Najd, it is worth noting the pilgrimage and its benefits for the region's inhabitants; for although the greatest economic benefit of the pilgrimage was in the Hijaz, and especially its main cities, Najd was not excluded from its positive effects.

Some Najdi towns lay on the pilgrimage routes leading to the Hijaz from the east and north-east of the Arabian peninsula and beyond. Often the pilgrim caravans stopped in those towns to purchase necessary foodstuffs and other commodities or to exchange an exhausted camel for a fresh one. The members of those caravans, on their part, might also sell some of what they had with them to local people.[28] The available sources concerning this period do not give enough information for us to form an opinion on the ratio of sedentary Najdis working in agriculture against those practising commercial and other business activities. But it is certain that the inhabitants of some areas were more active than those of others in the field of trade, and external trade in particular. Nor do the sources provide sufficient information about standards of living; but it may be assumed that this was generally low, in view of the lack of the stability needed for economic prosperity, and because of the natural conditions of the region at times, which caused permanent or temporary migration of some individuals or groups away from Najd.

The proportion of wealthy people in society at this time was probably small. Manifestations of wealth were numerous, and included owning slaves and keeping horses. The linkage of settled persons with the land changed the loyalty of those descended from Arab origins from tribalism to familialism because of changes in their social and economic circumstances; but genealogical authenticity remained a crucial factor in the assessment of an individual's social status, in addition to other factors such as economic standing and political or religious leadership. This resonates in the poetry of some poets of the period which suggests the power of the economic factor in determining social outlooks. Ḥumaydān al-Shuwayʿir says:

> Wealth raises the status of people obscure in descent,
> while poverty degrades those of noble blood.
> My son, amongst us gold coins
> elevate men who have little weight.
> Wealth may raise the sparrow's offspring
> high above the falcon's progeny.[29]

While admitting that material wealth is a significant factor, this statement should not be taken completely literally; for Ḥumaydān himself posits other, different qualities that raise the individual's position in society:

> Four things raise a man in people's eyes:
> victory, generosity, loyalty, and piety.[30]

It is clear that this latter view is a mixture of Arab ideals and Islamic values; in other words, it is the Arab-Islamic outlook.

One trait regarded as noble in Najdi society was benevolence, as represented by sympathy towards the poor, for instance the giving of food to the mosques for those fasting in Ramadan so they might break their fast at sunset.[31] One result of contacts between Najdis and people of other regions, through trade or otherwise, was the introduction of certain products into Najdi society, such as coffee. Al-Manqūr has quoted the views of jurists about this;[32] it seems that it did not enjoy an unqualified welcome. Mocking his son, Ḥumaydān associated coffee with smoking the hookah:

> The right hand holds the coffee cup,
> while the left grabs the hubble bubble.[33]

Thus the poet held hookahs and smoking pipes in low esteem. Both articles were brought into Najdi society through external contact. Again he says, defaming those he addresses:

> You offspring of regret, sucklings of servants,
> you who are fed by smoking pipes and hubble bubbles.[34]

The Najdi woman stood firmly beside her man in trying to overcome the difficulties of life. She would undertake household chores, care for the children, help with cultivation and sometimes go out to collect grass or firewood. The sources also point to some women who distinguished themselves in important social fields.[35] But of course the man retained the leading role. Early marriage was also a common practice in this society, especially within well-to-do families.[36]

When we try to familiarize ourselves with the way of life in the Najd desert at that time, through the available information, we find that the Najdis' life did not differ from that of their fathers and forefathers throughout various periods of history. Environmental circumstances compelled them to continue and preserve the traditional way of life. The desert, with its pasture lands, its tents and camels, remained the most important element. The Bedouin saw in the desert the most suitable place for his life, as he saw in it a guarantee for preserving his personality and traditions (as was noted earlier). In addition to providing a wide scope for his movement, it was also a zone of defence against any enemy from outside. The tent was the appropriate shelter for someone who led an unsettled life, whose circumstances forced him to move from one place to another in search of good grazing land to sustain and develop his livestock, and consequently to preserve his economic existence.

While rain was important for urban life, it was the most important factor directly affecting the Bedouin's life. It was the source of their prosperity and wealth, just as drought was their bitter enemy, which forced them to seek shelter in towns and villages to save their threatened lives. Shortage of rainfall was not uncommon, and drought often caused many problems for the Bedouins, especially economic problems, such as the death or weakening of livestock, or problems manifested in wars. Tribes that did not enjoy sufficient rainfall in their own areas would attempt to enter others that had received rain, even if these belonged to other tribes. Sometimes the latter tribes would allow entrance into their own areas, either gratis or in return for something specific; but sometimes they would not, which would lead to intertribal warfare.

Camels were the most important element in the Bedouin's economic life. They provided milk and meat and the means of transport and communication. Moreover, they constituted a standard for many aspects of his social life; blood money and dowries, for example, were priced at a certain number of camels. The status of camels to the desert nomad was even higher than that of the palm tree to the inhabitants of towns and villages. It is no wonder then that he placed them on an equal footing with his sweetheart in terms of defending them and willingness to die for them, as in the following verses:

We fight for the sake of the one whose eyes shed tears;
she weeps, and after weeping we reconcile.
She says: 'O you for whom victory is one of your habits,
attack in the hope that some remnants of you may survive.'
We also fight for the sake of the she-camel that yearns for her
offspring,
a she-camel with soft hair that loves comfortable summer pastures.[37]

One may recall here that Najd had a surplus of camels, as was noted above.

Horses were also so plentiful among Najdis that profits were made in selling or exporting them to other regions. Horses were very useful to the Bedouin, especially because his life often had call for sudden raids, defensive as well as offensive, which required swift mounts. Apart from their usefulness, keeping horses was also a source of pride. Sheep were also economically important for nomadic tribes, who often bought their necessities, such as food, clothing and weapons, by selling sheep products, in addition to making their tents from wool and meeting their needs for dairy products and meat. It goes without saying that Bedouin economic life is largely based on pasturage. But there are other sources of living; one of the most important being raids, a double-edged weapon by means of which one who is wealthy today may be reduced to poverty tomorrow. Other sources included the tributes which some tribes extorted from some town- and village-dwellers.

We have already mentioned the benefits to the settled inhabitants of Najd from the passage through their territory of caravans heading for the Hijaz. The Bedouins benefited more than the townspeople, because pilgrims sometimes hired camels from them, and gave presents to tribal chieftains in an attempt to ward off the dangers of attacks. Sometimes they also paid specific tributes in return for safe passage. They might also hire guards and guides from these tribes, or buy sheep, fat and the like. Despite all this, however, the caravans were sometimes targets for Bedouin raids.[38]

The special circumstances of the Bedouin's life, particularly with regard to lack of permanent settlement and conflicts over water sources and grazing grounds, made him feel closely attached and extremely loyal to his own tribe. As long as he was a member of the tribe in terms of genealogical descent, he saw no difference between himself and other fellow-tribesmen. Disparity in status was founded on personal qualities such as bravery and generosity. There is no doubt that those who demonstrated these qualities to the highest degree held positions of leadership and deservedly enjoyed the respect accorded them by Bedouin society. Nor is it strange that heroism and liberality were the chief virtues that paved the way towards leadership, since a Bedouin's life frequently encountered both raids and guests. Whoever was able to carry out the duties of such circumstances was qualified to occupy a leading position. Other figures who were respected by the society, apart from tribe and clan chiefs, were minor chiefs, men who were conversant with traditions, tribal laws and conventions, and tribal poets. Finally, having dealt with the social aspects of the Najdi desert, one must note that the Bedouin woman was by no means inferior, if not in fact superior, to her sedentary sister in contributing to public life and social distinction.

Political Conditions

It may be said that the elements which Najdi sedentary society felt should be present in the political leadership did not, on the whole, differ from the well-known elements of traditional Arab leadership, among which were noble lineage, bravery and generosity. In the period under discussion, the leadership of Najdi towns belonged to various Arab tribes, and it was not surprising that the Tamīm tribe occupied a prominent position due to its numbers and its tendency from an early period towards settlement. Among the emirs who belonged to that tribe were those of al-ʿUyayna, the strongest Najdi city at that time, and those of Tharmada, Rawdat Sudayr and Burayda.

The families who controlled Najdi towns came to power in different ways. One was that the family's forefather established the town, or revived it after it had been deserted. This often happened by buying the place from its former owner, as in the case of al-ʿUyayna,[39] or by seizing the town by force: those in authority from outside took it from its leaders. Examples were the seizure of al-Bīr by the Āl Ḥunayḥin (a branch of the

Dawāsir) from the tribe of Subayʾ in 1015/1605–6,[40] and the Hazāzina's taking of Namām and al-Ḥarīq from Subayʾ in 1040/1629–30.[41] In both cases the emirate was traditional and hereditary in the family, or went to a specific person from among its members, following their acceptance and approval, with the exception of conflicts that might sometimes break out within the family.

Contests for power are a familiar phenomenon in the history of all family dynasties in various parts of the world and in all historical periods; but the frequency of such conflicts varies according to circumstances. Consequently, the conflict for power within the ruling dynasties in Najd which the reader observes in the sources is not surprising.[42] These conflicts sometimes extended to involve close relatives. In 1101/1689–90, for example, Ibrāhīm ibn Waṭbān killed his brother Mirkhān over the leadership of ad-Dirʿīyah.[43] In 1111/1698–99, the sons of ʿUthmān ibn Nuḥayṭ, the Emir of al-Ḥuṣūn, arrested their father and expelled him from the city, with the encouragement of the Emir of Jalājil.[44] This was alluded to by Humaydan al-Shuwayʿir, in these lines:

> Like the ruler of Jalājil with Ibn Nuḥayṭ:
> he caught him at last after long plotting against him.
> He exposed him to fate from his high hiding place,
> then overcame him on the high peak.
> Then he said, 'Attack him, my sons,
> let one of you catch him and another wound him.'[45]

In 1138/1725, ʿUthmān ibn Ibrāhīm killed his son Ibrāhīm, who was then an emir in al-Qaṣab.[46]

At times the authorities outside the towns played a role in internal conflicts and in the change of leadership, as in the case of Ibn Nuḥayṭ, and as happened in 1052/1632, when Ibn Muʿammar drove Rumayzān ibn Ghashshām from Umm Ḥimār and when, later, Sharīf Zayd ibn Muḥsin killed Māḍdī ibn Muḥammad, the Emir of al-Rawḍa, and installed Rumayzān in his place.[47] As long as these circumstances prevailed, and because power struggles reached such an extent, it was not surprising to find conflict over authority among various families within the same town.

Such was the case in Āl Mazrūᶜ, when Dawwās wrested from them the rule of Manfūḥa in 1095/1684.[48] Nor was it surprising that tribal kinship ties, which might exist between the emirs of one town and another, proved useless in creating an atmosphere of harmony or unity within the region; such blood relations did not prevent the eruption of wars between those emirs. Political disintegration was the natural outcome, so that each town became independent, and was in most cases on unfriendly terms with its neighbours. This made it necessary for every emir to be in a state of constant military preparedness, either ready to attack his opponent and obtain as much booty as he could, or to defend his town against attacks that might be launched by others. Hence military strength was a much-admired quality, which society saw as a solution to many of its political problems. Thus Rumayzān ibn Ghashshām addresses Jabr ibn Sayyār as follows:

> O Jabr, the sword's edge is the key to relief;
> it overcomes difficulties which men face.[49]

Ḥumaydān al-Shuwayᶜir says:

> There is no doubt that the Indian sword decided
> every difficult issue,
> and drank cups from the flowing blood of foes.

And also:

> The cutting sword, coupled with determination
> brings the foes' necks to their senses.
> A rabbit lies down harmlessly to sleep,
> and no one is concerned about it.
> But the rapacious lion never sleeps,
> nor moves about in the land of his prey.[50]

The Najdi emirates had periods of weakness and of strength. The strongest emirate to appear in the region was al-ᶜUyayna, especially during the time of its chief, ᶜAbd Allāh ibn Muᶜammar, who ruled from 1096 to

1138/1680 to 1725. Ibn Bishr states that he never recalled anyone like him, 'either in his time or before in Najd, in terms of leadership, strong character, number of followers, equipment, property and possessions and paraphernalia'.[51] However, it is obvious that such grandeur never reached a degree that would have enabled al-ʿUyayna to make the political and military balance of power tilt in its favour.

As for the relationship between ruler and ruled, this varied from one prince to another. A general quality which Ibn Bishr describes in relation to the emirs of Najd was injustice. He states: 'As for the heads of the towns and their injustice: they know nothing but oppression and cruelty towards their subjects.'[52] One might say that this historian – a staunch supporter of Muḥammad ibn ʿAbd al-Wahhāb's *daʿwa* (mission) – exaggerated in this passage, in the introduction to his book, in order to show the difference between what the country was before that mission and what it became subsquently. But Ibn Bishr was not alone in giving a gloomy picture of the emirs of the period. The contemporary poet Jabr ibn Sayyār says:

The chiefs, when you consider them well,
are sly foxes who corrupt and abuse the realm.
They commit injustice towards their subjects; their nature
is shown to you by its signs and phantoms even after their death.[53]

General conditions in the region helped to produce various types of injustice, since sheer force and murder were regular means of attaining power. Fear of retaliation might necessitate taking unjust measures. Economic conditions also influenced the situation. The scarcity of resources available to some emirs, coupled with the demands of defence and hospitality, contributed to taking economic actions that to many seemed unjust. Some emirs extracted annual sums of money from their followers, in addition to the regular *zakāt* (ritual almsgiving).[54] Subjects had to endure some of these oppressive measures because of the nature of their economic life, which relied chiefly on fixed assets and wealth. This led the individuals to think that if they tried to escape from this injustice, they might lose some of their immovable assets. There were, however, some just emirs who behaved well towards their subjects and treated them kindly. They settled individual issues in a legal manner; and, without doubt, some judges had a significant influence in this regard.

The qualifications for obtaining political leadership in the Najd desert were the same as those required among Arab tribes throughout history. While it was taken for granted that noble lineage was present in each tribe's families, variation among individuals resulted from other factors, such as hospitality, bravery, forbearance and sound opinion. The more these qualities were found in one of the tribe's members, the higher his chances were for assuming leadership of the tribe. Although the tribe's chief was chosen on the strength of his personal qualifications for leadership by the heads of its clans and sub-clans, and eventually by the rest of its members, his relative proximity to the former leader was a point in his favour. Therefore leadership did not, in most cases, go outside the former leader's family, so that among many tribes it became a traditional, hereditary affair.

One might say that the road to leadership among the Najdi Bedouins was closer to democracy than it was among the settled population. It was a successful democracy characterized by amity and admiration of individuals for their leadership and sacrifice and the loyalty of that leadership towards them. One might expect such a difference between the relationship of tribesmen and their chieftains, on the one hand, and that between town-dwellers and their emirs on the other, because of the difference in the political and economic conditions of each group. Some roads to leadership among sedentary groups involved the use of force or murder. The wealth of individuals consisted mainly of immovable assets. Thus the relationship of the emirate with its individual subjects was sometimes characterized by injustice, and the necessity of enduring such. The path to leadership among the Bedouins, on the other hand, was free choice. Therefore the chieftain had always to think of the support he might receive from heads of clans and other dignitaries of the community, just as the latter also felt confident in themselves and in the importance of their role in the choice of tribal leadership. Moreover, the Bedouins' wealth was movable. If an individual felt he was under pressure, he could drive his camels and sheep to wherever he wished without suffering serious economic harm, as he would if his wealth consisted of immovable assets. It was also easy for such a migrant to find asylum with another Arab tribe. In fact it was easy – in accordance with the well-known convention regarding one seeking protection or refuge (*dakhīl*) – for even a criminal to enjoy the political protection of those with whom he seeks refuge. As a result, the relationship of the tribal chief with his tribesmen was characterized by flexibility, and by providing a living example of the submission of his admirers to loyal leadership.

It is also clear that there was a hierarchical political system among tribes. There were individuals, headed by clan and sub-clan chieftains, who were led by the tribal chief. These chieftains, along with the tribe's chief, constituted the tribe's council, which discussed important matters such as war and peace with other tribes and movement from one place to another in search of grazing land, as well as disputes within the tribe. It seems that the tribe's chief did not receive annual tributes from his tribesmen, but would meet his expenses from his own resources, whether inherited property, wealth acquired as booty from raids, or duties imposed on caravans passing through his sphere of influence. Intertribal relationships in Najd were mostly unfriendly, especially between neighbouring tribes. Force was the decisive factor in settling differences, according to the famous proverb: 'Najd belongs to the one with the longest lance'. Many tribes contested water resources or occupying first place at grazing grounds. At the beginning of the tenth/sixteenth century some branches of the famous Lām tribe were highly influential, as were the Banū Khālid. The poet Juʿaythin al-Yazīdī, praising Muqrin Āl Ajwad (killed in 927/1521) states:

> And the blooming open spaces of Najd he grazed
> in defiance of the chiefs of Lām and Khālid.[55]

Had those two tribes not been influential, it would have been pointless to praise Muqrin for his defiance of them. But any reader of the history of Ibn Bassām, in particular, and other Najdi histories in general, will note that the ʿAnaza tribe had also proven its strength, for it maintained its predominant position in the region throughout the period dealt with in this study. This is clear from its numerous attacks against other tribes, and its victories in most cases. Among the most famous tribes whose might is referred to by the historical sources that narrated their numerous wars were al-Dawāsir, al-Ẓafīr and al-Fuḍūl. Next to these, in frequency of mention, were āl Mughīra, Subayʾ, al-Suhūl, Qaḥtan and Muṭayr.

It is well known that it was Muṭayr who later removed the power of ʿAnaza from the main grazing grounds of Najd, and that it was Qaḥtan who succeeded Muṭayr in spreading its influence over those regions, as is clear from these verses by Muwayḍī al-Barāziyya:

> Najd we have protected against Wāʾil's offspring;
> today our enemy lives in Wādī al-Rāk.[56]

The first time Muṭayr appears in the sources is in 1022/1613;[57] its first war against ʿAnaza was when it participated with al-Ẓāfīr in the battle of Wathāl in 1061/1658.[58] Then it raided ʿAnaza on its own in 1078/1667.[59] After that, the sources that tell of the conflict during this period, when ʿAnaza was defeated some time after the rise of Sheikh Muḥammad, are silent on this tribe.

Just as it has been observed that some Najdi towns did not become powerful enough to make the political and military balance tilt in their favour, the same can be said about the powerful tribes just mentioned. Thus conflict among the Bedouins continued, as it did between urban groups, although it was more frequent among the former because of the absence of an effective central authority in the region.

Religious Conditions

Before discussing religious conditions in Najd in terms of belief and practice, it is worth addressing the status of religious scholarship there, and the sectarian affiliations of its scholars. It is clear that education at that time existed only on a narrow scale; it was totally absent among the majority of the population, who were Bedouins, and limited among the minority, who were town-dwellers. The general harshness of economic life, the fact that most people were preoccupied with obtaining sustenance, and the lack of financial support and patronage for education, were for most people obstacles to seeking knowledge.

Yet despite these difficulties there were attempts to learn and to teach, subject to the available resources. It seems that those heads of families who could afford to do so would have their sons taught to read the Qurʾan, or at least parts thereof. The religious factor also influenced those endowed with knowledge to do their best to teach others the Sharīʿa (Islamic law) that they themselves knew. The desire of some Najdis to seek learning and to disseminate knowledge is evidenced by the travels they made inside and outside their region in order to acquire knowledge and deepen their learning.[60] One aspect of that desire was their attempt to meet scholars travelling through the region on their way to perform the pilgrimage. They also bequeathed books as religious endowments (*waqf*) for seekers of knowledge, in addition to their own efforts at teaching.[61]

There is no doubt that there were scholars in Najd before the tenth/sixteenth century. The clearest indication of this is the legal documents written by such scholars that have been handed down to us. One of these is the well-known Ṣubayḥ document (*wathīqat Ṣubayḥ*), which dates to about the middle of the eighth/fourteenth century.[62] Another indication is the fact that Aḥmad ibn ʿAṭwa, who studied first under the scholars of al-ʿUyayna, went to Damascus for more advanced studies.[63] One of his teachers there, ʿAlāʾ al-Dīn al-Mardāwī, died in 885/1479–80;[64] this means that there were scholars in Najd prior to that date.

The sources do not provide us with sufficient information about scholars during the eighth/fourteenth and ninth/fifteenth centuries. However, there is much information about the region's scholars from the beginning of the tenth/sixteenth century to the middle of the twelfth/eighteenth. Important sources for this information include references in the histories written by Najdis such as Aḥmad ibn Bassām, Aḥmad al-Manqūr, al-Fākhirī, Ibn Bishr and Ibn ʿĪsā. There are, in addition, the jurisprudential views and *fatwas* (legal opinions) contained in al-Manqūr's *al-Fawākih al-ʿadīda fī al-masāʾil al-mufīda*, which includes opinions issued by Najdi scholars who preceded or were contemporary with the author, as well as other matters such as mention of their teachers, their pupils, and the certificates for transmitting books on religious learning (*ijāzāt*) which they obtained.

In 1978 Sheikh ʿAbd Allāh ibn ʿAbd al-Raḥmān al-Bassām published his valuable book on biographies of Najdi scholars over six centuries.[65] Here he gives the biographies of about seventy scholars who flourished in the region from approximately the beginning of the tenth/sixteenth century until the rise of Muḥammad ibn ʿAbd al-Wahhāb's *daʿwa*. Undoubtedly there were some other Najdi scholars who were contemporaries of these, but the author did not write their biographies, perhaps because he lacked adequate information about them.[66]

It is noteworthy that more than half of the Najdi scholars who preceded the advent of Ibn ʿAbd al-Wahhāb were born and educated in Ushayqir, and that others who were not born in that town went there to study with its Sheikhs. It is also noteworthy that more than half of the Najdi scholars of the period belonged to Āl-Wahhāb, a clan of the Tamīm tribe. Nearly half of these descend from one branch of Āl-Wahhāb, Āl Mushrif, the family of Muḥammad ibn ʿAbd al-Wahhāb. This shows that at that time Ushayqir was a centre of learning, and that Āl-Wahhāb in general, and Āl Mushrif in particular, belonged to the highest rank of scholarship in Najd.

On the other hand, we find that the number of eleventh/seventeenth-century scholars was nearly double that of scholars in the previous century, and that the number of scholars in the first half of the twelfth/eighteenth century was nearly equal to the total number of scholars in the century before. This shows that the inclination towards scholarship was continually progressing. We also find fifteen Najdi scholars who were not content to study in Najd, but travelled to other regions to increase their knowledge. Five of these were scholars from the tenth/sixteenth century, six from the following century, and four from the first half of the twelfth/eighteenth century. This means that the proportion of Najdi scholars travelling beyond Najd gradually decreased. This may be due to two reasons: first, a rise in the number of scholars in Najd, some of whom were outstanding; this provided an opportunity for Najdi students to study in their homeland. Second, outside Najd, from the mid-eleventh/seventeenth century onwards, there were only a small number of prominent scholars of the legal school (*madh-hab*) to which the Najdis belonged; for while we note the rise of gifted Najdi scholars during the eleventh/seventeenth century, men such as Muḥammad ibn Ismāʿīl, Sulaymān ibn ʿAlī and ʿAbd Allāh ibn Dhahlān, we also note the deaths of some famous Ḥanbalī senior scholars outside Najd. Al-Ḥijjāwī, for example, died in 968/1561, Marʿī ibn Yūsuf in 1032/1623, and Manṣūr al-Bahātī in 1052/1642.

The Academic Status of Najdi Scholars and Their Relations with Others

ʿAbd Allāh al-Bassām states that there were forty scholars living in al-Ushayqir at the same time, 'all of whom were qualified for judgeship, at a time when only the most distinguished and proficient scholars could be appointed to this position'.[67] There may be some exaggeration in this statement, since the author, a respected researcher on Najdi scholars during this era, wrote the biographies of no more than forty scholars from al-Ushayqir covering a period of nearly three centuries. It is unlikely that information about such scholars would have disappeared completely. The accounts of *fatwas* issued by Najdi scholars before the rise of Ibn ʿAbd al-Wahhāb show that some enjoyed high scholarly rank; but this group does not represent a majority by any means. Only a very few scholars stood out from among those distinguished enough to be termed first rate.

Among these few was Sheikh Aḥmad ibn Yaḥyā ibn ʿAṭwa, the most famous scholar of his home town during the tenth/sixteenth century. Ibn ʿAṭwa was born in al-ʿUyayna. After a period of study there, he decided to leave Najd. It seems that this decision resulted from his inability to find anyone in his homeland who could satisfy his scholarly aspirations. He studied actively under such renowned Ḥanbalī scholars in Damascus as Ibn ʿAbd al-Hādī, al-Mardāwī and al-ʿAskarī. He was so successful in his studies that his colleague, the famous Ḥanbalī jurist Mūsā al-Ḥijjāwī, studied under him and benefited from his learning.[68] Upon Ibn ʿAṭwa's return to Najd, students thronged to him and benefited from his knowledge to such a degree that some, like Aḥmad ibn Mushrif and ʿUthmān ibn Zayd, became leading scholars. His work in Najd was not confined to teaching; he was a *muftī* (giver of legal opinions) and an author. His works included *al-Tuḥfa al-badīʿa*, *al-Rawḍa al-anīqa* and *Durar al-fawāʾid*.[69] He was thus the most illustrious scholar in Najd during the tenth/sixteenth century.

The eleventh/seventeenth century witnessed the distinction of three Najdi scholars in three different cities: Muḥammad ibn Ismāʿīl in Ushayqir, Sulaymān ibn ʿAlī in al-ʿUyayna, and ʿAbd Allāh ibn Dhahlān in Riyadh. Ibn ʿĪsā expressed the high status of Muḥammad ibn Ismāʿīl by saying: 'He is the leading scholar in Najd.'[70] Sulaymān ibn ʿAlī said, 'He is the trustworthy Sheikh and the shining beauty spot of both worlds.'[71] Sulaymān ibn ʿAlī's scholarly attainment was described by Ibn Bishr: 'Najdi scholars used to resort to him for the resolution of any problem in *fiqh* [jurisprudence] and other fields.'[72] Muḥammad ibn Fayrūz called him 'the peerless scholar of Najd in his time'.[73] Ibn Dahlān's high scholarly status is clear from the statements about him by his pupil, Aḥmad al-Manqūr, in his *al-Fawākih al-ʿadīda*.

It is clear that Najdi scholars before Ibn ʿAbd al-Wahhāb emphasized *fiqh*. The perfection of this discipline was sufficient to provide various Najdi towns with the *qāḍīs* (judges) they needed. In rare cases, however, some scholars abandoned this discipline and devoted themselves to other branches of learning. Among these were ʿUthmān ibn [Aḥmad ibn] Qāʾid, who was born in al-ʿUyayna and studied in both Damascus and Cairo. His written works include *Najāt al-khalaf fī iʿtiqād al-salaf* ('Salvation of Successors Through [Adopting] the Belief of Predecessors').[74] This scholar died not in Najd but in Egypt. His interest in questions of *ʿaqīda* (Islamic creed) was perhaps a result of his debates with scholars outside of Najd.

The relationships of Najdi scholars with those of other regions were not confined to studying with those scholars. There were other mutual contacts between the two groups. Some Najdi scholars tried to buttress their views on certain legal matters with the opinions of scholars from outside their region, against their local opponents. An example was the contribution of some Makkahan *faqīhs* (jurisprudents) to the dispute among Najdi scholars about the *waqf* (religious endowment) of al-Saʿdūnī in al-ʿUyayna,[75] and that of the Shāfiʿī *muftī* of Laḥsā (al-Aḥsāʾ, in Bahrain) in his opinion on the dispute between Aḥmad ibn Bassām and one of his Najdi opponents.[76] Contact between these groups is also shown by Marʿī ibn Yūsuf's sending a copy of his famous work *Ghāyat al-*

muntahā to Najd, at the end of which he wrote: 'Written by Marʿī ibn Yūsuf . . . who sends abundant greetings and good will to our brother in God Khamīs ibn Sulaymān and conveys all grace and reverence to Sheikh Muḥammad ibn Ismāʿīl'.[77]

Judgeship

Judgeship (*qaḍā*) is clearly linked to scholarship, since attaining this position depends upon adequate knowledge of the Sharīʿa. Religious learning among the Najdis was restricted to those disciplines. As noted above, the main emphasis was on *fiqh*, full knowledge of which was sufficient to qualify one to assume a judgeship. It is clear that there was self-sufficiency in terms of Najdi judges in most towns of the region. Information on the exact incomes of these judges is not available; it is clear, however, that they did not receive cash salaries, and it appears that their sources of income were diverse. There were some local *waqfs* whose yield, or part thereof, went to the judge. Some judges practised trade or agriculture, by one means or another. Others would charge fees from litigants in return for settling differences between them. Ibn ʿAbd al-Wahhāb considered this as tantamount to bribery, and it was one point of disagreement between him and his opponents.[78] It appears that the income of judges was sufficient to provide them with a comfortable standard of living, and to provide their children with the opportunity for study, an opportunity not available to many Najdi families at the time. Because of the sense of justice and beneficence which most Najdi judges possessed, they were highly respected and appreciated by society as a whole. Their word was heeded by most people, and their good offices in mediation were accepted by politicians in their disputes with others. For example, Ibn Bishr refers to the journey of Sheikh Sulaymān ibn ʿAlī, together with Ibn Muʿammar, to al-Bīr, and explains this as an endeavour to bring about reconciliation between the two conflicting parties.[79]

Some Najdi judges lacked the noble qualities that graced the majority of their colleagues. Therefore they were subjected to severe social criticism, especially by that most sensitive group of society, the poets. Ḥumaydān al-Shuwayʿir described them as unjust and venal bribe-takers.[80]

While it is true that there is often much exaggeration in what the poets say, which must be cautiously received and carefully scrutinized, the fact remains that some Najdi judges used to legitimize for themselves what others – foremost among them Ibn ᶜAbd al-Wahhāb – regarded as bribery. It is common knowledge that judgeship and related matters were largely restricted to the urban parts of Najd; the desert nomads had no Sharīᶜa judges, but resorted to the conventions and traditions of their tribes.[81]

Religio-Legal Affiliations of Najdi Scholars

Sharīᶜa documents written by Najdi scholars before the ninth/fifteenth century show that the Ḥanbalī *madh-hab* (legal school) existed in Najd at that time. The travels of Najdi scholars to regions where leading Ḥanbalī scholars lived, in order to study with them, provide further evidence for their affiliation with this *madh-hab* before leaving their country. One of the earliest Najdi scholars to travel for this purpose was Aḥmad ibn ᶜAṭwa, discussed above. It may be noted that all the Najdi scholars during the period before the rise of Muḥammad ibn ᶜAbd al-Wahhāb whose biographies were written by ᶜAbd Allāh ibn Bassām belonged to the Ḥanbalī school. If we add to these scholars those whose biographies have not been dealt with here (and they are not many) the following facts will be confirmed: (1) there was not a single Najdi scholar who did not belong to one of the four well-known Sunnī schools; (2) no Najdi scholar belonged to the Ḥanafī school; (3) there is no reference to any Najdi scholar who embraced the Mālikī school except for Rashīd ibn Khunayn, who in any case was later, and was a contemporary, not a predecessor, of Ibn ᶜAbd al-Wahhāb; (4) Sheikh Ḥusayn ibn ᶜUthmān ibn Zayd was the only Najdi scholar reported by the sources to have left the Ḥanbalī for the Shāfiᶜī school.[82] But while Najdi scholars followed the Ḥanbalī *madh-hab*, this does not mean that they did not read and profit from the books of *fiqh* of other Sunnī schools. This also applies to others elsewhere who belonged to this school, just as those who adhered to other schools read and benefited from Ḥanbalī *fiqh*. This was perhaps one reason why some Najdi scholars, in their local legal disputes, sought help from scholars outside their region who belonged to other Sunnī schools.

If the predominance of the Ḥanbalī school in Najd during this period is clear, the way in which this *madh-hab* entered the region is clouded with obscurity. It is well known that the Ḥanbalīs encountered pressures in some major Muslim capitals, as in Baghdad during the fourth/tenth century, and that some of their scholars fled to other Muslim countries.[83] It is possible that Najd was one place where some of those fugitives sought asylum, and on their arrival sowed the seeds of Ḥanbalism. It is also likely that a Najdi, or a group of Najdis, studied under a Ḥanbalī scholar outside of Najd, and began to teach this *madh-hab* after returning home, thus leading to its spread. Nor was it surprising that the Ḥanbalī *madh-hab* found fertile soil in Najd, as it is the closest of the four Sunnī schools to the exoteric and literal aspects of the Qur'an and *ḥadīth*. As such, to some extent it represents simplicity. Simplicity was a favourite course taken by the Najdi, who was the least affected by outside influences among the inhabitants of the Arabian peninsula. Moreover, Najdis always admired those who stood firmly by their beliefs. It was perhaps the steadfastness displayed by the Ḥanbalīs – for example, by their leader Aḥmad ibn Hanbal and later by Ibn Taymiyya – that made Najdis admire them. Thus there are two factors coinjoined with Najdi psychology: the nature of the Ḥanbalī *madh-hab* itself, and the firm stand taken by some of its scholars. This, in turn, led to the dominance of this *madh-hab* in Najd.

Belief and Practice

The sources at our disposal disagree in their descriptions of the situation of the Najdis in terms of belief and the performance of the pillars of Islam during the period dealt with in this chapter. The sources that support Ibn ʿAbd al-Wahhāb's *daʿwa* present a gloomy picture; however, they differ on how gloomy that picture was. Ibn Ghannām, for example, passes a sweeping judgement on the Najdis to the effect that they practised all kinds of *shirk* (polytheism or paganism). He gives details about their practices at the graves of some of the Ṣaḥāba (the Prophet Muḥammad's Companions) who were killed during the War of Apostasy (*ridda*); these graves and shrines are found in al-Jubayla and the surrounding area. He also gives an account of their practices near some trees in that area. He concludes by describing a man called Tāj, whom the people of al-Kharj believed to be a saint, and visited him with votive offerings and supplications.[84] In his own sweeping judgement, Ibn Bishr also states that *shirk*, in both its major and minor categories, had become widespread in Najd, and gives examples of common practices. But he does not mention the names of shrines, except for that of Zayd ibn al-Khaṭṭāb in al-Jubayla.[85] Both historians agree on labelling this period as *jāhiliyya* (a 'period of ignorance').[86]

Ibn ʿAbd al-Wahhāb, for his part, gave an account of the belief of some of these 'ignorant people' in certain individuals such as Tāj, Shamsūn, Ḥaṭṭāb, Ḥusayn and Idrīs.[87] He also stated that one of his opponents, a Najdi scholar, made magical talismans,[88] and that there were Sufis or mystics at Miʿkāl (part of the present city of Riyadh) who followed the path of Ibn ʿArabī and Ibn al-Fāriḍ.[89] Further, he pointed out that the majority of some Najdi tribes did not perform the main pillars of Islam and denied resurrection after death.[90] He also asserted that the Bedouins had rejected the entire Book (the Qurʾan), rejected religion, and ridiculed those town-dwellers who believed in resurrection.[91]

Some sources, however, stress that Najd was the homeland of important scholars, most of whom were graced by piety and righteousness. They also depict most of its urban inhabitants (at least) as faithfully adhering to the rules of Islam and carrying out its duties and practices.[92] In this context, the poetry of this period contains nothing that conflicts with sound Islamic belief or is incompatible with the general rules of Islam. In fact, the poems emphasize the adherence of their poets to their faith and their commitment to Islam, and demonstrate that the society in which those poets lived was largely traditional in terms of action and conduct.[93]

A careful reader of Ibn Ghannām's history clearly sees his enthusiasm for Ibn ʿAbd al-Wahhāb's *daʿwa*. Knowing the author's attitude helps in assessing the information he provides. The success of Ibn ʿAbd al-Wahhāb's *daʿwa* cannot be denied; but perhaps Ibn Ghannām's staunch support of this mission led him to make a general judgement on all the people of Najd before it took place, in order to demonstrate its merits. One may note that the things mentioned by Ibn Ghannām are confined to a certain area in Najd, and that he did not refer to their existence in other areas. But is the absence of such references evidence that they did not exist, or (at least) that they did not reach the degree they attained in the region of al-ʿArīḍ? It is common knowledge that the region of al-Jubayla was the site of the graves of some martyred Companions. The existence of such graves may have led to their sanctification by some ignorant people; and falling into such a pitfall might well have led to other practices, such as worship of trees and the like. Whatever the case, one can say that Ibn Ghannām's generalization cannot be assumed to be historically correct.

Ibn Bishr, as is seen from a careful reading of his history, was also a zealous advocate of Sheikh Muḥammad's *daʿwa* and of its followers. Such a position might well lead to judgements lacking in accuracy. If we consider his account of what happened after the collapse of the first Saudi state, for example, we find evidence of this. He says of the people of Najd: 'They fought one another over practices not revealed on God's authority. Many abandoned ritual prayer and renounced fasting during Ramadan. In gatherings the sounds of the rebec and of singing were common. Wind scattered dust over mosques and *madrasas;* gatherings for entertainment after the call to prayer flourished; while questions about the principles of Islam and religious observances disappeared.'[94] It is clear that some of these statements are inaccurate, and were made in order to demonstrate the merits of the *daʿwa* and its adherents during the days of the first Saudi state and to clarify the important role played by Turkī ibn ʿAbd Allāh later on. But it may also be noted that Ibn Bishr did not generalize the practice of *shirk* among all Najdis before the rise of Ibn ʿAbd al-Wahhāb. He used the term 'spread' (*fashā*), which does not imply generality. It might be expected that Ibn Bishr, despite his exaggeration, would not attribute *shirk* to all these people generally, since he had stated earlier, in speaking of them, that which implies the impossibility of making such a generalization.

As regards the statements of Ibn ʿAbd al-Wahhāb, it is clear that his reference to 'talismans' refers specifically to one of his opponents. In his *Fawākih*, al-Manqūr records that some Najdi scholars did not content themselves with hating talismans (or 'cryptic charms'), but banned them completely.[95] Moreover, the names of the mystics in Miᶜkāl to whom Sheikh Muḥammad referred are not found among those of Najd religious scholars. In any case, what the Sheikh said about Najdi Bedouins deserves attention, and shows how ignorant the Najdis were of religious matters and how neglectful they were of religious duties.

From a comparison of various sources it seems that the religious situation in Najd was not conformant with the picture given in those sources that supported Ibn ᶜAbd al-Wahhāb's reformist *daᶜwa*. It clearly does not agree with the statements of those who said that the people of the region had rejected Islam and religion,[96] and is far from the allegation that all traces of Islam had vanished from Najd, and that recitation of the Qurᵓan, performance of ritual prayer, payment of *zakāt* (ritual alms) and pilgrimage had been forgotten by its inhabitants.[97] The picture presented in poetic sources may have been a closer reflection of reality. There were, indeed, ignorant people who performed polytheist or paganist rites, but their number was apparently small. There were many Bedouins who did not fully observe the fundamental pillars of Islam, simply because they were ignorant of them. The attitude of the region's religious scholars towards this situation was generally passive. But there were also strict observers of the Sharīᶜa, and those who adhered to the religious principles of Islam and the duties and practices it enjoins.

In any case, it is clear that the pious felt that Najd was in need of a reformist movement that would clarify for the ignorant what was obscure to them, remove all that would damage their faith, and oblige those who neglected the pillars of Islam to perform them. Najd seems to have been a suitable place for the success of such a movement, for Sufism was not deeply rooted there, as it was in many other Muslim countries. Najd was also devoid of non-Sunnī *madh-habs*. Many of the Bedouins had little idea of religion; therefore it was unlikely that they would resist any religious *daᶜwa*, especially if jihād ('holy war') was one of its objectives.

Najd was also ripe for a political movement that would unite its various emirates and tribes under one banner, in order to achieve security and stability. It provided fertile ground for the success of such a movement, for it was remote from the control of a strong central authority.

Thus it was possible for a movement to achieve at least initial success without drawing the attention of outside powers. Moreover, the diversity of Najd's emirates and tribes provided a further reason for the potential success of such a movement; for if a leader failed in one place, his chances of success in another place nearby were strong, because any local ruler would welcome a person who was rejected by his neighbouring ruler. The *daʿwa* of Muḥammad ibn ʿAbd al-Wahhāb is a good case in point.

Notes:

1. ʿUthmān ibn Bishr, *ʿUnwān al-majd fī tārīkh Najd* (Riyadh, 1391/1971), II, p. 189.
2. Ibrāhīm ibn ʿAlī ibn ʿIsā, *Taʾrikh baʿḍ al-ḥawādith al-wāqiʿa fī Najd* (Riyadh, 1386/1966), pp. 32, 36.
3. *Ibid.*, p. 50.
4. *Ibid.*, pp. 30–1.
5. *Ibid.*, p. 32.
6. *Ibid.*, p. 32.
7. Fahd Mārik, *Min shiyam al-ʿArab* (Beirut, 1383–5/1963–5), III, p. 99.
8. *Ibid.*
9. Khālid al-Faraj, *Dīwān al-Nabi* (Cairo, n.d.), I, p. 43.
10. See Aḥmad ibn Muḥammad al-Manqūr, *al-Fawākih al-ʿadīda fī al-masāʾil almufīda* (Damascus, 1383/1963), I, Introduction, p. *wāw*.
11. *Ibid.*, I, p. 156.
12. Al-Faraj, *Dīwān al-Nabi*, I, pp. 44, 64.
13. Ibn Bishr, *ʿUnwān*, II, p. 235.
14. *Ibid.*, II, p. 230.
15. Ibn ʿĪsā, *Tārīkh*, p. 89.
16. *Ibid.*, p. 66.
17. Ibn Bishr, *ʿUnwān*, II, p. 238.
18. *Ibid.*, II, pp. 216, 219.
19. *Ibid.*, II, p. 231.
20. Al-Manqūr, *Fawākih*, I, p. 235. (The weights referred to are variable, and do not have precise equivalents; nor does the coinage.)
21. Ibn Bishr, *ʿUnwān*, II, pp. 219, 232, 216; see also al-Manqūr, *Fawākih*, I, p. 158.

22. J. L. Burckhardt, *Notes on the Bedouins and Wahábys* (London, 1831), I, p. 69.
23. *Ibid.*
24. Ahmad Mustafa Abu Hakima, *A History of Eastern Arabia (1750–1800)* (Beirut, 1965), p. 4.
25. Al-Manqūr, *Fawākih*, I, p. 197.
26. Burckhardt, *Notes*, II, p. 29.
27. Ibn Bishr, *ʿUnwān*, II, p. 209.
28. *Ibid.*, II, pp. 228, 232.
29. Al-Faraj, *Dīwān al-Nabi*, I, p. 51.
30. *Ibid.*, I, p. 41.
31. Al-Manqūr, *Fawākih*, I, p. 440.
32. *Ibid.*, I, pp. 410–13.
33. Al-Faraj, *Dīwān al-Nabi*, I, p. 61.
34. *Ibid.*, I, p. 21.
35. Ibn Bishr, *ʿUnwān*, II, p. 237.
36. Husayn ibn Ghannām, *Rawḍat al-afkār wa-al-afhām li-murtād āl al-Imām waiʿdād ghazawāt dhawī al-Islām* (Cairo, 1368/1948–9), I, p. 26.
37. ʿAbd Allāh al-Khālid Ḥātim, *Khiyār māyultaqat min shiʿr al-Nabat* (Damacus, 1387/1966–7), II, p. 256.
38. Aḥmad al-Manqūr, *Tārīkh al-Sheikh Aḥmad al-Manqūr* (ed. ʿAbd al-ʿAziz al-Khuwaytir, Riyad, 1390/1970), pp. 67, 75; Ibn Bishr, *ʿUnwān*, II, pp. 220, 239, 240.
39. ʿUthmān ibn Bishr, *ʿUnwān al-majd fī tārīkh Najd* (Riyadh, 1391/1971), II, p. 189.
40. Ibrāhīm ibn ʿIsā, *Tārīkh baʿḍ al-ḥawādith al-wāqiʿa fī Najd* (Riyadh, 1386/1966), p. 50.
41. *Ibid.*, p. 51.
42. *Al-Dāra* 3.3, 1977.
43. Ibn Bishr, *ʿUnwān*, II, p. 220.
44. *Ibid.*, II, p. 224.
45 Al-Faraj, *Dīwān al-Nabi*, I, pp. 30–1.
46. Muḥammad al-Fākhirī, *Tārīkh al-Fākhirī*, ms., fol. 20b; see also Ibn Bishr, *ʿUnwān*, II, p. 226.
47. Al-Fākhirī, *Tārīkh*, fol. 8b; Aḥmad ibn Muḥammad al-Manqūr, *Tārīkh* (ed. ʿAbd al-ʿAzīz al-Khuwaytir, Riyadh, 1390/1970), pp. 45, 47; Ibn ʿIsā, *Tārīkh*, pp. 5–50. Ibn Bishr (*ʿUnwān*, II, p. 208) names the person killed by Sharīf Aḥmad ibn Mādī.
48. Al-Manqūr, *Tārīkh*, p. 60; Ibn Bishr, *ʿUnwān*, II, p. 115.

49. ʿAbd Allāh al-Khālid Ḥātim, *Khiyār māyultaqaṭ min shiʿr al-Nabaṭ* (Damascus, 1387/1967), I, p. 80.
50. *Ibid.*, I, pp. 109, 121.
51. Ibn Bishr, *ʿUnwān*, II, p. 226.
52. *Ibid.*, I, p. 20.
53. Ḥātim, *Khiyār*, I, p. 104.
54. Ibn Bishr, *ʿUnwān*, I, p. 25.
55. Quoted from *Majallat al-ʿArab* 7 (1387/1967), p. 607.
56. Muḥammad ibn ʿAbd Allāh ibn Bulayḥad (ibn Bulayhid) al-Najdī, *Ṣaḥīḥ al-akhbār ʿammāfī bilād al-ʿArab min al-āthār* (Beirut, 1392/1972), II.
57. ʿAbd Allāh ibn Muḥammad Bassām, *Tuḥfat al-mushtāq fī akhbār Najd wa-al-Ḥijāz wa-al-ʿIrāq*, ms., fol. 36b.
58. *Ibid.*, fol. 44b.
59. *Ibid.*, fol. 47a.
60. Aḥmad ibn Muḥammad al-Manqūr, *Tārīkh* (ed. ʿAbd al-ʿAzīz al-Khuwayṭir; Riyadh, 1390/1970); see also Ibn Bishr, *ʿUnwān al-majd fī tārīkh Najd* (Riyadh, 1391/1971), II, p. 194.
61. ʿAbd Allāh ibn ʿAbd al-Raḥmān Bassām, *ʿUlamāʾ Najd khilāl sittat qurūn* (Beirut, 1398/1978), I, pp. 5–216.
62. For a study of this document see ʿAbd al-ʿAzīz al-Mubārak in *Majallat al-ʿArab* (1387/1967), pp. 51–9.
63. Bassām, *ʿUlamāʾ Najd*, I, p. 199.
64. *Ibid.*, I, p. 201.
65. This book comprises three volumes and includes the biographies of 338 scholars (see n. 3 above).
66. These include Aḥmad ibn Fayrūz ibn Bassām, Manṣūr al-Bāhilī, ʿAbd al-Raḥmān al-Bāhilī, Sulṭān ibn Mughāmis, ʿUthmān ibn ʿAlī ibn Zayd, Aḥmad al-Murshidī, Ḥusayn ibn ʿUthmān ibn Zayd, ʿAbd al-Wahhāb ibn Mūsā, Muḥammad ibn Manṣūr and Aḥmad ibn Mūsā al-Bāhilī. See Ibn Bishr, *ʿUnwān*, II, pp. 194, 206; ʿAbd Allāh ibn Muḥammad Bassām, *Tuḥfat al-mushtāq fī akhbār Najd wa-al-Ḥijāz wa-al-ʿIrāq*, ms., fol. 23; Aḥmad al-Manqūr, *al-Fawākih al-ʿadīda fī al-masāʾil al-mufīda* (Damascus, 1380/1960), I, pp. 223, 360, 512; II, p. 324.
67. Bassām, *ʿUlamāʾ Najd*, I, p. 15.
68. *Ibid.*, I, pp. 200–10.
69. While Bassām calls Ibn ʿAṭwa's works *al-Tuḥfa fī al fiqh, al-Rawḍa fī al-fiqh* and *Durar al-fawāʾid wa-al-iqyān* (see *ʿUlamāʾ Najd*, I, pp. 2–203), al-Manqūr calls the first two *al-Tuḥfa* and *al-Rawḍa* and the third *Iqyān al-qalāʾid wa-durar al-fawāʾid* in one place (*Fawākih*, I, p. 126) and *Durar*

al-fawāʾid wa-iqyān al-qalāʾid in another (*ibid.*, I, p. 189).
70. Bassām, *ʿUlamāʾ Najd*, III, p. 788.
71. Al-Manqūr, *Fawākih*, I, p. 506.
72. Ibn Bishr, *ʿUnwān*, II, p. 210.
73. Bassām, *ʿUlamāʾ Najd*, I, 311.
74. ʿUthmān ibn Aḥmad al-Najdī, *Najāt al-khalaf fī iʿtiqād al-salaf* (Damascus, 1350/1952).
75. Al-Manqūr, *Fawākih*, I, p. 514.
76. *Ibid.*, I, p. 510.
77. Ibn Bishr, *ʿUnwān*, II, pp. 7–198.
78. Ḥusayn ibn Ghannām, *Rawḍat al-afkār wa-al-afhām* (Cairo, 1368/1949), I, pp. 113, 133.
79. Ibn Bishr, *ʿUnwān*, II, p. 209.
80. ʿAbd Allāh al-Khālid Ḥātim, *Khiyār mā yultaqaṭ min shʿir al-Nabaṭ* (Damascus, 1387/1968), I, pp. 216, 121.
81. *Lamʿ al-shihāb fī sīrat Muḥammad ibn ʿAbd al-Wahhāb* (ed. Aḥmad Abū Ḥakīma; Beirut, 1967), p. 33.
82. Al-Manqūr, *Fawākih*, I, p. 223.
83. Muḥammad Abū Zahra, *Ibn Ḥanbal* (Cairo, 1947), pp. 399–400.
84. Ibn Ghannām, *Rawḍat al-afkār*, I, pp. 7–8.
85. Ibn Bishr, *ʿUnwān*, I, pp. 19, 22.
86. Ibn Ghannām, *Rawḍat al-afkār*, I, p. 14; II, p. 3.
87. *Ibid.*, I, p. 219.
88. *Ibid.*, I, p. 142.
89. *Ibid*, I, p. 147.
90. *Ibid.*, I, pp. 108, 144.
91. *Ibid.*, I, 163.
92. One sees this clearly in the histories of Ibn Bassām, al-Manqūr, al-Fākhirī and Ibn ʿĪsā, as well as in al-Manqūr's *Fawākih* and in the earlier works of Ibn Bishr.
93. See Ḥātim, *Khiyār*, I, pp. 89, 2–113, 138.
94. Ibn Bishr, *ʿUnwān*, II, p. 7.
95. Al-Manqūr, *Fawākih*, I, p. 150 n. 1.
96. See e.g. ʿAbd al-Raḥmān Āl al-Sheikh, *ʿUlamāʾ al-daʿwa* (Cairo, 1386/1966), p. 12.
97. Cf. William G. Palgrave, *Narrative of a Year's Journey across Central and Eastern Arabia* (London/Cambridge, 1865), II, p. 370.

Chapter 5

MUḤAMMAD IBN ʿABD AL-WAHHĀB AND HIS CALL FOR MONOTHEISM

Al-Tihāmi Nuqrā

The heart is, arguably, the most sublime part of the human being, the abode of knowledge and certitude. For the believer, the best part of this certitude is a divine belief that he nurtures with his acts and worship, which grants him all that is most worthwhile in life, opening in front of him the treasures of faith, the wellspring of elevated feelings and the source of noble sentiments.

According to the Prophet, the best fruits of this faith are good deeds. He said: 'Faith does not reside in wishing, but in what has established itself in the heart and been confirmed in deeds.' The divine principle is simply the principle of the oneness of God, which message he entrusted to his prophets and revealed in his books, making it his commandment in the beginning as at the end.

In this light, from the start until the final revelation, from the time of Noah's message through to Muḥammad's message, paganism can be seen merely as an extraneous phenomenon that worked against these beliefs.

It is recounted from ʿIyādh al-Majāshi that the Prophet said in one of his traditions: 'Verily, my God has commanded me to teach you what you know not. What he has taught me is: "All My worshippers I have created true, and then devils came to them and made them stray from their belief, and forbade them what I had allowed, and ordered them to follow polytheism which I had not so ordained."'

And believers still hold that devils, or evil, still lies in wait for man on all roads, attempting to block him from the path of God, turning him away from His Oneness, and luring him to polytheism.

According to Islamic belief, in all ages the religion of God resides in the singularity of his divinity, and in the surrender to Him alone in worship. So long as God is one, then religion too must be manifest in but one faith. However, people may be lured by illusions, sentiments and philosophies, masking the truth that the prophets revealed with the untruths that their doubts and minds create.

The Arabs and the Belief in the Unity of God

In Islam, the unity of God is at the core of its system of belief, and the centre of its worship. Its specificity lies in man's worship of God alone. That is why such care was taken to liberating the faith from superstition and illusion, and towards specifying the form that the truth of divinity should take within human consciousness, as the Qurʾan ordains: 'Whomsoever We sent before you of prophets but We revealed to him that there is no God but I, so worship Me' (Sūra 21, Al-Anbiyāʾ [The Prophets] 25).

When Islam was revealed in the Arabian peninsula the area was a veritable crucible of beliefs – from Christianity, from Judaism, from the Persians and from ancient heathenism. Some worshipped idols, taking them as images of angels, or for their own sake. In the Kaaba, erected for the worship of the one and only God, there were up to 360 idols. The Qurʾan has revealed the different forms of idolatry that were prevalent in the pre-Islamic age in numerous verses (sūras).[1] Most of the revelations of the earlier Makkahan period aimed to sow belief in the unity of God, addressing a people who, in an age of prophets that extends from Ishmael to Muḥammad, a period that spans more than 3,000 years, had never been charged to follow any particular creed. Then, the Qurʾan relates, the Almighty said to the Prophet Muḥammad: 'But (you are sent) as a mercy from your Lord, to give warning to a people to whom no warner had come before you' (Sūra 28, Al-QAṢAṢ [The Narration] 46).

With the succession of generations, heredity and traditions, the original beliefs became overlaid with what came to be seen by the pious as false beliefs. Yet the unity of God was often reiterated: 'Has he made the gods into one God, verily, this is a wonder' (Sūra Ṣād, verse 5). The Qurʾan offered many examples of this principle and set out many proofs of the unity of God, countering opposing beliefs. Indeed, this is why everything in the Qurʾan is based on the oneness of God, and is inspired by it. The Muslim is driven from within himself, not by external forces. According to Islam, faith is what should cast its shadow on his life, which is why the Qurʾan regarded this as a noble aim in itself. Ibn al-Qayyim said:

> Every verse in the Qurʾan carries within itself [a sign of] the oneness of God, is witness to it, and calls for it . . .[2] The recourse to God alone, in what is permitted and what is forbidden, in the laws, in the way of life, the weight of values and concepts, turning only to Him in requests, worship, hope, fear, and piety are the requirements for holding to the) unity of Divinity and the power of God. He is the Ever Living, the only God, so invoke Him, making your worship pure for Him alone . . . (Sūra 40, Ghāfir [The Forgiver], 65)

The Power of Monotheism

According to Islam, there is no power on earth that can match the power of monotheism, for this power frees spirits from submission to anything other than God and worship of any other save Him. It shields deeds from the sin of hypocrisy. One of its early fruits were those models of human perfection provided by men whose spirits were too proud to accept humiliation and quietude, refusing to follow the oppressor no matter how mighty and powerful on earth, seeking succour and support from God, fearful of Him and not of people even when they were told: 'People have united against you, so be fearful'. This only strengthened their faith, and they replied: 'Sufficient unto us is God, none better than Him as our Trustee.'

Believers hold that because of this and because their faith in God reached a certain level of certitude, God gave them victory in their confrontation with despotism, and led them to overcome all ordeals. This is what the Prophet had planted in their hearts. He said to Ibn ʿAbbās when he was still a youth, 'Uphold God and he will uphold you, uphold God and you will find Him next to you. If you ask something, ask only God; and if you seek anything, then it is from God that you must seek it. Know that even were the whole people to act to benefit you, they will not be able to benefit you except with what God has already ordained for you, and if they all agreed to harm you, they will not be able to harm you except with what God has already ordained for you'(related from at-Tirmīdhī).

It is this creed that the Prophet proclaimed to his Companions and followers, and which made them disregard mundane things and answer God when He summoned them to what gives them life. They were not tempted by the pleasures of mortal life because they were confident that what God offers is superior and longer lasting.

It is often held that the Muslims failed to be victorious only when their belief was shaken or their faith wavered.

The Dangers of a Corrupted Faith

If the belief in the unity of God has such an impact on spiritual and material life, then any deviation from it is seen as a turning away from the path of the cherished faith, and results in the loss of the path of God, and in the corruption of true instinct: 'Judgment is for none but God. He has commanded that you worship none but Him; that is the true religion, but most men know not' (Sūra 12, Yūsuf [Joseph], 40.) 'False' beliefs can only create dissension in the mind and life of the Muslim, and he becomes conflicted in his direction and prayer, emotion and hope.

The object of prayer and invocations is He Who possesses the key to granting them; He is the giver of life, not he to whom it was given.

The perceptivity of Islam in examining the heart and warning against whims is extremely acute and sensitive, so how can it be acceptable for one who believes in the creed of the one God to give himself over to other than God, or to place hope in someone else, or to abase himself to a creature like him who has no sway over things?

It is for this reason that Islam has cautioned against polytheism in all its manifestations – and they are many forms, sometimes too imperceptible to be visible, so that only he who has given God His due can see them. It was related in the Prophet's traditions that polytheism is more imperceptible than the creeping of motes over hard rock on a pitch-dark night.

Yaḥyā bin Muʾādh said, 'With monotheism comes light, and with polytheism comes fire. The light of monotheism burns more the vices of the believers in the one God than the fire of the idolaters burns their virtues.'

With the passage of time some Muslims simply forget what is right and become familiar with what is wrong, especially if they do it frequently or if it is frequently practised before them, with the exception of those pious and strong whom God has fortified with virtue so that, in their obedience to God, they do not heed any censure or blame. Such believers do not hesitate to tell or support truth, because they are not influenced by fear, flattery, concession or far-fetched interpretation. They are not tempted by the praise of others; nor are they deterred by censure levelled against them. Some of these righteous people are encouraged by God to reform the faith and they are determined to stand firm until Allah alone is worshipped, even if this means their suffering harm and hatred by upholders of what they regard as falsehood.

Muḥammad ibn ʿAbd al-Wahhāb: the Preacher and Reformer

One such reformer was Sheikh Muḥammad ibn ʿAbd al-Wahhāb. He was born in the town of al-ʿUyayna, Najd, in the year 1115/1703, where he was brought up, learned the Qurʾan by heart and was taught basic religious studies and Ḥanbalite *fiqh* (jurisprudence) by his father who was the *mufti* (giver of formal legal opinions) and judge of al-ʿUyayna. Then he travelled to Hijaz and Basra in search of further learning, dedicating himself to the study of the books of *tafsīr* (Qurʾanic exegesis), *ḥadīth* (Prophet Muḥammad's traditions) and the works authored by the high-ranking scholar ibn Taymiyya and the works of his disciple Ibn Qayyim al-Jawziyya. These works left a deep imprint on him, in his writings, ideas and arguments.

When he returned to al-ʿUyayna, Sheikh Muḥammad ibn ʿAbd al-Wahhāb was well received by its emir at that time, ʿUthmān ibn Muʿammar. During that period the town had many trees and stones that were held sacred by its inhabitants, who sacrificed to them. Examples of these sanctified objects included the Dome of Zayd ibn al-Khaṫṫāb and the tree of Abū Dujāna. The Sheikh was outraged by this behaviour, which he considered a deviation from true religious principles. So, together with the emir and accompanied by some troops, he cut down the trees that the people had worshipped and pulled down the shrines and domes. The people of al-ʿUyayna complained to the governor of al-Qatīf and al-Iḥsā provinces against the Sheikh. The governor accordingly instructed the emir to order the Sheikh out of al-ʿUyayna; and so the Sheikh left for ad-Dirʿīyah in the year 1157/1744.

When he knew of his arrival, Muḥammad ibn Saʿūd, the Emir of ad-Dirʿīyah, visited the Sheikh. They discussed the idolatry and polytheism that was rampant among the people of Najd, keeping them away from true monotheist belief. The Najdis at the time used to frequently visit a grave which, they alleged, belonged to Pap Dirār, the well-known Ṣaḥābi (Companion of Prophet Muḥammad), asking him to fulfil their wishes, and dispel their distress. There was also a tree called al-Ṫarafiyya to which they accorded a sanctity similar to that endowed by the pre-Islamic people to the tree that was called Dhāt Anwāạ. A third example was a cave called Maghārat Bint al-Amīr, which was frequented by women who could not have children or were not married, as well as for other matters that were contrary to the essence of monotheism and attributed good or harmful deeds to agencies other than God.

He found the emir to be an avid listener, willing to support what the Sheikh intended to do in advocating reform, resisting harmful innovations and wiping out idolatry and polytheism. This was certainly not an easy task, especially among people who had other beliefs.

In this reformist movement the Sheikh had supporters as well as opponents. But he was fortunate to find strong backing and unqualified sponsorship from Emir Muḥammad ibn Saʿūd.

In the year 1199/1784 Imām Muḥammad ibn Saʿūd died and was succeeded by his faithful son, ʿAbd al-ʿAzīz. Abdul Aziz was equally supportive to Sheikh Muḥammad ibn ʿAbd al-Wahhāb. Abdul Aziz conquered Riyadh, Tihāma and parts of Yemen and Hijaz. Najd also proclaimed allegiance to him. All this resulted in the predominance of the Sheikh's *daʿwa* (call) after twenty years of incessant strife. He died in the year 1206/1792 at the age of about 90, nearly twenty-seven years after his victory.

The Sheikh's Advocacy of Monotheism

Most of the Sheikh's works pivoted around his call to the oneness of God, a right which men owe their Lord. In Islam, the word *tawḥīd* (monotheism), that is, the profession of the unity of God, implied negation of the divinity of any being other than God for those who seek refuge with Him, ask for His help or support or appeal to Him. Thus is the divine oneness which God has commanded in His Holy Book when He says: 'Yet when God's slave [i.e. the Prophet Muḥammad] stood to invoke Him, they crowded around him. Say: "I do no more than invoke my Lord and I associate none as partners along with Him." Say: "It is not in my power to cause you harm or to bring you to the rightful path." Say "No one can deliver me from God's punishment [should I err], nor would I find refuge except in Him, unless I proclaim what I receive from God and His message"' (Sūra 72, al-Jinn [The Jinn], verses 19–22).

In this context, the Prophet Muḥammad says: 'Do not extol me as Christians extol Jesus, the Son of Mary; for I am merely a servant of God. Describe me, therefore, as God's Servant and His messenger.'

In the same context a man once said to the Prophet Muḥammad: 'As long as God and you intend.' Whereupon the Prophet retorted: 'Have you made me equal to God? You should say "As long as God alone intends."'

Accordingly, and in the same vein, Sheikh Muḥammad ibn ʿAbd al-Wahhāb says in the section where he discusses *al-ʾaqīda* (the Islamic faith), 'It is a part of polytheism to ask help from or invoke anyone other than God; this means that one would be bestowing divine attributes on those other than Him. No one should transgress these limits and turn to a created mortal and address him with what he would address the Creator only; this would mean a denial of God's divinity and an equating the God of the universe [with His creatures]: "Is then He Who creates like one who creates not? Will you not then remember?"' (Sūra 16, Al-Naḥl [The Bees], verse 17).

In *ḥadith al-Ifk* (the story when ʿAisha, Prophet Muḥammad's favourite wife, was unjustly accused of having had an affair), when ʿAisha was acquitted by a Qurʾanic verse and the Prophet informed her of that, her mother told her to go to him. But she said: 'By God I will not do that nor will I thank either him or thank you two, [meaning her parents]. I thank God alone Who has sent down my exoneration.'

In another version she is quoted as having said: 'Praise be to God and not to you'.

In his *sanad* (tracing back the Prophet's tradition or *ḥadīth* through a chain of authorities), al-Bayhaqi quoted Muḥammad ibn Muslim to have said: 'I heard Hayyān, the friend of Ibn al-Mubārak, say: "I said to ʿAbdallah ibn al-Mubārak: I feel that ʿAisha exceeded her bounds when she said to Prophet Muḥammad: 'I thank God and I do not thank you.' Whereupon ʿAbdallah replied: "Well, she bestowed praise on Him Who duly deserves it."'

Moreover, the pagans whom the Prophet Muḥammad fought, all believed in the oneness of God – that is, that no one creates, sustains, brings to life, causes death and disposes of affairs except God alone; and this we can also see in the Qurʾan in the following verse: 'Say: Who provides for you from the sky and the earth? Or who is it who owns hearing and sight? And who is it who brings out the living from the dead and the dead from the living? And who is it who regulates all affairs? They will soon say: "God"' (Sūra 10, Yūnus [Jonah], verse 31).

The Sheikh replied to the people who make untenable justifications and excuses when he said: 'If one of the idolaters says: we know that it is God who creates, sustains and regulates affairs; however, these righteous people are His favourites. Thus we call on them and make vows to them; take refuge with them thereby we want to obtain their favour and intercession.' In this case you have to retort by saying to such people: 'Your talk is similar to that of Abu Jahl and his likes. They call upon Jesus, and Lazarus, the angels and the saints seeking, as the Qurʾan has related, 'Those who seek others than God for protection, in order to bring them nearer to God' (Sūra 39, Al-Zumar [the Groups], verse 3). 'They worship, besides God, those that neither can hurt nor profit them and they say: "These are our intercessors with God" . . .' (Sūra 10, Yūnus [Jonah], verse 18). What made these people atheists is that they did not testify to the oneness of God for none but God is to be beseeched and invoked for help. Vows and immolations must not be made except to Him.[3] He believed that it is misleading enough for this world to be blind to the shining light of monotheism. In this lies a corrupted faith, a corrupted life and a miserable end.

God articulates through the holy *ḥadīth*: 'I wonder at the attitude of human beings and Jinns: I create, but others are worshipped, and I provide yet others are thanked.'

The Sheikh's call for unadulterated monotheism was heard beyond Najd, crossing the borders to embrace the entire Muslim world, reaching out to people who invoked not God's but fellow human beings' help. They made vows to them (asking them to intercede with God on their behalf); they even made them the equals of God.

In this connection, according to a *ḥadīth* narrated by al-Bukhāri on the authority of ʿAbdallah ibn Masʾūd, the Prophet Muḥammad was quoted as saying: 'Anyone who dies while he sets up equals to God will go to Hell.'

Definition of a Polytheist

Careful study of the messages and sermons of Sheikh Muḥammad ibn ʿAbd al-Wahhāb on monotheism and polytheism reveals that the Sheikh backs up his call with solid arguments that bolster his belief and faith (*ʿaqīda)*; he also refutes the arguments of his opponents, and bases his own 'proofs' on the Qurʾan and Sunna.

He often assumes a question to be asked by way of objection and, therefore, he replies to make the enquirer more convinced and to instruct the preachers what they should be equipped with in terms of traditional and rational evidence in their preaching of monotheism where he says in his seventh treatise, 'The fundament that combines causes of worshipping God alone': 'If someone asks "what is the foundation for worshipping

God alone?", I will say: "Obeying Him through compliance with what He enjoins and avoidance of what He forbids." Again, if somebody asks about the types of worship that do not befit anyone except God, I will say: "These types include supplication, asking for help, slaughtering sacrifices, making vows, showing fear of God, expressing hope, reliance, turning repentantly to God, showing awe and displaying inclination towards Him; kneeling, prostration, submissiveness, humility to and glorification of God, all of which are exclusively duties towards God. Evidence of invocation is found in the following Quranic verse 'And the places of worship are for God alone: so invoke none along with God'" (Sūra 72, al-Jinn [The Jinn], verse 18). Evidence of imploring assistance occurs in the verse where God says: 'Remember ye implored the assistance of your Lord and He answered you . . .' (Sūra 8, al-Anfāl [The Spoils of War], verse 9). In his definition of *shirk* (polytheism), the Sheikh mentions three types, as follows:[3]

1. *Shirk Akbar* (major polytheism) which includes worship, intention and love: Polytheism in worship is self-evident. Intention and love polytheism, on the other hand, is to seek, through one's obedience, the pleasure of others than God.

   There is no controversy among believers with regard to obedience in polytheism, which involves humans' obedience to commit sinful deeds. In this context, the Prophet Muḥammad explained this to ʿUdayy ibn Pap Hātim when the latter, in answer to a query, said to the Prophet: 'We do not worship them.' To this the Prophet said to ʿUdayy that worshipping those [other than God] is obeying them in committing sinful deeds. (This *ḥadīth* was narrated by al-Tirmīdhi.) Love in polytheism is illustrated in the following verse where God says: 'They love them [i.e. those others who are regarded as equal to God] as they should love God. But those who truly believe overflow with love for God alone' (Sūra 2, al-Baqara [The Cow], verse 165).
2. *Shirk Asghar* (minor polytheism): is hypocrisy or dissimulation. In this connection, al-Pap Hakīm (a *ḥadīth* narrator) quoted Prophet Muḥammad to have said: 'Even a small amount of hypocrisy is polytheism'.
3. Concealed polytheism is a state into which a true believer may unwittingly lapse. Therefore, the Prophet Muḥammad used to say when supplicating God:

'O God: I seek refuge with You lest I associate anything with You while I know that, and I ask Your forgiveness for the guilt which I may have unknowingly done.'

Sheikh Muḥammad dealt at length with doing work that sincerely seeks God's pleasure, and spoke in great detail about the necessity of freeing the heart from preoccupations that could distract one's attention from God, or keep one away from God. Such things are felt only by those who have actually practised the Islamic faith and lived its spiritual experience.

Works Authored by al-Sheikh

Among the Sheikh's most highly regarded works one may mention *Kitāb al-Tawḥīd* (book of monotheism); *Kitāb Usūl al-Īmān wa Fadāʾil al-Islām* (book on foundations of belief and merits of Islam); *Kitāb Aḥādīth al-Fitan* (accounts of seditions); *Mufīd al-Mustafīd fī Hukm Tārik al-Tawḥīd* (the useful source for judgement on those rejecting monotheism); *Kitāb Nasīḥat al-Muslimīn bi-Aḥādīth Khātam al-Mursalīn* (advice to Muslims through the sayings of the Seal of Prophets [i.e. [the Prophet Muḥammad]; *Majmūʾ al-Pap Hadīth Murattaban ʿalā abwāb al-Fiqh* (a compendium of *ḥadīth* arranged according to sections of [Islamic] jurisprudence). In addition to these he abridged versions of some important sources such as *Mukhtasar Zād al-Ma ʿād li ibn al-Qayyim* (a summary of ibn al-Qayyim's book, Zād al-Maʾād [provisions for the hereafter]; al-Mardāwi's *Mukhtasar al-Insāf fị Maʾrifat al-Rājiḥ fi al-Khilāf* (a summary of the preferable side in matters of controversy) and *Mukhta-Papsar al-Sharḥ al-Kabīr li ibn Qudāma al-Maqdisi* (an abridgement of ibn Qudāma al-Maqdisi's major work).

Imām Muḥammad ibn Saud University has made valuable contributions to this field, especially to the Islamic library which has critically edited, printed and published the numerous manuscripts of this celebrated preacher and reformer. Thanks to the University's dedicated scholars, this corpus of work has enabled students to access the writings of the Sheikh and provided valuable information about his movement as al-madh-hab al-Wahhābi (i.e. the Wahhābi sect), despite the fact he has no independent school of *fiqh* or for the *ʿaqīda* (Islamic faith). He was simply a reformer scholar, a sincere preacher and a traditionalist follower of the Ḥanbalī *madh-hab*. In fact, his *daʿwa*, the preaching of monotheism, was nothing but a revival of the path followed by the venerable forefathers who rejected the claim that Almighty God had allocated a special place for a select group of people with whom God accepts that men can seek protection, supplicate and ask assistance, making them intermediaries between them and himself.

The following Qurʾanic verse is relevant in this regard: 'When God alone is mentioned, the hearts of those who believe not in the Hereafter are filled with disgust and horror; and when other gods than Him are mentioned, behold, they are filled with joy' (Sūra 39, al-Zumar [The Groups], verse 45).

Al-Qushayri says in his *exegetic commentary* on the story of testing prophet Ibrāhīm when he was ordered by God to sacrifice his own son, Ismāʾīl: we read in the Qurʾan 'and, when he was old enough to walk with him . . .', pointing to Ibrāhīm's doting on his son, and his strong feelings of attachment to him. It is related: that he saw him one day mounting a pale grey horse, he found him handsome and eyed him with admiration, then God ordered him to slaughter him. When Ibrāhīm complied with God's order and drove Ismāʾīl out of his own heart, surrendering him to God, redemption came about. It was as if all that was intended was for Ibrāhīm to turn his heart to God and away from his son.

Having referred to some of the works of the Sheikh, one should not neglect also to pay tribute to some of his sons and grandsons who dedicated their entire lives to spreading his *daʿwa* and religious knowledge through books like *ta ʾsīs al-taqdīs fi al-Radd ʿalā Dawūd ibn Jirjīs* (fundaments of sanctification in replying to Ibn Jirjis) by al-Imām al-Sheikh ʿAbd al-Latīf ibn al-Sheikh ʿAbd al-Raḥmān; *Taysīr al-ʾ Azīz al-Hamīd fī Sharḥ Kitāb al-Tawḥīd* (facilitation by the Almighty, the Most Praiseworthy in explanation of the book of monotheism) by Sulaimān ibn al-Sheikh ʿAbdallah, and *Dawrunā fi al-Kifāḥ* (our role in the struggle) by H. E. Sheikh Hasan ibn ʿAbdallah Āl al-Sheikh, Minister of Higher Education.

Ad-Dirʿīyah Pact

It is reported that at the historic meeting between Prince Muḥammad ibn Saʿūd ibn Muqrin, Emir of Dirʿīyah, and Imām Sheikh Muḥammad ibn ʿAbd al-Wahhāb, the emir said:

'This [Islam] is the faith of God and His Apostle (Prophet Muḥammad) no doubt about that. So rejoice at victory and the support I will extend to you for the fulfilment of your call, and strive through jihad against those who oppose you. But I have the two following conditions to make:

First, if we support you and strive through jihad in the way of Almighty God, and he then enables us to capture the country and emerge victorious, you shall not desert us and make alliances with others instead.

Secondly, the people of Dirʿīyah owe me taxes which I will collect at harvest time So do not deprive me of that.'

The Imām and Sheikh said: 'As regards your first condition, please extend your hand to me', which Emir ibn Saʿūd did and the Sheikh held the emir's hand and said:

'Blood for blood and destruction for destruction (i.e. unconditional support). But as for the second condition, it may happen that God will bestow victory upon you and thus enable you to obtain, through spoils and booty, a better substitute for the taxes you expect to collect from the Dirʿīyah people.'

The Imām wrote to the people, judges, chiefs and scholars of the neighbouring cities and districts asking them to join the *daʿwa* (the calling). Some of them responded favourably and followed the path he had laid down, while others remained aloof, were sarcastic and critical, and persuaded others to keep away. The Sheikh's response to this was to declare jihād (holy war) and the *daʿwa* adherents raised its banner and followed suit. The first detachment of *daʿwa* supporters consisted of seven female camel mounts. They raided the enemy as far as they could, and faced much resistance. The first encounter they had with the enemy was in the year 1159/1746 when they fought in close combat with men who rallied around Daḥḥām ibn Dawwās, the Emir of Riyadh. Daḥḥām was a major adversary of the *daʿwa* and of the Emir of ad-Dirʿīyah. Ad-Dirʿīyah itself was a target of the attacks made by the adversaries, the most serious of which was that launched by Daḥḥām ibn Dawwās, the Emir of Riyadh, backed by his own townspeople and al-Sumādaḥ of Wādi al-Zafīr. He led his men up to Manfūḥa, which he captured.

But ʿAli ibn Mazrūʾ, together with a group of fighters, staged a stiff resistance against Daḥḥām. ʿAli also sent a message to Dirʿīyah asking for reinforcements from Muḥammad ibn Saʿūd, the emir of the city, who sent an army led by his own son, ʿAbdallah ibn Muḥammad. Ibn Dawwās retreated before Ibn Saʿūd's troops and asked for a truce, undertaking to establish the laws of Islam. He also asked for a preacher to teach the people of Riyadh about *tawḥīd* (monotheism). Sheikh ʿEissa ibn Qāsim was accordingly sent to perform the task. But the truce did not last long. The *daʿwa*, on the other hand, spread rapidly, forging its way either by persuasion or by the use of force.

In the year 1168/1754 Huraymila surrendered. A delegation also came to Dirʿīyah from al-Quwayʾiyya and pledged to act in accordance with the tenets of Islam and to be faithful and loyal to the *daʿwa* and its upholders. By the year 1170/1756 the *daʿwa* had extended far and wide to cover the regions of al-Washm and Sudayr. Thādiq also capitulated and ad-Dirʿīyah sent Sheikh Aḥmad ibn Suwaylim to teach *tawḥīd* to the people of Thādiq.

Notes:

1. Like Sūra 39, al-Zumar (The Groups), verses 3 and 4; Sūra 43 al-Zukhruf (The Adornments), verses 62–5; Sūra 34, Sabaʾ (Sheba), verses 40–6; Sūra 37, Al-Sāffāt (Those Ranged in Ranks), verses 149–59; and Sūra 53 al-Najm (The Star), verses 19–28.
2. Ibn Qayem al-Jauziyah. *Madarej al-Salkeen* (Cairo, 1331/1912) Vol. 3, p. 289.
3. Works of Sheikh Muḥammad ibn ʿAbd al-Wahhāb, Part One, pp. 363–6.
4. Al-Sheikh al-Imām's *Works*, Part One. 1/379–80.

Chapter 6

THE PERSONAL LETTERS OF SHEIKH MUḤAMMAD IBN ʿABD AL-WAHHĀB

ʿAbd Allāh al-Ṣāliḥ al-ʿUthaymīn

The *daʿwa* (mission) of Muḥammad ibn ʿAbd al-Wahhāb had a far-reaching influence on the course of modern Islamic history; hence the considerable interest in all that is related to its leader. Much has been written about his life, his mission, and the consequences of these. Indeed, the success of this movement has led some writers to research the scholarly figures who proceded him and who preached something like, or some of, the principles he advocated. Writing about Ibn ʿAbd al-Wahhāb vary in their degree of depth or superficiality, fairness or bias, novelty or lack of such. It is hoped that one result of these varied studies will be to produce works that combine depth with impartiality and creativity, and that at the end of the day, we will not be repeating what the ancient Arab poet says:

> I see that we only say what we have borrowed,
> or merely repeat what we ourselves have said before.

Much has been written about Sheikh Muḥammad as a young man seeking knowledge wherever he could find it, as the advocate of a *daʿwa* determined to do whatever would secure its success, and as a leader who contributed greatly to directing legal issues. Much has also been written about the origins of his *daʿwa* and its effect on his own and other Muslim societies. This modest study does not offer a detailed or independent account of any of these aspects; it is, rather, an attempt to clarify the importance of the Sheikh's personal letters, especially with regard to his personality and the circumstances surrounding his mission.

The Letters in Terms of Authenticity

One of the most significant matters with which any researcher in the humanities must concern himself is to confirm the authenticity of the text which he attempts to study. If he is not convinced of the authenticity of that text it will be useless to try to draw conclusions from it. This is what I will attempt to call attention to in the introduction to this study.

Muḥammad ibn ʿAbd al-Wahhāb lived a long life filled with varied activities. His life as leader of a mission, and as a partner in directing a state for nearly sixty years, would make one expect him to have written a large number of personal letters. But what is actually known about his personal correspondence does not match this expectation. Consequently, this researcher is almost certain that many of his personal letters have been lost.

Here one may suggest that the attitude of Husayn ibn Ghannām, to whom most of the credit goes for presenting those letters that have survived, calls for contemplation. He recorded letters which vary in length as well as in content, and in some cases quoted some letters from the Sheikh's opponents as a preliminary to writing down replies to them. But he also stated that he did not record many of the Sheikh's responses to some questions, for fear of falling into prolixity.[1] Did Ibn Ghannām treat some of the Sheikh's personal letters in the same way that he treated some of his responses, or did he find only the letters he included in his book? Whatever the case, what he has attributed to the Sheikh seems to be authentic.

But there are other sources that ascribe to the Sheikh letters not mentioned by Ibn Ghannām. These letters have been published in the fifth volume of the Sheikh's works, which collects all the personal letters attributed to him. The writers of this volume have taken Ibn Ghannām's history as the primary source, with which they compared, and to which they added, things that it did not include. Careful scrutiny of this collection leads us to two observations:

First, there is a difference in some expressions and phrases between the letters presented here and the originals as cited by Ibn Ghannām, with no indication of the points of difference. An example is the Sheikh's letter to the scholars of Makkah, and his letter to the Sharīf Aḥmad ibn Saᶜīd.[2] Second, some letters added to those cited by Ibn Ghannām contain nothing to suggest they are in fact attributable to the Sheikh himself. Take, for example, the letter which the Sheikh is said to have sent to a scholar from Madinah. This letter is found only in the compilation (by Ibn Qāsim), *al-Durar al-saniyya*, and the name of the scholar to whom it was addressed is not mentioned. It is unlikely that the Sheikh would have sent a letter to a scholar of that city without mentioning his name; moreover, there is no indication that it was from the Sheikh. Whoever studies the Sheikh's letters sees that they begin, 'From Muḥammad ibn ᶜAbd al-Wahhāb to so-and-so, son of so-and-so'; this particular letter does not begin with such a phrase, but is in a style quite different from the Sheikh's usual style.

Something similar can be said about the letter which the Sheikh is said to have sent to Sheikh ᶜAbd Allāh al-Ṣanᶜānī. This too is found only in *al-Durar al-saniyya* and the name of its sender is not mentioned. When compared with the letter written by Sheikh Muḥammad's son ᶜAbd Allāh upon his entry into Makkah with Suᶜūd ibn ᶜAbd al-ᶜAzīz, it reveals much similarity between parts of both letters in terms of style and content.[3] It is possible that the person who wrote to al-Ṣanᶜānī was ᶜAbd Allāh and not his father.

As for the letter which Sheikh Muḥammad is said to have sent to the people of the Maghreb (North Africa), it is clear that it was not written by him, for several reasons. First, because the two aforementioned letters attributed to him appear only in *al-Durar al-saniyya*, and the name of the sender is not mentioned. Second, it is unlikely that the interest of the leaders of the Najdi reformist *daᶜwa* in the Maghreb began before their conquest of the Hijaz, the meeting place of people coming on pilgrimage. Third, and most important, is the fact that this letter reached Tunis during the time of (the vizier) Ḥammāda Pasha (ibn ᶜAbd al-ᶜAzīz). Tunisian sources mention its arrival after discussing the achievements of Suᶜūd ibn ᶜAbd al-ᶜAzīz in the Hijaz.[4] This agrees with the second reason, in that interest in the Maghreb was a result of the Saudi presence in the Hijaz. This letter, too, may have been written by ᶜAbd Allāh ibn Muḥammad, who accompanied Suᶜūd ibn ᶜAbd al-ᶜAziz when the latter entered Makkah, as stated above.

In the fifth volume of the Sheikh's works there is another letter which is said to have been a reply to a letter whose sender is not named. This letter was mentioned in Ibn Muʿammar's *Majmūʿat al-rasāʾil wa-al-masāʾil* as well as in *al-Durar al-saniyya*. Its style is similar to the Sheikh's in many of his works; but there is a phrase that attracted this researcher's attention. It reads as follows: 'It is the purport of what you mentioned in your letter to the effect that Sheikh Muḥammad prescribed three fundamental principles for you.'[5] It might seem that the author of this phrase was not Sheikh Muḥammad; but the Sheikh may have cited the phrase written by the person by whom this letter was sent. In this letter the following passage also occurs: 'This is what Ibn ʿAbd al-Wahhāb advocates.' [6] Had the writer been a pupil or a follower of the Sheikh, he would more likely have written 'the Sheikh' before 'Ibn ʿAbd al-Wahhāb'. The Sheikh's designation of himself as 'Ibn ʿAbd al-Wahhāb' is found in other letters.[7] There is also an indication that this letter was written while ʿAbd Allāh al-Muways (one of Ibn ʿAbd al-Wahhāb's opponents) was still alive: 'Notwithstanding, your devil al-Muways tells you that his respected females and their relatives know about *tawḥīd*, to say nothing of their men.'[8] But the following statement also occurs in the letter: 'What about one who has a relative who has been reviling God's religion for forty years?'[9] If it is assumed that the Sheikh's preaching began in Najd around 1145/1733, this letter would have been written around 1185/1775. It is well known, however, that al-Muways died ten years earlier.[10] It is clear that despite the paucity of Ibn ʿAbd al-Wahhāb's personal letters, a small portion of this handed-down tradition requires careful study and re-examination.

The Style of the Letters

If the writer's style plays a role in revealing features of his personality, his personal letters are more eloquent than his other writings in shedding light on those features. Perhaps the most significant point which may be noted by one who contemplates the style of the Sheikh's letters is (his) originality and simplicity. Most letters start with a phrase such as: 'From Muḥammad ibn ʿAbd al-Wahhāb to so-and-so, son of so-and-so. Peace be upon you together with the mercy of Allāh and His blessings . . . To begin with [*baʿd*] . . .' This style is in complete harmony with the Arab milieu in which the Sheikh lived, an environment which had not yet seen the incursion of foreign influences, and completely agrees with the styles of the forebears (*salaf*) of the Muslim community. This explains the Sheikh's desire to follow in the footsteps of those forebears. Yet although adherence to authenticity and simplicity was the main characteristic of the Sheikh's style, he was, apparently, ready to compromise if he thought that this would be in the general interest of his *daʿwa*. For example, he was well aware of the prestige of the Makkahan scholars and their influence, negative or positive, on the *daʿwa*'s progress. Thus his style in his letters to them diverged from his usual style, and his preambles included a type of affected rhymed prose (*sajʿ*), such as: 'From Muḥammad ibn ʿAbd al-Wahhāb to the illustrious scholars in the City of God. May Allāh bestow victory on the [Prophet Muḥammad, the] Lord of Mankind, on whom be the best of prayers and greetings, and on the followers of the celebrated imāms; greetings to you, and God's mercy and blessings.'[11]

He also appreciated the status of the governor of the holy city, and his influence, should he choose to support the Sheikh's mission. Thus he began his letter to him with phrases that show a certain skill in flattery. But the Sheikh did not content himself with showering honorific titles and lavishing good wishes on the addressee both in this world and the hereafter; he went beyond this by the subtle intimation that the Sharīf, because of his kinship to the Prophet Muḥammad, was the most likely person to support the *daʿwa*:

> In the Name of God, the Merciful, the Compassionate. I take leave to submit to your honourable self (may God continue to shower His favours and blessings on you), your Excellency Sharīf Aḥmad, son of Sharīf Saʿīd (may Allāh honour him in both worlds, and may He exalt him through the religion of his ancestor [Muḥammad], the master of humans and of jinns, that when your letter reached your humble servant, and he contemplated its beautiful words, he raised his hands in supplication to God to confer His gracious support upon you.[12]

When hoping to win over the chieftain of a large tribe to his *daʿwa*, the Sheikh adds to the beginning of his letter to him what he believes to be affective elements. Thus when he writes to the chieftain of a tribe in Syria, he says: 'From Muḥammad ibn ʿAbd al-Wahhāb to the meritorious Sheikh of Āl Mazyad (may Allah increase his faith and protect him against the intrigues of the devil . . . To begin with . . .'.[13]

A careful examination of the Sheikh's style will note how he sticks to authenticity and simplicity. He will also note the Sheikh's astuteness and his attempt to make use of whatever he sees as beneficial to the interest of his mission. So, when he wished to win over the people of Manfūḥa and Riyadh via the Qāḍī (judge) of ad-Dirʿīyah, he described this person in his letter to them by saying, 'We know no scholar among all the learned men of Najd, al-ʿArīḍ, or elsewhere, who can surpass ʿAbd Allāh ibn ʿĪsā.'[14] Yet in another letter he addresses the same judge as follows: 'You and your Sheikhs have not understood the religion of Islam, nor have you distinguished the faith of Muḥammad from that of 'Amr ibn Luḥayy.'[15]

He also seeks to arouse the magnanimity and sense of honour in his addressee. He tries to persuade Muḥammad ibn ʿĪd by saying, 'You certainly have an intellect, and personal honour, which you do not compromise. We believe that if you find the right to be on your side, you will never sell it in return for trifles.'[16] Further, he stirs up the zeal of the people of Shaqrāʾ against the *daʿwa*'s opponents by saying, 'I swear by God Almighty that women in their homes disdain you, not to mention the swords of Banū Zayd.'[17]

Indeed, the Sheikh's desire for the success of his mission led him to make hope outweigh despair. Thus he addresses ʿAbd Allāh ibn ʿAbd al-Laṭīf al-Aḥsāʾī: 'How great you will be if in this late period you will distinguish truth from falsehood in religion as did ʿUmar [ibn al-Khaṭṭāb] at the beginning.'[18] However, he apparently had little hope of ʿAbd Allāh's favourable response, as he says in the same letter: 'I have written this to you seeking God's forgiveness and calling upon you to follow God's path. There is no reward for those who call upon God. But I think that you will not accept it [the mission], and see it as a grave abomination.'[19]

One feature noted by a reader of the Sheikh's letters is that he is sometimes harsh. He himself acknowledged this trait in his letter to ʿAbd Allāh ibn ʿĪsā and his son ʿAbd al-Wahhāb.[20] This harshness usually appeared when dealing with a very active opponent or an enemy whom there was little hope of convincing. For example, the Sheikh begins his letter to his arch-enemy Sulaymān ibn Suḥaym as follows: 'What Sulaymān ibn Suḥaym knows is that you pestered him with a scroll containing strange ideas. If this is how you understand things, then you have a most corrupt understanding.'[21] He also tells him, 'You and yours seem to have followers among the dregs of Miʿkāl, butchers and their like, who believe that you are scholars'; and 'You are an ignorant pagan and hateful to God's religion.'[22] The Sheikh sometimes expresses his reactions with scathing sarcasm. He describes ʿAbd Allāh al-Muways as someone who exclaims: 'Know me! Know me! You see that I am coming from Damascus!'[23] Sometimes he does not mention al-Muways's name, but alludes to him as 'that one from Damascus' or 'your Damascene'.[24]

In his personal letters the Sheikh's style is, on the whole, restricted to classical Arabic and its rules of vocalization. But on a few occasions he rejects these constraints and uses expressions or terms that may be classed as colloquial. This is a common trait in his letters to the Najdis in particular. In his letter to Muḥammad ibn ʿAbbād we read: 'Remember that we are ready to explain anything to you if you do not see it clearly.'[25] He wrote to ʿAbd Allāh ibn Suḥaym, 'When God afflicted you with the son of al-Muways . . . [a bride] without a fair face or noble lineage.'[26] His letter to the Qāḍī of ad-Dirʿīyah contains even more such expressions, which constitute most of its contents.[27]

The Letters and the Circumstances Surrounding the **Daʿwa:** *Religious Conditions in Najd at the Beginning of the Sheikh's* **Daʿwa**

Ibn Ghannām, Ibn Bishr and other supporters of Sheikh Muḥammad's *daʿwa* tell of the conditions under which the Najdis lived before his mission began. They present a gloomy picture of those conditions, although Ibn Bishr pointed to the existence of Najdi scholars with noble qualities. Those who, like al-Manqūr, studied the works of those scholars, clearly saw such good qualities in them. Whoever looks closely at Ibn

Bishr's predecessors will note that the urban areas of Najd, at least, used on the whole to perform such religious obligations as public prayer, fasting, *zakāt* (almsgiving) and pilgrimage. Moreover, the poetry of the period, such as that of Jabr ibn Sayyār, Rumayzān ibn Ghashshām and Ḥumaydān al-Shuwayʿir, does not conform with the bleak image of Najdi conditions as depicted by some sources. Nevertheless, what is found in Sheikh Muḥammad's letters helps to clarify many aspects of the religious situation in Najd shortly before the beginning of his *daʿwa*.

It is well known that the issue of belief in the *awliyāʾ* ('saints'; sg. *walī*), or those who are believed to be saints, was one of the major issues over which a sharp controversy broke out between Sheikh Muḥammad and his opponents. His personal letters are full of discussions of this issue from different angles. They include the names of some in whose sainthood some Najdis believed, among them Shamsān, Idrīs and Tāj.[28] The letters also say that those who bore these names would be given votive offerings by people.[29] They also mention the names of some who believed in these saints.[30] We can gather from the Sheikh's letters that such affairs were widespread in certain Najdi areas, but not in others. Al-ʿArīḍ and the southern districts, especially al-Kharj, were affected by them, while al-Qaṣīm, for instance, was not. In his letter to ʿAbd Allāh ibn ʿAlī and Muḥammad ibn Jammāz the Sheikh says, 'The people of al-Qaṣīm have no shrines or lords', but that they were obliged to avoid being hostile to the pagans.[31] The Sheikh's letters also clearly show his attitude towards those who accept people's belief in [the saints] and accept votive offerings for them. He denied [the holy men] and described them as false gods or seducers to error, and sometimes as evil spirits, demons or dogs.[32]

The subject of Sufism (or mysticism) is also related to this issue. The Sheikh's opposition to Sufism, or at least to some of its manifestations, is well known. Perhaps the most interesting indication of this is his taunting of his opponent ʿAbd Allāh al-Muways by saying that one of his teachers was a Sufi nicknamed al-ʿĀrif billāh ('one who knows God').[33] One might expect that a milieu like that of Najd at the time would be devoid of Sufi orders. But the Sheikh's letters to certain Sufi individuals who followed Ibn al-ʿArabī and Ibn al-Fāriḍ, such as the sons of Mūsā ibn Jawʿān and Salāma ibn Māniʿ[34] and other such obscure persons, reveal the apparently strange fact that such people had a relation of some sort with a philosophical school of thought. But if we admit the truth of what is said in the Sheikh's letters, we will see that this phenomenon was confined to Miʿkāl (part of the present city of Riyadh). The Sheikh's letters also point out that Sulaymān ibn Suḥaym used to attend the Mawlid (celebration of the Prophet Muḥammad's birthday) and would read and chant its songs publicly. He also inscribed amulets that contained magical charms.[35] Sulaymān, it may be recalled, was a former resident of Miʿkāl. What the Sheikh says does not specify that the Mawlid was celebrated in Najd; but it is the sole indication, from the Sheikh or anyone else, which suggests that this event took place in the region.

Among matters related to mysticism and saints discussed in the Sheikh's letters are the books *Dalāʾil al-khayrāt*[36] and *Rawḍ al-rayāḥīn*.[37] One understands from this discussion that they were among the books read in Najd at that time. Sulaymān ibn Suḥaym, in his letter to scholars outside Najd, claimed that the Sheikh had ordered them to be burned.[38] The Sheikh, in his letter to al-Suwaydī, denied that he had burnt the first book, and said that the cause of rumours about this matter was that he had told those who accepted his advice, and who thought that reading it was more useful than reading the Qurʾan, that nothing should be more revered in their hearts than the Book of God.[39] Ibn Ghannām also denied that the Sheikh burnt the *Rawḍ al-rayāḥīn*.[40] It may seem strange that the Sheikh gave this explanation for the rumours concerning the *Dalāʾil al-khayrāt;* but to burn a book is one thing, to suggest that nothing should be more revered in the hearts of people than the Qurʾan is another. It is worth nothing that al-Ṣanʿānī praised the Sheikh in the following verse:

> He deliberately burnt a copy of the *Dalāʾil;*
> he did right, and merits innumerable praises.

Neither Ibn Ghannām nor Ibn Bishr, who quote this verse in their histories, make any comment about it.[41] It is also worth noting that ʿAbd Allāh ibn Muḥammad ibn ʿAbd al-Wahhāb, talking about the *daʿwa*, said 'We never order the destruction of any books except those which mislead people into polytheism, like *Rawḍ al-rayāḥīn*.'[42]

Bedouin Conditions

Sheikh Muḥammad's letters point to an extremely important topic, albeit one about which there was not much controversy between the *daʿwa*'s supporters and its opponents. The Sheikh states that many of the Bedouins did not practice religious observances and, indeed, that many did not even believe in one major article of faith: resurrection after death. In his letter to Muḥammad ibn ʿĪd he says, 'The practices of the Bedouins, or of most of them, are well known both to the elite and to ordinary people ... Among them there are more than a hundred violations of Islam.'[43] He writes to Sulaymān ibn Suḥaym, 'It is well known that the people of our land and of the Hijaz who deny resurrection are more numerous than those who believe in it, that those who are knowledgeable about religion are fewer than those who are not, that those who neglect ritual prayers are greater in number than those who practice them regularly, and that those who do not pay the *zakāt* (alms-tax) are more numerous than those who do.'[44]

Given that at that time the Bedouins constituted a large proportion of the inhabitants of Najd, one can see how serious this question was. But such a state of affairs was to be expected, since ignorance of religion was prevalent among them (as indicated by the passage just quoted) and because there was no authority concerned with this issue. This may be the fundamental reason why the Sheikh refrained from passing judgement on those characterized by the qualities mentioned above at the beginning of his *daʿwa*, as Ibn Ghannām stated.[45] But it is certain that this situation could not last, as they had fulfilled the conditions enumerated by the Sheikh in his letter to Aḥmad ibn Ibrāhīm: 'You know that the Bedouins have denied the entire Book [the Qurʾan], and have renounced religion altogether. They have ridiculed the town-dwellers who believe in resurrection. They preferred the rule of false gods over God's Sharīʿa, and have mocked it, despite their admission that Muḥammad is God's Messenger and that God's Book is found among town-dwellers. Yet still they belied, disbelieved, and ridiculed out of sheer obstinacy.'[46]

The Beginning of the Daʿwa *in Najd*

It is well known that the Sheikh's *daʿwa* began in Najd before his father's death in 1153/1740. Ibn Bishr states that he had founded the *daʿwa* several years before his father's death.[47] This means that it began around 1150/1737, if not earlier. But he does not specify the year of its beginning, and there is nothing in the Sheikh's letters that can elucidate this matter, although there are some things that shed some light. He states in his letter to ʿAbd Allāh ibn ʿAbd al-Laṭīf al-Aḥsāʾī (according to Ibn Ghannām), 'We met about twenty years ago.'[48] But in the fifth volume of his collected works, containing his letters, this statement occurs in some copies (of the letter) as follows: 'I met you nearly ten years ago.' It seems clear that this statement is more correct than that in Ibn Ghannām's history.[49] If its authenticity is accepted, the Sheikh was in al-Aḥsāaʾ ten years before he wrote this letter. So when was this letter written?

There is no specific text in Ibn Ghannām's history about the time or place of its writing; but a careful reader of the Sheikh's letters can conclude certain things which may be helpful on this point. In his letter to ʿAbd Allāh [ibn ʿAbd al-Laṭīf] the Sheikh states that he felt pained at the latter's correspondence against him with the people of al-Aḥsāʾ.[50] In two letters sent from al-ʿUyayna to ʿAbd Allāh ibn ʿĪsā and his son ʿAbd al-Wahhāb, he states that they had mocked Ibn Fayrūz's reply, and that the trouble caused by ʿAbd al-Wahhāb was harder for him to bear than that caused by the people of al-Aḥsāʾ.[51] If ʿAbd Allāh ibn ʿAbd al-Laṭīf had corresponded with the people of al-Aḥsāʾ, and if this correspondence took place when the Sheikh was in al-ʿUyayna, it would be likely that the Sheikh's letter to him was written from that town. But although it is known when the Sheikh travelled from al-ʿUyayna to ad-Dirʿīyah, it is not certain when he came from (his home town of) Ḥuraymila to al-ʿUyayna.[52] His arrival there might have been some months after his father's death, or even one or two years later. Thus it is possible that his stay in al-ʿUyayna was between 1153/1740 and 1157/1744–5, that the letter in question was written during this period, and that his meeting with ʿAbd Allāh ibn ʿAbd al-Laṭīf took place between 1143/1731 and 1147/1735.

But since the Sheikh probably did not stay long in al-Aḥsāʾ, his return to Najd from his travels abroad would also have been in the same period. It is known as a historical fact that he began his *daʿwa* in Huraymila immediately after his arrival there.

There is no doubt that the opposition of some Najdi scholars to the Sheikh began when he embarked upon his *daʿwa*. The sources note that opposition to him took place before his father's death; and his letters support this. One of his letters from al-ʿUyayna mentions that ʿAbd al-Wahhāb ibn ʿĪsā had been working against the *daʿwa* for more than five years.[53] This means that opposition to him had begun at least by around 1152/1739.

The Daʿwa's *Methodology*

The Sheikh's letters show that one method of propagating his *daʿwa* was through correspondence with those whom he believed had influence on people, both from the area's princes and its scholars, as well as through his responses to questions from those who wrote to him enquiring about the truth of the *daʿwa* or about some aspect of it.[54] Another means was through the activities of his supporters and propagandists in the various towns of Najd in expounding the *daʿwa* or disputing with its opponents. For example, Ibn ʿĪdān was one of its proponents in al-Washm;[55] Mūsā ibn Salīm (from the region of al-ʿAriḍ) would read a letter by the Sheikh, with comments on it by one of his opponents, explaining its correctness, while Ibn Ṣaliḥ debated with Sulaymān ibn Suḥaym in a council of leaders from Riyadh.[56]

The Sheikh's letters support Ibn Ghannām's assertion that, at the beginning, he would preach to his opponents in a patient style. He says in his letter to Aḥmad ibn Yaḥya, 'This Ibn Ismāʿīl, al-Muways and Ibn ʿUbayd: we have received their letters, in which they reject the faith of Islam. We wrote to them, quoted exemplary passages, and addressed them in the best manner; and yet they become more and more refractory.'[57] He also says about ʿAbd Allāh al-Muways: 'I summoned him at first in a gentle manner, and tolerated monstrous things from him.'[58] It seems, however, that this mild approach was adopted at a very early stage of the *daʿwa*'s activities. This was necessary for several reasons, one being the expectation that opposition at the beginning would not be very violent, because the *daʿwa* had not yet been successful enough to make its opponents sense its dangers and push them towards strong opposition. Thus it would be expected that its founder himself would not take a strong position against them. Another reason was that the Sheikh hoped to win over some opponents to his side, and a mild method is clearly one factor in attracting others. Also, the Sheikh understood the strangeness of some of the things he advocated to members of his community, so it was necessary to follow a mild method, at least temporarily, lest the reaction to the *daʿwa* be unfavourable. In one of his letters the Sheikh says, 'Were it not for the fact that until now people have not known the religion of the Prophet, and that they disapprove that with which they are not familiar, things would be different. By Allāh, other than Whom there is no god, if people knew things as they really are, I would have issued a *fatwā* legalizing spilling the blood of Ibn Suḥaym and his like and the obligation to kill them.'[59] It is of course well known that when they found the circumstances favourable, the *daʿwa*'s leaders adopted the most significant method of its propagation: jihād, 'holy war'.

The Najdi Opposition

It is clear from the Sheikh's letters that his *daʿwa* was fiercely opposed by some Najdi religious scholars. More than twenty scholars, or 'seekers of knowledge', stood against his mission at any one time. Foremost among these were ʿAbd Allāh al-Muways, from Ḥurma, and Sulaymān ibn Suḥaym, from Riyadh. It can be gathered from the letters that those Najdis who opposed the Sheikh took different stands. Some opposed him from the beginning and continued to do so.[60] Others at first admitted that some or all of what he preached was right, but changed their position over time.[61] Still others vacillated between support and opposition.[62] The letters show clearly that the opposing Najdis gave different names to the *daʿwa:* they called it 'the religion of the people of al-ʿArīḍ',[63] termed it 'a fifth *madh-hab*ʾ,[64] or claimed it was a *bidʿa* (heretical innovation) which came first from Khurasan.[65] It seems that there were several reasons why those Najdis opposed the *daʿwa*, some of which were present among all opponents, while others existed at the individual level. It is unfair to overlook the element of personal conviction among those opponents who believed that some of the Sheikh's preaching was not correct. Nor should one ignore the changing attitudes of some opposition leaders subsequent to the transformation of the *daʿwa* from one stage to another, its advocacy of elements that it had not previously proclaimed, or its adoption of practices that it had not previously followed. Perhaps the most striking evidence of this is the Sheikh's own statement in one of his letters: 'Those who claim to be scholars, in all places, affirmed me with respect to *tawḥid* and the denial of *shirk* (idolatry, paganism), but rejected my call for considering (dissidents) as unbelievers and fighting them.'[66] In another letter he says, 'They say that if the people of al-ʿArīḍ ceased charging others with unbelief and fighting them, they would be following the religion of God and His Prophet.'[67]

It is well known that the war waged by the *daʿwa*'s supporters against their opponents did not take place from the start. In one of his letters the Sheikh gives two fundamental reasons why some scholars changed their position from supporting the movement to opposing it. The first reason was that the common people would say, 'If what the Sheikh preaches is right, why did you not call us to it earlier?' That they did not ask this question does not, however, justify the scholars' silence. In other words, these opposition leaders were afraid of losing their social prestige because the common people might question their learning and their sincerity. Thus if they did not know the correct judgement before the Sheikh, their knowledge would be (deemed as) little, and if they knew it and concealed it, their sincerity would be (considered) non-existent. In either case their prestige would have been weakened.

The second reason for changing their stand was, according to the Sheikh, his rejection of their taking illicit money and bribes.[68] One can accept this second reason, because this subject was, in a way, one of the questions mentioned by Ibn Suḥaym in his letter to scholars outside Najd urging them to oppose the *daʿwa*.[69] But the first reason cannot be accepted without reservation. For if Sulaymān ibn Suḥaym, and others like him, felt that their admission of the *daʿwa*'s truth might damage their social status, they would not have admitted its truth at the beginning. Perhaps the real reason for changing their stand was the *daʿwa*'s transformation from one stage to a rather different one. The letters also indicate that the change in position of some Najdi opponents resulted from the influence of others, as in that of al-Muways on ʿAbd Allāh ibn Suḥaym.[70] They further show that the abstention of some scholars from joining the *daʿwa* was the result of their inability to convince the ruling princes of its worth.[71]

The Sheikh's letters also reveal that the activities of the Najdi opposition were quite varied. Foremost among them was writing against the *daʿwa*. An examination of these letters shows just how copious this literature was, although, as might be expected, most of it is not lengthy in terms of content. Sulaymān ibn Suḥaym, ʿAbd Allāh al-Muways and Sulaymān ibn ʿAbd al-Wahhāb rank first among these writers. It is worth noting that most of what was written by Najdi opponents (except for the last three mentioned) has been lost. If their original writings were to be found, the researcher's reliance upon them would doubtless be greater. However, the Sheikh's letters shed light on some of these writings.

His letters say that Sulaymān ibn Suḥaym wrote four important letters: (1) a letter to scholars outside Najd, included by Ibn Ghannām in his history,[72] in which he cites fifteen issues on which he considered the Sheikh's opinions defective; (2) a letter to ʿAbd Allāh ibn Suḥaym, which is said (by the Sheikh, in his letter to the same person) to have included twenty-four questions[73] (this letter includes some, but not all, of that which is found in the letter to scholars outside Najd, as is clearly seen from the Sheikh's reply, and also questions not found in the previous letter[74]); (3) a letter referred to in his letter to Sulaymān, saying, 'You have disturbed us with a sheet of paper which included strange things'[75] (what the Sheikh discussed in this letter makes it clear that Sulaymān's letter, or 'sheet of paper', is neither of the two previous letters[76]); (4) papers which the Sheikh said he had perused, and whose content differs from that of the above-mentioned letters.[77]

As for al-Muways, in his letter to ʿAbd Allāh ibn Suḥaym the Sheikh pointed out that he had written a book which he sent to the people of al-Washm, comprising three topics: (1) the study of (God's) names and attributes, or beliefs (*ʿaqāʾid*); (2) *tawḥīd* and *shirk* (monotheism and idolatry); and (3) emulating the example of learned scholars. The Sheikh discussed the first two topics in his letter to ʿAbd Allāh, but left aside discussion of the third because, as he says, he had sent his opinion to al-Muways himself.[78]

The second type of Najdi opposition was debating with the *daʿwa*'s supporters in various towns: for example, that of Ibn Ismāʿīl with the Sheikh's supporters in Tharmada, and that of Sulaymān ibn Suḥaym with Ibn Ṣāliḥ at the council of scholars in Riyadh.[79] The third type comprised contacts with scholars and influential people outside Najd, instigating them against the Sheikh and his *daʿwa*. Another example is the letter sent by Sulaymān ibn Suḥaym to scholars outside Najd, and his complaint to the people of al-Ḥaramayn (Makkah and Madinah).[80] Al-Muways and his close supporters went to the people of the shrines of al-Kuwwaz and Rajab, telling them of the Sheikh's condemnation of their practices and trying to arouse them against him, just as al-Muways, Ibn Rabīʿa and Ibn Ismāʿīl went to the people of the shrine of Abū Ṭālib and incited them against the Sheikh's followers.[81] This tendency to seek help from outside shows clearly the Najdi opponents' realization of their weakness before the Sheikh's *daʿwa* and their inability to stop it. The fourth type of local opposition was the circulation of books by non-Najdi scholars against the *daʿwa;* al-Muways and Ibn 'Ubayd promoted one such book by al-Qabbānī al-Baṣrī, and al-Muways and Ibn Ismāʿīl another by Ibn Afāliq.[82]

Al-Aḥsāʾ Scholars and the **Daʿwa**[83]

The Sheikh's letters shed light on the activities of some scholars from al-Aḥsāʾ with regard to his *daʿwa*. These activities included sending letters against him to the Najdi opposition leaders expressing their support, or trying to persuade those who sided with the Sheikh to abandon him. These letters also clarify some points made by those scholars. Among these was the issue of *ijtihād*, which, they stress, the Sheikh was not qualified to practise.[84] The Sheikh also made clear in his letters his position on this subject.[85] It appears that foremost of the Aḥsāʾī scholars who wrote against the Sheikh was the judge ʿAbd Allāh ibn ʿAbd al-Laṭīf; it is also clear that the Sheikh was anxious to win over that scholar to his side, or at least to oblige him to observe neutrality between himself and his opponents.[86] Another scholar was Muḥammad ibn Afāliq, of whom the Sheikh states that in his book he claimed that *tawḥīd* was the creed of Ibn Taymiyya, and that when he delivered his legal opinion on this subject the religious scholars accused him of unbelief and launched arguments against him.[87]

Other opponents included Ibn Muṫlaq and Ibn Fayrūz. In one of his letters the Sheikh cites two lines of poetry, saying that one occurred in the *Muṣannaf* of Ibn Muṫlaq and the other in the *Muṣannaf* of Ibn Fayrūz.[88] The first three opponents, in the Sheikh's view, were more hostile than Ibn Fayrūz, for he said of them, 'As for Ibn ʿAbd al-Laṫīf, Ibn Afāliq and Ibn Muṫlaq, they have revealed their own filth: meaning that they revile *tawḥīd* and permit shedding the blood of those who believe in it or those who reject idolatry.' But Ibn Fayrūz was, according to the Sheikh, the closest to Islam.[89] It seems that the Sheikh realized the danger of those Aḥsāʾī scholars, because he warned Muḥammad ibn Sulṫān against them after hearing that the latter would present his teachings before them.[90] Another matter referred to in the Sheikh's letters was the graves or shrines in which some people of al-Aḥsāʾ believed.[91] And there were other issues that ran counter to the roots of Islam according to his interpretation.[92] Under such circumstances it was not surprising that the Sheikh considered this area to be the land of idolators.[93]

The Sharīfs and the Daʿwa

It has been noted that the Sheikh realized the importance and influence of the Makkahan scholars, and was well aware of the prestigious status of that city's governor. The complimentary manner in which he dealt with them all is manifest in his style. His letters reveal that the Najdi opposition also realized the status and importance (of the Makkahans), and that their leaders made great efforts to win over the Makkahan dignitaries to their side. It is clear from the letters that their efforts bore fruit; for the Makkahan scholars sent letters to Najd expressing their support for those who opposed the *daʿwa*.[94] The Makkahan authorities took a hostile position towards the *daʿwa*'s supporters, imprisoned some of them when they came to perform the pilgrimage, and for a long time prevented its followers from performing that obligation.[95]

The Sheikh, on his part, recognized the right of the Āl al-Bayt (the Prophet Muḥammad's family), to whom the Sharīfs of Makkah belonged, saying, 'God honoured them above all others on earth.'[96] Indeed, he blamed some of his supporters who criticized one Sharīf for allowing his hand to be kissed and for wearing a green turban, pointing out that wearing green had begun much earlier, in order to distinguish them should they do wrong, or in case someone who did not know them failed to show them due respect. However, this position did not prevent him from attacking those practices among them which were related to the faith, but which also indicated moral decline. In his letter to Ibn al-Bukaylī he says, 'Some women who are well known for prostitution come in groups on the day of the Great Pilgrimage, and it is publicly known what the Sharīfs want from them.'[97] The generalization in this passage was clearly motivated by a deep feeling of having been wronged by the person who had written to him. Yet the existence of moral decline among some, at least, is a matter that attracts attention.

The content of this chapter represents only a part of what is included in the Sheikh's personal letters. It does not address some of the well-known fundamental principles of the *da'wa*, nor the discussions about them found in the letters. Yet there is no doubt that those interested in such matters will find much of interest in the letters.

Notes:

1. Ḥusayn ibn Ghannām, *Rawḍat al-afkār wa-al-afhām li-murtād ḥāl al-imām wata'dād ghazawāt dhawī al-Islām* (Cairo, 1368/1948–9), I, pp. 81, 114; henceforth referred to as *Rawḍa*.
2. Muḥammad ibn 'Abd al-Wahhāb, *Mu'allafāt*. V. *al-Rasā'il al-shakhṣiyya* (Riyadh, 1981), p. 175; henceforth referred to as *Shakhṣiyya*.
3. See *ibid*., pp. 100–1; compare 'Abd al-Raḥmān ibn Muḥammad ibn Qāsim, *al-Durar al-saniyya fī al-ajwiba al-Najdiyya* (Riyadh, 2nd edn, 1385/1964), I, p. 127.
4. See, for example, Aḥmad ibn Abi al-Ḍīyāf, *Itḥāf ahl al-zamān bi-akhbār muluk Tunis wa-'ahd al-amān* (Tunis, 2nd edn, 1976), II, pp. 82–5.
5. *Shakhṣiyya*, p. 172.

6. *Ibid.*
7. *Rawḍa*, I, p. 122. (It is common for writers of letters to refer to themselves in the third person.)
8. *Shakhṣiyya*, p. 173.
9. *Ibid.*
10. ʿUthmān ibn Bishr, *ʿUnwān al-majd fī tārīkh Najd* (Riyadh, 2nd edn, 1391/1971), I, pp. 4–55.
11. *Rawḍa*, II, p. 144. (It is not possible to render the rhyming prose effectively. -Ed.)
12. *Ibid.*, II, p. 80. It may be noted that the word *haḍrat* ('excellency'), in the sense it has here, is used in the Sheikh's writings in only two places: in this letter, and in his letter to al-Suwaydī in Iraq. His use of it in only these places stemmed from his belief that this style was manifest in the Hijaz and Iraq.
13. *Rawḍa*, I, p. 151.
14. *Ibid.*, I, p. 146.
15. *Ibid.*, I, p. 155. (ʿAmr ibn Luḥayy was 'the legendary founder of polytheism in Arabia' and ancestor of the important Makkahan tribe of Khuzāʿa; see *EI2*, s.v.)
16. *Ibid.*, I, p. 107.
17. *Shakhṣiyya*, p. 292. (The Banū Zayd are a tribe in central Najd.)
18. *Rawḍa*, I, p. 54. (ʿUmar ibn al-Khaṭṭāb was a companion of the Prophet and the second caliph.)
19. *Ibid.*, I, pp. 3–54.
20. *Ibid.*, I, p. 157.
21. *Ibid.*
22. *Ibid.*, I, pp. 138 and 142.
23. *Ibid.*, I, p. 100.
24. *Ibid.*, I, pp. 19–121.
25. *Ibid.*, I, p. 104. (Translation cannot replicate this register.)
26. *Ibid.*, I, pp. 102–16.
27. *Ibid.*, I, pp. 6–157.
28. See *ibid.*, I, pp. 130, 155, 178, 180, 188, 216, 226. It is noteworthy that the Sheikh sometimes says Awlād (sons of) Shamsān and Awlād Idrīs (I, p. 216), and at others Shamsān and his sons (I, p. 22) or Muḥammad ibn Shamsān (I, p. 22).
29. *Ibid.*, I, p. 21.
30. For example, Ṭālib al-Ḥumḍ; see *ibid.*, I, pp. 10, 154, 156.
31. *Shakhṣiyya*, p. 232.

32. See *Rawḍa*, I, pp. 178, 217.
33. *Ibid*., I, pp. 120.
34. *Ibid*., I, p. 147.
35. *Ibid*., I, p. 140.
36. *Dalā'il al-khayrāt wa-shawāriq al-anwār fī dhikr al-ṣalat ʿalā al-nabiyy al-mukhtār*, a popular devotional work by Muḥammad ibn Sulaymān al-Juzūlī (d. 854/1465).
37. *Rawḍ al-rayāḥīn fī ḥikāyāt al-ṣāliḥīn*, by ʿAbd Allāh ibn Asʿad al-Yāfiʿī al-Yamanī (d. 768/1357).
38. *Rawḍa*, I, p. 112.
39. *Ibid*., p. 153.
40. *Ibid*., I, p. 129.
41. *Ibid*., I, p. 47; Ibn Bishr, *ʿUnwān*, I, p. 69.
42. Ibn Qāsim, *Durar*, I, p. 127.
43. *Rawḍa*, I, p. 108.
44. *Ibid*., I, p. 33.
45. *Ibid*., I, p. 144.
46. *Ibid*., I, pp. 3–164.
47. Ibn Bishr, *ʿUnwān*, I, p. 21.
48. *Rawḍa*, I, p. 50.
49. *Shakhṣiyya*, p. 250.
50. *Rawḍa*, I, p. 150.
51. *Ibid*., I, pp. 7–158.
52. *Ibid*., I, p. 157.
53. This is clear in most of his letters. This method seems to have achieved a good deal of success, as in the case with the Qāḍī of ad-Dirʿīyah, who said that it was one of the main reasons why people accepted religion. See *ibid*., I, p. 156.
54. *Ibid*., I, p. 97.
55. *Ibid*., p. 140.
56. *Ibid*., I, p. 141.
57. *Ibid*., I, p. 172.
58. *Ibid*., I, p. 103.
59. *Ibid*., I, pp. 6–157.
60. One of these was al-Muways.
61. For example, Ibn Suḥaym.
62. For example, ʿAbd Allāh ibn ʿĪsā.
63. *Rawḍa*, I, p. 167.
64. *Ibid*., p. 139.
65. *Ibid*., I, pp. 102, 116.

66. *Ibid.*, I, pp. 7–108.
67. *Ibid.*, I, p. 150.
68. *Ibid.*, I, p. 114.
69. *Ibid.*, I, p. 113.
70. *Ibid.*, I, p. 116.
71. *Ibid.*, I, pp. 119, 162.
72. *Ibid.*, I, pp. 11–113.
73. *Ibid.*, I, pp. 13–122. Ibn Ghannām cited the Sheikh's letter as replying to Sulaymān's letter addressed to the scholars outside Najd.
74. Compare the two letters in *ibid.*, I, pp. 11–113 and II, pp. 13–122.
75. *Ibid.*, I, p. 138.
76. Cf. *Ibid.*, I, p. 11–113, pp. 138–41, and II, pp. 13–122.
77. *Ibid.*, I, pp. 18–220.
78. *Ibid.*, I, pp. 97–103.
79. *Ibid.*, I, pp. 106–41.
80. *Ibid.*, I, p. 139.
81. *Ibid.*, I, pp. 109, 160.
82. *Ibid.*, I, p. 106.
83. Al-Aḥsāʾ (also known as al-Ḥasā or Laḥsāʾ) is a group of oases in eastern Arabia known for its religious scholars. See *EI2*, s.v.
84. *Rawḍa*, I, p. 52.
85. *Ibid.*, I, p. 51.
86. See the praises which the Sheikh showers on Qāḍīʿ Abd Allāh and his attempts to ingratiate himself with him in his letter to him (*ibid.*, I, pp. 50–60).
87. *Ibid.*, I, p. 106. The written works of Ibn Afāliq include a treatise entitled *Taḥakkum al-muqallidīn bi-man iddaʿā tajdīd al-dīn;* this may be meant here. He sent another treatise to ʿUthmān ibn Muʿammar which includes many statements cited from Ibn Taymiyya.
88. *Rawḍa*, I, p. 161. (The works cited are collections of *ḥadīths*.)
89. *Ibid.*
90. See *Shakhṣiyya*, I, pp. 4–145.
91. *Rawḍa*, I, p. 165.
92. *Ibid.*, I, p. 59.
93. *Ibid.*, I, p. 166.
94. *Ibid.*
95. *Ibid.*, I, pp. 109, 160.
96. *Ibid.*, I, p. 81.
97. See *Shakhṣiyya*, p. 97.

Chapter 7

THE EFFECT OF MUḤAMMAD IBN ʿABD AL-WAHHĀB'S SALAFIYYA *DAʿWA* ON RELIGIOUS AND SOCIAL REFORM IN EGYPT

ʿAbd al-Raḥīm Abdulrahman ʿAbd al-Raḥīm

Foreword

Muḥammad ibn ʿAbd al-Wahhāb was active in the middle of the twelfth/eighteenth century, calling on people to dedicate themselves to the worship of Allāh alone and to return Islam to its earliest origins. His *daʿwa* (call) spread, and became widely publicized.[1] It was at the forefront of events that put an end to the stagnation that had prevailed over the Arab world in general, and the heart of the Arabian peninsula in particular, despite the difficult conditions under which it worked. But thanks to the efforts of the Sheikh and his disciples, and to the political support they received from Āl Saʿūd,[2] the *daʿwa* became a model to be followed by subsequent religious and social reform movements all over the Muslim world. Thus it could be said to be the parent movement of those later movements, or like a great river from which smaller tributaries branched off.

There is no disputing the fact that this *daʿwa* played a significant role in the civilizational transformation of the Arab region beginning in the last quarter of the twelfth/eighteenth century.[3] For through the call to *tawḥīd* (the profession of God's Unity), the crushing of the myths and superstitions that had become attached to Islamic doctrines, the attempts to liberate thought and open the door of *ijtihād* (independent judgement), the encouragement of study, and the search for and refinement of the fundamental rules found in the original religous sources, the Muslim region witnessed an intellectual ferment that had long been absent.[4] In conjunction with this was a political development which kept abreast of this religious call, and an attempt to achieve Arab unity.

It is therefore necessary to look at the principles on which the *daʿwa* was based, if we are to see the extent of its influence on later Salafiyya ('forebears') reform movements, and the religious and social reform movement in Egypt in particular. This can be done through a comparative study of the principles of the two movements. Here we should note that the principles and thought of the Salafiyya movement enjoyed the support and admiration of Egyptian scholars from the beginning of the nineteenth century. Thus we find the Egyptian historian ʿAbd al-Raḥmān al-Jabartī (d. 1241/1825), who was contemporary with the spread of the Salafiyya movement, admiring and supporting it, as did some of al-Azhar's scholars. But opposition to the Salafiyya's principles in Egypt was stronger than the sympathy and admiration shown by Egyptian thinkers, mainly because the provincial ruler of Egypt led this opposition, having been charged by the Ottoman Empire to fight the *daʿwa* and its supporters.[5]

When this religious and social movement began in Egypt in the last quarter of the thirteenth/nineteenth century, led by Sheikh Muḥammad ʿAbduh and his pupils, it was based on the same principles advocated by Ibn ʿAbd al-Wahhāb. Muḥammad ʿAbduh grew up in Egypt at a time when the teachings of Ibn ʿAbd al-Wahhāb filled the air; and his reasoning and study led him to the two bases on which the former had built his teachings: (1) fighting the heretical innovations and corruption which had infiltrated Muslim belief through the association of saints, graves and shrines with God; (2) opening the door of *ijtihād*, which had been closed by weak-minded traditionalists. ʿAbduh devoted himself completely to serving these two objectives.[6]

This is the reason behind our search for aspects of the influence of the principles of the Salafiyya movement, and for the scope of the two principles on which Salafiyya reform movements in the Muslim world were based. It is clear that Muslim reformers perceived that the secret of the weakness that had befallen the Muslim world, and the position of Muslim peoples as easy prey for colonialist powers, was fundamentally traceable to the Muslims' remoteness from the true teachings of their religion. Hence their perception that progress and development would not come to the Muslim *umma* (community) unless it returned, and adhered to, the principles of Islam in their essential form, as defined by Qurʾanic texts, Prophetic *ḥadīth*, and the sayings of the *salaf* (forebears), and the adoption of these principles as a starting point for a renaissance (*nahḍa*).

1. *The Call for Tawḥīd*

The call for *tawḥīd* (the greatest distinguishing feature of Islam), was the first principle upon which the Salafiyya movement was founded, and which influenced reformist movements in Egypt and throughout the Muslim world. According to this doctrine, God alone is 'the creator and controller of this world. He is the giver of the laws by which the world moves, and the legislator for this world. No one ordains laws in this world save Him; no one deserves worship and glorification save Him.'[7] In his call for *tawḥīd*, Ibn ʿAbd al-Wahhāb relied firstly on Qurʾanic texts, Prophetic *ḥadīth*, and the works of the forebears (*salaf*), which he extracted from their sources and compiled by topic. His book *al-Tawḥīd alladhī huwa haqqu Allāh ʿalā al-ʿabīd* ('Profession of God's Unity, Which Is Obligatory on His Servants'),[8] is filled with such proofs, so as to leave no opponent with a valid argument. The book further states that God says, 'Say: He is God the One and the Only; God the Eternal, the Absolute; He begetteth not, nor is He begotten; and there is none like unto Him',[9] and, 'Thy Lord hath decreed that ye worship none but Him, and that ye be kind to parents';[10] and, 'Say: O People of the Book!! Come to common terms as between us and you: that we worship none but God; that we associate no partners with Him; that we erect not from among ourselves lords and patrons other than God. If then they turn back, say ye, Bear witness that we are Muslims [bowing to God's Will]'.[11] The Prophet Muḥammad said, 'If you ask for anything, ask God';[12] and 'Whoever says there is no god but Allāh, and rejects anything that does not come from God, has secured his property and life, and his final account is with God, the Mighty and Exalted.'[13]

Ibn ʿAbd al-Wahhāb called his contemporaries and those living in his milieu to a pure and unadulterated *tawḥīd*, having seen the elements of *shirk* (polytheism, paganism) which his contemporaries had attached to Islamic beliefs. After him came Muḥammad ʿAbduh; and after Abduh became aware of the Sheikh's views, he called on his own contemporaries, urging them, if they wished to progress and to free themselves from sin, to return to the early principles of Islam. He expressed his dissatisfaction with the narrow milieu in which he had grown up, and the way towards reform, saying,

> I found that I grew up in the same way as did the majority of the Egyptian middle class, and was involved in the same things. But after a while I came to detest continuing in this familiar way, and hastened to seek out things which they did not know. I discovered what they had not found, advocated the best of what I found, called on (others) to adopt it, and raised my voice clamoring for two great things: Liberation of thought from the shackles of tradition and understanding religion as it was understood by the forebears of the *umma* before the outbreak of disagreement, and returning, in the acquisition of knowledge, to its earliest sources; and considering (thought) to be among the methods of human reason, established by God to control its excesses, reduce its confusion, and regulate it so as to complete God's wisdom in maintaining the order of the human world.[14]

If Ibn ʿAbd al-Wahhāb, in his call for *tawḥīd*, exposed the Qurʾanic proofs and Prophetic *ḥadīth* which point to it, Muḥammad ʿAbduh was also influenced by this trend, and began to call on his pupils in particular, and people in general, to learn the meaning and foundations of *tawḥīd*, relying on much the same evidence. But he also presented his own philosophy in this summons, saying,

> The religion of Islam came to profess the Unity of God Almighty in Himself and His actions, and to negate His resemblance to His creatures. The proofs testify that the universe has only one Creator, Who is characterized by the sublime attributes manifested by the effects of His making, such as knowledge, power, will, and so on; and that nothing He has created resembles

> Him, and there is no relation between Him and them except that He is their Creator and that they will return to Him. 'Say: He is God, the One and the Only; God the Eternal, Absolute; He begetteth not, nor is He begotten, and there is none like unto Him.'[15]

He then states, 'The Book [the Qurʾan] states that the religion of God at all times is to single Him out for lordship, show submission to Him alone in worship, and obey His commands and prohibitions; this serves the best interests of people and provides a mainstay for their happiness in this world and the hereafter.'[16]

Outstanding evidence of the influence of the Salafi *da'wā* and its thought on ʿAbduh is that he wrote his *Risālat al-Tawḥīd* after Ibn ʿAbd al-Wahhāb had written on this topic. Does this not show that ʿAbduh was influenced by the Salafi *daʿwa*'s thought and content? For if Ibn ʿAbd al-Wahhāb had announced earlier that 'the *tawḥīd* preached by all prophets from first to last is to single out God to receive all worship, with no right thereto to any king or prophet, to say nothing of anyone else',[17] ʿAbduh, who came after him and was influenced by him, declared: 'God's religion has at all times singled Him out for lordship, submission to Him alone in worship, and obedience to His commands and prohibitions'.[18] A century before Muḥammad ʿAbduh, Ibn ʿAbd al-Wahhāb opposed acts that violated *tawḥīd*, such as visiting shrines and using them as places of worship, saying, 'Whoever worships God day and night, and then appeals to a prophet or to a saint at his grave, has taken two gods, and has not testified, "There is no god but Allāh". For that (other) god is the one appealed to, as the polytheists do today at the shrines of al-Zubayr, ʿAbd al-Qādir, and others.'[19] He also rejected seeking intercession through others besides God, belief in the saints' ability to perform miracles and supernatural acts, and seeking their help to bring about either good or harm. He said, 'Whoever exaggerates (the power of) a prophet, a Companion, or a pious man, and attributes to him some sort of divinity, such as saying "O my Lord So and So, help me", or, "I take refuge with you", or the like, is an unbeliever (*kāfir*); he should be asked to repent, and if he does not, he must be killed. For God has sent prophets and revealed scriptures so that He, and no other, may be worshipped.' He also said,

'Know that the polytheists of our time have surpassed the unbelievers in the time of the Prophet in invoking pious saints in times of both ease and hardship and asking them to relieve adversities and to fulfil their needs.'[20] In the context of his rejection of polytheism and his call to appeal to no one but God to bring about good or ward off evil, he says, 'No one is called on to remove harm save Him, or to bring about good save Him. Vows are made only to Him. No oaths may be sworn except by Him. Sacrifices are to be dedicated to none save Him. All religious observances are proper for none save Him, Who has no partner.' He relies in this on Qur'anic texts such as 'Nor call on any, other than God, such will neither profit thee nor hurt thee: if thou dost, behold: thou shalt be certainly one of those who do wrong. If God do touch thee with hurt, there is none can remove it but He: if He do design some benefit for thee, there is none can keep back His favour: He causeth it to reach whomsoever of His servants He pleaseth. And He is the Oft-Forgiving, Most Merciful.'[21] He states that God also says, 'The things that ye worship besides God have no power to give you sustenance: then seek ye sustenance from God, serve Him, and be grateful to Him: to Him will be your return';[22] 'And who is more astray than one who invokes other than God, who will not answer him on the Day of Judgement, and who are unconscious of their prayers, and who, when mankind are resurrected, will be hostile to them and reject their worship.' The Prophet Muḥammad said, 'Appeal for aid is not made to me, but only to God'. Other Qur'anic texts and Prophetic *ḥadīths* were included in the Sheikh's numerous letters to his contemporaries explaining his *daʿwa*.

In some chapters of his book, Ibn ʿAbd al-Wahhāb allocated a dedicated section for each heretical innovation which he felt was in contradiction with *tawḥīd*, establishing proofs and the lessons to be learnt from them. It can safely be said that *Kitāb al-Tawḥīd* is an encyclopedia of this branch of learning, and reveals the Sheikh's thorough knowledge of the sources, as well as his broad-mindedness and careful reasoning. After him came Muḥammad ʿAbduh, who was influenced by the approach followed by the founder of the Salafiyya movement, and who drew attention to the way polytheism had led believers away from the early tenets of Islam, and observed that the unhappy events that had befallen Muslim countries might be the results of digression from 'God's commands'. Other factors may also govern actions that are beyond created beings' powers, including the belief in someone, or something, greater than God, and seeking their help in matters which humans cannot cope with: for example, reliance on elements other than military power in war; seeking cures for diseases other than the medicines towards which God has guided us; and attempts to attain happiness in this world or the next through ways other than those prescribed for us by God.[23]

This is the *shirk*, or polytheism, which idolaters and their like practised. The Islamic Sharīʿa came to wipe out this *shirk*, claiming that anything that exceeds human abilities and material causes to be the work of God alone and to establish two major points, which are the twin pillars of felicity and the support of human actions. First, the believer gains, through his will and ability, the means to happiness; second, God's power is the last resort of all beings. Some of the effects of that power prevent a person from doing what he wishes; but only God can provide the believer with the help to attain anything. The Sharīʿa came to establish this principle and to prohibit believers from seeking help from anyone or anything other than their Creator for success in accomplishing their aims, and to oblige man to raise his hopes by seeking help from God alone after he has exhausted his own efforts towards 'correct' thought and good performance. Neither reason nor religion, it is claimed, allows anyone to follow any other path. The forebears of the *umma* were guided by this and performed deeds which astonished other nations. ʿAbduh states:

> I repeat that belief in God's Unity requires nothing from the obligated person except his belief that God has disposed in his power to him, and that he acquires (his acts) through his belief, and through other acts with which God has charged him, and with the belief that God's power is above his own and that it alone has supreme authority in fulfilling the believer's wishes by removing obstacles or by preparing other ways and means. This is neither known to man nor under his control.[24]

Thus we see that both reformers believed the conditions of the Muslim *umma* could not be put right except through that which was right for it at its beginning, that is, through sound belief, free from polytheism, and by abstaining from a return to Jāhiliyya (pre-Islamic) customs, attempts to extinguish the roots of *tawḥīd*, 'dependence on others besides God, endeavours to glorify what is useless and to provide that which does no harm; for this harms all Muslims in the greatest way. Therefore their society has become backward, ignorance has spread among them, and they have suffered humiliation while others have surpassed them, and their countries have become colonized so that they are ruled by those inferior to them in number and weaker in belief'.[25]

2. *The Call to Open the Door of Ijtihād*

If we move to the second major principle on which the Salafiyya movement was based, and which constituted one of the mainstays of the reform movement in Egypt – opening the door of *ijtihād* – we find that Ibn ʿAbd al-Wahhāb advocated that *ijtihād* which does not contradict the texts of the Qurʾan, the Prophet's *sunna*, or the works of the *salaf*. 'It is the right – nay, the obligation – of every responsible person who possesses the tools for *ijtihād* to practise it, and to deduce judgements according to his understanding of scripture and what he considers correct of the *sunna*, as his reasoning directs.'[26] The Sheikh and his followers did not make adherence to the school of Aḥmad ibn Ḥanbal – which they themselves followed – obligatory in all cases; on some subsidiary questions supported by the Qurʾan, *sunna*, and the opinions of the other three imāms, they adopted the latter's views and abandoned that of Ibn Ḥanbal. 'This was the case concerning the question of the inheritance of grandfather and of brothers, and which party has precedence over the other. They dispute the opinion of Ibn Ḥanbal and follow that of the other three imāms, preferring the grandfather, because this is what they consider correct.'[27]

The Sheikh called for the liberation of thought, declared his conflict with the stubborn traditionalists, stood firm against them, and continued in his *ijtihād*, maintaining that the door of *ijtihād* was open to anyone who desired to pursue it. He clarified Islam's position on many current practices, criticized them, and fought against them, declaring that they ran counter to the doctrines of Islam. One sees that the Sheikh, through his call for opening the door of *ijtihād*, intended to 'renovate and develop the Islamic mind within the framework of the Qurʾan and *sunna*', realizing that closing the door of *ijtihād* leads only to the stagnation of thought and the suppression of sound deduction. This, in turn, leads to the backwardness and ignorance of Muslims, and drives them 'to belief in myths, acceptance of innovations, and becoming susceptible to errors. These myths and innovations soon become tradition and convention, and will quickly develop into a belief system or something like it.' By opening the door of *ijtihād* it seems that the Sheikh intended to 'move by means of it towards the renovation of religious thought'.[28]

Then came Muḥammad ʿAbduh, who lived in a milieu filled with the teachings of Ibn ʿAbd al-Wahhāb. He was deeply involved in political life; he travelled to Europe, studied French culture, and mingled with western academics and philosophers. When exposed to problems similar to those faced by Ibn ʿAbd al-Wahhāb, he philosophized the *daʿwa*, 'basing it on psychological and social foundations, as well as on religious principles'.[29] As a judge, he distinguished himself for seeking truth and valuing justice over the strict observance of legal texts. This was due to his open mind, his study of Islamic Sharīʿa, and to the fact that he himself had not been exclusively trained within the legal mould. He also manifested numerous characteristics of *ijtihād*, as seen in the *fatwā*s (legal opinions) he issued when he occupied the position of *muftī* in Egypt. He also used his *tafsīr* (exegesis) of the Qurʾan as a means of achieving his goal for reform and *ijtihād*. If the *āya* (Qurʾanic verse) was related to morals, he clarified the effect of this moral on the welfare of nations, and the effect of its absence manifest on their decay. If the *āya* was related to a social situation, he demonstrated the effect of this situation on the life of nations, seeking guidance from what takes place in the world – all this with fluent rhetoric, an eloquent tongue, and an attractive tone. In his exegesis he was a pragmatist, explaining reality and showing its causes, as well as a moralist who advocates working in accordance with the principles of Islam. He also tried to reconcile Islam with modern theories of civilization, and adopted methods of interpretation (*taʾwīl*) to find agreement between religion and scientific theories, thereby elevating the position of reason in Qurʾanic interpretation. He opined that the vision of the early exegetes should be presented in a way that allows for a modern, enlightened interpretation of the Qurʾan. But anyone who undertakes such a difficult task must be adequately equipped with 'linguistic weapons and tools, some knowledge of the causes of revelation, information about the Prophet's life, and the contents of human history concerned with the life of the universe and the peoples dealt with in the Holy Qurʾan'.[30] Thus we find him urging the Muslim individual to 'read the Qurʾan continuously, understand its injunctions, prohibitions and the lessons learnt from it, just as it was recited to believers and unbelievers at the time of revelation'.[31] He also advises: 'Beware of overapplying yourself to the diverse commentaries, unless in order to understand a term whose original meaning for the Arabs you cannot grasp, or to comprehend an obscure linkage between one term and another.' He tells the reader: 'Go towards what the Qurʾan dispatches you to, accustom yourself to what the Qurʾan means, and combine that with reading the Prophet's *sīra*, pausing at that which is correct and reasonable, and shielding your eyes from weak and valueless statements.'[32] He says the Muslim must follow this course (of *ijtihād)* using reason, which is the path to knowledge of God. For reason 'is the pivot and mainstay of human powers, while the universe is the page at which reason looks, the book which it reads. Everything which is read therein is guidance towards God and the path which leads to Him.'[33] Thus God has freed human reason to follow the path which nature has prescribed, without restrictions. 'In his letters and actions the Sheikh continually urged the use of reason and *ijtihād* to understand the Qurʾanic text, which is "a book of religion first and foremost".'[34] Hence the necessity of *ijtihād* to understand it (the Qurʾan) and to remove the obstacles posed by the stagnation, superstition and traditionalism which dominated the Muslim mind and caused its backwardness.

Thus we see how Egypt's contact with the principles of the Salafiyya movement was strong and direct, so much so that one feels that the call to those principles was renewed by Muḥammad ʿAbduh and his pupils. While it is said that the Egyptian reform movement had its own particular approach, it did not lack the spirit of the Salafiyya movement, whose influence continued to manifest itself until the defence of the movement and its followers became the dominant current of Egyptian intellectual life among both its supporters and its opponents in the first quarter of the twentieth century. Support of the Salafi movement in Egypt was led by Sayyid Muḥammad Rashīd Riḍā, proprietor of the newspaper *al-Manār*, and his associates. An intellectual debate arose among Egyptian scholars in clubs and in periodicals about the truth and essence of the Salafiyya movement; this, in turn, enriched religious thought, and awakened certain people to the importance of returning to the early teachings of Islam.

Rashīd Riḍā wrote about Ibn ʿAbd al-Wahhāb, reminding people of his role in ridding Islam's teaching of the flaws that had become attached to it, saying: 'Sheikh Muḥammad ibn ʿAbd al-Wahhāb was a renewer of Islam in Najd, by turning its people away from polytheism and the (heretical) innovations which had spread among them and back to *tawḥīd* and *sunna* as conceived by Ibn Taymiyya.'[35] He began writing about such innovations as visiting shrines, making votive offerings to beings other than God, and seeking the help of human beings instead of God. He debated with the al-Azhar scholars and others who opposed the Salafiyya principles, asserting that the roots of the Salafiyya movement did not diverge from the path followed by the people of the *sunna* and *ijmāʿ* (consensus). He tells of one stand that he took with the scholars of al-Azhar:

> I was in a meeting with the Grand Sheikh of al-Azhar Mosque, and I mentioned the Wahhābīs (meaning the followers of the *daʿwa*) and the reason for defaming them. Those present at the meeting included Professor Sheikh ʿAbd al-Majīd al-Labbān, Professor Sheikh Muḥammad Shākir, Professor Sheikh Aḥmad Hārūn, Professor Sheikh al-Ẓawāhirī, and other prominent religious scholars. I explained to them the history of the movement and the views of the historians who had written about it at the time that Prince Suʿūd captured the Hejaz. Then one of the messengers of the Azhar Secretariat went to the bookshop of *al-Manār* and brought back dozens of copies of (the book) *al-Hadiyya al-saniyya* ('The Splendid Gift'), and distributed them among those present. The Grand Sheikh read the passages which we have quoted here, and others which we have not. He

> admitted that this was the *madh-hab* followed by the people of *sunna* and consensus, until he observed that the *ḥadīth*, 'Mounts are harnessed only for three mosques: this mosque of mine (at Madinah), the Haram (the sacred mosque of Makkah), and the Aqṣā Mosque (of Jerusalem)' had been interpreted by [other] religious scholars. I replied, 'They interpreted it literally, following some of their scholars [meaning the Ḥanbalīs]; and some Shāfiʿīs and Mālikīs have prohibited saddling mounts to visit the shrines of pious men such as al-Imām al-Juwaynī, the father of Imām al-Ḥaramayn [al-Juwaynī]. It [the *ḥadīth*] was chosen by Qāḍī ʿIyāḍ in his commentary on the *Ṣaḥīḥ* of Muslim. Al-Nawawī copied it from him. Thus the Wahhābis had forerunners in this respect, and were not the first to espouse it.[36]

Rashīd Riḍā's efforts, and his defence of Salafi ideas and principles, were not confined to the articles he wrote for the newspapers *al-Ahrām* and *al-Manār*. He was also able, through *al-Manār*'s press, to publish letters and books by the prominent scholars of the Salafiyya movement. This made the publishing house of Dār al-Manār the bastion of the movement's principles, led by the newspaper *al-Muqattam*. The battle polarized two parties of scholars, each defending its stand, and bore fruit in the huge quantity of books and articles which are, without doubt, important for the study of the religious reform movements in Egypt and the rest of the Muslim world.

Interestingly, the intellectual debate about the principles of the Salafiyya movement was not confined to the capital (Cairo) alone, but extended to all parts of the country. It reached its peak in Alexandria, where violence was resorted to in some cases. Disagreement between the movement's followers and their opponents was based on three issues: *shafāʿa* (intercession), *tawassul* (supplication), and loud invocation of prayers and peace on the Prophet Muḥammad after the *adhān* (call to prayer). Both parties appealed to the Mashyakha (council of Sheikhs) of Alexandria, after the police had intervened, and the Mashyakha put an end to the affair. Sheikh Muḥammad Tāj al-Dīn, one of the Alexandrian scholars, wrote a treatise entitled *al-Risāla al-Ramliyya fī faṣl al-khilāf bayna ahālī al-Raml wa-duʿāt al-Wahhābiyya* ('The Ramliyya Treatise, on Settling the Dispute between the Inhabitants of al-Raml Quarter and the preachers of Wahhābism'); one of the *daʿwa*'s followers, Sheikh Muḥammad ʿAbd al-Ẓāhir Abū al-Samḥ, responded with *al-Risāla al-Makkiyya fī al-radd ʿalā al-Risāla al-Ramliyya*, in a refutation of this treatise.

Sufficient evidence of the escalation of the conflict between the movement's followers and their opponents is that writing on both sides on topics treating the *daʿwa*'s principles witnessed unprecedented activity. In Cairo, the works of Ibn ʿAbd al-Wahhāb and his adherents, their letters and other Najdi works, were published either individually or in collections. This activity continued as the Jamāʿat Anṣar al-Sunna al-Muḥammadiyya ('Society of Supporters of Muḥammad's Sunna') sponsored their publication and distribution in their belief in the importance of publishing these works to help people in religious matters.[37]

We can leave the preceding presentation with the following facts. First, Egypt was never remote or isolated from the thought of the Salafiyya movement, even from the movement's inception. Regardless of the attitude of the political authorities in Egypt at any given point in time, the movement continued to spread and gain momentum until it acquired a large number of supporters. Second, when the religious reform movement in Egypt began in the nineteenth century, it did so on the basis of Salafiyya principles. Thus Muḥammad ʿAbduh began to call people to believe in the tenets of their religion following traditional foundations, so that these might help them to combat colonialist attempts to control the Muslim peoples and weaken their religion. His own aims and principles derived from those of the Salafiyya movement (*tawḥīd* and *ijtihād*). He also called for resistance to the same innovations that Ibn ʿAbd al-Wahhāb had warned against before him. He wrote his *Risālat al-Tawḥīd* in emulation of Ibn ʿAbd al-Wahhāb's treatise on this topic, although each dealt with the subject in the manner he himself deemed suitable. But a comparative study of these two books shows that their sources are the same. Third, the leaders of the reform movement in Egypt realized that for the movement to continue it had to espouse the principles of the Salafiyya movement as a basis for its own work; hence its open advocacy of the Wahhābī *daʿwa* and the sharp conflict between its proponents and opponents as referred to above. From this we can safely conclude that the Salafi reform movement in Egypt was greatly influenced by the Salafiyya movement as has been outlined in this chapter.

Notes:

1. This *daʿwa* (literally, call or preaching) is called *al-daʿwa al-salafiyya* and *al-daʿwa al-Wahhābiyya*. See Aḥmad Amīn, *Zuʿamāʾ al-iṣlāḥ fī al-ʿasr al-ḥadīth* (Cairo, 1948), p. 10; ʿAbd al-Raḥīm ʿAbd al-Raḥmān, *al-Dawla al-Suʿūdiyya al-ūlā* (Cairo, 2nd edn, 1975), Ch. 2; William Yale, *The Near East, A Modern History* (Ann Arbor, 1958), pp. 62–4.
2. An agreement was concluded between Ibn ʿAbd al-Wahhāb and Prince Muḥammad ibn Saʿūd in 1158/1745; see ʿAbd al-Raḥmān, *Dawla*, pp. 40–3; S. N. Fisher, *The Middle East* (New York, 1959), pp. 280–1.
3. For the role of the Salafiyya movement in civilizational change, see Muḥammad Aḥmad Khalafallāh, 'al-Wahhābiyya', and Muṣṭafā al-Shakʿa, 'al-Wahhābiyya: Manhaj wa-taṭbīq', papers presented to the Symposium on Civilizational Change in the Middle East Region in Modern Times, Middle East Research Center, ʿAyn Shams University, Cairo, 11–14 December 1976.
4. Studies on the modern period of the history of Arab thought have dealt with the role of the Salafiyya movement. See, e.g., ʿAlī Muḥāfiẓa, *al-Ittijāhāt al-fikriyya ʿind al-ʿArab fī ʿaṣr al-nahḍa 1798–1914: al-ittijāhāt al-dīniyya wa-al-siyāsiyya wa-al-ijtimāʿiyya wa-al-ʿilmiyya* (Beirut, 1975), pp. 39–44; Aḥmad ʿAbd al-Raḥīm Muṣṭafā, *Ḥarakāt al-tajdīd al-Islāmī fī al-ʿālam al-ʿArabī al-ḥadīth* (Cairo, 1971); ʿAbd al-Karīm al-Khaṭīb, *Muḥammad ibn ʿAbd al-Wahhāb: al-ʿaql al-ḥurr wa-al-qalb al-salīm* (Cairo, 1960); Albert Hourani, *Arabic Thought in the Liberal Age, 1789–1939* (New York, 1962), pp. 37–8.
5. See especially Muḥammad Maḥmūd al-Surūjī, 'ʿAbd al-Raḥmān al-Jabartī wa-mawqifuhu min al-daʿwa al-Wahhābiyya' (paper delivered at the International Symposium on the Sources of the Arabian Peninsula's History, Riyadh University, April 1977); al-Shakʿa, 'al-Wahhābiyya', p. 15. (See also *EI2*, art. 'Salafiyya'.)
6. Amīn, *Zuʿamāʾ*, p. 23.
7. *Ibid*., p. 11.
8. See Muḥammad ibn ʿAbd al-Wahhāb, *Muʾallafāt*, I: *al-ʿAqīda wa-al-ādāb al-Islāmiyya* (Riyadh, 1981), pp. 7–151. All references are to this edition.

9. Qur᾿an 112.1–4.
10. Qur᾿an 17.23.
11. Qur᾿an 3.64. All these Qur᾿anic texts are cited in Ibn ʿAbd al-Wahhāb's *Kitāb al-Tawḥīd*.
12. In ʿAbd al-Wahhāb, *Mu᾿allafāt*, I, p. 34.
13. *Ibid.*
14. Muḥammad ʿAbduh, *al-A'mā al-kāmila* (ed. Muḥammad 'Imāra; Beirut, 1972–4?), I, p. 181; Muḥammad Rashīd Riḍā, *Tārīkh al-ustādh al-imām al-Sheikh Muḥammad ʿAbduh* (Cairo, 1324–50/1906–51), I, p. 11.
15. Muḥammad ʿAbduh, *Risālat al-Tawḥid* (ed. Maḥmūd Abū Rayya; Cairo, 1966), p. 135.
16. *Ibid.*, p. 144.
17. Ibn ʿAbd al-Wahhāb, *Mu᾿allafāt*, V: *al-Rasā᾿il al-shakhṣiyya*, p. 66: letter sent to Muḥammad ibn Rabīʿa, *mutawwi'* (religious monitor) of the people of Thādiq.
18. ʿAbduh, *Tawḥīd*, p. 144.
19. Ibn ʿAbd al-Wahhāb, *Mu᾿allafāt*, V, p. 166.
20. Muḥāfiẓa, *Ittijāhāt*, p. 42. For further details about these issues see Ibn ʿAbd al-Wahhāb, *Mu᾿allafāt*, V.
21. Qur᾿an 6.14, 10.107–8.
22. Qur᾿an 29.17.
23. ʿAbduh, *Tawḥīd*, p. 65.
24. *Ibid.*, pp. 65–6.
25. Al-Shak'a, 'al-Wahhābiyya', p. 14.
26. *Ibid.*, p. 15.
27. Muḥammad ʿAbd Allah Māḍī, *al-Nahḍāt al-ḥadītha fī Jazīrat al-ʿArab* (Cairo, 1951), I, p. 39.
28. Al-Shakʿa, 'al-Wahhābiyya', p. 11.
29. Amīn, *Zuʿamā᾿*, p. 23.
30. Muḥammad ʿImāra. *Ibid.*, p. 183.
31. *Ibid.*
32. *Ibid.*
33. *Ibid.*
34. *Ibid.*, p. 185.
35. Abd al-Raḥīm, *Muhadhrat fi tarikh Alalam alarabi al hadith wa almasser*, pp. 72–89. M. Rida, *Almanar*, vol. I, pp. 468–9. *Encyclopaedia Britannica*, vol. 23, pp 144–5.
36. See Muḥammad Rashīd Riḍā, *al-Wahhābiyyūn wa-al-Ḥijāz* (Cairo, 1925–6), p. 6.

37. Works published during that period included: (1) Opponents: Muḥammad Ḥasanayn Makhlāf, *Risāla fī ḥukm al-tawassul bi-al anbiyāʾ* (on supplicating prophets); Muṣṭafā ibn Aḥmad al-Shaṭṭī, *al-Nuqūl al-sharʿiyya* (on legal traditions); Muḥammad al-Amīn al-Ḥusaynī, *ʿUqūd al-diyya* (on blood money); *Kashf al-irtiyāb fī atbāʿ Muḥammad ibn ʿAbd al-Wahhāb* (on the disillusionment of some of Ibn ʿAbd al-Wahhāb's followers; Muḥammad al-Ḥusayn al-Kāshif, *Naqḍ fatāwā al-Wahhābiyya* (refutation of Wahhābī legal opinions); Muḥammad Ḥasan al-Qazwīnī, *al-Barāhīn al-jalīla* (proofs against the movement); Muṣṭafā al-Karīmī, *Risālat al-Sunniyyīn fī al-radd ʿalā al-mubtadiʿīn* (Sunnī refutation of innovators). (2) Supporters: Muḥammad Rashīd Riḍā, *al-Wahhābiyyān wa-al-Ḥijāz;* Muḥammad Ḥāmid al-Faqī, *al-Najdiyya* (on Najdis, Najdism); ʿAbd Allāh ʿAlī al-Qusaymī, *al-Thawra al-Wahhābiyya* ('The Wahhābī Revolution'); *al-Burūq al-Najdiyya* ('The Najdi Lightning-Bolts'); Sulaymān ibn Saḥmān, *al-Ḍiyāʾ al-bāriq* ('The Sparkling Light'); *Tanbīh dhawī al-albāb al-sālīma* ('Admonition of Those With Sound Minds'). These were in addition to the works of Ibn ʿAbd al-Wahhāb and other Najdis published by al-Manār Press and al-Salafiyya Press.

Chapter 8

The Rise of Muḥammad ibn ʿAbd al-Wahhāb's *Daʿwa* in the Southern Arabian Peninsula

ʿAbd Allāh ibn Muḥammad ibn Ḥusayn Abū Dāhish

Shortly before the rise of Ibn ʿAbd al-Wahhāb's *daʿwa*, intellectual and literary life in the southern Arabian peninsula was characterized by disparity and confusion. It had witnessed active religious conflict,[1] political instability and disunity,[2] as well as involvement in heretical innovations and beliefs.[3] If news of the *daʿwa* came early to these countries, this was because it came as a response to the desire of many scholars in Tihama and Yemen who found themselves strongly inclined towards the Salafiyya movement,[4] as they were living in true religious exile. Another factor was the intellectual contact that began during this period between these regions and ad-Dirʿīyah (the capital of the first Saudi state). The pilgrimage may also have had some, albeit a limited, effect.[5] But even if one can point to a need for reform, the main factor in the rise of the *daʿwa* later on, in the second decade of the thirteenth/nineteenth century, was the role of the political propagandists who undertook the tasks of carrying out and disseminating its principles.[6] By following the history of the movement in ʿAsīr, Tihama and Yemen one can learn much about the rise of the Salafiyya movement in these regions.

1. *ʿAsīr*

The sources differ in their dating of the beginning of Ibn ʿAbd al-Wahhāb's *daʿwa* in ʿAsīr. Nevertheless, they all agree that it was quickly espoused by the people of that region. This may have been due to the ʿAsīrīs' hatred of the Zaydis and their imāms in Yemen,[7] and also to the absence of a fertile scholarly milieu that might have rejected any inclination towards its acceptance. (This also applies to similar towns of the Arabian peninsula.) Other contributing factors include the political aspirations of the senior leaders of the *daʿwa* and of others in ʿAsīr.[8] This appears clearly in the town of Ṫabab and the surrounding areas, and among some other ʿAsīrī tribes.[9] These factors may not be applicable to Najrān, although Najrān was one of the regions most aware of the *daʿwa*'s emergence in Najd.

Najrān and Its Surrounding Areas[10]

The tribes of Najrān were amongst the first to become aware of the Salafiyya *daʿwa* in Najd. A handwritten document refers to the alliance concluded in 1175/1761 between the Qāḍī al-Hasan ibn Hibat Allāh al-Mukarramī and Muḥammad ibn Suʿūd in ad-Dirʿīyah.[11] We do not know the terms of that alliance, but it seems to have been a political reconciliation between the two parties. That peace, however, did not last long, because al-Mukarramī attacked ad-Dirʿīyah in 1177/1763, thereby violating his former agreement.[12]

The actual appearance of the *daʿwa* in Najrān was perhaps in 1189/1775, when some tribes from Najd raided the Bedouins of Najrān, an act regarded 'as the first action taken by this group [*ṭāʾifa*] in Yemen'.[13] Following this, the tribe of Wādiʿa accepted the *daʿwa* in 1212/1797.[14] Its adoption by the 'Ajmān and Āl Murra tribes took place in 1215/1800,[15] the year that IbnʿAbd al-Wahhāb's *daʿwa* began to spread throughout the countries of the southern Arabian peninsula. Yet despite these efforts, the Najrānīs continued to maintain strict secrecy with respect to their extremist Bātinī Ismāʿīlī sect.

Ṫabab and the Surrounding Areas

The town of Ṫabab is considered one of the most favoured parts of this region in terms of spreading the Salafiyya *daʿwa* in ʿAsīr, for it was the seat of the emirate and the stronghold of the Salafi missionaries. While historians give different dates for the appearance of the *daʿwa* in this part of the Arabian peninsula, the consensus is that it was around 1213/1798 or 1215/1800. This still conflicts with 1177/1763, the date established by Jaʿfar al-Ḥifẓī in his memoirs, when, he states, a number of ʿAsīrī notables, and some scholars from Rijāl Almaʿ, went to ad-Dirʿīyah to study.[16]

Other ʿAsīrī Tribes

The other tribes of ʿAsīr varied in their acceptance of the *daʿwa*, although they were already aware of its principles. The *daʿwa* appeared among the Khathʿam and Banū Taghlib in 1196/1781, when these tribes began attacking Yemeni pilgrims to Makkah and forcing them to accept it.[17] Attacks by the *daʿwa*'s leaders on the remaining tribes of ʿAsīr continued actively. The Najdis attacked Bīsha in 1209/1794, and Qaḥtan in 1210/1795;[18] Shahrān witnessed frequent Saʿūdī raids from 1211/ 1796.[19] The Ghāmid tribe recognized the *daʿwa* around 1212/1797, as is stated in a handwritten document whose scribe writes: 'Islam appeared in the territories of Ghāmid in 1212.'[20] The *daʿwa* also appeared in Tanūmat Banī Shahr in 1215/1800, as a scholar of āl al-Ḥifẓī states (speaking of the events of that year): 'The people of al-Sārā were converted in Tanūma.'[21] It is clear that these tribes were among the first to come under Saudi rule and accept the *daʿwa*. The remaining tribes of ʿAsīr embraced it, in succession, from the time of the rise of the Abū Nuqṭa emirate.

These brief historical references show that ʿAsīr was not like other regions in the southern Arabian peninsula in terms of the spread of the *daʿwa*, as it depended on its political propagandists, such as Muḥammad and ʿAbd al-Wahhāb, the sons of ʿĀmir al-Muthami in Ṭabab, Sālim ibn Shakbān in Bīsha, Muḥammadibn Dahmān[22] in Banī Shahr, and other emirs in Tubāla and Zahrān. These propagandist princes had been working since 1215/1800 on spreading and preaching the *daʿwa*; this makes this date the starting point for the practical, political appearance of the movement, which is linked to ad-Dirʿīyah and its princes. The ʿAsīrīs' acceptance of Ibn ʿAbd al-Wahhāb's *daʿwa*, and their coming under the rule of Āl Saʿūd, helped to spread its tenets and to support it.

2. *Tihama*[23]

During the second half of the twelfth/eighteenth century Tihama was known for its scholarly awareness and distinguished intellectual activity. It contained a large number of scholars, as well as a variety of religious sects; this was the reason for the rise of the *daʿwa* in most of its towns being both late and limited. Yet it did not lack scholars who supported the *daʿwa*, such as the Bakrīs in Rijāl Almaʿ. Perhaps the Shāfiʿī *madhhab*, which most of Tihama's towns embraced, helped to facilitate the rise and support of the *daʿwa*; for during this period these areas saw active sectarian conflict between the Zaydis in Sanaa and the Shāfiʿīs in Tihama. The *daʿwa*'s most well-known centres in Tihama were perhaps Rijal Almaʿ, Bāriq and al-Mikhlāf al-Sulaymānī.

Rijāl Almaʿ

The *daʿwa* enjoyed the support of the scholars of Āl Bakrī in Rijāl Almaʿ, who hastened to accept it.[24] This may have been because of the religious vacuum and political void in the town, which made the early scholars of Āl Bakrī direct themselves towards the east and to adopt and support the *daʿwa*. It is likely that contact between these scholars and ad-Dirʿīyah had begun early on. But it does not seem to have assumed the form indicated by Jaʿfar al-Ḥifẓī in his memoirs, in which he enumerated a group of Bakrīs who migrated to ad-Dirʿīyah in 1177/1763.[25] The true situation may be as Muḥammad ibn Aḥmad al-Ḥifẓī stated in his *Nafḥ al-ʿūd*: 'When that call reached us and came to our ears, we could not but join those who heard and obeyed . . . This took place in the year one thousand two hundred and five.'[26]

While the appearance of the Salafiyya *daʿwa* in Rijāl Almaʿ had begun in the early thirteenth/nineteenth century, this date marked the start of its dissemination in those areas, for it is after this that we find Muḥammad al-Ḥifẓī writing books and corresponding with scholars. In his *al-Lijām almakīn* he refers to his pleasure in accepting the *daʿwa*, and states that he wrote the book for its sake in 1212/1797.[27] What furthered the *daʿwa*'s spread among the Āl-Ḥifẓī scholars was the presence of political propagandists in ʿAsīr from 1215/1800 onwards, the date which the historian

Luṭf Allāh Jaḥḥāf considered the starting point of its acceptance by Aḥmad ibn ʿAbd al-Qādir al-Ḥifẓī.[28] From then on the Ḥifẓī scholars backed the Salafi emirs of ʿAsīr and began to spread the principles of the *daʿwa* in their territories.

Bāriq and Surrounding Areas[29]

The few available sources do not agree on the precise date of the *daʿwa*'s appearance among the tribes of Bāriq, al-Rīsh and Hily in Tihama. While Ibn ʿAbd al-Shakūr suggests 1214/1799,[30] the anonymous author of *Umarāʾ Makkah wa-al-Ḥijāz* put it at 1215/1800.[31] There is disagreement about the name of the tribal chief of al-Rīsh who was considered the first to accept the *daʿwa*. Ibn ʿAbd al-Shakūr calls him Maʿaddī ibn Shār and states that he induced his fellow tribesmen to embrace the *daʿwa:* 'when he was converted, so was the whole tribe'.[32] The author of *Umarāʾ Makkah* calls him Sheikh Manṣār, and says that formerly he was accountable to 'Sheikh Ghālib, the ruler of Makkah'.[33] Despite the discrepancy between these two historians, it is clear that these dates are chronologically close and in agreement as to their purport. It seems that both chiefs belonged to Tihama, as Ibrāhīm ibn Aḥmad al-Ḥifẓī mentions a message from Suʿūd ibn Abdul Aziz addressed to 'ʿAbd al-Wahhāb, ʿArār, Manṣūr and Maʿaddī'.[34] Perhaps he meant by these ʿAbd al-Wahhāb al-Mathamī, ʿArār ibn Shār al-Shaʿbī and Manṣār ibn Nāṣir al-Ḥasanī.[35] In this case Ma'addī ibn Shār was really the Sheikh or chief of al-Rīsh, as Ibn ʿAbd al-Shakūr stated. Whatever the case, the year 1216/1801 was followed by the embracing of the *daʿwa* by a number of Tihama tribes.[36]

Al-Mikhlāf al-Sulaymānī

Ibn ʿAbd al-Wahhāb's *daʿwa* began in the towns of al-Mikhlāf al-Sulaymānī in the same way as it had in Rijāl Almaʿ, in terms of the religious scholars' response to it and in terms of migration. Both ʿArār ibn Shār al-Shaʿbī and Sharīf Aḥmad ibn Ḥusayn al-Falqī went to ad-Dirʿīyah in Najd, motivated by their desire to know the truth of the *daʿwa* and to learn from its genuine preachers. Al-Falqī returned in 1215/1800 with a letter from ʿAbd al-ʿAzīz ibn Saʿūd to the people of al-Mikhlāf al-Sulaymānī inviting them to accept and support the *daʿwa*.[37]

Most of the Yemeni and al-Mikhlāf al-Sulaymānī historians agree on the date when the *daʿwa* appeared in those regions. Jaḥḥāf states that in 1215/1800 'the Mawhiba affair emerged in the coastal area and won over the people of al-Darb'.[38] Al-Hasan ibn Aḥmad ʿĀkish, referring to the Sharīf Ḥamūd Muḥammad al-Ḥasanī,[39] states, 'He began to rise with the acceptance of the Najdi man's *daʿwa* in these regions.'[40] This makes that date a starting point for the *daʿwa* in this area in the light of the activity of the earliest Salafi preachers. Acceptance of the *daʿwa* by the Mikhlāf al-Sulaymānī emirs was delayed until 1217/1802, when Sharīf Ḥamūd Abū Mismār was converted to it. Al-Ḥasan ibn Aḥmad ʿĀkish ascribes this initiave to a poem sent by Muḥammad ibn Aḥmad al-Ḥifẓī to Qāḍī ʿAbd al-Raḥmān ibn Hasan al-Bahkalī in which he attempted to win him over to the Wahhābī *daʿwa*.[41] However, it seems more likely that it was the fierce battles that preceded his conversion, rather than this poem, that led him to accept the *daʿwa*.

3. *Yemen*

Yemeni historians wrote in detail about Ibn ʿAbd al-Wahhāb's *daʿwa*. More often than not, they showed their aversion to the mission, without either scrutiny or investigation. The reason for this attitude may in some cases be ascribed to the conduct of some of the *daʿwa*'s leaders in the southern Arabian peninsula, and in others to biased accounts brought to Yemen by migrants there.[42] Whatever the case, Yemen never lacked genuine scholars who did justice to the *daʿwa* and worked for its propagation.

The city of Sanaa may be considered one of the earliest in the southern Arabian peninsula to become aware of the rise of Ibn ʿAbd al-Wahhāb's *daʿwa* in Najd. It is also one of the few cities which the *daʿwa*'s military forces did not reach,[43] although Yemeni Tihama, Hadramawt and Aden witnessed many attacks by Salafi missionaries. Its appearance in Yemeni cities came about chiefly through the efforts of religious scholars, as is seen clearly in Sanaa and the surrounding areas.

Sanaa and Its Surroundings

The beginning of the Salafiyya *daʿwa* in Sanaa dates back to 1160/1747, the year to which the emir Muḥammad ibn Ismāʿīl referred when he said, 'Since 1160 we have received news that a man appeared in Najd calling on people to follow the Prophet Muḥammad's *sunna*.'[44] This led the emir to write to Ibn ʿAbd al-Wahhāb in 1163/1749–50.[45] This date may correspond to ʿAbd Allāh ibn ʿĪsā's statement in his *al-Sayf al-Hindī* that the beginning of the *daʿwa* in the region had been 'known to proficient historians for years', and that it was 'around the mid-sixties of the twelfth century'.[46] Scholars in those areas continually received news from later comers to Yemen, such as Mirbid (or perhaps Mayzad) ibn Aḥmad al-Tamīmī, who came to Sanaa in 1170/ 1786.[47] Those scholars wrote to the authorities in ad-Dirʿīyah asking them about the *daʿwa*.[48]

If this earlier scanty information circulated in Sanaa and its surroundings, actual information on the *daʿwa*'s appearance in that part of the Arabian peninsula dates it to 1215/1800, the year of the arrival of the two letters from ʿAbd al-ʿAzīz ibn Saʿūd to the (Zaydi) imām of Yemen.[49] News and correspondence were not confined to Sanaa alone; the cities of Dhamar, Su'da and others were in the same position.[50] There is some disagreement among historians as to the exact date of the spread of the *daʿwa*; Ṣiddīq Hasan al-Qannawjī said that it did not reach its climax 'until about the year twelve hundred'.[51] Perhaps the researcher should not worry about the lack of reliable sources, since there was scarcely any other means for the rise of the *daʿwa* in the southern Arabian peninsula except through Salafi scholars and preachers.

Al-Ḥudayda and Its Surroundings

The sources also differ on the precise dates of the rise of the Salafiyya *daʿwa* in Yemeni Tihama. Some suggest that it first appeared in 1216/1801,[52] while others give dates varing between 1217/1802, 1220/1805 and 1221/1806. In any case, 1216/1801 may be viewed as a starting point for its emergence in those areas, since, as in similar cities in the Arabian peninsula, it was not then accompanied by any political aspects. The sources further disagree in dating the subsequent stage, after 1216/1801. While Muḥammad Zabāra states that al-Luḥayya, Zabīd, al-Ḥudayda, Bayt al-Faqīh, Zubayda and other similar towns had been aware of the *daʿwa* since 1217/1802,[53] Ibn Bishr says that al-Ḥudayda, Bayt al-Faqīh and Zubayda joined it in 1220/1801, after a series of continuous military engagements.[54] Aḥmad ibn Aḥmad al-Niʿmī dates the beginning of these battles to 1221/1806,[55] while al-Fākhirī fixed 1225/1810 as the date when the Salafiyya *daʿwa* arose in al-Luḥayya.[56] All this shows that this later period is regarded as the actual stage of the *daʿwa*'s rise in Yemeni Tihama, especially if we consider 1216/1801 as its starting point.

Aden and Hadramawt

The sources indicate that the *daʿwa*'s preachers had appeared on the coast of Aden in 1219/1804; however, they did not enter the city, but returned home.[57] The actual appearance of the *daʿwa* in Hadramawt was in 1224/1809, when the preacher ʿAlī ibn Qamla and a number of his companions came to that area.[58] Notwithstanding the benefits which the inhabitants of Hadramawt reaped from the presence of those preachers, the latter did not remain among them, but left after forty days. It is said that they returned to Hadramawt later, in 1226/1811, but were received with hostility and opposition.[59] Despite frequent campaigns, Hadramawt did not accept the *daʿwa* of Muḥammad ibn ʿAbd al-Wahhāb.[60]

Notes:

1. The conflict between various legal schools and religious sects, such as Shāfiʿīs, Zaydis, Sufis, Ismāʿīlīs, Bāṭinīs and others, was clearly evident.
2. These regions of the Arabian peninsula were divided into various petty states, emirates and sheikhdoms. The Zaydi Imams ruled Yemen; Sharīfs from Āl Khayrāt ruled al-Mikhlāf al-Sulaymānī; ʿAsīr and Hadramawt were ruled by various emirates and Sheikhdoms; while Najrān belonged to the Mukarramiyya family.
3. The effect of the Salafiyya *daʿwa* on southern Arabia was clearly evident in this field, as will be explained in later studies.
4. For example, Sheikh Muḥammad ibn Ismāʿīl al-Amīr and Sheikh Aḥmad ibn ʿAbd al-Qādir al-Ḥifẓī, who, on finding a political and educational vacuum, went to ad-Dirʿīyah instead of Yemen.

5. See Muḥammad ibn ʿAlī al-Shawkānī, *al-Badr al-ṭāliʿ fī maḥāsin mā baʿd al-qarn al-sābiʿ* (Beirut, n.d. [photo reproduction of the first edn, Cairo, 1348/1929]), II, pp. 5, 6.
6. This was seen clearly in preacher-princes in ʿAsīr and elsewhere.
7. ʿAbd al-Fattāh Ḥasan Abū ʿĀliya, *al-Iṣlāḥ al-ijtimāʿī fī ʿahd al-malik ʿAbd al-ʿAzīz* (Riyadh, 1396/1976), p. 105.
8. See Maḥmūd Shākir, *ʿAsīr* (Beirut/Damascus, n.d.), pp. 149–52.
9. Ṭabab: a village in the Rufayda area which lies in the well-known Wādī Ṭabab. It was the seat of political authority in ʿAsīr during the first third of the thirteenth/nineteenth century.
10. Najrān lies in the south-western Arabian peninsula. It comprises a wide valley extending from the east towards al-Rubʿ al-Khālī (the 'empty quarter'). (See *EI2*, s.v.)
11. Al-Ḥasan ibn Hibat Allāh al-Mukarramī, covenant between the Mukarramīs in Najrān and Muḥammad ibn Suʿūd, photocopy of ms. in Muḥammad ibn Ḥasan Gharīb's private library, Riyadh (no. 48). The Qāḍī is called *al-dāʿī* ('the preacher/missionary') by the Mukarramīs in Najrān.
12. Muqbil ibn ʿAbd al-ʿAzīz al-Dhikkīr, *al-ʿIqd al-mumtāz fī akhbār Tihāma waal-Ḥijāz*, ms., Documents Division, Dārat al-Malik ʿAbd al-ʿAzīz, Riyadh, no. 569, fol. 13.
13. Luṭf Allāh Jaḥḥāf, *Durar al-ḥūr al-ʿīnbi-sīrat al-imām al-Manṣūr wa-aʿyān dawlatihi al-mayāmīn*, ms., Western Library of Sanaa Great Mosque, History, no. 85, fols. 9–11. (This library houses three other copies; another is in the Manuscripts Division, King Saud University, no number.) *Ṭāʾifa* is given in the source. A number of historians and scholars in southern Arabia have traditionally used such terms, giving the *daʿwa* and its preachers titles such as *al-mawhiba* ('the gift'), *al-madīna* ('the city'), *al-khāwarij* ('dissenters'), *al-daʿwa al-Najdiyya* ('the Najdi *daʿwa*'), *al-fitan al-Najdiyya* ('Najdi seditions'), *dīn al-Wahhābī* ('the Wahhābī's religion'), *daʿwat al-Najdi* ('the Najdi's call'), *al-shurūq* ('sunrise'), *al-mashāriqa* ('the easterners'), *al-tadayyun al-tawahhub* ('Wahhābī piety'). See e.g. Jahhāf, *Durar*, fols. 535, 466; al-Ḥasan ibn Aḥmad ʿākish, *al-Dībāj al-khusruwānī bi-dhikr mulūk al-Mikhlāf al-Sulaymānī*, photocopy owned by Ḥijāb Yaḥya al-Hāzimī, Ḍamad, no number (original ms. at the ʿUqayliyya private library, Jāzān, no. 42; another defective manuscript owned by ʿAbd Allāh Abū Dāhish), fol. 16; *idem., Hadāʾiq al-zahr fī dhikr al-ashyākh aʿyān al-dahr*, ʿUqayliyya private library, Jāzān, no. 38, fol. 55; Aḥmad ibn Aḥmad al-Niʿmī, *Tārīkh al-Niʿmī*, ms., photocopy belonging to Muḥammad ʿAbd Allāh al-Zalāfa, fol. 2. See also ʿAbd al-Raḥmān ibn Aḥmad al-Bahkalī, *Nafḥ al-ʿūd fī sīrat dawlat al-*

Sharīf Ḥammūd (ed. Muḥammad ibn ʿAbd al-Raḥmān al-ʿUqaylī, Riyadh, 1402/1982).

14. Jaḥḥāf, *Durar*, fol. 268.
15. *Ibid.*, fol. 312.
16. See Maḥmūd Shākir, *ʿAsīr*, pp. 149–50; see also the genealogical table of Āl Bakrī of Rijāl Almaʿ, ms. owned by this author, which contradicts what Shākir states in terms of the time frame of this event and the ages of those involved.
17. See Jaḥḥāf, *Durar*, fol. 102.
18. *Ibid.*
19. See Shākir, *ʿAsīr*, pp. 151–2; ʿUthmān ibn ʿAbd Allāh Bishr, *ʿUnwān al-majd fī tārīkh Najd* (Riyadh, 1982), I, p. 117.
20. Anonymous diary, private library of Muḥammad ibn Saʿd al-Barakī, Baljurashī.
21. Anonymous diaries belonging to this author.
22. This prince was nicknamed 'Abū Nuqta' to distinguish him from his brother ʿAbd al-Wahhāb, and was traditionally known to historians by this name. See Muḥammad Aḥmad al-Ḥifẓī, *Nafḥ ūl-ʿād fī al-ẓill al-mamdūd fī tārīkh Āl Saʿūd*, ms. fol. 2. Some elderly people of Tanūmat Banī Shahr said that Ibn Dahmān had sought to spread the *daʿwa* among his countrymen, and would invite religious scholars to his emirate, particularly from the territories of the ʿAbs in Tihama, to whom the famous family of learned jurists known as the Banū Shahr is related.
23. Here Tihama refers to the level plains on the Red Sea coast, which become wider as they extend toward the western slopes of the Sarā mountains, from the furthest parts of Yemeni Tihama to al-Qunfudha in the north.
24. They were descended from Sheikh Bakrī ibn Muḥammad ibn Mahdī ibn Mūsā ibn Jaghtham ibn ʿUjayl. The surname al-Ḥifẓī became prevalent in this family, as Aḥmad ʿAbd al-Qādir assumed it, and the family became known by it later, although this name was originally restricted to Aḥmad ʿAbd al-Qādir and his offspring. See the (anonymous) genealogical tree of Āl Bakrī of Rijāl Almaʿ, manuscript owned by this author; see also the introduction to Muḥammad ibn Aḥmad al-Ḥifẓī, *Dhawq al-ṭullāb fī ʿilm al-iʿrāb* (ed. ʿAbd Allāh Abū Dāhish; Riyadh, 1401/1980), p. 6.
25. See Shākir, *ʿAsīr*, p. 149.
26. Muḥammad al-Ḥifẓī, *Nafḥ al-ʿūd*, fol. 1.
27. Muḥammad ibn Aḥmad al-Ḥifẓī, *al-Lijām al-makīn wa-al-zimām al-matīn*, ms. belonging to this author, dated 1212/1797, fols. 1, 4.
28. Jaḥḥāf, *Durar*, fol. 312.

29. Bāriq is a wide area in Tihama regarded as the homeland of one of the most famous Azd tribes in the region.
30. ʿAbd Allāh ibn Muḥammad ʻAli ibn ʿAbd al-Shakūr, ʻMin maṣādir tārīkh al-dawla al-Suʿūdiyya al-ūlā', *Majallat al-ʿArab* 10.11–12 (1396/1976), pp. 820–1.
31. Anonymous, *Umarāʾ Makkah wa-al-Hijāz*, ms., Manuscripts Division, Imām Muḥammad ibn Saʿūd Islamic University, no. 143, fol. 2.
32. Ibn ʿAbd al-Shakūr, ʻMaṣādir', pp. 820–1.
33. So in the source; the correct wording is ʻthe Sharīf who is Ghālib ibn Musāʿid' (*Umarā' Makkah*, fol. 2).
34. Al-Ḥifẓī, Aḥmad ʿAbd al-Qādir, Ibrāhīm ibn Aḥmad *et al*. Handwritten book catalogues belonging to ʿAbd al-Khāliq ibn Sulaymān al-Ḥifẓī.
35. These were among the most prominent preachers of the *daʿwa* in ʿAsīr and al-Mikhlāf al-Sulaymānī; see al-Bahkalī, *Nafḥ al-ʿūd*, pp. 91, 101.
36. *Umarā' Makkah*, fol. 2. See also Ibn ʿAbd al-Shakūr, ʻMaṣādir', pp. 821ff.
37. See al-Bahkalī, *Nafḥ al-ʿūd*, pp. 68ff.
38. Jaḥḥāf, *Durar*, fol. 314; the Darb (road) is Darb Banī Shuʻba.
39. He is Ḥamūd ibn Muḥammad ibn Aḥmad al-Khayrātī. He was nicknamed Abū Mismār (ʻthe man with the nail') because of a nail which pierced his neck in one of the battles he fought. He was born in 1170/1756–7 and died in 1233/1817. He accepted the *daʿwa* of Ibn ʿAbd al-Wahhāb in 1217/1802 and as a result became the Emir of al-Mikhlāf al-Sulaymānī; he remained in this position until he died in the village of al-Mallāḥa in ʿAsīr. See his biography in al-Bahkalī, *Nafḥ al-ʿūd*, p. 70.
40. ʿĀkish, *Dībāj*, fol. 16.
41. *Ibid.*, fol. 19. ʻĀkish states, ʻWhen the emirs of Najd arrived in this country, Sharīf Ḥamūḍ did not surrender power to them until a poem arrived from Muḥammad al-Ḥifẓī of Rijāl [Almaʿ] addressed to the learned Qāḍī ʿAbd al-Raḥmān ibn Ḥasan al-Bahkalī urging the people of the region to submit to the Najdi's call.'
42. Muḥammad Ṣiddīq Ḥasan al-Qannawjī, Nawab of Bhopal, *Abjad al-ʿulūm al-musammā bi-al-Washy al-marqūm fī bayān aḥwal al-ʿulūm* (Beirut, 1975–6), III, p. 196.
43. Muḥsin ibn ʿAbd al-Karīm ibn Ahmad ibn Isḥaq, *Lafaḥāt al-wajd min fiʿlāt ahl Najd*, ms. in the Western Library, Sanaa Great Mosque, fol. 3.
44. Muḥammad ibn Ismāʿīl al-Ṣanʿānī, *Irshād dhawī al-albāb ilā ḥaqīqat aqwāl Muḥammad ibn ʿAbd al-Wahhāb*, ms. in the Western Library, Sanaa Great Mosque, fol. 393.
45. *Idem, Dīwān*, ms. owned by this author, copied 1351/1932, fol. 56. See also

the genealogical tree of the Sharīf ʿArīf ibn al-Ḥasan ibn Zayd, manuscript, private library of Ḥasan Ibrāhīm al-Faqīh, al-Qunfudha, copied 1220/1805.

46. This work is referred to by Muḥsin ibn ʿAbd al-Karīm in his *Lafaḥāt al-wajd*, fol. 2. In his *Abjad al-ʿulūm* al-Qannawjī states that he wrote it in 1218/1803. This shows that Ibn ʿĪsā was biased against the *daʿwa* at that time, which was filled with sectarian and political conflicts.
47. See al-Ṣanʿānī, *Dīwān*, fol. 58; Muḥsin, *Lafaḥāt*, fol. 4; al-Qannawjī, *Abjad*, p. 196.
48. Among these scholars were Aḥmad ibn Muḥammad al-ʿAwbalī and Ismāʿīl al-Jarrā'ī. See information about their letters in Muḥammad ibn ʿAbd al-Wahhāb, *Mu'allafāt*. V. *al-Rasā'il al-shakhṣiyya* (Riyadh, 1981).
49. Al-Shawkānī, *al-Badr al-ṭāliʿ*, p. 7.
50. See *ibid.*, p. 263; Muḥammad ibn Nāṣir al-Sharīf al-Tihāmī al-Ḥāzimī, *Iqāẓ al-wasnān ʿalā bayān al-khalal alladhī fī ṣulḥ al-ikhwān*, ms., Manuscripts Division, King Saud University, Riyadh, no. 554, copied 1359/1940, fol. 31.
51. Al-Qannawjī, *Abjad al-ʿulūm*, p. 194.
52. ʿAbd al-Wāsiʿ ibn Yaḥyā al-Wāsiʿī, *Tārīkh al-Yaman al-musammā Furjat al-humūm wa-al-ḥazan fī ḥawadith wa-tārīkh al-Yaman* (Cairo, 1366/1947), p. 60.
53. Muḥammad ibn Muḥammad Zabāra, *Nayl al-watar min tarājim rijāl al-Yaman fī al-qarn al-thālith ʿashar* (Cairo, 1348/1929), II, p. 420.
54. Ibn Bishr, *ʿUnwān*, p. 138.
55. Al-Niʿmī, *Tārīkh*, fol. 2.
56. Muḥammad ibn ʿUmar al-Fākhirī, *al-Akhbār al-Najdiyya* (ed. ʿAbd Allāh ibn Yūsif al-Shibl, Riyadh, n.d.), p. 138.
57. See Hamza ʿAlī Ibrāhīm Luqmān, *Tārīkh ʿAdan wa-janūb al-Jazīra al-ʿArabiyya* (Cairo, 1379/1959–60), p. 181; Aḥmad ibn Faḍl ibn ʿAli ibn Muḥsin al-Abdalī, *Hadiyyat al-zaman fī akhbār mulūk Lahj waʿAdan* (Beirut, 2nd edn, 1400/1980), p. 136.
58. Ṣalāh al-Bakrī, *Fī janūb shibh al-jazīra al-ʿArabiyya* (Cairo, 1368/1949), p. 140. Ibn Qamla may have come from Wādī Khubb in Yemen; see Jaḥḥāf, *Durar*, fol. 354.
59. Al-Bakrī, *Junūb*, p. 141.
60. ʿAbd al-Karīm Rafīq, *al-ʿArab wa-al-ʿUthmāniyyūn 1516–1916* (Damascus, 1304/1984), p. 41.

Chapter 9

Glimpses of Hijazi History at the Beginning of the First Saudi State

Aḥmad Fuʿād Mitwallī

The Hijaz region was beset by disturbances and revolts during the early period of the first Saudi state. This was a time characterized by bitter struggle between certain nobles (*ashrāf*) over the rulership of Makkah. Often bloody, as is recorded in some contemporary books, whose writers sympathized with the holy city concerning these disputes, the struggles generally took the form of armed conflict with varying degrees of violence.

It was during this period, however, as the struggle in the Hijaz became more intense, that the Saudis appeared in Najd. Their power increased swiftly, as did the number of their supporters and followers. Yet the nobles not only considered them to be enemies but also enemies of the true religion, even though the Salafiyya movement, which they supported, did not transgress the tolerant boundaries of Islam and was considered a revival of, and a return to, the teachings of the true religion. Despite a bitter struggle for leadership, the nobles initiated hostile and inflammatory measures against the followers of the Salafiyya movement, one of which was to forbid the Najdis from fulfilling the obligation of the pilgrimage, especially during the time of Sharīf Aḥmad ibn Saʿīd.[1]

As for Sharīf Sarūr ibn Musāʿid (r. 1186–1202/1772–88), he was not hostile to Najd in the early period of his rule,[2] and allowed Najdis to perform the pilgrimage, although later he reneged on this and prohibited them.[3] Ottoman Turkish documents tell us about the correspondence from Sharīf Sarūr ibn Musāʿid to the Ottoman sultan, urging him to be wary and careful, to begin preparations to repel an expected attack from what he called the Wahhābīs against the Hijaz, and asking the sultan to send both equipment and other forms of military aid to enable him to resist and expel the Saudis.[4] He also sent appeals for help to the governors of Baghdad, and later Damascus, in an attempt to avert the anticipated danger from the Āl Saᶜūd, as he expressed it.[5]

Turkish sources show that no help materialized for Sharīf Sarūr ibn Musāᶜid, and that all his efforts met with failure. The Ottoman state received his requests with a coolness, for the sultan believed that the conflict between Najd and the Hijaz was no more than a difference of opinion that would not lead to hostility between the two parties. Further, the Ottomons were preoccupied at this time with war with Russia, Austria and Venice.[6] The governors of Baghdad and Syria, likewise, did not consider the matter urgent and made no move to help, a stance driven largely by fear of the possible consequences.[7]

The nobles followed the progression of the Salafiyya movement with interest, although, like most people at the time, they did not expect it to succeed. But their views changed with the passage of time, after the movement expanded, subjecting to its authority most Najdi regions and establishing a new state.[8] Any survey of the history of the Hijaz nobility will observe that it was a history filled with bloodshed and strife, with families divided and the quest for power paramount.[9]

In the fifth volume of his *Taʾrīkh Jawdat*, the Turkish historian Aḥmad Jawdat Pasha[10] records the following observations on the nobles of the Hijaz at the time of Sharīf Ghālib ibn Musāᶜid:

> Much blood flowed because of the wars that took place between the nobles in Makkah, the place where the divine inspiration descended. When the brothers of Sharīf Ghālib ibn Musāᶜid, the amir of Makkah, exceeded all bounds in their conflict with him in the preceding year (1203/1789), both sides prepared their armies and violent battles took place. The judge of Makkah and the muftis of the four legal schools sought to mediate between the two antagonists and finally succeeded in bringing about a truce between them.[11]

The reports that arrived for Āghā Dār al-Saʾāda in 1204/1789 show that a bitter war took place in Makkah between Ghālib, the Emir of Makkah, and his nephew, Sharīf ʿAbd Allāh, on the 29th of Ṣafar. Due to the intensity of rifle and cannon fire – and the volleys continued for three days – the call to prayer could not be made, and prayer was suspended nineteen times. A piece of the Black Stone, about three fingers wide, was broken off due to the bullets that rained down on it; the stone itself finally broke, but was restored after the battles had ended, pasted together with limestone mixed with oil. After that, the people gathered angrily and advised the nobles: 'If you fight, fight outside the Haram, as was the ancient custom, and resolve your conflicts either through war or peace.'

Sharīf ʿAbd Allāh took refuge with the Hudhayl tribe. He re-entered Makkah with a great crowd of supporters. When he settled at the place called al-Mu'ābdeh, Sharīf Ghālib set out to meet him with many troops, and a fierce battle took place in which many from both parties fell. Yet the outcome was inconclusive and Sharīf Ghālib withdrew to Makkah, while Sharīf ʿAbd Allāh seized Ṭā'if.[12] As the stalemate continued, Sharīf Ghālib received an order from higher authorities instructing him to avert the conflicts and remove any threat to the poor of the two holy shrines. At the same time, an order was sent to Uzun Ibrāhīm Pasha, the leader of the pilgrimage (Emir al-Hajj), urging him to advise the two parties and persuade them to exercise self-control and settle the dispute between them.[13]

According to the historian ʿAbd al-Shukūr Effendi, these disturbances began from the time when (the deceased) Sharīf Sarūr, the brother of Sharīf Ghālib, had an aide called Yaḥyā Saltūḥ whom Sharīf Ghālib had imprisoned, being certain that he was involved in the revolts and disturbances. But, some time later, Saltūḥ escaped and took refuge in the house of Sharīf Sarūr's sons. Despite intensive searches, Sharīf Ghālib was not able to discover his whereabouts, and so assumed he had fled to a distant place. However, Yaḥyā Saltūḥ had worked secretly to foster sedition by tempting Sharīf ʿAbd Allāh, Sarūr's son, with the emirate. Although ʿAbd Allāh was under age, not yet being 12 years old, he was taken in by these words, and became obsessed with the idea of the emirate. He ordered a siege around the house of Sharīf Ghālib, and the house came under fire.

The two (Sharīf Ghālib and Sharīf ʿAbd Allāh) confronted each other somewhere in Makkah, and firing went on between them for a period of four days and nights, during which the streets were emptied of people, and prayers ceased at the holy shrine; even the Friday prayer could not take place.

After that Sharīf ʿAbd Allāh, together with his brother Sharīf Muḥammad and many of the nobles who supported him, left for al-Muʿāyida. Yaḥyā Saltūḥ, and a number of (the late) Sharīf Sarūr's slaves and devotees followed him. Sharīf Ghālib meanwhile prepared his troops and set out to confront them. Having defeated them he went on to Ta'if, seized it, and then set out once more for Makkah after raising a sufficient force from a number of different tribes. From Makkah, Sharīf Ghālib set out to fight the epic battle that took place in the Rayyan valley.[14] He seized Sharīf ʿAbd Allāh and his brother and scattered and dispersed their troops. Despite this, Sharīf Ghālib later forgave his nephews and treated them well, allocating them both salaries and positions.

After this defeat, Yaḥyā Saltūḥ escaped to Damascus by way of Madinah. When he arrived there, he wrote a petition seeking that the emirate be granted to Sharīf ʿAbd Allāh. He then went to Istanbul, where he submitted his petition to the higher authorities; receiving no response, he left in despair for Egypt.[15] Aḥmad Jawdat Pasha, commenting on these events, stated: 'Had control in Makkah passed to that young boy, corruption and chaos would have overwhelmed that safe city where divine inspiration first appeared.'

Notes:

1. Aḥmad al-Sibāʿī, *Ta'rīkh Makkah* (Cairo, 1952), I, p. 302.
2. See Munīr al-'Ajlānī, *Ta'rīkh al-bilād al-ʿArabiyya al-Suʿūdiyya* (Beirut, n.d.), I, p. 136.
3. See al-Sibāʿī, *Ta'rīkh Makkah*, p. 345.
4. See document 3453 in the Topkapi Museum, Istanbul.
5. See document 6821 in the Topkapi Museum, Istanbul.
6. Bir Heyet, *Mufassal Osmanli Tarihi* (ed. S. R. Iskit and Z. Orgun, Istanbul, 1962–3), V, p. 2703.

7. See Aḥmad Jawdat Pasha, *Taʾrīkh Jawdat* (Istanbul, 1303/1886), V, p. 92.
8. Amīn Saʿīd, *Taʾrīkh al-dawla al-Suʿūdiyya* (Beirut, 1964), pp. 62–3.
9. Ḥāfiẓ Wahba, *Jazīrat al-ʿArab fī al-qarn al-ʿishrīn* (Cairo, 1967), p. 150.
10. Aḥmad Jawdat Pasha was born in 1237/1822 at LovḌa (Lovec) in northern Bulgaria, when it was still part of the Ottoman Empire. He was appointed by Sultan ʿAbd al-Ḥamīd II (1293–1327/1876–1909) as official chronicler (and occupied various positions under the Ottomans), and was later commissioned to write the history of the Ottoman state. He began his book on Ottoman history in 1270/1854, entitling it *Taʾrīkh Jawdat*, co. Its twelve volumes covered the years from 1188/1774 to 1241/1826, and it is considered one of the main sources for the history of the Ottoman state in that period. The historian spared no effort, relying on the documents and manuscripts that his official position as state chronicler allowed him to access. He also consulted Arabic, English, French and German sources. The book was published many times in Ottoman Turkish script. The first volume was translated into Arabic by ʿAbd al-Qādir al-Danā and published in Beirut in 1308/1890. It has been reprinted using modern Turkish script, in five volumes, by Dündar Cünday, edited and revised by Muʾmin Juwayk, published in 1972 (see the introduction by Dündar Cūnday, *Tarihi Cevelet*, V, pp. 1–12).
11. Aḥmad Jawdat Pasha, *Ta'rimacr;kh Jawdat*, V, pp. 30–1.
12. Bir Heyet, *Mufassal Osmanli Tarihi*, V, p. 2703. See also Yilmaz Öztuna, *Osmanli Tarihi* (Istanbul, 1967), XI, p. 124.
13. See *ibid*. See also Ismail Hami Danişmend, *Izahli Osmanli Tarihi Kronolojisi* (Istanbul, 1972), IV, p. 85.
14. Munīr al-ʿAjlānī states: ‘In 1203 a supporter of Sharīf Sarūr tempted one of his sons, Sharīf ʿAbd Allāh ibn Sarūr, a child no more than twelve years old, to seek the emirate. He gathered 500 slaves and fired at the house of Sharīf Ghālib, and blocked the streets of Makkah for many days, after which they were overpowered’ (*Taʾrīkh*, I, p. 138).
15. *Mufassal Osmanli Tarihi*, V, p. 2704.

Chapter 10

ORIGINS OF SAUDI HISTORY: AN INTRODUCTION TO METHODOLOGY AND ATTITUDE

ᶜAbd al-Hafiz ᶜAbd al-Fattah Qari

In this chapter my aim is to carry out a theoretical experiment to explain the rise and continuity of the early Saudi State. The research techniques I call upon are those described by the American educationist and thinker John Dewey.[1] While the foregoing is a preliminary attempt to achieve this goal, it will be followed by other attempts which will no doubt benefit from further insights, the general progress of human knowledge and the advance of science.

The chapter arises from a need to deal with early Saudi history by means of a study that functions within the framework of a particular attitude towards the interpretation of history. For as long as any general theory has not attained a sufficient degree of perfection, and the rules of this theory have not been defined, I think it unfair that the historical study of this period comes as mere application of the present technical parameters of historical methodology, given that the question is fundamentally a philosophical one. So, in order to bring sufficient theoretical consideration to bear on the conclusions we arrive at, we must first define our interpretation of history.

Consequently we have to conduct primary research that starts from the root of the problem and uses probability methodology in dealing with its limits.

- A significant factor controlling the findings of research is how to start. For this is related to two fundamental things: (a) axioms – and the problem in this case lies in the absence of historical axioms, and (b) the logical structure of research – which depends on the start because start involves a definition of the historical attitude irrespective of the latter's causes and philosophy.

- Thus the choice of an appropriate starting point is the choice of one's theoretical interpretation of history. For what makes one issue have priority over another in discussing the perspective of the gravity of logical structure in formulating the results? To my mind at least, it is the theoretical attitude itself towards interpretation of history. For example, to choose the principle of freedom differs from choosing the principle of determinism. It should be noted that the outcomes are ultimately related to choosing or rejecting one of these two principles.[2]
- The initial attitude is based on pre-judgement. In this case axioms will be assumed ones; this requires us to follow a pragmatic logic. But the method I adopt will simply conform with this approach. Otherwise, every hypothesis will turn into an axiom in order to discuss issues within its sphere in a general experiment that aims at the deduction of the scientific attitude towards interpretation of history. The difference here lies in the final structure and in the method itself: to transform axioms into hypothetical truisms for the sake of a general experiment primarily aims at the choice of an attitude or, rather, the choice of the logically probable starting point. And the chapter as a whole offers no more than an introductory methodology and attitude.
- It is not very important, therefore, whether we choose issues at random or according to a prearranged order so long as the situation ultimately resolves defining the limits of the issue and coming to a final conclusion.
- It follows from this that every issue defining the beginnings and discussing the issues of the other problem within its own limits will represent an advance in its outcomes and one of its methodological necessities. Without it research is a beginning without a beginning or, to put it more clearly, a beginning from the middle of the road.
- Let us, therefore, hope that this chapter, which starts from the necessary beginnings and chooses a probable stand in the problem, will be comprehensive.
- But, on the other hand, the chapter is defined by an applied limit, or, let us say, it lies within the boundaries of an example the reasons for the choice of which are not as important as its being a practical example; for its scientific problems are more serious and important than its theoretical problems.

- For it is limited by the earliest development of Saudi history and its progress over one hundred years. But, although this cannot make us dispense with research deprived of outside actual practice, it is still not less important, taking into account the difference between the social theory that requires future application for knowing validity and soundness on the one hand and the historical theory that finds application ready, on the other, because it is an integral part of the theory.
- The issue we choose in this part is the aim lying behind the interpretation and development of Saudi history as a constituent of discussing general historical theory.

We will not use qualitative or historical classification as a framework but objective classification only.

We shall see a difference between the general reader's and the academic researcher's interpretation of history. For to readers who contributed in different degrees to history-making, the aim is not more than learning lessons from and getting acquainted with the experiences of others. This is a naive or rather a simplistic attitude resulting from a non-technical understanding of the function and social value of knowledge. It goes without saying here that reading the annals of former peoples and nations, strange events, the vicissitudes of time and accounts of states, sovereigns and countries was, to ancient people from the time of the ancient kings of Persia until the age of the Arab thinker Ibn Khaldūn (732–808/1332–1406), regarded as a vehicle for examining social and cultural behaviour and political, administrative and military techniques. While this has been the view of the majority of kings, caliphs, princes, military commanders, men of letters and commoners in all ages, it was also the view of traditional scholastic historians. In Ibn Bishr's book such history is described as 'an honoured branch of learning with admonition, contemplation and acquaintance with events of time and conditions of bygone people, which awakens intellect and thought and enables sane people to compare themselves with those peers of theirs who preceded them in this world'.[3] Thus historiography to them is a direct means to present a cultural model for straightforward emulation. This is also the apparent viewpoint of Ibn Khaldūn when he says

'. . . So that the benefit of emulation from that is realized for those who aspire for it in spiritual as well as in temporal affairs.'[4]

Here we notice a simple, natural recognition or admission of the time-honoured attitude towards the interpretation of history, that is, history as governed by laws and norms and seen as a scientific phenomenon verified through repetition. But if the views of traditional scholars and readers in general were natural and naive, Ibn Khaldūn was the first outstanding theoretician and pioneer of this well-known historical attitude.

Many contemporaries had not gone further than this approach when Langlow and Seniobus described history as a tool for scientific culture,[5] which shows that the actions of history are deducible and theorizable, especially while they emphasize that history is an important complementary link in the chain for the completion of political and social sciences, comprehension of the underlying factors of the present and a cure of the fear of changes. History is a human experience that helps to complete these sciences which are still in the origination stage; because it is a study of the development of social phenomena in time. It also accustoms us to the diversity in these phenomena and helps us understand the present since it explains the roots of the present state of things.[6]

I, for one, consider this to be no more than rhetoric because it does not result from a systematic scientific attitude. The beginning of modern attitudes to explaining history, other than with Ibn Khaldūn, came from questioning the nature of historical events. Are historical events scientific phenomena or do they differ from scientific phenomena because of the recurrence of results? This attitude sees the recurrence and exact equivalence of objective conditions and circumstances as supporting the view that history and its events can be listed as theoretic laws and rules.

The other attitude, however, emphasizes human free will and consequently the possibility of difference of decision (and action) under similar objective circumstances and conditions – that is, the belief that the history of mankind is governed by human free will and free action, and not by laws.

In other words, the former (first) attitude explains history through determinism while the latter (second) attitude explains history through human beings' will and actions.

The aim of historians in writing history has varied in accordance with their attitude and choices in regard to these two principles.

Thus history in Ibn Khaldūn's opinion is the discovery of the nature of civilization and the dialectic of nomadic evolution and the civilizational pyramid. For Ibn Khaldūn believed in determinism according to his own interpretation. He says in his *Muqaddimah* (introduction) 'to measure the unseen thereof in accordance with the seen and judge the present according to the bygone'.[7]

The discovery of the natural qualities of civilization and the dialectic of the evolution of the state as viewed by Ibn Khaldūn provides the most striking example: advanced scientific technical terms are not used to relate the logical start, or the logical preliminary choice, on the one side to the attitude and the goal of historical research on the other.

This idea is formulated as follows: measurement of the unseen through the seen and the present in accordance with the bygone means absence of change because the conditions of analogy, if applied with correct methodology, imply congruity or exact equivalence, and with the presence of the exactly equivalent relation the difference disappears in the evaluation of the issue's consituents.

Conversely, the presence of difference in the constituent elements, and consequently in judgement, necessitates dissimilarity. This in turn means that a historical event is either identical or non-identical with other events of history belonging to the same time and theme.

Hence, to compare the events of history with one another means in the interpretation of history nothing but consistent results, which necessarily implies the inability to act and to change. This in turn negates man's ability, will and action.

The problem was discussed during the time of the Muslim philosophers as part of the issue of fate and divine decree and of predestination and free will, or innate tendency and choice, as the First Teacher Ibn Taymiyah put it. But here it is reduced by one degree that will come later by God's Will.

In our present research the choice of this principle of identicalness in historical events leads to many results:

1 Historical events are repeatable, i.e. can be recurrent.

2 Recurrence possibility necessitates identical results.

3 Identical results necessarily involve their predictability.

4 In this case is prediction the goal of history?

5 Does the goal of history involve prediction of what will happen, or, to put it more clearly, a knowledge of the future depending on the present which implies the identicalness of the data of a past historical context?

6 If it is right to forecast what will happen is it possible to plan it, or, rather, change it? Is history ahead of us more than it is behind us?

The various schools of thought concerned with the interpretation of history according to the validity of events aim at scientific goals that adopt degrees of predictive sequence.

This author is not concerned with analysis of all these schools of thought. A quick review of the books specialized in this field is sufficient to define the names, limits, horizons and proofs of these schools.

In all this, we should notice that the primary principle is the kind of historical issue. Ibn Khaldūn was not innovative at this level but one of its founders; his theoretical innovation lay in the delicate relations he established between the historical issues discovered by his inventive intellect.

Spengler agrees with Ibn Khaldūn in this type of thinking, and in this school of thought, the civilization cycles theory, the distinctive traits of civilizations, and the theory of destiny present a structure based on the first principle as summarized in the well-known attitude adopted towards the type of historical issue. According to Spengler, this principle takes him to the furthest extent to which scientific imagination can go. He did not acknowledge that principle in his serious solid statements for which he exchanged the trait methodology. But his theory is based on the attitude of this school of thought, which Carl Bauber called the historical school or historicism. At the height of his claims for the potential of history as a discipline, he says that its ability includes 'by-passing the present as a final end of knowledge and making an estimate in advance of the spiritual form, continuity, rhythm, meaning and outcome of the still incomplete stages of our western history and reconstruction of unknown stages that disappeared a long time ago, and even rebuilding complete civilizations of the past through morphological kinships'.[9]

Other theories occupy a lower level of prophetic sequence, adding a new element with unique principles although not independent in accordance with the conditions of the unity of human knowledge. This new element is that of religious interpretation, Toynbee's theories of challenge and response and the fate of modern civilization, and modern Islamic theories of historical interpretation, which are based on the discovery of divine norms in the universe.

The aim of historical meditation in these theories is to discover God's inventiveness in His creation and the establishment of man and future civilization for the attainment of human perfection and supreme humanity, or discovery of divine norms in the universe.

This is an aim for planning the future of mankind founded on the basis of former experience and as a result of the methodology of historical events.

This aim reflects a dream of scientists for the rationalization of human behaviour and for planning its phenomena and practices on higher bases selected in accordance with science and careful consideration. This requires the discussion of human history as characterized by lapse of time. But the leaders of this school do not find this characteristic effective and believe that there is no difference between temporal and non-temporal experience. Hence came the recurrence of this theory as something actually possible; and thus this school has produced the hackneyed dictum 'history repeats itself'.

Subsequent reflections within the framework of this school have added to historical events a claim for discovering great facts, one of which is the theory of evolution in both its selective and materialist dialectic forms. This theory has also been followed by another claim of discovery which is still more valuable, namely, the theory of change.

According to both these theories, history aims to discover how effective are the evolution forces or dynamism of human changes.

But the most important opposing principle in this question is that of human freedom and the negation of general necessities with all their interpretations and various degrees.

We will begin our explanation of this school of thought through showing its sequence within a theoretical context; for historical theories within the framework of this school vary according to their place in the theoretical sequence of the problem according to their school.

To start with, the historical question differs from the material (physical or natural) one, for understanding the relation between the human mind and the natural material phenomenon is a free understanding with regard to man and fixed from the materialistic side. No dialectic interaction between them can happen while the historical exposition differs from the one which is characterized by dialectic understanding between the historian and his historical topic.

To put it clearly, planning for the future of the matter cannot be abrogated by the matter itself, while planning for the future of man may very likely be abrogated by man. A plan for building a city is one of diminishing probability of failure, while the plan drawn for the organization of its society is one of an escalating possibility of failure. This is one point.

The other point is that the constituent elements of the material issue are possible and constant in terms of species, kind and determination, while the historical issue is always defective in terms of constituent elements and mostly dissimilar in this issue.

In this respect intervention of human will and awareness in diverting historical progress (development) constitutes a censure of the methodology of the historical case. Assuming, in this connection, that the law of history necessitated the disappearance of the Saudi state after the fall of Dirʿīyahh in Ibrahim Pasha's hands – with what that reflects in terms of triumph and the ascendancy of one party and the destruction, break-up and cultural decline of the other party – why did the Saudi state come to exist again? And assuming that the rule of history dictates that the Saudi state disappears after the departure of ʿAbd al-Rahman ibn Saʿūd from Riyadh and its capture by al-Rashid who controlled affairs and gained influence, what were the factors underlying ʿAbd al-Aziz ibn ʿAbd al-Rahman's return to Riyadh and his establishment of the modern Saudi state?

In this case, we cannot but state a remark to the effect that the rule of history is defective and the historical case is logically unsound, for we cannot say that the historical rule is truthful in all cases.

The problem may be put forward thus. The historical context is not rationally governed by, nor is it subjected to, necessity, because a historical event is a human action and human action is characterized by flexible probability. It may take place and it may not; because it can exist or happen but, owing to human will, human action is neither an obligation nor a necessity. Thus when what happened has happened it is not necessary that what is expected to happen will actually take place, because it is subjected to what is willed and not to what will necessarily take place and one may or may not want what will happen. One may want something else. The necessity existing between will and action or incidence is an inconstant perfection except in the case of God as is stated in the following Qur᾽anic verses: (because God does what He wants), (Your Lord does certainly do what He wants), (He is the Owner of the Throne, the Glorious One, Who does what He wishes), (Verily Allah enjoins what He wishes), (If He wishes a thing, He only says to it 'Be!' and it shall be).

Then the separation of human action from human will, and consequently of the human event from those who cause it, means a decline in the probability of the historical event, and constitutes an abrogation of the historical context.

This discovery requires that the aim of history is not to know the future but to monitor or observe human freedom during the period of time which precedes the moment of observation.

Accordingly, history is not a necessary explanation of the past as much as it is knowledge of it, and knowledge does not come about of the necessity alone.

What concerns me in this research is to explain the views of two thinkers who can be classified as proponents of the freedom of a historical event. They will enable me to dispense with investigation because my methodology in this research is not based on review.

The first view was recorded by the British thinker Collingwood in his *The Idea of History*. We will extract from this work only what is related to the aim of the historian. We will return to this in the coming sections because it is full of reflections and meditations.

Collingwood established his theory on a unique foundation, although it was not a new theory at all. Most of his discussion related to the nature of history as a history of thought, and consequently his methodology was based on knowing human history through knowing human thought.

To him, the aim of history is to make a man try to know himself; and it is only our discovery of history that has made us realize that human activities emanate from free will. Thus Collingwood is one of those who assert that the activity displayed by man's attempt to erect the monument of his ever active historical world is an activity that results from human free will. Meanwhile, within the limits of his specialization as a historian man aims at the discovery of human free will as a (force) that plays its role in historical events.

A reading of Collingwood's book suggests to this author that his rich intellectual gifts were suffering from sterility. For this reason his theory of attitude summarizes the relation between human free will as an effective force in historical events on the one side, and necessity on the other. But what he says has been mere prose rhetoric in this respect. Be that as it may, the peak of his activity lay at the beginning of the theory and perhaps his attention was mainly centred on the path of historical insight and the type of the historical event.[10]

The other thinker with technical dimensions is the novelist Leo Tolstoy, whose ideas on history are expounded in his masterpiece, *War and Peace*.

In our analysis of Tolstoy's structure, let us begin with a question he asked:

How should we start our looking at the past life of peoples and humanity at large? Is it an outcome of people's free or fettered activity? Because history generally aims at studying the movement of humanity and peoples.

1. Tolstoy's proofs, however, are not convincing to us, because when he wanted to summarize his idea in methodical phrases he could not free himself from technical restrictions, but he explained the evidence supporting his idea in the remainder of the four parts of his novel in a more profound and original way. His viewpoint, in brief, is:

2. History studies the demonstrations of human freedom.
3. History studies the movements of peoples.
4. We will never end up with a complete freedom or an unqualified necessity.
5. History deals with the demonstrations of human freedom in its relations with the outside world, with time and with the freedom's dependent status in terms of causality. In other words, he defines freedom in accordance with the laws of reason.

This is the historian's aim, and Tolstoy explains the historian's programme at the core of his novel. But, surprisingly enough, he says in another passage: 'In history also we call what is known to us the laws of necessity and we term what is undesirable as freedom. Freedom with regard to history is but an expression of the remaining unknown effect of the norms of human life which are known to us.'[11]

In the following passage, he puts his viewpoint in a nutshell: 'If it [history] aims at studying the movements of peoples and not describing certain specific sections of animals, it should exclude the concept of causes in order to search for the rules which are common to all the infinitesimal, but equal and inseparably coherent and undissolvable constituents of freedom.'[12] This has been the foundation on which he constructed the events of his novel and according to which he formulated its events.

What has been said above has analysed the case in its abstract form divided into two approaches. By this means it can be said that the issue of the aim of history has been deductively presented through these two thinkers or presented as a whole but according to their two schools of thought.

Historical thinkers, on their part, constructed various theories in complex structures with the methodologies chosen by them, varying with the degree of their intellectual stamina. But, according to this, we cannot take a stand vis-à-vis this issue by means of a unilateral abstractionist analysis.

Let us take the first steps of discovering the special attitude towards the question by a very brief critique of the two approaches mentioned above. In this context it should be said that many of the thinkers' approaches in this case are not concentrated purely on one of these two sides nor do they reject the addition of a part of the other side to construct thereby their own theories. In fact, many schools of thought embody in the essence of their theories a strong consideration of the opposite theory, whether this consideration is a mere intrusion or a genuine component. Indeed, most of these schools are forced to adopt and add this consideration in building up their theories in an excusatory, fabricated and apologetic form.

The most illustrative example of that is the historical materialism which faced the freedom predicament and most spuriously and belatedly added it to its own theory.[13]

In this part of the research I will leave aside the criticism of the roots of the theory because it is devoted to the discussion of the aim of history and the task of this field of human learning. Criticism in this section, therefore, will be confined to the aim and through assumptions.

The first group of the schools of thought aiming at the discovery of the laws, trends or fate of history is based on projection. They start with general statements similar to prejudgments in certainty, and may start in the form of an implicit conviction followed by a selective induction of historical phenomena within the framework of this conviction. The outcome of the search will inevitably be an adjustment to this conviction, and an enforcement of its details to comply with this certainty; in which case the task of history will be the discovery of those laws that are presupposed to be an established and complete certainty and to project them on to each and every case, period and history whether particularized or total and comprehensive.

Here I will deal with two examples only. For we have already said that the limits of this chapter stop at the roots of the schools of thought without proceeding to investigate forms and structures.

In the first example conflict will be a historical image of the principle of contradiction that constitutes the logical foundation of the theory. In this case materialist interpretation becomes the sum total of the historical elements of the philosophical solution of the problem of development based on the projection of material incidence on the historical human development.

According to the leader of the school, philosophers have differed on the explanation of the world and, importantly in his eyes, the change that comes from this. The traditional objection to this school is that the explanation of the world necessarily entails no change in it. Thus if the dictum of materialist interpretation of history is correct in any sense of the word, this means impossibility of change because change per se has abrogated the validity of the theory.

To put it more clearly: historical contradiction, assuming its validity, has necessitated that any change would be futile because it would lead to the historical contradiction itself, and thereby cease to be a change. If a true change has taken place, on the other hand, this would put an end to the statement of historical contradiction or conflict, and consequently implies its invalidity.

What is strange here is that Spengler, who belongs to the group that advocates the logical origin of this school, says in his traditional objection to it, 'Because lights were focused on this pragmatic theory in history and on the mental structure thereof, Jean-Jacques Rousseau and Karl Marx were able to convince themselves that they could change the course of the world by means of a theory.'[14]

In the following parts of this study I will prove that change is quite different from explanation in principle as well as in nature. Here I also suggest two comments about this school and traditional assumptions about it, including Spengler's objection. Both the comments will be embodied in the questions that follow.

What would happen if the proponents of this school abandoned the idea of change and contented themselves with their dictum about interpretation of history? Who and what would prove its validity or falsity?

But the correct form of this objection lies in the advocates of this school assuming the validity of two separate questions, the question of the philosophical interpretation of history in the form of, let us say, a category and the question of change, while the validity of either necessarily negates the other.

Thus history will be changing according to a law that denies the ability to change it, while the possibility of changing this conscious world negates, in turn, the existence of a law that controls it.[15]

Within the framework of the set historical categories this school of thought assumes that knowledge of the future is possible, while knowledge of the future is radically limited. According to their school, the future is restricted to the concept of materialist conflict. Therefore, I will put forward an interesting dialectical objection far removed from traditional ones. This objection has been made by Carl Bauber, the opposing British thinker.

This opposition is based on two foundations: first, the provision of a convincing proof of the development of human knowledge (which is not denied but claimed by the proponents of materialism and let us assume here that it is a fact in human existence). Secondly, the interpretation of history as a statement or category and consequently, cognizance of the future. There is also a third level to Bauber's opposition (which he deferred explanation of in his book), namely: 1. human history is affected by the development of human knowledge; 2. and since human knowledge is developing, history itself has been developing too; 3. it is impossible to predict the form which human knowledge will assume. (As Bauber explains, the prediction of its development requires that it should take place in its own time; or, to explain it through the concept of contrariety, if prediction of human knowledge were possible, it would be necessary for it to exist, which means that it does not exist in the future); 4. this means that it is impossible to know future history, Bauber's objection.[16] This counter-argument means that history as a category has to be established in the past as well as in the future. It follows that if it ceases to be valid in the future, it is not fit to be a comprehensive category, for history is not a law.

In this regard Bauber's opposition is still within the framework of a combination of the questions of interpretation and change of history with a radical difference in the second question, that is, replacing change through outside force by spontaneous or automatic change.

This second type of similar historical thinking is a theory that still maintains its lustre and attraction among Westerners. It was not for sheer wittiness that Churchill made it a title for his memoirs; for this theory was meant to be a counterpoise to historical materialism with all its comprehensiveness and encyclopaedic treatment of the subject and perfecting the semantics of discourse. It is the theory that was expounded by Toynbee in twelve volumes of his *Study of History*.

Regardless of some western observers' comments that Toynbee's *Study of History* is an encyclopaedia of historical information rather than a study, it is clear that this amount of knowledge, which is as wide as Spengler's *Decline of the West*, has been coordinated within the framework of a general theory.

Toynbee starts the journey of his theoretical structure with an eternal truth when he says: 'In brief, one cannot be destined to being labelled as historian without being motivated by curiosity.'[17] This avidity for learning motivated by major social changes – such as disasters, for example – entails that the historian has one angle of vision among other innumerable ones. This angle, as viewed by Toynbee, requires that the historian should offer us an image of God's creativity in His creation.

From this literary point of departure Toynbee began, having been aroused by the great social catastrophes and particularly the disastrous predicament in western civilization with its failure, even though – according to his assumption – it is the cream of human experience, to attain the terrestrial paradise.

Following this line, let us assume that Toynbee embarked on his task without any preconceived ideas about the general points of the following historical research. Let us also suppose that the indications of his long historical research constituted his own theory about history (generalizations).

Yet the questions that were raised and are still being raised in the course of historical research still remain unanswered by Toynbee despite his twelve volumes.

Assuming that he started and continued his research influenced by the presence of attitudinal precedents, his final theory will still remain not more than a special stand taken with a limited vision. Meanwhile, his interpretations of events and recorded history will be mere projection.

Relying on the second assumption, one can say that Toynbee had to perfectly forge his philosophical attitude (general theory) after having solved the problem of freedom and necessity; otherwise this general theory per se will be a directly treated solution of the problem of freedom and necessity.

This is because the problem of freedom and necessity is a starting point and a 'given' for every reasonable and probable end. Toynbee, however, does not solve this problem but offers us an interesting romantic escape through his claim that the law of nature conforms with freedom which, in his opinion, is the law of divine will. This conformity lies in the law of divine love. [18]

Thereby Toynbee would bypass the problem of individual and general or both the atomic and the generalization principles as described by Max Weber. [19]

This in turn leads to the question of how Toynbee distributes past human events according to the rules of his theory, especially while he emphasizes that history does not repeat itself; even if research in history were true, it would be done through the higher facts. Moreover, while human societies are the possible scope for that research, classification of historical events and data is done by structuring them through selection. Consequently, his study is but an empty emphasis of a previous theory, as Bauber puts it.[20]

The following objections to this question may be cited:

Let us leave aside the queerness of the imaginary sources of the challenge – and – response theory and let us treat it as if it were a hypothesis and take it as a sample of the rest of his huge theoretical structure, challenge, which entails hard conditions, rouses a response which is a psychological reaction (its source comes from above and is related to divine will). This factor is an explanation of the beginnings of civilizations through the transfer of societies from a state of stillness to a state of motion, while this interaction is followed by formidable generalities in the movement towards civilization.

The first objection to this basic assumption is that response as explained by Toynbee himself is multifarious. But is this response optional or is it necessary? If this response is automatic, then where is the position of choice in his theory? And if response is optional, but to various conditions, or varying precursors, future and actual interactive types, Toynbee should have defined how each of these conditions takes place. For the three states are choices (probabilities of freedom) that can be independent and isolated but they are (necessary likelihoods) within the general context of his theory.

The second objection, which is an extension of the first, is that Toynbee did not intend to elucidate the aim of the historian in a logical and orderly manner. It seems that he, like Spengler in using the trait direction and methodology, has mixed history with science and fictitious authored works by resorting to an interesting device, i.e. to ignore scientific facts for a short period.[21] But this oversight cannot be utilized without disregarding the basic problem of historical knowledge and sinking into the predicament of verbal effect on the logic of ideas. In this regard, when we fail to establish consistent relationships between various issues, we can interpret and explain it away by saying that the rest of what we have not proved is a specious type of fictional writing.

But for that, Toynbee would have been forced to show clearly the place of his general theory vis-à-vis the basic problems of knowledge – and, in particular, knowledge in the human field (a field characterized by following the trend about which the advocates of this view are almost unanimous).

To make this clearer it should be said that disregard of the lower facts of research and attempts to generalize verbal abstractions such as challenge and response or dialectic conflict among its proponents are but a theoretical fallacy still lacking the certain rational tie 'to the extent that humans can talk about certainty',[22] which links knowledge as a certainty (scientific laws – logical generalities) with matter or incidence as a reality that lies outside the mind and acts as a field for its consideration.

But once again I go back to the basic objection that recurs in this chapter, that is, the discussion method within the framework of the revelation of general laws. The problem is like this:

1.1 Assuming a solution for the problem of the quality of the historical case, that can recur and that it is a material incidence,

1.2 The outcome of discussing one event would lead to the general theory itself in any other event, and consequently any other discussion of another event would not be more than simply an add-on.

1.21 According to the rule of probability, types of judgement acquire a high ratio of probability, near the ratio of the certainty of each judgement in each category.

1.22 This means that incidence is identical in its several occurrences.

1.3 The contradiction of this finding comes from various sources

1.31 through theoretical contradiction which is discussed in the following parts of the article. The clearest part thereof is the question of transgression and the question of causality or relation between action and reaction, or, as the ancients put it, the relation between the effect and the influencing factor;

1.32 through the reality of development in knowledge which is the following part of this chapter;

1.33 through application, that is, according to the rule which says that application is the condition which proves the validity of the theory.

It is this contradiction which shows that Toynbee has been able to claim that he has discovered his broad theory by using a literary method of overlooking scientific facts – for a short period of time – and entrusting fictitious written works with filling the gaps of generalization and ignoring what has really happened throughout the long history of time if it is not consistent with his theory of actual incidence. This oversight is based on the claim that it comes within the period of the outweighed probability. This made him add marginal enlargements to the structure of his theory, such as the stakes of Faust, as an explanation for moving from the stage of stillness to the stage of motion.

The basic problem of these two models is that they regard the results which the historian arrives at – in terms of objective and the job of discussion – as general and all-embracing, and that every future incidence lies within the framework of these results and should be formed according to their necessity. To put it more clearly, the task of the historian moves from revealing what has happened to the revelation of what will happen. This is what has been cited by most of the pioneers of this school of thought; for to them the aim of history is to know the future. It is a knowledge that comes next to knowing the past because to these pioneers the space between the two is quite void. In addition, it is impossible in terms of logic, which is what Laplace meant when he said: 'Had there been a mind that can observe the site and speed of each atom and solve all mathematical equations, the future would have been, like the past, present to this superhuman intellect, and it would have been able to define in the minutest details all events whether they took place thousands of years after us or ahead of us. This physical determinism is the most important result of Newton's Physics.'[23]

Now let us move to the second approach:

First of all, to regard human freedom to be 'an absolute beginning'[24] implies a contradiction because it is a role.

1.1 To regard freedom to be an absolute beginning means that it is an absolute generalization.

1.11 It will be the same if freedom is alive (in the future) or dead (in the past).

1.2 But freedom requires the negation of absolute generalization (categories – laws).

1.3 Therefore, freedom cannot be an absolute beginning.

Within the framework of examples, for man to look absolutely at himself as a master of his own self means that this is the general law (for the past and in the future) in human history (human life) and the mere application of general law or comprehensive dictum or category abrogates the basic objective, freedom.

Thus the assumption that man can do what he wants in the past and in the future requires that there should be no limits for his will and action and that he wills and acts, which makes history happen. As long as man is characterized by this quality, any beginning that is not free is null, void and impossible because it contradicts the basic principle.

Let us assume that a person wanted to realize his will in an affair which we do not care to describe: this necessitates free will, freedom of action and then freedom of occurrence. Here two situations crop up: either each of the three steps is necessarily successive to the other, which is consistent with the basic objective; or the necessary succession is rejected by the material fact because human will, human action and human event are successive within the framework of the principle or liberty in the sense that if one of them actually happens it is not inevitable that the next one takes place.

For example, if a certain leader or head of state wanted to destroy a state other than his own, the rule of absolute liberty says that this leader willed to do the evils he had intended to do and then carried out the evils he willed. The necessary sequel is that what he had carried out did actually take place and the state was destroyed. But is it not likely that he would fail to carry out what he wills? And if he did carry it out, is it not possible that destruction will not actually take place?

Absolute liberty may be abrogated by another means, i.e. differentiation between the one single existence (unity) and the multiple existence (multiplicity). Thus the assumption of absolute freedom requires that existence is one, and humanity be one single person. Otherwise, where is absolute liberty if humanity were two human beings?

And since existence is actually multiple units, freedom means numerous liberties, while the multiplicity thereof necessarily means absence of absoluteness, because each freedom is limited by the borders of the other freedoms. In other words, its presence in one field, which is human community, creates meeting points for this multitude which are border points, while limitation or definition negates absoluteness.

In this case the task of the historian cannot be to uncover absolute freedom in human history, for absolute freedom is theoretically defective; therefore, the historian cannot discover it because it is in fact non-existent.

This is the beginning. So if the question was placed within the assumption that human liberty is the ability to do and the ability to cause – Raymond said that 'the quality of historical judgements is possibility' – the task of the historian cannot possibly be complete.

For human possibility is based on the three constituent elements, the first of which does not enable us to dispense with the next. These constituents are consciousness, attention, determination or will – in brief, intellectual presence with its various conditions; then action (application); and realization among other events.

Necessity among these three elements is an inverse presence. For the existence of action requires the presence of will and attention (intellectually existent) and its incidence requires doing it (its application). But necessity in its normal course is void theoretically as well as materially. Thus the existence of will does not necessitate the existence of action; both of them do not necessitate incidence.

This is an obvious gap in this state of assumption (knowing freedom as a possibility).

Next, to go back to the beginning, the task of the historian cannot possibly be to have a complete knowledge of potential freedom, because if he could get a highly probable knowledge in an inverse direction of the elements of this possibility, this would be a diminishing probability. The likelihood of knowing events may be high but knowing human actions in itself is less correct, while knowing the intention itself (the will) is almost impossible because it has low probabilities.

1. This has a theoretical proof which is also a new start, and means briefly that knowing freedom before its incidence contradicts the principle of freedom even if it lay within the framework of the concept of possibility. This can be expressed in two ways.
2. First, to know freedom before its incidence means that is an absolutely limited freedom if knowledge were complete and confirmed (inevitable); but if it were not it would be mere guess and conjecture; so complete and confirmed (inevitable) knowledge is a negation of freedom. To be an absolutely limited freedom means, according to correct definition, that its incidence is inevitable; otherwise how can I completely know what actions you will do if that still remains within the confines of your intellect and has not turned into an actually physical incidence?
3. Secondly, free will means that it is impossible to know future actions now and they can be known only if the process is an internal necessity while myth lies only in the belief that causal (internal) link exists.[25]

Therefore, and within the limits of these questions, the historian's task does not lie in monitoring the movement of human freedom, whether it be absolute or conceived as possible, because the knowledge of freedom is theoretically impossible as detailed above. It is also impossible subjectively from inside the issue as it consists of three elements.

'This eternal silence of these infinite spaces certainly terrifies me.' This is what Pascal said,[26] while more awe-inspiring than that is to offer answers and explanations for eternal silence (history).

But I must offer answers because love of knowledge is always overwhelming 'for if it is not possible to tell anything about the most dangerous questions which preoccupy humanity, it will not be worth one hour of the trouble we take'.[27] It is of course futile for anyone to claim that his answer will be definitive and conclusive and that it will put an end to all talk, because talk will never end.

But one has to stop somewhere, and there is no controversy about that; for a beginner has to come to an end. In any case, the issue is not settled. But it should be discussed from various perspectives because outlines of an answer may eventually be formed.

O time: Look at this peace.
You have seen the beginning,
So have a look at the end.[28]

Notes:

1. John Dewey, *Essays in Experimental Logic*, Mineola, NY, 1970, p. 752.
2. I cite a text by Carl Bauber in his book *Open Society and Its Enemies*, London, 1973, which says: 'In fact any theory or hypothesis can be described as a crystallization of the Point of View', part II, p. 260. 'And to this extent the situation in history is identical with that in natural sciences – such as Physics. But if we compare the visible part in the historical point of view with the one visible in the physics point of view, we will notice a big difference. For in Physics – as we see – the point of view is usually obtained by a theory which can be chosen through research and search for new facts. In history, on the other hand, the matter is not so simple.' Part II, page 261.
3. Ibn Khaldūn, ed. Eve Lecouste, p. 219, Beirut 1974.
4. Ibn Bishr, *Title of Glory* [unwan al-majd], part II, p. 6, Riyadh.
5. Ibn Khaldūn, *Muqaddimah*, part I, p. 216, ed. Ali Wafi, 1384/1964.

6. Langlow and Seniobus, *Historical Criticism*, trans. Badawi, pp. 250–1.
7. Ibn Khaldūn, *Muqaddimah*, part II, p. 263. It is impossible to judge Ibn Khaldūn so simplistically for elsewhere he makes an astonishing statement: 'One of the occult errors in history is to be distracted from the changing conditions of nations and generations by the change of time. It is a very serious and mysterious disease; for it only occurs after a lengthy period and perhaps only individuals in our world are aware of it; because conditions, customs, and creeds of the world at large and those of nations do not stay as they are. Things do change throughout time, *Muqaddimah*, part I, p. 399.
8. Muḥammad al-Talibi, 'al-Tarikh wa Mushkilat al-Yawm wa al-Ghad' (History and the problems of today and tomorrow), *Majallat A'alam al-Fikr*, vol. V, No 1, p. 42.
9. *The Decline of Western Civilization*, part I, p. 227.
10. For this, see specifically chapters 6 and 7, part II, of the *Idea of History*, by Collingwood, Egypt 1968.
11. *War and Peace*, part IV, p. 548 (Syria: Dar alyaqadah).
12. *Ibid.*, part IV, p. 551.
13. Zakariya Ibrahim, *The Problem of Freedom* (mushkilat al-hurriyyah) p. 79.
14. *The Decline of Western Civilization*, part I, p. 277.
15. I present here a play on words (paronomasia) in the Arabic words 'taghayyur' i.e. a change from inside, and 'taghyir', change owing to an outside agent or force.
16. Carl Bauber, *Futility of Historicism* (uqm al-madhab al-tarikhi), trans. Dr Sabrah, Egypt, 1959.
17. Toynbee, *A Short Study of History*, part IV, p. 235.
18. *Ibid.*, part IV, p. 141. The English origin may have been more successful in formulation. But here I rely on the abbreviated translation. Al-Aqqad took exception to the translation.
19. Julian Fronde, Max Weber's *Sociology*, London 1972, p. 38.
20. *Open Society and Its Enemies*, part II, p. 260.
21. *A Short Study of History*, part I, p. 101.
22. Heinz Reichenbach, *The Rise of Scientific Philosophy, Cairo*, p. 153.
23. *Ibid.*, p. 101.
24. William James, *Philosophical Problems*, p. 54, quoted from Renoviyyeh.
25. This entire paragraph is copied from Ludwig Wittgenstein's *Logical Philosophical Treatise*, Cairo, 1968, p. 112.
26. Copied from Kasirer, 'A Treatise on Man', Beirut, p. 49.

27. Bergson, from Zakariyya Ibrahim, *Contemporary Philosophy* (al-falsafah al-Mu'asirah), p. 306.
28. Muḥammad Iqbal, *Poetry Book on Secrets and Symbols* (diwan al-asrar wa al-rumūz), translated by ʿAbd al-Wahhab Azzam, p. 154.

Chapter 11

SUCCESS OF KING ABDUL AZIZ IN UNIFYING THE COUNTRY

ʿAbd Allāh al-Ṣāliḥ al-ʿUthaymīn

The course followed by King Abdul Aziz to unify the country proved neither short nor easy. On the contrary, it was a task that took about a quarter of a century of continuous struggle. Initially, his material means were weak. Some writers, who were not familiar with the history of the country, were led to say that the king started from a void. In fact, his first steps were founded and guided by more than a century and a half of leadership, that had been based on a clear Islamic programme, aiming at the unification of the country into a state that propagates and protects its faith, applies and defends the Sharīʿa (Islamic law) and thus promotes security and peace.

While that programme remained basically unchanged throughout Saudi rule, the success in achieving its objectives differed at various times, in accordance with the abilities of the rulers and current circumstances. Under the first Saudi rulers the state included most areas of the Arabian peninsula, spread the Islamic monotheistic faith, especially among city-dwellers, and succeeded in applying the Sharīʿa in various fields of life. According to the works of Ibn Bishr and other historians, security and peace prevailed in the country at this time in an unprecedented manner.

The leaders of the second Saudi state, especially Imām Turki ibn Abdullah and his son Fayṣal ibn Turki, aimed to further the objectives set out by the leaders of the first Saudi state, but the circumstances they faced prevented them from achieving the same degree of power as their predecessors. It is not our concern here, however, to discuss the power and weakness of these states.

When King Abdul Aziz embarked on his mission, his thoughts focused on the state of his predecessors who unified the country, propagated the faith and applied Sharīʿa for the preservation of peace and security. This was his aim, which he never failed to proclaim. The factors behind his success in achieving his goals come under two headings: his leadership, and the circumstances surrounding his course of action.

1. *Leadership*

Of the many attributes that strengthened his leadership were:

a. *Religious Commitment*
In his personal conduct the king was meticulous about religious rites and duties. He also proclaimed Islam as a personal commitment. Religious devotion can undoubtedly be a source of power that lends the individual certain qualities, such as faith in God, that help him to face danger and persevere in hard times. The king's religious devotion had a profound effect in attracting people in the area where he started his rule. The people in the Najdi townships felt a special respect for religion. The religious direction adopted by the two earlier Saudi states was still alive in their memory. An outstanding proof of that love and respect is seen in the poetry of that time: poems celebrating the faith and its defenders.

b. *Generosity*
King Abdul Aziz was generous without ostentation. He very much enjoyed receiving guests and giving gifts. He was never known to have liked saving money or indulging in trade. While the love and respect of a generous person is common to the nature of human beings, a generous person has a special standing among the Arabs, in particular. Traditionally, the Arabs celebrate chivalry, but their celebration of generosity is no less typical, perhaps it is even more common. There is no doubt that the

generosity of King Abdul Aziz was a strong factor in his gaining the admiration and support of the people.

c. *Courage*

The king's courage was balanced and thoughtful, not rash or reckless. He never hesitated to fight battles, as his many wounds attest. But he took to warfare only when he thought it was necessary and useful. His courage won him the admiration of the people while still a young man, at the battle of Riyadh, then of Dalam, for example. When he came to Qasseem in early 1322/1904, he was accompanied by some Najdis, mainly from Arid and the chieftains of Qasseem, who were refugees in Kuwait. The king was then in his thirties. The poet Ibraheem al-Qadi celebrated the occasion in a fine poem in vernacular Arabic.

The king realized, from the beginning of his rule, that he should plan not for the immediate future but for the long term. Therefore he did his best to avoid war. He always preferred to win supporters without war, rather than fight and defeat his opponents. This was not only because he wanted to save the lives of his supporters, but also because he wanted to save the lives of those who, for special reasons, joined his rivals.

One reason for this was that he aimed to win those rivals to his side, sooner or later, as he had previously done with others – and all would form his future nation. This is why he trusted those nearest to his rivals who, after victory, would form his special guards. A third reason was that he did not find it below him to admit that his rivals too were chivalrous. Abdul Aziz ibn Rushaid, a famous knight from Najd, set out alone from his Shinana camp and reclaimed his flock of sheep ransacked by about twenty knights from the king's army. The king did not belittle Ibn Rushaid's knighthood, but praised his courage and success.

d. *Personality*

King Abdul Aziz had a distinguished personality. He was tall, with a smiling face and brilliant eyes full of resolve, and a strong and confident voice. In addition to that he had a friendly disposition, yet was able to scrutinize people before him. He was intelligent, clear thinking, and could make convincing arguments. This was admitted not only by local people, but also by many foreign leaders. Among those was the Dutch consul in Jeddah who said, 'He looks royal all around, and demandingly attractive.' The British representative in the Gulf said, 'The King has many aspects of greatness. He is strong, fearless, and clear in thinking, and he knows what is good for him.' US President Roosevelt said, 'Of the Arab problem, the Islamic problem, and the Jewish problem, I learned from Ibn Saʿūd in five minutes much more than what I learned from the exchange of dozens of letters.' His impression was that, 'He was an excellent example of a fighter-king.'

Undoubtedly, those qualities impressed others and won them to his side.

e. *Competent Administration*

The king's wars with his rivals were not all victories. Although he won many battles, he also suffered various setbacks. But he knew how to deal both with victory and defeat. Victory did not make him arrogant: he would not put the conquered to the sword and frighten the survivors and their relatives beyond redemption. Defeat did not make him despair, nor undermine his morale or will. Often, he crowned his military success by offering pardons, so he could win to his side those who were against him. From defeat he made sure he learnt the appropriate lessons, enabling him to improve his future plans. His strong will kept him steadily working towards his aim, unless he found out a better course, when his flexibility of approach would allow him to follow the better plan.

f. *Consultation*

The king's willingness to consult others in various affairs was another of his strengths. This quality brought people closer to the king and deepened their trust in him. It also made the consultants feel their own importance in pushing the wheel of progress.

He consulted experts in various fields, as individuals or groups. Then he would consider their opinions and decide on what he considered most suitable. He used to accept advice, if he found it sound, even when he did not ask for it. For instance, he accepted the opinion of Muḥammad ibn Hindi, the Barqa chief, to move to Bkairiyya to prevent Abdul Aziz ibn Rushaid from capturing the township. He also listened to his advice to try to conclude a truce with that prince when he approached Shinana.

g. *Secret Movement and Camouflage Tactics*

These two tactics were employed inside and outside the Arabian peninsula, past and present. Imām Saʿūd ibn Abdul Aziz was known to have favoured these activities, but King Abdul Aziz excelled in them. He would often conduct a raid northwards, for instance, and give the impression that he was targeting a town or a tribe in that area. Soon he would change his direction and pounce on a town or a tribe in the opposite direction. That would give him the benefit of surprise and win him a quick victory. Another ploy was to prepare a large army and give the impression that he intended to confront a strong rival. But, instead, he would surprise a weak rival and achieve a resounding victory that would shock a powerful rival. Alternatively, he would prepare a small army to give the impression that he was attacking a weak rival, but he would then take by surprise a strong rival and achieve success.

In addition to the secrecy of movement and camouflage tactics, the king was very wary of his rivals. His wariness took two forms: one was vigilance against rival movements; another was being constantly on the alert for any possible attack. As soon as he entered Riyadh, he started to build walls around the town to guard against an attack by Ibn Rushaid or others. Again, he did not start attacking the areas north of Riyadh, once he established himself there, before securing his back. So he moved southwards, to areas relatively far from Shammar Mount, the centre of Rushaid power.

h. *Knowledge of History*

King Abdul Aziz was interested in the lessons that could be learned from history. He was mainly concerned with the history of his nation and homeland, in order to see what was behind the success or failure of his predecessors in the Saʿūd family. He realized that the secret behind their success in establishing security and peace was their support for their faith.

Hence his allegiance to that faith and his resolve to apply the Sharīʿa.

He also realized that the backbone of his predecessors' military power was formed by the city-dwellers, since the nomadic tribes that had supported the Saudis in times of victory were soon to change allegiance when signs of weakness were discerned. He also realized that the former Saudi leaders did not pay enough attention to the nomadic Bedouins. It is true that they sometimes sent preachers to those nomads to educate them in religious matters, but their efforts were not constant enough. In his first ten years of experience, the king became convinced more and more that the nomads could not be stopped from what they had been doing for years, namely raids and attacks on caravans, and that they were not as reliable as city-dwellers. So he adopted a pioneering project: to settle the Bedouins in certain areas and inject them with the religious spirit. And to a large degree he was successful in putting an end to their mutual aggression, turning them into military units that fought for his own objectives. The efforts of these new powers between 1335 and 1344/1916 and 1925 to unite the country proved his plan was sound.

The king was aware, from his knowledge of history, that military victory alone was not enough to achieve firm political success. More vital in this respect was to know the power of one's rivals, to weigh up the various circumstances, and deal with every rival and situation in a manner that suits it best. He found out that some of his predecessors went too far in punishing their local rivals and in challenging others, and that such policy was partly behind the temporary failure of Saudi rule. Hence, he adopted a policy of leniency towards local rivals. His policy towards Britain, the major power surrounding him at the time, was friendly, especially when that did not interfere with his plans for the unification and independence of the country in the long run.

i. *Choice of Men*

King Abdul Aziz carefully chose the men who worked with him. It cannot be said that they were all equal to the responsibility they were charged with, but most of them were, given the prevailing circumstances.

Among the men who worked with the king were natives, in addition to men who came from other countries to escape the oppression of colonial powers. Some of the king's men proved resourceful in times of crises, like his finance minister Abdullah ibn Sulaiman. Before the battle of Sabla, the king was badly in need of money to pay his followers, especially the new city-dwellers. He asked his minister for whatever money he had, but there was not enough to answer the immediate need. So, the minister bought all the goods brought by Qasseem merchants to Makkah at 40 per cent profit, provided that the payment be made six months later. Then he redirected the goods to the local markets and sold everything immediately at a much lower price than what he had promised to pay, because he needed that money immediately. In two days, the money was on its way to the king, who resolved a problem that otherwise could not have been solved.

Another example of resourcefulness was provided when the king was about to conduct a raid. He was in Braida and did not have enough money. He had already borrowed a great deal from the merchants of the area, and could not ask for more. He was worried about the situation, but Shalhoub assured him that things would be all right.

An hour later, Shalhoub went to al-Rabadi, a wealthy merchant in Braida, with a few heavy sacks. He said to the merchant that Abdul Aziz was intent upon a raid, the result of which no one but God knew. Shalhoub told al-Rabadi that he wanted to leave sacks of money with him in trust, and that there was a note with the name of each owner inside the sacks. Shalhoub explained that, if God brought him safely back from the raid, he would reclaim the money and return to each owner his due; otherwise the al-Rabadi was to open the sacks and return the money to the proper owners. Al-Rabadi did not suspect Shalhoub. A day later, Shalhoub said to the credulous merchant that the king needed 2,000 Rials, but did not like to break the seals of the sacks. The merchant said he was willing to lend funds, now that he had the sacks of money as a trust. The money loaned solved the problem of providing for the raid, which turned out to be successful, and booty helped to pay back the money to al-Rabadi.

The merchant asked Shalhoub to take back the so-called money sacks. Shalhoub answered with a grateful smile: 'Keep it. It is all yours!' The sacks turned out to be full of horse and camel gear with some tent-wedges, wrapped up inside in such a way that they could not be discerned by touch, giving the impression that the borrower was financially reliable. Thus a cunning trick by a man loyal to Abdul Aziz saved a critical situation.

j. *Knowledge of His People*

The king's knowledge of his people, in town and desert, attracted the attention of many authors and chroniclers. He knew all the chieftains and the bases of their election as chiefs. He knew, also, the eminent city families as well as the branches of the various tribes. That knowledge earned him the admiration of all. It also earned him skill in dealing with individuals and groups in the manner most suitable. He was aware of the fact that his people did not like there to be a barrier between them and the ruler. Therefore, he kept his doors open to his people, which won him their love and appreciation.

k. *The Mass Media*

Communication was an essential tool in the unification of the country, especially in the military field. On several occasions, King Abdul Aziz proved that he was an expert in the arts of mass media. When he established himself in Riyadh, his father came to him from Kuwait. When southern Najd fell under the king's power, he set a rumour in the town to the effect that a misunderstanding had broken out between him and his father, the result of which was that they had parted company. The aim was to entice Ibn Rushaid to confront him on a solid ground where the king was in control. Ibn Rushaid believed the rumour and came to the area to capitalize on the alleged rift between father and son. When he approached Riyadh he was disappointed when he discovered that it was a trap to lure him in. The king fought Ibn Rushaid and defeated him, thus becoming his equal.

When the king was defeated by Ajman, his brother Saᶜd was killed. The king himself suffered a serious wound, following which a rumour broke out to the effect that he had been killed. What the king did next was unexpected – he immediately married a woman, and ordered that marriage to be widely proclaimed. Though on his wedding night his wounds were still very deep, people concluded that he was in good health. Thus the rumour of the king's death died out and the morale of his followers was restored.

1. *Luck*
City-dwellers and Bedouins alike believed that luck was a necessary quality for any leader under whom they fought. The luckier the leader the more his army was prepared to fight under his banner. Luck has two aspects: one is the leader's success in his plans, his tactics and the results of his movements. Another is when his rival is too disrupted to pull himself out of traps. There were many occasions on which the king appeared to be lucky, and he himself used to speak of such occasions to prove that God was with him, and to explain why he was often victorious. To say that King Abdul Aziz had great luck does not belittle his greatness. His qualities, planning and achievements are all indications of his outstanding personality. Yet, a leader who has no luck can never be successful.

2. *Circumstances*

The ability and competence of any leader are tested in the way he addresses various situations. A competent leader can use a helpful situation to the utmost in the service of his objectives. He can also mitigate adversities so that their negative effect on his career will be minimal.

King Abdul Aziz was a competent leader who could use favourable situations to his benefit. He could also mitigate adverse situations quite admirably. Here are some of the former situations:

a. *Historical Heritage*
King Abdul Aziz came from a ruling family that had established a state such as had not been known in the Arabian peninsula since the early days of Islam. It covered a wide area, was committed to the monotheistic faith

and applied the divine law, as has been explained. There is no doubt that the majority of the people in the area, especially the city-dwellers, became highly respectful of this family, having experienced at the hands of its early leaders the benefits of unity and the justice of Sharīʿa. Therefore, they were willing to support any Saudi leader as long as he enjoyed the required qualities of leadership. A proof of this is the fact that the leaders of the Saudi state could not unite the Najdi territories except after forty years of continuous struggle. This is because those people had not experienced the benefits of living under the power of a state. But their attitude changed a great deal when they experienced those benefits. Hardly two years passed by after Imām Turki ibn Abdullah entered Riyadh, and evacuated the remaining fighters of Muḥammad Ali's army from the area, when most Najdis came peacefully under the power of his state.

When King Abdul Aziz initiated his plan to unify the country, the majority of the people found in him the desired leader, because of personal qualities on the one hand, and, on the other, because he belonged to the Saudi family for whom they had great love and respect. Some of the Najdi areas were under the control of the Rushaids when the king launched his unification project. This delayed those areas from joining the new state, at first, though it did not hamper the king's efforts in the long term.

b. *Rushaid Rule*

In most of the Najdi areas, Rushaid rule did not have deep roots, as it did not cover the whole of Najd except during the ten years before King Abdul Aziz entered Riyadh. Prince Abdul Aziz ibn Mutʾib himself was not qualified to face the new stage of development. He was not a seasoned politician who could win people by his wisdom. He was rather a courageous fighter who tended to rule people by force. It is said that when his uncle Muḥammad ibn Abdullah died, he sent a message to the tribal chieftains saying 'Muḥammad died and I am in charge; I have nothing for you except the hoof and the sword.' Another indication of his arrogance and faith in his power was his rash remark when he heard of the king's seizure of Riyadh: he referred to the king as 'a rabbit entrapped'.

Moreover, some of the Najdi princes had special problems with the Rushaidi family. Among them were the princes of the two major Qasseem towns, Braida and Unaiza, who had been in exile in Kuwait, from around the time of the Mulaida battle until the king's entrance into Riyadh. The inhabitants of those two townships were supporters of their traditional princes, and were thus disgruntled with the Rushaidis, who had killed many of them in the Mulaida battle. The support of the majority of Najdis for the king and their desire to get rid of the Rushaidi rule was evident in the ease with which the king joined to his rule the south of Najd and the areas between Riyadh and Qasseem. He found great cooperation from the Qasseemis when he approached with his followers along with the exiled princes of the two major townships returning from Kuwait. Ibn Rushaid realized that the majority of Najdis were supporters of King Abdul Aziz, so he found himself obliged to ask the Ottomans for arms and men.

Though such Ottoman support benefited Ibn Rushaid in the short term, his dependence on foreign power gave the local population a clear indication that he was becoming weak and that his rule was coming to an end. The poet al-Awni describes that situation in touching poems in the vernacular. It is known that the Najdis did not like the Turks, since they had suffered from Turkish oppression in former days. Three years after the king's seizure of Riyadh, the entire area of Najd came under his rule, except Shammar Mount, the centre of the Rushaid power. The Najdis contributed towards the king's objective in unifying the country.

The greatest indication of the king's good fortune and the change of situation in his favour was the internal differences in Shammar Mount itself, which began to disrupt the rule of the Rushaidis, after the death of Prince Abdul Aziz ibn Mut'ib.

c. *Success in al-Aḥsāʾ*

The progress of Saudi rule shows that Najd was a starting point, from where the movement progressed towards al-Aḥsāʾ. When the king started his unification activities the area was under the rule of the Ottoman Turks, but their military presence was weak. The nomadic tribes had a free hand in the towns and villages outside the walls. As the Turks were unable to take any measure against those tribes, the local inhabitants were looking for a power to save them from their unenviable situation. Hence, some of the local chieftains made contacts with King Abdul Aziz, encouraging him to come to their rescue, and promising their support. To unify that area of Najd, he had only to defeat the Turks and the tribes that exploited the dominant situation. The king convinced the largest of those tribes to move away from the area, promising to support them against a rival tribe. Once he secured the removal of that large tribe, he pounced on the Turkish garrison in al-Aḥsāʾ, who had to surrender, leaving al-Aḥsāʾ to join the union.

d. *Aseer and Jazan*

It is known that the call of Sheikh Muḥammad ibn ʿAbd al-Wahhāb was well received by the inhabitants of these two areas which formed part of the first Saudi state. This was felt in the heroic stand taken by the people of Aseer, particularly, against the forces of Muḥammad Ali, which came to the Arabian peninsula to put an end to Saudi rule. The friendly relations continued between the leaders of this area and the Saudis. When the Turks withdrew after World War I, Hasan ibn Ayid became the prince of the area. But the chieftains of some large tribes disagreed with him. Because those chieftains had always been on good terms with the Saudis, and because of what they saw of the king's success, especially after the victory of his followers in the Turba battle in 1337/1918, they found in him a leader who could solve their problems with their prince. So, they asked the king for help, and he sent a delegation to Prince Hasan of Aseer to negotiate a peaceful solution; but to no avail. The king therefore attacked Aseer, which soon fell under his rule.

Jazan was then ruled by the Idreesis. The great-grandfather of that family was a Moroccan Sufi (mystic) who settled in Sibya in 1246/1830 and had followers in the area. But this family came to rule Jazan, first at the hands of a resourceful grandson of that Moroccan, named Muḥammad ibn Ali, who was born in 1293/1876. That was taken to be the same year of King Abdul Aziz's birth. Muḥammad allied himself with the Italians against the Turks until he became ruler of the country. Then he found himself between two neighbours who had ambitions against his country:Yemen and Hijaz. So he concluded a treaty with King Abdul Aziz, hoping for his help. After the death of Jazan's ruler, a family dispute broke out between his son Ali and his brother al-Hasan ibn Ali, and the latter became the ruler. But the situation at home and abroad led him to seek the protection of King Abdul Aziz in 1345/1926. When he failed to run the country he conceded Jazan to King Abdul Aziz; thus Jazan became part of the kingdom.

e. *Hijaz*

The situation that led Hijaz falling under the rule of King Adbul Aziz is similar to that which led to its fall under the first Saudi state. King Abdul Aziz did not start war against the King of Hijaz: it was the latter who invaded Najd, in the same manner that the predecessors of both kings had done. Al-Sharīf Ghalib opened war against Imām Abdul Aziz ibn Muḥammad ibn Saʿūd. Then a difference emerged between King Abdul Aziz and King al-Hussein ibn Ali about the oases of Turba and Kharma, where the majority of the inhabitants supported the Saudis. The Prince of Kharma al-Shariif Khalid ibn Louay had a dispute with the King of Hijaz, so he joined forces with King Abdul Aziz. This dispute was similar to that between the two relatives, Uthman al-Madaifi and Ghalib, when the former joined Imām Abdul Aziz ibn Muḥammad ibn Saʿūd. The joining of Madaifi to the first Saudi state was a gain to that state, as was the Ibn Louay's joining them. Al-Madaifi's contribution was the bringing of Hijaz under the rule of King Abdul Aziz. The old Sharīfs had prevented the Saudis from performing pilgrimage, as did Sharīf Hussein to the followers of Abdul Aziz. That was the gravest of Sharīf Hussein's political mistakes, as it provoked the king's followers to fight al-Hussein evermore.

Among the factors that helped King Abdul Aziz to bring Hijaz under his rule was that Hijaz became surrounded by Saudi areas on the eastern and southern sides. Moreover, Hijaz was no longer under Turkish rule, as the Ottoman Turks were chased out by al-Hussein ibn Ali with British help. King al-Hussein ceased to receive help from the British once they had realized their objective. Favourable politial situations, at home and abroad, thus helped King Abdul Aziz to unify Hijaz with the rest of the kingdom.

Thus a variety of factors, including luck, strong leadership, favourable political and social circumstances – and, according to the faithful, divine help – all contributed to the unification of the country.

Chapter 12

King Abdul Aziz: His Style of Administration

ᶜAbd Al-Aziz ibn ᶜAbd Allāh al-Khwaiter

The king's style of administration may be approached from various starting points. Yet one should be aware of the aspects of administration dominant in his time to recognize what had been inherited from ancient times, Abbasid or Umayyad; or from recent times, for example from the Ottoman era. Some of those starting points may be defined as his style of administration:

- in the desert areas
- in the townships
- in times of war
- in times of peace
- in his early days
- after unification of the kingdom
- towards the men he trusted
- towards the new in allegiance.

These points intermingle or branch out into various areas covering different cases and events; yet a general rule may be established concerning the king's style of administration.

1. *The State of Administration in the Peninsula before the Reign of King Abdul Aziz*

Before the reign of King Abdul Aziz, the peninsula was ruled by the following traditions:

In the townships, villages and oases, which represent the settled population, Islamic teachings and the traditions that developd from them were in control of the administrative system. Power was in the hands of the prince, the *qadi* (religious judge), with the dignitaries influencing the conduct of the prince in many cases. This was the class of the major merchants, landowners and farmers.

In the desert, the dominant traditions which developed with time were not always compatible with the Islamic religion. Some of those traditions have even been identified with despotism. The judge in such cases may have been a man of wisdom and insight into the psychology of people in order to reach a fair judgement acceptable to his rivals, and saving face for the wrongdoer. The tribal chief played an important part in the affairs of his tribe; and, in major cases, he consulted a council of mature men who shouldered the responsibility with the chieftain.

Some of the townships knew some aspects of Turkish administration, represented in an administrative government heading a number of employees to supervise the application of certain regular instructions.

2. *Early Experience of the Desert in Times of War*

The early years of the king's relations with the desert people were of a military nature. They were either friendly or half-hearted relations. With a trusted friend, the king gave a free hand in the administration, as well as exercising his general policy of help in carrying out the military plans.

With new allies, on the other hand, the king was wary, strict and vigilant. He would keep significant aspects of power in his own hands, and relinquish what could be relinquished according to custom. He was very cautious not to displease, in order to retain what he had gained and to reassure the defeated person and lead him to a position of constant trust.

This balance between yielding power and providing trust, between wariness and vigilance was not exercised only with tribal chieftains, but also with the emirs of towns. There were towns known for their friendship and loyalty to the Saudi rulers before him, and they showed the same feelings to the king, so he trusted them and kept their emirs in their positions, and relieved some of their burdens demanded by the war situation at the time, such as sharing in war expenditure and providing fighters.

As for other towns not known for their loyalty, the situation demanded a tight grip and the appointment of a trusty ruler to manage their affairs.

But this situation lasted for a short period only, after which there was a growth of mutual trust among the parties, as those towns realized that the king's rule was just, firm and strong, not like the transient rule of others in that period. They found it in their interest to be faithful to the king, and to support him, in order to enjoy the privileges that entailed: mainly stability and security. These privileges were proffered to them to an unexpected degree. So they yielded power to him willingly, and gained trust in return.

So much for political administration and rule. In civil administration, the executive civil power was in the hands of the emir who represented the king within the limits marked out for him. The legislative power was in the hand of the *qadi* (religious judge) according to the Islamic Sharīʿa, which rules the emir as well.

The election of the tribal chief was mostly undertaken by the tribe, and governed by its traditions and customs. But, because of his relation with the tribes, and his knowledge of their men and customs, King Abdul Aziz was able to enlist the tribal chieftains to his support in solving the problems of those tribes.

Selecting a town emir was not a problem for the king, since he had full authority to appoint an emir according to the importance of the township, its situation and liability to an attack. The qualities needed in an emir were loyalty, truthfulness, vigilance and vitality. Although these were features required of any administrator, the king had a special need for men of such qualities at that period. He was intent upon winning able men to his side, and did not hesitate to punish anyone who violated those qualities in his conduct.

He could feel the ability and importance of the faithful men among his emirs, and expected their full support for his administration, because he believed they shared with him a realization of the importance of security and stability, and that any relaxation of control might destroy all efforts, and may lead to a setback. Therefore, he could not tolerate any negligence in supporting and protecting the achievements attained. The king's style with his emirs stems from the fact that he was familiar with their history, psychology and aspirations, so he could use a style of address and management that would guarantee success.

3. *With Bedouins in Times of Peace*

In times of peace, the reins of power fell into his hands gradually, a situation which the tribal chieftains accepted wholeheartedly. They did not resent the fact since the king had put an end to rebellions and provided them with unprecedented calm. Therefore, they shouldered with him the burden of administration. Their control of their followers was characterized by the principles of Islamic Sharīʿa. What was left to the king was to handle certain individual cases which went off the line and to decide where Sharīʿa rules would be applied to deter wrongdoers in a newly formed society, not quite free from chaos. It was clear that the king had meant to build his rule upon strong foundations.

Security and peace brought a new factor into the desert areas, as they allowed larger tribes to divide into smaller groups. This helped the king to relocate those groups across the kingdom, according to a certain system. The best sign of administrative obedience was the prevalence of peace among tribes, their spread over a large area, and their settlement in new areas. The payment of *zakāt* to the person in charge remained a certain sign of complete allegiance.

4. *Urban Areas in Times of Peace*

Some new developments began to be seen in townships when the wars came to an end: the roads became peaceful, trade flourished with security and stability, towns grew larger, new villages and townships burgeoned on the main routes. The king's administration of some towns, in wartime, was characterized by vigilance, caution, suspicion, alertness, quick reaction, insightful treatment of events, over-concern with appearance and hidden implications and a tendency to severe punishment. In times of peace, that administration became more patient, forgiving, looking at the various sides of events, relying more on consultation, good faith, tolerance and disregard of minor offences.

a. *Facilities of Administration*

The means and facilities of administration were not available in a manner that would help in perfecting the work of the administrator. This made the king resort to any means available, as planning facilities were not developed at the time. The general plan was present in his mind, and its execution tool, the form of partial plans, sometimes changed by unexpected developments.

Camels and horses were the means of transport. Messengers carried letters, handwritten on any paper available, and with any kind of pen. Letters were dictated directly by the main responsible person, who could be the king himself or his representative. With the advent of the telegraph and cars the administration advanced. When the king entered Hijaz, new aspects of administration followed him through experienced employees and better facilities, such as the typewriter, registration and book-keeping, classification systems and so forth. A reliable postal service, stamps, customs offices, police, checkpoints, a regular army, coastal guards, organized foreign relations, ambassadors, consuls and roads opened up in the mountain areas, along with systemized finance, main and secondary depots . . . all added to higher standards of administration.

Another aspect of the king's administration when matters cleared up before him was his efforts to settle the Bedouins, educate them and establish means for selecting emirs of various areas, to specify their terms of office and the observation of their activities.

b. *After Unification of the Kingdom*

Generally speaking, in the administrative system in Najd the king was the source of power. He had the final word, which was bound solely by the power of the Sharīʿa. He relied on no systematic administrative bodies other than the employees in his council, whose job was to submit to him the various matters that were raised in council, then to carry out his orders in addressing those matters. The king decided on administrative, political, military, economic and social matters, and referred what concerned the Sharīʿa to the relevant authorities.

The administrative departments in Najd were: the emirates, the finance departments and the *qadi* (religious judge) who sat next to the emir. After he took control of the Hijaz, the king introduced to Najd some administrative systems, and used some trained employees to implement those systems, adding some of the educated locals as a support.

Hafiz Wahba relates that the king introduced the modern health system to Najd and al-Aḥsāʾ by increasing the number of doctors and mobile hospitals to treat patients across the country. He also introduced smallpox vaccination, encouraged education, built schools and used the wireless to stop some rebellions in the north and south.

In Hijaz, the king found traces of the Ottoman systems modified by the Sharīfs. He abolished some of those systems such as the position of *wali* (ruler), governor, provincial divisions of *qada* and *nahiya*, and replaced them by the emirate, both large and small. But he retained the current administrative division after some modifications.

Perhaps the first order he issued after he entered Hijaz was the Constitution of 21 Safar 1345/September 1926. Then came the royal decree to unify the name of the kingdom on 17 Jumada al-Ula 1351 to come into effect on 21 Jumada al-Ula 1351/1933. The constitution assigned six basic functions to the state: Sharīʿa, internal, external, financial, education and military. These departments are headed by directors acting under the deputy of the king. Then came the formation of the Consultation Council, the Ministry of Finance and the Ministry of Foreign Affairs. In Ramadan 1350/1932 the Council of Deputies was formed to parallel the Council of Ministers, headed by the deputy of the king, comprising the deputies of foreign affairs, finance and consultation. The council derived its authority from the king, and the deputies were collectively responsible before the king.

In the light of these basic regulations, the central administrative formations changed into: the Head of the Council, the Ministry of Foreign Affairs, of Finance, of Internal Affairs and the Consultation Councils.

The following administrations were attached to the Ministry of Internal Affairs: Public Health and Relief, Public Education, Telegraph, Post and Telephones, Chief of Justice, Military Affairs, Endowments and Holy Sanctuary, Municipalities, Water and Zubaida Spring, Marine Rockeries, Coastal Guards, Public Police, Directorate of Attachments.

Chapter 13

Early Roots of Projects to Settle the Bedouins in the Arabian Peninsula

ʿAbd al-Fattāḥ Ḥasan Abū ʿAliyya

Projects to settle the Bedouins in the Arabian peninsula stretch back to the enterprise undertaken by King Abdul Aziz ibn Saʿūd, which is considered to have achieved many of its religious, social, economic, political and military aims. Thus it is an important landmark in modern Arab history.

The idea of settling the Saudi Bedouins originated with King Abdul Aziz himself, whose efforts enabled him to bring this project out of the domain of ideas into the phase of implementation, cutting through all obstacles until he was able to achieve the greatest and deepest social transformation that the Arabian peninsula had seen in many centuries. Robert Ernest Cheesman states, 'The project to settle the Bedouins that the European newspapers made much of, was evidence of the great intelligence of Sultan Abdul Aziz, clearly showing his vitality and energy.'[1] The idea of resettling the Bedouins stemmed from King Abdul Aziz's appraisal of the civil, economic and social aspects of Bedouin society and his intent to improve conditions generally; in this his foresight and breadth of vision are clear.

A number of related factors contributed to the success of the settlement project, among them the role played by the religious scholars or 'volunteers' (*al-mutawwiʿūn*) and those with moral authority (*al-murshidūn*) in persuading the Bedouins to build agricultural villages and to begin farming. Such activities are considered socially necessary for development and construction. By 1920, under the rule of Abdul Aziz, most of the Bedouin population had abandoned their nomadic lifestyle and joined the new settlement project.[2]

For the first time there appeared in the Arabian peninsula a great number of agricultural settlements called *al-hijar* (sg. *hijra*), whose nomenclature refers to the Prophet Muḥammad's migration (*hijra*) from Makkah to Madinah. Amīn al-Rīḥānī comments: 'Migration here is migration to God's Unity, but also to civilization, from tents to houses of mud and stone, from poverty and raiding to the land that does not betray its master if he takes the plough to it; it is a migration from fear and apprehension to a security that does not desert he who works productively for himself and his country.'[3]

King Abdul Aziz managed to persuade the chiefs of the Bedouin tribes to come to Riyadh in order to study in its great mosque with a number of religious scholars who were appointed by the regime to instruct the tribal chiefs in religious matters and urge them to abandon the nomadic life for agriculture and settling near water sources. Al-Rīḥānī comments: 'Ibn Saʿūd began his great reform through religious means. He sent the "volunteers" to the desert to teach its inhabitants about the Unity of God, and religious precepts, and to exhort them to leave their (present) condition for the sake of belief in their faith, a home in which to take refuge, and a land to cultivate.'[4] The king bestowed many gifts and grants on the Bedouin chiefs; he also issued an order granting them houses in the city of Riyadh. From those chiefs he formed the military command of the irregular Saudi army. With these methods the king was able to persuade most of the desert Bedouins to accept his project.[5]

The settlement allowed the larger Bedouin tribes that participated in it to let some of their numbers remain in the settlement to attend to farming, and some to remain in the desert to maintain their flocks. This flexibility of the settlement project was one of the factors that encouraged the Bedouins to accept it.[6] The king succeeded in persuading the tribes to sell their camels ('the symbol of nomadism'), and to take up farming instead of grazing flocks, to gather into settled agricultural communities instead of leading a nomadic pastoral life. He was helped in establishing his idea of this society by those groups who were responsible for educating the Bedouins, for the king had mobilized the efforts of religious scholars and prepared many of them for this purpose. The Englishman Harrison, who visited Riyadh in 1918, describes the preparations for the project: 'People in Riyadh live for the next world, and hundreds study in the mosques to become teachers and religious instructors for the Bedouin tribes. Riyadh was the centre which produced religious scholars who were trained to be dispersed throughout the country in order to instruct the Bedouin.'[7] Amīn al-Rīḥānī commented, 'The religious scholars brought history, with tales of the forebears, with which the "volunteers" were armed in order to fight against indolence and laziness. They taught the settled tribes that farming, trade and industry did not contravene religion, and that the rich believer was superior to the poor believer.'[8]

Among the reasons for the success of this project were the many gifts and grants that King Abdul Aziz presented to the Bedouins in the form of money, food supplies and the means necessary for farming. The distribution of lands adjoining the agricultural settlements to the Bedouins who had migrated there, and which accompanied the settlement project from the start, was an important incentive that helped the project to succeed. For the individual Bedouin, this was the only way he could obtain a share in the distribution of land, especially since ownership of land, water and grass in the tribal system was collective and not individual. Thus the individual Bedouin, who benefited greatly from the project, was obliged to support it.

The Bedouins had tired of nomadic life, so the establishment of the settlement project offered them security, which they preferred to nomadism. Their reorientation to a settled life was influenced by the many years of drought that had made their pasture lands arid and destroyed the traditional sources of their livelihood. Additionally, they came to prefer settlement because it allowed them more flexibility in their lives than did a nomadic existence.

One possible way of evaluating the task faced by King Abdul Aziz in trying to make this project succeed is to measure the resistance that was put up by the Bedouin tribes, attached as they were to their nomadic existence. We will give one example here: the Ruwala tribes in the northern part of the Arabian peninsula always preferred to return to their traditional areas in the centre of the peninsula rather than to move into the settlement project.[9] When King ʿAbd al-ʿAzīz invited the Bedouins in his kingdom to forsake their nomadic existence and to participate fully in a more secure life within settled agricultural communities, the al-ʿAjmān tribes in the region of al-Ḥasā (al-Aḥsāʾ) refused to accept these orders, believing that the settlement project would destroy their tribal society.[10]

Aims of the Settlement Project

The major aim of the first stage of King Abdul Aziz Āl Saʿūd's settlement project was to civilize the Bedouins in the full sense of the word, in terms of its political, cultural, military and economic elements, and to gather the Bedouin tribes, who were scattered and dispersed across the Arabian peninsula, into agricultural settlements, and so make the individual Bedouin feel the responsibility of citizenship and implant in him the love of stability. Through this project the king aimed to 'develop the Bedouins beyond their instinctive warlike nature, and make them feel part of one nation'. He wanted the Bedouins to 'feel that the settlements he had built for them were like a small homeland for them within the larger homeland'.[11]

The king also aimed at developing his country economically, by creating agricultural villages by means of which the economic conditions of the Bedouins would be improved. The project was to transform the cultural, social and economic life of the Bedouins 'when they learned religious principles, agriculture, and the building of houses and mosques'.[12] Thus the agricultural settlements were to form a single independent and autonomous administrative and economic unit.

Likewise the king, through the settlement project, aimed at giving the Bedouins an Islamic religious education based on the Ḥanbalī principles chosen by the mission of the reformer Muḥammad ibn ʿAbd al-Wahhāb. Thus one can state that the settlement movement was a coherent totality in its religious, economic, social, political and military goals, as the Bedouins became a major military force in the Arabian peninsula, performing their military duties until the regular army was formed. Because of their economic obligations, the settled population was occupied year round in their commercial, agricultural and industrial activities. These activities demanded all their time. Farmers, for example, could not leave their fields, nor could the urban population close their shops and set off for war whenever the need arose (which was often in those days), as soldiers were not paid, except for whatever booty they could take after a battle. King Abdul Aziz states: 'The Bedouins come to us in peace and we give them whatever they need of clothing, sustenance, and money; but in days of war they ask nothing of us. In days of war each one girds himself with a cartridge belt and sets out with his rifle, riding his camel and carrying a few coins and dates . . . What is little to us is worth a lot to others.'

Unlike the settled population, who could not leave their fields and shops because economic life in the country would come to a standstill, the Bedouins were a military force ready to go to war at any moment. The economy was the true lifeline of the country. Moreover, in Najd the Bedouins outnumbered the settled population. Through his settlement project King Abdul Aziz was able to redirect the nomadic Bedouins towards military and administrative functions that were a preamble to their acceptance of the regime and to becoming disciplined, thus turning the Bedouin tribes away from their former lifestyle of conducting tribal raids in the desert, which disturbed the local authorities. Al-Rīḥānī mentions that King Abdul Aziz was able to call up 76,000 soldiers in 1344/1926 from among the settled Bedouins in response to a general mobilization.[13]

Most historical sources agree that the establishment of the first agricultural settlement for the Bedouins in Saudi Arabia took place in 1330/1913 and that the first settlement was that of al-Artāwiyya.[14]

Settlements and the Tribe

The process of resettling the Bedouins and gathering them into agricultural units was one of the most important means of weakening their tribal affiliations. After the success of the project, and with the transfer of the Bedouins from the desert to agricultural villages, actual authority was no longer in the hands of the tribal chiefs, but had been transferred to the central authorities in Riyadh. Likewise, the religious re-education of the Bedouins that accompanied the resettlement project made them a God-fearing community, and religious ties became stronger than tribal ties.

Both the resettlement drive and the accompanying re-education campaign succeeded in breaking the traditional tribal structure, and indeed put restrictions on Bedouinism. Loyalties were transferred from tribal sheikhs to the ruler, and tribal conflicts, which had dominated nomadic society in the desert and worked against peace in the area, were ended.

The resettlement project was based on the principle of integrating the tribes, since they came to live together in a single settlement. This intermingling heralded the weakening of the principle of tribal unity, and thus settlement became one of the most important means for merging the Bedouins into a single agricultural community, and consequently into the social melting-pot of the state, which became a substitute for the tribal social structure.[15]

When the Bedouins settled in the agricultural villages, their economic function changed from that of grazing animals to farming. As a result their social condition changed, especially with respect to the individual's tribal loyalty. The concept of desert life, which had imposed solidarity and loyalty, was weakened; the Bedouin, now settled, began to build new social and economic relations with others outside his original community. The Bedouin was thus no longer focused on his tribe and its chief, since his new economic condition naturally reorientated him to a new outlook on life. The tribe now became secondary, while the new regime began drawing the individual Bedouin closer to the state and the ruler. His affiliation to the nation now became closer than that to his tribe, a situation added to by the new customs and culture that he began to adopt from his new environment.

The Importance of the Settlement Project and its Outcome

The settlement project initiated by King Abdul Aziz in the Arabian peninsula occupies a central position in modern Arab history because of the important consequences that stemmed from it, which greatly influenced the social, cultural and economic life of the Bedouins in particular and the life of the peninsula's inhabitants in general. The project's ramifications included the fact that the Bedouins' acceptance of settlement was the beginning of the transformation of their life from a nomadic one to one of security and civilization. The project's first phase involved the resettling of fifty Bedouin families from the desert into an agricultural village, the first step towards its wider implementation. Within a short time, the idea of settlement caught on so widely among the Bedouins that later villages housed more than ten thousand inhabitants.[16]

To a certain extent, the settlement project allowed the replacement of Bedouin society by a settled society living around water sources in oases, where the inhabitants practised farming. This was the major social and economic change that occurred in the Arabian peninsula in the 1920s. This transformation had a wide impact on the life of people in the new Saudi state; settlement, and its civilizational and social consequences, influenced the future of this then still youthful kingdom, after its doors were opened to the social development resulting from settling the Bedouins in agricultural villages.[17]

The settlement project made the individual Bedouin accept the concept of citizenship. From this emerged the individual Bedouin's recognition of the concept of an organized state as an alternative to tribal authority. Thus King Abdul Aziz created stable religious agricultural communities which owed their allegiance to the state instead of to the tribe. Peace reigned in the country, and the trade routes between the different regions of the Arabian peninsula on the one hand, and Iraq, Kuwait and Syria on the other, became secure. Security and peace led to an economic boom that, in turn, led to the prosperity of Saudi society and also of other societies in the peninsula. Moreover, settlement took Bedouin society from a state of anarchy and tribal conflict to one of security, the normal state of civilized societies. The success of the settlement project also led to the creation of a strong military force in the Arabian peninsula and marked the beginning of the merging of the Bedouin tribes into the Saudi regime's united society.[18]

The settlement project established among Bedouin groups a sense of responsibility towards their fellow citizens. This feeling was a contributing factor in the later unification of the different regions of the Saudi kingdom. This sense of citizenship replaced traditional tribal and individual affiliations that had prevailed within Bedouin communities. The Bedouin was passionately attached to his freedom, which made him feel the singularity of the tribe. Settlement was a strong factor in dissolving this individuality and incorporating it within the framework of the state. Settlement also created from the Bedouins a religious military force that imprinted a religious character on the wars they waged both internally and externally. This was due to the religious groups that controlled the project.

The settlement project transformed the mentalities of the Bedouins once they saw that a settled life was far preferable to a life of constant wandering. They accepted the practice of the new means of civilization that had attracted large numbers of Bedouins to the settlements.[19] The project produced new responsibilities and values among the Bedouins. They developed a deeper outlook on life, and many of their habits changed, as well as many of the traditional social customs of the Arabian peninsula. There also appeared the idea of establishing semi-fixed and stable borders between the new Saudi state and nearby Arab countries, such as Kuwait, Qatar, Iraq and eastern Jordan. Settlement restricted the seasonal migrations of the Bedouins, which had always led to a lack of stability with respect to borders. Once the Bedouins were settled, treaties were signed which fixed these borders with special provisions organizing the movement of the Bedouin tribes within the boundaries of these states.

One can say that the settlement project marked the end of the migrations of the Bedouin tribes outside the Arabian peninsula, since King Abdul Aziz's rule was based on the Islamic Sharīʿa. This system was preferred by the Bedouin tribes to that of rule in other neighbouring Arab countries, which at that time were either protectorates or under British and French mandates, and which therefore gave rise to a different course of development, establishing a way of life far removed from the life of the Bedouin tribal groups.[20] One important result of the project was that the settled population became the real force in political and economic life. Moreover, the settlement project led to the decrease of the Bedouin population and the increase of the settled population, which in turn changed the face of social and economic life in the country.

Thus the settlement project achieved some of its goals, both politically and militarily and, to a lesser extent, culturally. But we must note here that other, secondary issues emerged that brought difficulties leading to the failure of the project in achieving some of its goals. Among the social difficulties that hampered the course of the project was that the Bedouin inhabitants of the agricultural villages did not reside in them all year long, but often left to return to the desert for part of the year, coming back to the villages especially at harvest time, and during Ramadan to observe their religious duties.[21] Nor was the project successful economically, for the agricultural villages came to resemble housing projects because the Bedouins became dependent on the gifts, grants, foodstuffs and other facilities bestowed by the state.

Even though a strong religious and political impulse was at the root of this experiment to settle the Bedouins of the Arabian peninsula, it could not develop economically due to the harsh living conditions. These included the unsuitability of the soil for farming and for long-term residence, because of the lack of water sources, poor health conditions, lack of opportunities for work and livelihood, and poor transport systems.[22] While the establishment of the Saudi Arabian kingdom allowed peace and coexistence to pervade relations between the tribes, the settlement project did not proceed according to its fundamental plan, because many Bedouins returned to their original regions once peace and security spread throughout the Arabian peninsula. And once the tribes returned to their old habitats, their old forms of life also re-emerged.

One reason why the settlement project weakened is that the 'brothers',[23] the inhabitants of the agricultural villages, lacked proper religious education, or indeed education in general. Few of them could read or write. Had they absorbed the religious teachings in their original sense and avoided prejudice and zealotry, they could have formed the kernel of a true spiritual and social renaissance in the Arabian peninsula. But despite all this, the settlement project undertaken by King Abdul Aziz was a daring experiment in this field, from which other plans for settling the Bedouins can benefit. It sheds much light on King Abdul Aziz's plans to develop the country socially, economically and culturally.

Notes:

1. Major Cheesman was a high-ranking British officer in the region, and among the officials who had special knowledge of the issues in the Arabian peninsula. He visited the region at the time of King Abdul Aziz, when this project was being translated from idea to action. See his report in FO 686, vol. 18, p. 108; see also R. E. Cheesman, *Unknown Arabia* (London, 1928).
2. See FO 686, vol. 18, p. 111.
3. See Amīn al-Rīḥānī, *Ta'rīkh Najd wa-mulḥaqātuh* (Beirut, 1971), p. 261.
4. *Ibid.*
5. See Don Peretz, *The Middle East Today* (New York, 1978), p. 304.
6. See H. R. P. Dickson, *Kuwait and Her Neighbours* (London, 1956), p. 330.
7. See Harrison's article in *The Moslem World* 22 (1930); see also his *Wahhābism and Ibn Saʿūd*, p. 242.
8. Al-Rīḥānī, *Ta'rīkh Najd*, p. 262.
9. See American Geographical Society, *The Geographical Review* 20 (1930), p. 497.
10. FO 686, vol. 18, p. 111.
11. See Benoist-Mechin, *ʿAbd al-ʿAzīz ibn Suʿūd: sīrat batal wa-mawlid mamlaka* (trans. from the German by ʿAbd al-Fattāḥ Yāsin, Beirut, 1965), p. 120.
12. See D. van der Meulen, *The Wells of Ibn Saud* (New York, 1957), p. 63.
13. *Ibid.*, p. 454. To know the names of the settlements that responded to the general mobilization and the number of fighters in each settlement see *ibid.* For the rulers of these agricultural settlements see the newspaper *Umm al-Qurā*, no. 218 (1347/1928).
14. George Antonius mentions that the first *hijra* was established in 1910. The fact is that there was no mention of the settlements and their inhabitants before King Abdul Aziz entered al-Aḥsā' in 1913; nor did they play any military role in the wars that the king waged before that year. See Antonius, *The Arab Awakening* (New York, 1939), p. 348. Al-Artawiyya is 300 km north of Riyadh.
15. See H. C. Armstrong, *Lord of Arabia* (Beirut, 1966), p. 81. Armstrong was one of the British officers specializing in the military affairs of the Arabian peninsula; he wrote this book about King Abdul Aziz.
16. See Ḥāfiẓ Wahba, *Jazīrat al-ʿArab fī al-qarn al-ʿishrīn* (Cairo, 1961), p. 309.
17. See W. Thesiger, *Arabian Sands* (New York, 1964), p. 230.
18. Armstrong, *Lord of Arabia*, pp. 79–81.

19. See the magazine *al-Yamāma* 12 (1373/1954).
20. See the American Geographical Society, *The Geographical Review* 20 (1930), p. 497.
21. See India Office no. V16037, 'Report of a Trip to Southern Najd and Dawasir on Special Duty in Central Arabia', by H. St John Philby, 7 July 1918; printed at the Government Monotype Press, 1918.
22. See Muḥammad ʿAlī al-Jāsim, 'Tawṭin al-bādiya fi al-mamlaka al-ʿArabiyya al-Suʿūdiyya', *al-ʿArab* 8.11–12 (1393/1984), p. 878.
23. All the sources agree that the name 'brothers' (*ikhwān*) came from the first Islamic group who received Islam from the Prophet, formed the first Islamic community in Madinah, and were joined in God and by brotherly ties of solidarity. Bedouin brotherhood refers to the principle of fraternity practised by that first Muslim community. See the articles in *Umm al-Qurā;* al-Rīḥānī, *Taʾrīkh Najd;* Wahba, *Jazīrat al-ʿArab;* Dickson, *Kuwait*, p. 107 ('Notes on the *Ikhwān*'); FO 686, vol. 18.

Chapter 14

Arab Travellers in the Arabian Peninsula: Saudi Arabia 1901–1972

Manṣūr Ibrāhīm al-Ḥāzimī

Even in this age of aeroplanes and rockets, travel continues to be a source of delight, knowledge and culture, even though it has lost that lustre that surrounded it in the past, and the elements of imagination and adventure, when the world was remote and unknown, and the means of transport primitive and limited. Yet man is by nature a traveller, always keen for knowledge and the discovery of the unknown. If he is unable to travel, he listens closely to those who have had the good fortune to travel and observe, although those who hear are not like those who observe.

The traditions of all nations are filled with travel accounts, some of which time has preserved and whose records have reached us so that we may read and enjoy them and discern in them true pictures of the life of the ancients, and some pages about their struggles, morals and beliefs. Thus we see the ancient world as recorded by Herodotus, in his famous account of his observations in Egypt, Cyprus, Phoenicia, Assyria and Iran, and in what Plutarch, Julius Caesar, Tacitus and Ptolemy recorded about various regions and places, and accounts of nations and peoples.

As for the Arabs, they have outstripped the peoples who preceded them in terms of their legacy of travel literature. In this they were aided by the extensiveness of the Islamic empire, by flourishing agriculture and trade, and by an advanced scientific and cultural life. Religion was another important factor that drew travellers to the Hijaz to perform the duty of the *ḥajj* (pilgrimage) and to visit the holy sites. The Arabic libraries are filled with travel books, printed and in manuscript, that attest to the interest of the early Arabs in this attractive genre of writing, and to a great vitality and energy.[1]

Travel literature has not received enough attention from modern critics and researchers, despite its importance and its richness in the Arabic and Islamic heritage. Ḥamad al-Jāsir has frequently drawn attention to this in his journal *al-ʿArab*, and by publishing texts and studies has emphasized the importance of travel literature in revealing aspects almost lost and forgotten in the history of the Arabian peninsula.[2] In his writing on travel literature, Shawqī Ḍayf (*al-Riḥlāt*, 1956) summarized the major Arab travel accounts such as those of Ibn Jubayr, Ibn Baṭṭūṭa and al-Muqaddisī. Jūrj Ghurayyib followed the same path in his *Adab al-riḥla* (Beirut, 1966), but devoted most of his book to Amīn al-Rīḥānī. Ḥusnī Maḥmād Ḥusayn, in his short book *Adab al-riḥla ʿind al-ʿArab* (Cairo 1976) contented himself with discussing Ibn Jubayr and Ibn Baṭṭūṭa, adding Ibn Khaldūn, Rifāʿa al-Ṭahṭāwī and Aḥmad Fāris al-Shidyāq.[3]

There is no doubt that all these works are commendable, but they are not sufficient. For the most part they are merely introductory or short presentations and summaries that are incommensurate with the prodigious output that the Arab intellect has left behind throughout the centuries. Perhaps the most interesting book that I have come across in this field is the *History of Geographical Literature (Istoria arabskoi geografi cheskoi literatury* [Moscow, 1957] by the well-known Russian orientalist I. Kratchkovskiĭ; the Arabic translation is *Taʾrīkh al-adab al-jughrāfī* [Cairo, 1963–5]. Kratchkovskiĭ spent many years in collecting the material and in writing his book), tracing Arab travel literature from its beginnings until the eighteenth century. His methodology is distinguished by its scholarly precision, manifest in the way he gathers material together, his method of presentation, and his discussion and analysis. But Kratchkovskiĭ was not concerned with literature (*adab*, in the literary-critical meaning of the word), as it occurs in his title, but with its general sense, which includes the entire heritage of the (Muslim) community in all its creative aspects, and alludes to all that was produced by the Arabic-Islamic intellect in travel literature specifically.

Travel accounts constitute a wide field in which history and literature compete, and perhaps even many other arts and disciplines, too numerous to count; yet in some forms it is pure literature, or closer to literary art. I have searched for a definition of travel literature in its narrow sense, but found nothing that could give a complete understanding of the term. Perhaps the Arabs, in leaving us this rich heritage of travel books, never thought to include it in the circle of 'pure literature', and thus were not concerned to lay down rules for it, as they did for other arts of speech, such as poetry, oratory and letters. They also ignored the art of storytelling, despite their recognition of the *maqāma* and the great heritage of the storytelling tradition.

Perhaps the ancients had their own justification for ignoring travel literature and in not recognizing it as a literary form, for, as I have mentioned, travel accounts were a mixture of many arts, each being as different as its authors and purposes. For example, Ibn Jubayr's travel account was written as a diary, recounting the experiences of the author on his way to the holy sites to perform the pilgrimage and his return.[4] Ibn al-Mujāwir, on the other hand, was concerned in his *Ta'rīkh al-mustabṣir* with what he saw in the southern Arabian peninsula and the mid-Hijaz region with respect to differences in popular customs, as well as with describing different regions, roads and distances.[5] As for Ibn Baṭṭūta, who was greatly influenced by beliefs current in the Maghreb, he was noticeably interested in accounts of saints and dervishes and of their miracles and fabulous deeds.[6] A literary character dominated the account of Ibn Maʿṣūm, *Ṣalawāt al-gharīb wa-salwat al-arīb*, which was more of a personal account, with an occasional digression into literary matters, and which was written to describe his family's journey from Madinah to India.[7]

These are some examples of the differences between travel accounts in their style, methods and forms. For this reason, some researchers have classified them according to subject matter, and have divided them into fifteen kinds of accounts: (1) journeys to the Hijaz; (2) sightseeing journeys; (3) official journeys; (4) travel for study; (5) archaeological travel; (6) journeys of discovery; (7) visits to shrines; (8) political journeys; (9) visits to saints' tombs; (10) 'cataloguing' journeys; (11) scientific journeys; (12) guidebooks; (13) imaginary journeys; (14) ambassadorial journeys; (15) general journeys.[8] Even though such a classification is of some benefit to the researcher, it is not free from arbitrariness. One travel account can combine many different types. For example, Ibn Baṭṭūta's account combines a journey to the Hijaz, sightseeing, discovery, ambassadorial and scientific travels, visits to shrines and so on.[9]

There is another approach to the classification of Arab travel accounts, which is perhaps more precise, inclusive and flexible in terms of application. This approach is based on the relationship of the author to his account. Thus, the account is either subjective, concerned with whatever befalls the author, the events and conditions that had an impact on him, his beliefs, and his innermost self, or objective, focused on recording things apart from the self. Of the second kind are the books written by Arab geographers about knowledge of travel routes and kingdoms (*al-masālik wa-al-mamālik*) and which were concerned with the measurement of distances, roads and the description of the agricultural, economic, political and architectural aspects of regions. The 'objective' journey is in this sense closer to a scientific account in which the author is concerned with scientific precision and with communicating details without being concerned with literary style or self-expression.[10] But despite the value of this approach, and its closeness to the critical approach in interpreting texts, it is still not comprehensive. This is because two elements are usually combined in the travel account: the subjective and the objective. Many Arabic travel accounts begin with a personal account of the life of the traveller himself, but soon turn into a compendium in which the author interprets what he has heard from the Sheikhs and scholars he has met, or into literary selections which may help the researcher in ascertaining the popular tastes of the period.[11]

On the other hand, we have noted that the personal orientation and culture of the traveller, and the general conditions of his period, were important in directing his journey, and stamped it with the hue of both his individual impulse and objective general circumstances. We give as an example the interest of scholars in the Arabian peninsula during the age of codification. They needed to set down the language, establish its rules, and collect the literary heritage from the mouths of the tribesmen. When the principles of the language and the collection of this heritage were achieved, they no longer needed to set out on such difficult journeys. We may also note the interest of later travellers with the Sheikhs of the Sufi orders, holy men, dervishes and pious people, made on account of the rigidity that overcame Islamic thought in later periods, and the spread of ignorance, chicanery and charlatanry among the general population.[12] We have also seen how some travellers, impelled by their interests or special studies, were concerned with some specific aspects and ignored the rest. Al-Muqaddasī was greatly concerned with populations and their circumstances,[13] while Nāṣir-i Khusraw was keen to highlight his attitudes and impressions,[14] and al-Zamakhsharī was interested in places in the Arabian peninsula and their connection to the Qurʾan and the Prophet's life.[15]

This diversity and colourful variety of travel literature are still evident in modern journeys to the Saudi territories, journeys made from the beginning of the twentieth century until the present. Some set out to perform the pilgrimage and visit the holy places; such travellers are concerned to describe the route, the sites where water can be found, travel procedures, and the rituals and Islamic sites they saw. Others travelled for nationalist and political reasons, the most famous being Amīn al-Rīḥānī, whose experiences are recorded in his book *Mulūk al-ʿArab aw riḥla fī al-bilād al-ʿArabiyya* ('Arab Rulers, or a Journey in the Arab Lands'; Beirut, 1925–51). Naturally, al-Rīḥānī was not concerned with describing the route or visiting the sites, but was primarily interested in the personages he met and talked with, especially political personages. There were also writers or journalists who were drawn either by chance or by the occasion (because they chase news and collect it) and who recorded in semi-journalistic reports the signs of the renaissance that had occurred during the flourishing of the Saudi period.

But whatever the inclinations and fancies of different travellers, none could ignore their own curiosity; and so we find them, despite their different aims and orientations, writing little or much on customs and traditions that they observed and which aroused their interest. These might be a certain type of behaviour or customs or certain manners in eating, dress or drink. Some wrote on the dialects of town-dwellers and of some Bedouin tribes. Others recorded the texts of popular and Bedouin songs which they heard, as well as other curious phenomena they saw worthy of recording.

Thus the travel account becomes a mixed form, whose disparate elements can only be brought together by the author himself. He has the freedom to write what he pleases in whatever style he chooses. Indeed, the travel account is closer to the memoir in which the writer records, in a spontaneous manner, what has happened to him, or what he has heard or seen during a particular period of his life.[16] The journey spans a limited period in a person's life: it normally begins and ends on a specific date; it may continue for days, months or years. However, some travel accounts turn away from their initial spontaneous style to adopt the style of a scientific investigation, a style behind which we discern much effort and exertion. This is exemplified in the travel account of Muḥammad Ḥusayn Haykal, *Fī manzil al-waḥy* ('In the Abode of Revelation'), which runs to hundreds of pages, even though the traveller stayed there for only a few weeks. It is clear that the writer had prepared his material long before his arrival in the Hijaz. Such accounts may satisfy the reader who is seeking information only; but it will not satisfy his artistic feelings, for such accounts often lose the sense of spontaneity and surprise, and the human aspects of the writer largely disappear from view.

Few are the travel accounts where the author gives free rein to his nature without affectation or design. One of the exceptions I have come across is the account of the writer Ibrāhīm ʿAbd al-Qādir al-Māzinī's journey to the Hijaz in 1930. This work is imbued with al-Māzinī's personality, his vehemence, his impetuosity, his ridicule and his defiance. He frequently resorts to a storytelling style and deploys dialogue in a brilliant manner, so that one finds oneself looking at wonderfully artistic canvases, as if one were seeing a film reel bursting with life. It is clear that al-Māzinī did not intend to convey historical, archaeological or social information in his travel account, as did Ibrāhīm Rifʿat in his *Mirʾāt al-ḥaramayn* ('The Mirror of the Two Sanctuaries') or al-Batanūnī in *al-Riḥla al-Ḥijāziyya* ('Journey to the Hijaz'), but intended to amuse and delight the reader, which is in general the main aim of the storyteller or writer.

It is clear from the above that travel accounts have different aspects that attract literary scholars as well as geographers, historians, social researchers and others. Each looks at the account from his own specialism. It is because of this that in collecting the material for this study, I have attempted to extract, from all the intermingled mass of travel accounts, what concerns the literary scholar above all. I was eager to find what travellers recorded of our literature in the three periods of Turkish, Hashemite and Saudi rule. What little I found made me redirect my attention to their accounts of cultural life in general. The features recorded of social life, in its various forms, should be treated with caution, as they reflect the historical development our country underwent over a period of more than seventy years.

Modern Travel Accounts: Reasons and Types

The Arabs' connections to the Arabian peninsula were evident even before the appearance of Islam. They extend to the pre-Islamic era (al-Jāhiliyya), when waves of people from the peninsula spread beyond the borders of their homeland to live in Iraq and Syria. But after the Islamic conquests the Arabs, no longer content to live within the limits of the desert, penetrated into remote cities. They bore a new message that made them military leaders, after having been content to be subjects of the Persians and Romans.

Islam bestowed a special importance on the Arabian peninsula, which has made it the object of veneration down through the ages. On the one hand it was the birthplace of Islam, and on the other the source of the language in which the Qurʾan was revealed. It was natural that the Hijaz, which contained the holy sites, would enjoy pride of place in the minds of Muslims, and that the pilgrimage would be the main motive for their travel. Despite the neglect that the Arabian peninsula was subject to after the transfer of the seat of the caliphate outside its borders, the holy sites retained their religious pre-eminence. Makkah remained a distinguished centre, not simply because of its religious significance but because of its cultural role, as it was, and still is, a centre for the meeting of Muslims from the various Islamic regions. Thus it was one of the most important centres for spreading culture throughout those regions, and formed a connecting link between the scholars of the Islamic realm, east, west, south and north, throughout past ages.[17]

Pilgrimage was thus the main factor in the journeys of large numbers of Muslim travellers to the Hijaz throughout the centuries, men such as Ibn Jubayr, Ibn Baṭṭūṭa, Ibn al-Mujāwir, al- ʿAyyāshī and many others. Ḥamad al-Jāsir has noted the superiority of the scholars of the Arab west (Maghreb) over those of the east (Mashreq) in this field, as well as the deep cultural bonds that connected Maghrebis and the Andalusians with the holy regions. He enumerates the many scholars from the Maghreb who travelled to the Hijaz to learn and disseminate their knowledge there,[18] and mentions that Sheikh ʿAbd al-Ḥayy al-Kattānī recorded forty-six books of travellers from the Maghreb. He adds that there are scores more of these travel accounts still in manuscript form, preserved in private and public libraries in the Maghreb.[19]

If the pilgrimage, and perhaps the desire to seek learning, helped to preserve the history of the two holy cities of Makkah and Madinah, the same was not true of the rest of the Arabian peninsula, which lost its allure for travellers, and remained unknown and unnoticed until recent times. The city of Ṭāʾif, despite its historical links with the beginnings of the Prophet's mission, the spread of Islam, and its proximity to the holy city of Makkah, was mostly neglected, because travellers who came to perform the pilgrimage and visit the holy sites were mainly concerned with the two holy cities, with describing the routes to them, and other related matters. Their discussion of other issues was based more on hearsay than on experience.[20] It is safe to say that the more we penetrate into the interior of the Arabian peninsula, the more ignorant we are of its history, which results in a weakening of its links with the outside world.

This state of affairs continued until the beginning of the twentieth century. We do not intend here to follow all modern Arab journeys to the Arabian peninsula; our purpose, as stated in the title of this chapter, is to focus on the regions that are now part of the Saudi state. The reason for setting limits to this field is to enable the researcher to cover all aspects of the subject, which would prove too unwieldy were the study extended to the whole of the peninsula. Moreover, the Saudi kingdom incorporated most regions in the peninsula and its most significant and sacred sites. Many of the journeys of modern Arab travellers to these areas were simply a continuation of those of their predecessors; this fact will be of interest to those studying the historical links in the Arab spirit, as well as comparing old with new.

It is unnecessary to point out that the kingdom of Saudi Arabia, with its present borders, did not exist at the beginning of the twentieth century, which is the starting date of this study. This official designation was declared only in 1351/1932,[21] when King Abdul Aziz Āl Saʿūd wished to express the political unity that he had created for the first time in the history of the Arabian peninsula, and through which he united its weak, fragmented and warring regions.

Those regions consisted of small emirates, constructed for political rather than religious, linguistic, natural or social reasons, nominally independent but in fact subject to foreign domination. The Hijaz, Najd, al-Aḥsāʾ and the northern parts were controlled by the Turks, while Idrisid Tihama supported British policy. Following World War I, Britain was still the prime mover of events in the Hijaz and Tihama, while at the same time, ʿAbd al-ʿAzīz had succeeded in regaining Riyadh and annexing the eastern, northern and southern areas under his authority. Uniting these different emirates was not an easy task; it required a continuous struggle that lasted throughout the first quarter of the twentieth century, from the conquest of Riyadh in 1319/1902 by ʿAbd al-ʿAzīz until the seizure of the Hijaz in 1343/1924–5. The efforts to strengthen the pillars of that unity and to consolidate it continued beyond that time, until the proclamation of 'The Kingdom of Saudi Arabia' (al-Mamlaka al-ʿArabiyya al-Su'ūdiyya) on 21 Jumādā I 1351/22 September 1932.[22] Travellers to one or another of these emirates before their unification naturally could not give a true picture of their political, social and cultural situations after unification. For example, in the account of al-Batanūnī (1909) the Hijaz under Turkish rule was very different from the Hijaz at the time of Haykal's trip in 1936, at the beginning of Saudi rule. This difference does not lie in the realm of nature, history or archaeology, or in a sudden change in people's customs, morals or livelihoods. Rather, it lies in the new form of government that introduced fundamental reforms that allowed the country to enter a new age. One of the most important reforms, as we shall see, was the establishment of security, coupled with an educational renaissance. Al-Batanūnī was much concerned with the issue of security, as were many other travellers in the past; but this was no longer an issue for Haykal after security had been established and fears dispelled in the new Saudi era. This shows the necessity of distinguishing between different political periods when studying Arab travel accounts to the kingdom. But this political specification should not be forced or arbitrary, for we must distinguish between what changes suddenly, such as the issue of security, and that which requires time for change and development, such as education and other social issues.

Arab accounts of travel to the Hijaz in the twentieth century have portrayed three different political eras: the Turkish era, that ended in 1916 with the Arab Revolt; the Hashemite, from 1916 until King Abdul Aziz captured the Hijaz in 1924; and the Saudi era, that began then and continues until the present. The first era is represented here by two travel accounts: that of Ibrāhīm Rifᶜat Pasha, *Mirʾāt al-ḥaramayn aw al-riḥla al-Ḥijaziyya wa-al-ḥajj wa-mashāᶜiruh al-dīniyya*, an account of four journeys undertaken by the author during the pilgrimage season in 1901, 1903, 1904 and 1908;[23] and that of Muḥammad Labīb al-Batanūnī's journey as a companion of the Khedive ᶜAbbās Ḥilmī at the end of 1909, during the pilgrimage of 1327. Ibrāhīm Rifᶜat's journeys took place at the end of the reign of the Sharīf ᶜAwn al-Rafīq and continued during the reign of ᶜAlī Pasha, while al-Batanānī's journey took place at the beginning of the reign of Sharīf Ḥusayn Pasha, ᶜAlī Pasha's son, in 1327/1909.

The Hashemite period is represented by three travel accounts: that of Muḥammad Rashīd Riḍa at the beginning of al-Ḥusayn's revolt against the Turks (1916);[24] that of Khayr al-Dīn al-Ziriklī (*Mā raʾaytu wa-ma samiᶜtu*, 1920); and Amīn al-Rīḥānī's *Mulūk al-ᶜArab aw riḥla fī al-bilād al-ᶜarabiyya* (1922). The last two journeys took place at the end of the Hashemite period, a few years before the Saudis seized the Hijaz. Al-Rīḥānī's journey was not confined only to the Hijaz, but included most areas of the Arabian peninsula: Najd, ᶜAsīr, Yemen, Lahaj, the nine protectorates, Bahrain and Iraq.

During the Saudi period travel to the region increased and became more varied. It is sufficient to mention only a few accounts: Ibrāhīm ᶜAbd al Qādir al-Māzinī's *Riḥla ilā al-Ḥijāz* (1930), Amīr Shakīb Arslān's *al-*

Irtisāmāt al-liṭāf fī khāṭir al-ḥajj ilā aqdas maṭāf (around 1930) and Muḥammad Ḥusayn Haykal's *Fī manzil al-waḥy* (1936). Also worthy of mention are the journeys of ʿAbd al-Wahhāb ʿAzzām to the Hijaz and other regions of the Saudi kingdom at different times, beginning in 1937, Aḥmad Ḥusayn's *Mushāhadātī fī Jazīrat al-ʿArab* (1948), Bint al-Shāṭīʾ's *Arḍ al-muʿjizāt: Riḥla fī Jazīrat al-ʿArab* (1951) and Muḥammad Badīʾ Sharīf's *Fī mahbiṭ al-rūḥ* (1963).[25] It is important to note that most of these journeys during these three different political periods were mainly to the Hijaz and especially to the two holy cities. In this respect they continue the long series of pilgrimage journeys known by earlier Muslims. Few went beyond the boundaries of the Hijaz to neighbouring areas, or combined the performance of religious duty with the scientific imperative to reveal the truth or discover the unknown. Only one man, due to his own particular circumstances, and a pupil of western travellers, undertook such an adventure: Amīn al-al-Rīḥānī. Those who visited other areas in Najd and al-Aḥsāʾ, such as Aḥmad Ḥusayn and Bint al-Shāṭīʾ, did so for journalistic or touristic reasons, and their writings conform to those aims.

The fact that Arab travellers refrained from penetrating the unknown territories of the Arabian peninsula before the Saudi era can be attributed to many reasons, the most important of which was lack of security on the one hand, and lack of motivation on the other. During the Turkish and Hashemite periods security in the Hijaz was no better than in other areas, but there was motivation – a religious motivation – which bestowed on the adventure a noble aim for whose sake life and money were considered cheap. Apart from the two holy cities, there was nothing to impel an Arab traveller to strike out into the desert, suffer hardship and expose himself to danger. This was the opposite of what we see with western travellers who, since the sixteenth century, roamed through the whole of the Arabian peninsula, and who suffered, for the sake of their objectives, whether scientific or colonialist, much discomfort, sometimes leading to death, but who were sufficiently motivated to undergo such adventures.[26]

The Hijaz not only monopolized the religious centre but from the beginning of the twentieth century was also the pivot of Arab politics, especially after the outbreak of World War I and the declaration of the revolt against the Turks in 1916. For many Arab intellectuals outside the peninsula, it embodied two ideals: the religious and the Arab. The attempts to win independence from the Ottomans towards the end of the nineteenth century were sometimes joined to a call for closer relations with the peninsula, the cradle of Arabism and birthplace of Islam. Likewise, talk of an Islamic caliphate at the time of Sultan ʿAbd al-Ḥamīd had directed people's eyes towards the Arabian peninsula and to the possibility of establishing an Arab caliphate that would restore Islam to its glory and protect the rights of the Arabs. There is no doubt that ʿAbd al-Raḥmān al-Kawākibī in his book *Umm al-qurā* was influenced by this idea. He called for making the holy city of Makkah the centre for the *ʿumm al-qurāʾ* society that would include representatives of the entire Muslim world. Al-Kawākibī also believed that the Arabian peninsula was the best suited of the Islamic countries to be the centre of religious policies,[27] and that its inhabitants were the most suited to preserve the Islamic religion.[28]

When the Arab Revolt broke out in 1916, the hopes of the Arabs increased. They believed that their long-held dream of independence and unity was about to be achieved. Consequently, their attachment to the peninsula, and especially to the Hijaz, increased. Their writers and poets expressed this in dozens of poems and articles.[29] As for Amīn al-Rīḥānī, he preferred to leave America and go to the Arabian peninsula, after having followed the news about the Arabs and writing on them from afar.

> I accompanied the Arabs when they rebelled against the Turks during the war, I accompanied them in the English magazines and the Arabic newspapers. Through writing, I discharged part of the duty imposed by love and admiration. I was lucky during that period to visit Spain, and as I stood in the Alhambra, in the room where Washington Irving wrote his priceless book, I heard a voice calling me to the birthplace of inspiration and prophecy, in the name of nationalism and for the sake of the homeland.[30]

Al-Rīḥānī's wish was fulfilled when he visited the Arabian peninsula, meeting its rulers and writing about both. He aimed (as he says) at serving the Arab cause through introducing the different rulers to one another, in an attempt to establish accord between them.[31] However, such an accord did not take place, and al-Rīḥānī returned empty-handed.

During this time, King Abdul Aziz worked and planned, in silence and wisdom. Far from the lights and sounds, he fought for the sake of that unity which was so difficult to attain, and which aspirations and negotiations had failed to achieve. Through his victories in the military, political and reformist spheres, ʿAbd al-ʿAzīz succeeded in drawing the attention of the Arabs to the Arabian peninsula once again, after it had turned away in anger following al-Ḥusayn's failure and the division of the Arab countries between the Allies. Muḥammad Ḥusayn Haykal says that with the consolidation of ʿAbd al-ʿAzīz's rule in the Hijaz, 'Talk of this conqueror of the Arab lands from Najd began to recur in the press both in the west and in the east. I met one of those journalists, acclaimed for his precision and balance of judgment on things and people; how surprised I was on hearing one of them, the well-known German Von Weisel, sing the praises of Ibn Saʿūd to the extent of calling him the Bismarck of the East. Von Weisel had met and conversed with Ibn Saʿūd and had become acquainted with the goals of his policies.'[32]

By strengthening security and introducing developments in modern ways of life, Saudi rule was able to attract writers, thinkers and journalists to visit Saudi Arabia and write about it. King Abdul Aziz's generosity was legendary, and the state spent generously on its guests even before the discovery of oil, when its resources were still limited. Further, the state realized the vital importance of the media in revealing the truth and rebutting the falsehoods circulated by its enemies, particularly following the conquest of the Hijaz and the resulting tension in its relationships with some of the neighbouring Arab countries. It is for this reason that so many writers, journalists and scholars came to the kingdom during this short period of its history; the country had never known the like in its past.

From the preceding overview it becomes clear that modern Arab travel accounts can be classified according to the different historical periods in which the journeys took place, or through their content and the purposes for which they were written. Indeed, the researcher does not lack for other classificatory schemes, such as analysing the forms or styles of the travel accounts or the way they express the personality of their writers, or through investigating their historical errors and truths. While we concede the importance of different classificatory schemes, we prefer a classification according to subject matter, bearing in mind other aspects as much as possible, and fully realizing the extent of the difficulties the scholar may face by being constricted by narrow boundaries and divisions. Taking this into consideration, we can identify among modern Arab travel accounts three distinct types: (1) journeys for pilgrimage and sightseeing; (2) political journeys; and (3) journalistic journeys. We will explore each type briefly in order to reveal its objectives, historical conditions and general characteristics.

Pilgrimage and Sightseeing Accounts

We have already noted that the religious motivation is an ancient one, since God enjoined the pilgrimage on all Muslims, making it one of the pillars of Islam ('People will come to you on pilgrimage, on foot and on lean camels, and from every deep mountain pass' [Qurʾan 22: 27]). We also noted that the travel of modern Arabs to the holy sites is only a continuation of the journeys made by their predecessors. The motivation behind these journeys is expressed in the titles of their accounts: *Mirʾāt al-ḥaramayn* ('Mirror of the Two Holy Shrines'), *Riḥla Ḥijāziyya* ('Journey to the Hijaz'), *Fī manzil al-waḥy* ('In the Abode of Revelation') and so on. Often the introduction recounts the circumstances of the journey and the religious reasons why the author wrote his account. Ibrāhīm Rifʿat says:

> I was eager to go on pilgrimage, ardent to perform this religious obligation, and entreated God to grant me success in seeing His holy sanctuary and its rituals. God graciously answered my supplication, blessing it as he had blessed Abraham's prayer that brought forth a nation (that will endure) until the Day of Judgment, made its barren regions proper, and spread there true civilization and firm law. For in 1318/1901 I was appointed commander of the guards of the palanquin (*maḥmal*), and I knew that the only way I could show my gratitude for God's blessings was by recording

> my journey from the first step to the last, and publishing it for the benefit of people that they may be guided by its light should they make the pilgrimage to God's sanctuary or visit the peninsula. I neglected no detail, either small or large, of what I saw or heard, but recorded it (all).[33]

Rifᶜat was granted the blessing of making the pilgrimage three more times, as the leader of the [Egyptian] pilgrims (Amīr al-Ḥajj). He wrote of his enormous expenses on these four journeys and in publishing his accounts of them: 'The most serious consideration in publishing this account, and in suffering the enormous costs, is that it is the most articulate elucidation of one of the duties of religion, and the most faithful description of the birthplace of prophecy and the inspiration of the law, revealing to you the life of the Prophet and the places honoured by his presence as though you were to see them with your own eyes.'[34]

As for al-Batanūnī, he accompanied Khedive ᶜAbbās II on the pilgrimage as 'a special envoy of His Eminence during his journey to the Hijaz'. On his return, he was ordered by the Khedive to record something 'of this blessed journey'.[35] Al-Batanūnī says, 'Since these lands were still not known to the learned and wise as they ought to be . . . I saw fit to add to the Khedival journey a few words on sacral religious feelings.'[36] He adds, 'In performing this sacred duty I did not confine myself to discussing points of religion; my study treats what might concern the reader in terms of architectural, social, geographical and historical matters, which no one 6efore me who has written of these lands has written about.'[37]

It is clear from the introductions of both Rifᶜat and al-Batanūnī that they considered the writing of their travel accounts from a religious perspective, as a form of giving thanks to God for granting their wish to perform the pilgrimage, and as an effort to strive for rewards for good deeds and to enlighten Muslims on religious matters. That is why, despite all that has been written about Makkah and Madinah since the dawn of Islam until the present, they still perceive this region as 'unknown' and in need of rediscovery. Thus their accounts had to include a great many different ceremonies and rituals connected with the pilgrimage. This naturally led to the enlargement of the account, so that it became more akin to travel books and to historical and jurisprudential reference books. It is enough to look briefly at al-Batanūnī's account to discern this tendency in travel writing. He begins with a preface fifty-four pages long, in which he writes of the Arab *umma* (tribes and kings) before Islam: the ʿImlīqs, ʿĀd, the Muʿīnīs [?], Ṭasm, Jadīs, Thamūd, Sabaʾ [Sheba], and the ʿAdnānī kings (of northern Arabia). Then he writes of the Umayyads, the Abbasids, the Tatars, the Persians and so on. This is followed by a geographical section on the Arabian peninsula, its different divisions and its modern history. Frequently, not content with the preface, he interrupts the flow of events in his account to return to his historical sources at some length, talking also about rituals and prayers or devoting independent chapters to them.[38]

In addition to the religious motivation in both Rifʿat and al-Batanūnī's journeys, we should not ignore the worldly motivation, nor should we forget that both writers came to the Hijaz in an official capacity: Rifʿat was the chief of the guards of the *maḥmal* and later Amīr al-Ḥajj, while al-Batanūnī was assigned to accompany the Khedive on his sojourn in the Hijaz. It was natural that both should discharge their duties scrupulously, giving due care and attention to the official side. Al-Batanūnī's work was similar to that of a journalist accompanying the head of state, charged with covering his news and movements; he wrote his book at the official request of the Khedive himself.[39] As for Ibrāhīm Rifʿat, due to his position he was assigned to write long reports on his trips to present to responsible persons in the Egyptian government.

There is no doubt that the official aspect of the journeys of Rifʿat and al-Batanūnī had a great impact not only on their opinions and views about the lives of people in the Hijaz (of which more later) but also on the shape of their accounts in terms of form. Often the imperative of the report dominates the writer's style, and we often encounter long passages of official reports inserted between paragraphs and chapters. These may have significance for the historian or researcher, but not for the ordinary reader, and could become a source of boredom and frustration for those who seek artistic pleasure or look for aesthetic elements in the account.[40]

Travel accounts of the pilgrimage underwent a noticeable development with Muḥammad Ḥusayn Haykal. Such accounts were no longer concerned with accumulating information or quoting old and new sources haphazardly, but began to select what was appropriate and what could express the writer's personal stance. In his preference for contemplative thought, his literary bent and his use of western styles in his method and composition, Haykal differs totally from Rifᶜat and al-Batanūnī. His motive in visiting the holy places was not only his desire to perform the pilgrimage and visit the holy sites; he was concerned to uncover 'the truth of these lands, and why they were destined to be chosen for the revelation and the Prophet's message, in such a manner that could convince contemporary thought. What foreign scholars have written is far from the spiritual phenomenon that transformed history fourteen centuries ago, and which will continue to be influential in the life of the world as long as spiritual forces have influence and power over its direction.' The writer's visit thus had a specific purpose, a scholarly one that can be considered a continuation of his research into the life of the Prophet when he was preparing his book on this subject (*Ḥayāt Muḥammad*, 1954). Haykal wished to follow the ways of experimental scientists who relied only on what they themselves discovered and experienced with their senses. Reading cannot compensate for experience and first-hand observation. 'At the end, I felt that I would always lack the essence of what I was studying if I did not go myself to the land of the Arab Prophet, and did not stand in the same place he stood during the most crucial periods of his life.'[41]

Haykal was precise in defining the plan for his scholarly journey and in defining what he wanted from it. Thus his account, despite its bulkiness, has clarity, and its parts are largely well connected. The traces of the Prophet are many, and scattered throughout the Hijaz; the author succeeded in retracing most of these and connecting them together with precise artistic links. His method in connecting these historical truths is that of self-reflection and conjuring up images of the past so that we can see them like moving reels that we witness with our own eyes, react to the events and situations depicted, and participate with our own emotions and ideas.

Political Journeys

There is scarcely a travel account that is devoid of political aspects; but the only Arab travel account that from beginning to end is determined by its political character is Amīn al-Rīḥānī's *Mulūk al-ʿArab*, which recounts his travels through many regions of the Arabian peninsula, beginning in the Hijaz in Rajab 1340/February 1922. The author does not conceal his objectives, for he asserts in his introduction that he wrote the book to serve the Arab cause and to make Arab rulers familiar with one another, for 'among Arab rulers today there is none who has travelled through all the Arab lands, and not one who can say, "I know the Arab countries, their rulers, their inhabitants, their tribes, their economic and agricultural conditions, their internal and external political issues, from reports conveyed to me by knowledgeable persons, and information from those who are aloof from political aims and religious partisanship"'.[42] Al-Rīḥānī regrets this total ignorance of conditions in the Arabian peninsula, and the fact that the British Government's Colonial Department is the body specializing in these regions, producing a publication whose information is based on the reports of its political agents and the writings of western travellers, and regularly revised. But this publication is not free from mistakes, and its distribution is limited to official circles.[43]

Al-Rīḥānī does not deny the political task that he assigned himself and applied himself to carrying out. In addition to the main title of his book, *Mulūk al-ʿArab*, he declares frankly that his book contains a political aspect, and adds, 'There is nothing in the book, whether literary or political, descriptive or critical, that is not the truth, although not disinterested.'[44] After his visit to the Hijaz, Yemen and ʿAsīr, he says,

> Here in Yemen and ʿAsīr my political mission ends. I sought to serve the Imām Yaḥyā [of Yemen] by making his cause more comprehensible to the British and their interests, and by drawing them closer to his mentality, and paving the way for reconciliation between him and al-Idrīsī. So I suggested a conference in which he and his opponents could exchange views, get to know each other, and come to an agreement; but he declined, for reasons that I comprehend but that cannot be remedied. The Imām desires to conquer all of the Yemen, and desires as well, I believe, the title of King Ḥusayn, whom he does not recognize. I wanted to serve King Ḥusayn by concluding two pacts that, at first, would connect the Hijaz with Yemen and ʿAsīr by even the thinnest of threads, because I believed

> that His Majesty represented a noble Arab national idealist. He did not agree to either, and I do not think he approved the idea, for reasons I am aware of but that cannot be remedied. Neither Imām Yaḥyā nor al-Sayyid al-Idrīsī recognize his Royal Majesty al-Ḥusayn as the king of the Arabs. Nevertheless, they both extended their allegiance and assistance to him; but he refused them. Who then is the stumbling block in the way of an Arab renaissance?[45]

In spite of al-Rīḥānī's assertion in his introduction that he undertook this arduous task of reconciling the Arab kings voluntarily and in service of the Arab cause, suspicions were aroused about him and his undertaking, suspicions that he himself described in his introduction in recounting the words of King Abdul Aziz at their first meeting: 'They told us that you are an American who came to spread the Christian religion in the Arab countries. They said that you represent certain companies and came to gain some concessions. They said that you come from the Hijaz, that you support the Sharīf, and that you work to achieve his claim. They said other things as well. We replied, "If this man is harmful, we know how to guard ourselves against him; and if there is good in him, we know how to benefit from it." We know, sir, about your mission; may God bless your efforts.'[44] In another interview al-Rīḥānī mentions that King Abdul Aziz showed him a letter from King Ḥusayn asking his opinion of him, and quotes King Abdul Aziz: '"What is your opinion, sir? Do not tell me that you have no interest in politics and that your travels in our country are simply for the sake of knowledge. We sympathize [?]; we understand." He stroked his beard, smiling his charming smile.'[45]

The truth is that al-Rīḥānī's adventure does call for doubt and reflection. The author came to the Arabian peninsula at a crucial period in its modern history, when despair had set in after al-Ḥusayn's failure, Britain's breach of its promises and its division of the spoils of the 'sick man of Europe' (Turkey) with its French ally. Did al-Rīḥānī undertake his mission at the request of the British, who were at that time interested in settling the situation in the Arabian peninsula? This view is supported by several considerations. Firstly, this type of conduct was not foreign to British policy; Britain had acted in the same manner in preparing the way for the

Arab Revolt when it had sent its 'tools' (as Khayr al-Dīn al-Ziriklī says) to the princes of the peninsula to negotiate with one and correspond with another.[48] Further, it is difficult to believe that al-Rīḥānī would undertake such political consultations with Arab leaders in his personal capacity, for these talks went beyond what is normal in ordinary visits and journalistic interviews, to the extent of proposing pacts and making agreements between the Arab emirates. Moreover, al-Rīḥānī's ties of friendship with Britain's political emissary in al-Ḥudayda were swiftly consolidated,[49] and he accompanied him on his trip to meet al-Idrīsī in Jīzān.

On the other hand, in defence of al-Rīḥānī, it can be said that he was not the only one to be attracted by the political events taking place in the peninsula at that time. He was preceded by many Arab brethren who participated in the Arab Revolt, as both planners and instigators. Among them were both Muslims and Christians, who came to the Hijaz fleeing the oppression of the unionists and who saw in al-Ḥusayn the great saviour; they assisted him in the field of politics as well as in the field of war. Among them were ministers, ambassadors, leaders, consultants, journalists, administrators and so on. It is enough to mention Yūsuf Yāsīn, Khayr al-Dīn al-Ziriklī, Fuʿād al-Khaṭīb, Muhibb al-Dīn al-Khaṭīb, Nūrī Saʿīd, Kāmil al-Qaṣṣāb, Salīm Sarkīs and Constantine Yannī, among many others. Al-Rīḥānī was no exception; but he had enlarged his circle of connections to include all the Arab leadership, following the changes in political conditions during that period. For while Fayṣal ibn al-Ḥusayn had been appointed king of Iraq, and Transjordan had been apportioned to his brother ʿAbd Allāh ibn al-Ḥusayn, al-Ḥusayn's own fortunes in the Hijaz were waning, and many of the Arab politicians who had gathered around him during the Arab Revolt now abandoned him.[50]

It may also be said that in his book al-Rīḥānī did not introduce any aims or principles that he had not already declared. A partisan of the Arabs, he was passionate about all things Arabic, the people, the language and the history, to an almost fanatical extent. We see this in the events, images and ideas that he recorded in his book, so much so that at his hands pan-Arabism becomes transformed into the standard by which he distinguishes between right and wrong or virtue and vice.[51] This was not a sudden infatuation, but the result of long reflection and thought, a feeling of having been lost for many years in the American diaspora, and extensive reading of the accounts of western explorers who travelled widely in all regions of the Arabian peninsula (such as Burckhardt, Burton and Doughty) and the books of western historians who wrote about Islamic glories (such as Carlyle and Washington Irving), all combined with a limitless admiration for the classical Arabic heritage, and not least the thought of the poet Abū ʿAlāʾ al-Maʿarrī: 'I began to boast that I came from the nation that had produced this wise, brave and free poet.'[52]

Whatever the case, despite all obstacles and hardships, al-Rīhānī succeeded in penetrating for the first time the boundaries between the competing small Arab emirates, and in conveying his message to the Arab princes and kings. Although he failed in his political endeavours, in his travel writings he succeeded brilliantly in recording that important era in the modern history of the Arabian peninsula. Al-Rīḥānī's political travel account has a unique style, for he combined the past with the present, history with politics, and imprinted all with his personality, his philosophy and his ideas, enriched by his poetic imagination and his elegantly flowing literary style. Perhaps its most important aspect is his acute portrayal of political personalities and his attempts to fathom their attitudes and thoughts. He writes of particular personalities on more than one occasion, and is careful to convey the situation precisely, not omitting the circumstances in which the interview takes place or the person's individual characteristics in terms of appearance, posture or behaviour, recording expressions, movements and gestures. He uses short, graceful and suggestive phrases, and often brings the dialogue down to earth by employing the words the person himself used or the phrases he quoted. He is a master of the dramatic sketch, yet is also realistic, writing of his impressions in a direct and frank style.

Muluk al-ʿArab is an innovative work in its structure, style and impact, and has earned the admiration of many critics and scholars. Jūrj Ghurayyib has said of it, 'The least impression left by this book is amazement. Al-Rīḥānī is the first to unlock the East in a period when it was closed in upon itself, the first to fling open its doors in the face of time. In travelling from one minor ruler to another, the world is turned topsy-turvy, due to the wealth of al-Rīḥānī's reports, descriptions, and analyses that surpass the boundaries of history, description and analysis to incorporate philosophical, artistic, literary and social dimensions. Under his pen, the account becomes is unbridled, and thought is given free rein. His work is enveloped in sound scholarship and opinions supported by proofs, observations accompanied by scrutiny of hidden issues, and a literary style that elevates the account to its highest forms of expression.'[53]

We have noted that the political aspect dominates al-Rīḥānī's travel account. As for Khayr al-Dīn al-Ziriklī's *Mā ra'aytu wa-mā samiʿtu*, it is dominated by a scholarly bent, even though his coming to the Hijaz was more for the purpose of seeking political refuge. Al-Ziriklī states that he fled from Damascus following the defeat of the Syrians in the battle of Maysalān in 1920, going first to Egypt via Palestine. The French occupiers of Syria sentenced him to death *in absentia*, along with a number of other Free Syrians, amongst whom were Kāmil al-Qaṣṣab, Shukrī al-Quwwatlī and Tawfīq al-Yāzijī. After staying in Cairo for around two months, he went to the Hijaz at the invitation of Sharīf al-Ḥusayn. Al-Ziriklī had written a letter to al-Ḥusayn from Egypt, informing him of his situation and enquiring what the Sharīf intended doing to resist the French. He states that he travelled to the Hijaz with a Hijazii passport in Muharram 1339/September 1920,[54] and enjoyed the Sharīf's hospitality for three months,[55] after which he returned to Egypt in 1339/January 1921.[56]

Although, as evidenced by his writings, al-Ziriklī only came to the Hijaz to appeal for help from the Sharīf in support of Syria and for solidarity with her in her ordeal, he mentions nothing about what transpired between him and al-Ḥusayn on this issue, apart from what was contained in a poem that he presented to al-Ḥusayn on some occasion, in which he mentions Syria's suffering under the French occupation and urges him to come to its help.[57] Except for this poem, there is nothing in the travel account that indicates that al-Ziriklī had addressed al-Ḥusayn or negotiated with him over the Syrian question, even though he stayed at 'Government House' and met with His Majesty for two hours each evening throughout the period of his stay, which exceeded ninety days.[58] Even so, al-Ziriklī benefited from this long stay with al-Ḥusayn, for he wrote many valuable pages on him and his four sons (ʿAlī, Fayṣal, ʿAbd Allāh and Zayd) which the scholar of the history of this period cannot do without.

He also outlined the history of the Arab Revolt and the well-known events and developments that overtook it. The major part of the book is devoted to his trip from Makkah to Ṭāʾif,[59] in which we can see al-Ziriklī as the investigative scholar who is not content with what he sees or hears but must return to classical sources for verification, correction and comparison. In this he was, without a doubt, a pioneer for all later scholars interested in the history of the tribes and the verification of their locations.

In his journey al-Ziriklī was concerned with history, archaeology, and the traditions and morals of the Bedouins, rather than with politics. He may have despaired of al-Ḥusayn's ability to change the situation in Syria, or to annul the agreement between the two great powers, Britain and France. He expresses his disappointment by quoting a certain poet.[60] Perhaps his personal circumstances prevented him from clarifying his position clearly and frankly, in the way that al-Rīḥānī did. For al-Ziriklī was merely a militant writer, who fled for his life and freedom from colonialist repression. Moreover, he was a subject of the Hashemite state during its brief tenure in Syria. His relationship to al-Ḥusayn was more that of a subject to his patron; and it is not unlikely that al-Ḥusayn confided in him certain matters and assigned to him some tasks during his sojourn. This is indicated by al-Ziriklī when he mentions in his *al-Aʿlām* that after his return to Egypt he took Arabian citizenship in the Hijaz in 1921, and that al-Ḥusayn appointed him to assist his son ʿAbd Allāh in Transjordan. When the Hashemite government was established in Amman, al-Ziriklī was one of its first appointees, becoming a general inspector of education, and later head of the office (*dīwān*) of the prime minister from 1921 to 1923.[61]

Journalistic Travels

By this we mean the occasional short trips to the region undertaken by some Arab journalists and writers at one time or another to cover some important occasion or simply to gather information. These visits may have been prompted by an official invitation from the government, or undertaken on the writer's personal initiative. Sometimes these visits coincided with the pilgrimage season, enabling the writer to fulfil this obligation and combine a religious duty with journalistic work.

Perhaps the first important occasion that drew the interest of journalists during the Saudi period was the convening of the first Islamic World Congress in Makkah in 1344/1926, in response to the invitation of King Abdul Aziz āl Saʿūd. This conference was attended by a number of Arab journalists, among them Muḥammad ʿAlī Ḥasan, the proprietor of the newspaper and printing press of Nahḍat al-Sharq and the representative of the newspaper *al-Liwāʾ al-Maṣrī* which was affiliated with the National Party [al-Ḥizb al-Waṭanī]. He covered the conference and produced a short booklet on its proceedings (*Ṣaḥīfa muʾjiza bi-aʿmāl Muʾtamar al-ālam al-Islāmī al-Awwal bi-Makkah al-mukarrama ʿām 1344*). The booklet contained the opening address delivered by King Abdul Aziz at the start of the conference and his statement to the conference participants.[62] It is formal in tone, and we cannot consider it as a travel account; but it was the first of many journalistic accounts that were not content simply to report news but attempted to depict different aspects of life in the region and to express a specific viewpoint or position. In 1346/1927 Muḥammad Shafīq Muṣṭafa published his *Fī qalb Najd wa-al-Ḥijāz*, which he described as a 'series of political, social and religious articles containing facts and events witnessed in the heart of the Arabian peninsula that no traveller has previously recorded'; these were published serially in the newspaper *al-Siyāsa*.[63] The author states that the renaissance in the Saudi period, following the unification of the two Arab regions of Najd and the Hijaz under one rule, had inspired many to investigate and study the facts at close hand. He writes: 'During his visit to Egypt his Royal Highness Prince Saʿūd had invited Egyptian thinkers to visit his country, study its affairs, and publish the facts for Arabic speakers who were still ignorant of any knowledge of them.'[64]

In the year 1930, the well-known writer Ibrāhīm ʿAbd al Qādir al-Māzinī made a journey to the Hijaz that he later published as *Riḥla ilā al-Ḥijāz*. He did not mention the reason for the trip; however, he did note the celebrations of the confirmation of ʿAbd al-ʿAzīz as ruler of the Hijaz.[65] He also mentioned the banquet that Prince Fayṣal, ʿAbd al-ʿ Azīz's viceregent, held at the Kandara Palace, which was attended by the author and his companions from the Egyptian delegation, as well as by many foreign emissaries in Jeddah. He states, 'Fuʿād Bey Ḥamza gave a speech at the end of the banquet on the occasion of the first anniversary of the confirmation of Ibn Saʿūd as king of the Hijaz, pointing out the reforms undertaken by the Saudi government, and what it was considering doing in different areas.'[66] Among the colleagues who accompanied him from Egypt, al-Māzinī mentions Aḥmad Zakī Pasha, the foremost supporter of Arabism, Nabīh Bey al-ʿAẓma and Khayr al-Dīn al-Ziriklī.[67]

Muḥammad Ḥusayn Haykal's *Fī manzil al-waḥy* sheds some light on al-Māzinī's trip. Haykal notes that at the beginning of winter 1930 the Saudi government had extended an invitation to the Egyptian press to visit the Hijaz on the occasion of King Abdul Aziz's coronation, and that the invitation had originally been addressed to him as the representative of the newspaper *al-Siyāsa*, but he had apologized because of work and had nominated instead his friend and colleague Ibrāhīm ʿAbd al Qādir al-Māzinī.[68] Al-Māzinī states that he undertook this journalistic assignment, and that he and his fellow Arab journalists would telegraph their newspaper offices in Egypt from the Hijaz.[69]

ʿAbd al-Wahhāb ʿAzzām visited the Saudi region more than once and wrote about it in both his first and second travel accounts. On the first trip he came to the Hijaz in 1356/1937 along with other members of Fuʿād University sent to perform the pilgrimage,[70] and on his second, in 1367/1948, he came as minister plenipotentiary of the Egyptian government. On this occasion he was able to travel through the Hijaz and Najd and to record his observations (he states that he went from Jeddah to Madinah nine times by car and twice by plane[71]), while on the first short trip he could only describe, briefly and hastily, the rituals of the pilgrimage and impressions of some Islamic sites that he visited.

ʿAlī at-Ṭanṭawī's *Min nafaḥāt al-ḥaram* is much the same as ʿAzzām's in that it is a record of numerous journeys made by the author to the holy places at different times, the most important being the first, to perform the pilgrimage with the Syrian delegation in 1935, inaugurating the first land route for automobiles. Bint al-Shāṭī's journey in 1951, recorded in her *Arḍ al-muʿjizāt: riḥla fī al-Jazīra al-ʿArabiyya*, was born of her deep-rooted desire to visit the holy lands, although chance played a major role in it. She states:

> At the beginning of 1951, a number of teachers and students of Cairo University met together, and as they discussed the mid-year holidays that were approaching, some suggested travelling to the Sudan to meet our southern brethren, while others preferred to go on pilgrimage to the Hijaz to perform the lesser pilgrimage (*ʿumra*), a journey worthy of attracting all the Muslims amongst us, and to attract students of Arabic language and literature as well as of Islam and its history. However, the cost of participating in the journey was set at 45 guineas, a sum beyond the means of most of those eager to participate, and in the end there were only ten of us left.'

She goes on to say that the journey was supposed to include only Jeddah, Makkah and Madinah, with the aim of performing the lesser pilgrimage and visiting historical sites, but that on learning of their project, Prince Fayṣal āl Saʿūd took them under his care and enabled them to visit other areas of the kingdom that had not occurred to them. Thus they visited Najd, al-Dahnāʾ, and the eastern wing of the peninsula as far as al-Aḥsāʾ and Bahrain. She adds that as soon as they arrived in Jeddah they were surprised to be informed that they were the guests of His Majesty for the period of their stay.[72]

Naturally, these journalistic accounts differ in terms of subject matter, ideas and style from one writer to another, according to their circumstances and the differences in their inclinations and tastes. They may resemble pilgrimage accounts in their description of religious rites and in their expression of spiritual contemplations; some may share with scholarly accounts their interest in tribal conditions, dialects and so on. Despite this, they are united by the journalistic propensity for speed and digression. Many such accounts were published in instalments in journals that addressed the ordinary reader's desires for travel, colour and excitement. Prince Shakīb Arslān pointed to this journalistic aspect in his *al-Irtisāmāt al-liṭāf* when he noted that he had published this account as separate articles in *al-Shūrā*, and that this forced him into countless digressions in response to the readers' taste. He states: 'Sometimes I published [these accounts] in journals that were more like a newspaper than a book. If the writer writes from one week to the next, under the impact of external factors, taking into account daily changes, and being attentive to the psychology of his readers, he is liable to be carried away by digression, to stray from his topic, and to wander in every direction.'[73]

While Arslān wanted to inform his readers by gathering a wealth of varied information, geographical, historical, social, linguistic and literary, al-Māzinī wanted to amuse and stimulate them through descriptions of attitudes or social customs that seemed strange to him. He exaggerated his descriptions to the point that they became comical caricatures; and such depictions featured heavily in his account. They were in tune with his lively temperament, and with his tendency to criticize by way of exaggerated description and mockery.

Among the journalist travellers there were those who, in recounting the strange and the curious, made mistakes, either because of ignorance or extreme naivety or both. An example is Muḥammad Shafīq Muṣṭafa's claim in *Fī qalb Najd wa-al-Ḥijāz* that Fayṣal al-Dawīsh was chief of the al-Arṭawiya tribe and Sulṭān ibn Bijād the chief of al-Ghaṭghaṭ,[74] while it is well known that al-Arṭāwiya is the agricultural settlement of the Muṭayr tribe, and al-Ghaṭghaṭ is that of ʿUtayba.[75] Elsewhere, in the chapter on the beliefs of the Najdis on life and eternity, he states that it deserves mention that the people of Najd believe that the Najdi was born to worship God and obey His laws, that his lifespan is preordained, and that there is resurrection after death. He goes on to compare what he calls 'the beliefs of the people of Najd' with those of the Pharaohs concerning resurrection.[76] This claim needs no commentary, because it shows the writer's extreme ignorance; for these are the beliefs of all Muslims, and not just the people of Najd. He writes about 'the Najdis' as if he were writing about primitive tribes in Africa or the Far East.

In addition to being both digressive and exciting, the journalistic travel account is marked by its informative character in uncovering unknown facts, and its praise of countries undergoing renewal and development. Until recently Saudi Arabia lacked the means of effective and energetic communication that could convey the true image of life in the kingdom beyond its borders. Those journalists and writers undertook this task to the best of their abilities, and were able to communicate some of the positive aspects they had witnessed to their readers throughout the Arab world. Some aspects upon which they reflected at length were the issue of security, the advancement of education and the development of modern ways of life. Bint al-Shāṭī expressed her amazement at the tremendous advances the kingdom had achieved by 1951, when the aeroplane replaced the camel in connecting the remote regions of the country. The journey from Jeddah to Dhahran took only four hours, and the writer, sitting beside a Bedouin woman in the plane, voiced her amazement at that leap:

> Just like that, from the camel to the plane in one jump?
> Just like that, from the saddle to the Dakota and Bristol salons?
> Just like that, from rainwater and wells to pineapple juice and Coca-Cola?

> What a wonderful leap, that bypassed the stages of development we had passed through, for al-Dahnāʾ had not known the carriage of the automobile, and until today has not seen a train passing through its sand dunes and lowlands.[77]

But it is the 'land of miracles', Bint al-Shāṭī says, that fourteen centuries had, through Islam, transformed the history of the world, and had determined 'the destiny of nations, peoples, thrones, crowns, civilizations, and religions. Today it is destined to facilitate the flow of oil like warm blood through the world's veins, and shares in deciding the destiny of today's world.'[78]

On her second trip, in 1972, Bint al-Shāṭī is amazed at the great progress made by the Saudi Arabian woman in the field of education, for in 1951 she had experienced her as ignorant, lazy and backward, crouching behind walls. She comments:

> When I left the peninsula twenty years ago, there was not a single school for girls. Modern civilization had swept through the houses of Najd and al-Aḥsāʾ, permitting light, cinema, and radio into the harem, but not allowing books. After only one generation the doors of education, which were closed in the face of girls, were flung open, and they have passed through all the stages to higher education. In King Abdul Aziz University in Jidda,

they are about to complete their undergraduate studies, achieving [the project] which the late king had not dared to implement, but bequeathed it as a sacred duty to his son Faysal, who made the education of girls a special task, to compensate for what had been lost, and to connect with the ruptured past of this nation when women had shared effectively in the making of history in an effective manner, imposing their dynamic and influential presence on the life of the people, whether in the Jāhiliyya or in Islam.[79]

Notes:

1. Shawqī Ḍayf, *al-Riḥlāt* (Cairo, 1956), pp. 6–8.
2. Al-Jāsir says that travel was one of the most important aspects of Arabic culture and is still in need of the attention of researchers. The journal *al-ʿArab* led the way in this direction. See *al-ʿArab* 4.6 (1389/1970), p. 473; 9.5–6 (1394/1974), pp. 321–36.
3. Adab-al-rihlah ind al-Arab (Cairo: the General Egyptian Commission for Books, 1976).
4. Ḍayf, *al-Riḥlāt*, p. 71.
5. I. Krachkovskiĭ, *Taʾrīkh al-adab al-jughrāfī* (trans. Ṣalāḥ al-Dīn ʿUthmān, Cairo, 1963), I, pp. 349–51.
6. *Ibid.*, I, p. 428.
7. *Ibid.*, II, p. 728.
8. Muḥammad Adīb Ghālib, 'Ṫarābulus al-Shām fī al-riḥlāt al-ʿArabiyya' ('Syrian Tripoli in Arab Travels'), *al-ʿArab* 7.7 (1393/1973), p. 553.
9. *Ibid.*, p. 554.
10. *Ibid.*, p. 556.
11. See Krachkovskiĭ, *Taʾrīkh*, II, p. 735. We may give as an example Ibn Ma'ṣūm's *Sulāfat al-ʿaṣr fī maḥāsin aʿyān al-ʿaṣr.*
12. See Ḥamad al-Jāsir, 'Fī riḥāb al-ḥaramayn min khilāl kutub al-riḥlāt ilā al-ḥajj', *al-ʿArab* 9.5 (1394/1975), pp. 321–36.
13. Ḍayf, *al-Riḥlāt*, p. 15.
14. Krachkovskiĭ, *Taʾrīkh*, I, p. 260.
15. *Ibid.*, I, pp. 317–18.
16. [Khayr al-Dīn] ʿAbd al-Raḥmān al-Ziriklī expressed in the best possible way the nature of the travel account when he named his journey to the Hijaz in 1920 *Mā raʾaytu wa-ma samiʿtu* ('What I Saw and What I Heard'). In it he

says, 'I am only the transmitter of what I have heard and seen, transmitting as a narrator not as a historian, as a photographer and not as a writer, wishing to reveal the bare naked truth. If I could, I would take the reader by the hand to show him what my eyes have seen, and make him hear what my ears have taken in. But the account may make up for the experience, and the narrative for the sight' (*Mā raʾaytu wa-mā samiʿtu* [Cairo, 1342/1923], p. 111).

17. Al-Jāsir, 'Fī riḥāb al-ḥaramayn', pp. 321–2.
18. *Ibid.*, p. 322.
19. See al-Jāsir, 'Kutub al-riḥlāt', *al-ʿArab* 6.9 (1393/1972), pp.746–51. Al-Jāsir states that al-Kattānī did not make clear how many of these travel accounts were connected to the Hijaz. See also 'Jawla fī al-Maghrib al-ʿArabī', *al-ʿArab* 7.9 (1393/1973), pp. 641–2.
20. Al-Ziriklī, *Mā raʾaytu*, pp. 47–8.
21. See Fuʿād Ḥamza, *al-Bilād al-ʿArabiyya al-Suʿūdiyya* (Makkah, 1355/1937), p. 78.
22. It may be useful here to note the important events in the history of unification: the conquest of Riyadh (1902); the annexation of al-Kharj, al-Maḥmal, al-Shu'ayb and al-Washm (1902–3); the conquest of al-Qaṣīm (1903–6); suppressing local uprisings (1909); the conquest of al-Aḥsāʾ (1913); annexation of ʿAsīr (1921); conquest of Ḥāʾil and al-Jawf (1921); the capture of the Hijaz (1924–5); establishing Tihama as a protectorate (1926); defeating internal revolts (1928–32). See Ḥamza, *Bilād*, pp. 19–20.
23. Although Ibrāhīm Rifʿat preceded al-Batanūnī in his four trips to the Hijaz, he did not publish his accounts until some time after al-Batanūnī's book had appeared in print in 1925. This is why he refers to al-Batanūnī's book at some points.
24. Published in installments in *al-Manār*, 19–20 (1916–17, 1917–18); later collected, along with other travel accounts, in *Riḥlat al-imām Muḥammad Rashīd Riḍā*, collected and annotated by Yūsuf Ibish (Beirut, 1971).
25. The dates mentioned here indicate those of the authors' journeys, not the date of publication of their accounts. We should not forget to mention the journey of ʿAlī al-Ṭanṭāwī to the Hijaz in the company of the Syrian delegation in 1935; his account was published in 1940, and was reprinted with other articles in *Nafaḥāt al-ḥaram* (Damascus, 1960).
26. The author of this book on western travellers in the early twentieth century states that they completed the work begun by earlier travellers, but were more scientifically inclined and not romantics like their predecessors. Before

them lay many geographical, geological and other aspects of the Arabian peninsula that had not yet been investigated.

27. See ʿAbd al-Raḥman al-Kawākibī, *al-Aʿmā al-kāmila* (Cairo, 1970), pp. 301–4.
28. *Ibid.*, p. 300.
29. See Anīs al-Maqdisī, *al-Ittijāhāt al-adabiyya fī al-ʿālam al-ʿArabī al-ḥadīth* (2nd edn, Beirut, 1960), pp. 146–57.
30. See al-Rīḥāni, *Mulūk al-ʿArab aw riḥla fī al-bilād al-ʿArabiyya* (3rd edn, Beirut, 1951), I, introduction, p. 15.
31. *Ibid.*, introduction, p. 18.
32. M. Ḥ. Haykal, *Fī manzil al-waḥy* (Cairo, 1937), p. 144. At that time Haykal was an admirer of western leaders and thinkers. Bismark (1815–98) was the nineteenth-century German statesman who achieved the unification of Germany.
33. Ibrahim Rifʿāt, *Mirʾāt al-ḥaramayn aw al-riḥla al-Ḥijaziyya wa-al-ḥajj wa-mashāʿiruh* (Cairo, 1344/1925), introduction, p. 3.
34. *Ibid.*, introduction, pp. 3–4.
35. *Ibid.*, introd., p. 6.
36. Al-Batanūnī, *al-Riḥla al-ḥijāziyya* (2nd edn, Cairo, 1329/1911), introduction, p. 5.
37. *Ibid.*, introduction, p. 5.
38. See, for example, *ibid.*, pp. 69–73, 94–101, 101–33. See also the chapters: 'How the Muslim Should Go on Pilgrimage: Customary Prayers from the Beginning to the End' (pp. 172–6); 'The Laws of *Iḥrām:* Table of Observances of the Pilgrimage According to the Four Legal Schools' (pp. 176–9).
39. Krachkovskiĭ states that such travel accounts, written at the request of an important prince or in order to gain his favour, were quite common in past ages. Ibn al-Jiʿān's *al-Qawl al-mustaẓraf fī safar mawlānā al-ashraf* (ed. R.V. Lanzone, Turin, 1878), in which he describes the journey of [the Mamluk] Sultan Qāytbāy to Damascus, was of this kind. The writer was a member of the Sultan's retinue. Krachkovskiĭ says: 'This type of travel account flourished for many centuries. We even come across it in the twentieth century, in a similar vein, although on a totally different basis; I refer to al-Batanānī's account that he presented to the Egyptian Khedive ʿAbbās Ḥilmī' (*Taʾrīkh*, II, p. 476).
40. Cf. some examples from Ibrahim Rifʿat's reports (and these are only a few of many): 'Travel tickets of shipping lines' (*Mirʾāt*, II, p. 165); 'Schedule of what is due to every worker concerned with the *maḥmal* in terms of camels, tents, etc.' (*ibid.*, II, p. 162) and so on. The author could have

assigned a special section at the end of the book to collect all the reports and documents that he wanted to include.

41. See Haykal, *Fī manzil al-waḥy*, introduction, p. 10.
42. Al-Rīḥānī, *Mulūk al-ʿArab*, introduction, p. 18.
43. *Ibid.*, introduction, pp. 22–3.
44. *Ibid.*, introduction, p. 19.
45. *Ibid.*, I, p. 367.
46. *Ibid.*, II, p. 42.
47. *Ibid.*, II, p. 63.
48. Al-Ziriklī, *Mā raʾaytu*, p. 114.
49. Al-Rīḥānī, *Mulūk al-ʿArab*, I, pp. 222, 257ff.
50. See Ḥāfiẓ Wahba, *Jazīrat al-ʿArab fī al-qarn al-ʿishrīn* (Cairo, 1935), p. 240.
51. I will discuss this aspect in detail in the section on travellers and their positions.
52. Al-Rīḥānī, *Mulāk al-ʿArab*, introduction, p. 12.
53. Jārj Ghurayyib, *Adab al-riḥla: ta'rikhuhu wa-a'lāmuh* (Beirut, 1966), I, p. 105.
54. See al-Ziriklī, *Mā raʾaytu*, pp. 3–27.
55. *Ibid.*, p. 111.
56. *Ibid.*, p. 189.
57. *Ibid.*, p. 136.
58. *Ibid.*, p. 111.
59. *Ibid.*, pp. 27–109. See also al-Ziriklī's discussion of the peninsula, its traditions and literature, pp 137–86. The whole book is no more than 190 pages.
60. See *ibid.*, p. 108.
61. See his biography in Khayr al-Dīn al-Ziriklī, *al-Aʿlām: qāmūs tarājim li-ashhar al-rijāl wa-al-nisāʾ min al-ʿArab wa-al-mustaʿribīn wa-al-mushtashriqīn* (n.p., n.d.), X (Supplement), p. 257.
62. Muḥammad ʿAlī Ḥasan, *Ṣaḥīfa muʿjiza* (Alexandria, 1345/1926).
63. They were later printed by al-Manār press (Cairo, 1346/1927).
64. Muṣṭafā, *Fī qalb Najd wa-al-Ḥijāz* (Cairo, 1984?), p. 7.
65. Al-Māzinī, *Riḥla ilā al-Ḥijāz* (2nd edn, Cairo, 1973), p. 7.
66. *Ibid.*, p. 159.
67. *Ibid.*, pp. 10–11.
68. Haykal, *Fī manzil al-waḥy*, pp. 33–4.
69. Al-Māzinī, *Riḥla ilā al-Ḥijāz*, pp. 164–5.
70. ʿAzzām, *Riḥlat ʿAbd al-Wahhāb ʿAzzām* (2nd edn, 2 vols, Cairo, 1950–1); see also the introduction to the first edition (*al-Riḥla ūl-ālā* [Cairo, 1939]).

71. *Ibid.*, II, p. 363.
72. Bint al-Shāṭiʾ, *Arḍ al-muʿjizāt: riḥla fī Jazīrat al-ʿArab* (3rd edn, Cairo, 1969), pp. 7–9.
73. Shakīb Arslān, *al-Irtisāmāt al-lītāf fī khāṭir al-ḥajj ilā aqdas maṭāf* (Cairo, 1350/1931). Arslān states that after that he decided not to publish his articles in *al-Shūrā*, since this would take a long time and not be completed for two or three years. He proceeded to complete his compilation immediately; about one third of his articles had been published in *al-Shūrā*, and those not published there or elsewhere comprised about two-thirds (*ibid.*, pp. 4–5).
74. Muṣṭafa, *Fi qalb Najd*, p. 41.
75. See al-Rīḥānī, *Taʾrīkh Najd al-ḥadīth wa-mulḥāqātihi* (Beirut, 1928), pp. 412–14.
76. Muṣṭafa, *Fī qalb Najd*, pp. 42–3.
77. Bint al-Shāṭiʾ, *Arḍ al-muʿjizāt*, pp. 61–2. Al-Dahnā' had known the automobile long before Bint al-Shāṭiʾ's journey. F. Ḥamza points out in his *Qalb al-Jazīra al-ʿArabiyya* (Cairo, 1933) that he passed through al-Dahnāʾ on his way from Kuwait to Riyadh by car on 18 July 1932 (see the footnote, p. 32). He was not the first to undertake such an adventure. This means that automobiles were well known and widespread in Saudi Arabia before 1951, in contrast to what Bint al-Shāṭī' believed.
78. Bint al-Shāṭiʾ, *Arḍ al-muʿjizāt*, introduction.
79. Bint al-Shāṭiʾ, *Arḍ al-muʿjizāt wa-liqāʾ maʿa al-taʾrīkh* (Cairo, 1972), pp. 180–1.

Chapter 15

Soviet Diplomacy in Hijaz: First Move into the Arabian Peninsula 1923–1926

Vitali Naumkin

Immediately after the October 1917 Revolution, the Bolshevik government in Russia included the 'Islamic' current among the basic priorities of its foreign policy, which was, at that time, in a formative stage, open to many influences and concepts. In the early years of the rise of Soviet Russia, a period of foreign intervention and civil war, its activity in the East often was limited to propaganda calls and casual connections, mainly with personalities from the liberation movements. The main objective of Russian foreign policy in this respect was educational action among 'the masses suffering exploitation in the East', in order to lead them to revolt against the colonial powers and social injustice, as well as to spread revolutionary ideas. This was clearly seen in the call to 'all Muslim labourers in Russia and the East', issued on 20 December 1917, signed by Lenin and Stalin, as well as in the Comintern resolution concerning the colonies.

In 1921 Soviet Russia was able to conclude a treaty based on equal relations with Iran (26 February), a friendship treaty with Afghanistan (28 February) and a friendship and brotherhood treaty with Turkey (16 March), which can be regarded as brilliant diplomatic coups for Soviet Russia.

Russia was planning to expand its international relations with the East, and to approach the Arab world, where national feelings overwhelmed the population after the defeat of Turkey in World War I.

In the context of the Lausanne Conference of 1922–3, the Russian delegation made contacts with some Arab delegates, including that of

Hijaz. Representing al-Sharīf al-Ḥusain ibn Ali, the King of Hijaz, Naji al-Aseel discussed with Georgi Checherin, the people's commissioner for Russian foreign affairs (Foreign Minister), the establishment of diplomatic relations between the two countries. Commissioned by the foreign ministry, Checherin studied the consular reports from Jeddah, sent between 1890 and 1914, among other documents. Based on that information, he declared that he knew of other rulers in the Arabian peninsula, like al-Idrisi and Ibn Saʿūd, who did not recognize the authority of al-Ḥusayn, and rather considered him their enemy. At the same time, Checherin suggested to al-Ḥusayn the exchange of delegates by opening a Russian consulate in Jeddah.

In December 1923, Checherin wrote to Stalin, then the secretary general of the Russian Communist Party, saying,

> When I was in Lausanne, the Political Bureau adopted a resolution about the necessity of establishing relations with Hijaz, in order to put our representatives – even a consulate – close to Makkah, which is considered the centre of intellectual activity in the Islamic World. The negotiations started by comrade Vatslav Jordanski came to an end since his second trip to Lausanne. Now comrade Jordanski has discussed the matter with Prince Habeeb Lutfullah, the representative of Hijaz in Rome. The King of Hijaz is anxious to start relations with us. But because he fears England very much, he cannot consider our representative a commissioner, and suggests we should have a consulate in Hijaz (which is what we expected from the first moment).

Then he adds,

> Hijaz suggests we should accept a representative. The Committee of the People's Commissariat for Foreign Affairs considered from the beginning that this absence of representation is not congenial, and informed Comrade Jordanski of the suggestion. Now comrade Jordanski says that Prince Habeeb Lutfullah would very much like to come to us as a commissioner.[1]

Though Georgi Checherin gave a negative opinion about the personal qualities of this prince ('I had a long conversation with him and was convinced that he is a hopeless idiot'), the negotiations between the two men led to the idea of accepting this nomination. ('There is no doubt that penetration through Holy Makkah is highly important for us. If Comrade Ibraheemov could find a Muslim commissioner acceptable to us, who will carry the title of consul, but, in fact, he will be a commissioner, it would add to our weight and role exceedingly, not in the Arabian peninsula alone.')

On 3 April 1924 Checherin sent a letter to Constantin Joreniev, the commissioner of Soviet Russia in Rome, saying that

> The decision to enter into diplomatic relations with Hijaz was taken by a highly influential institution when I was in Laurence, realizing that Comrade Vorovski was asked to arrange that with the representative of Hijaz, who holds a document authorizing him that right. The execution of that decision was delayed because the representative of Hijaz was not in Rome at that time. The death of Comrade Vorovski delayed the execution even more. Jordanski executed that decision, as he arranged with the representative of Hijaz, Habeeb Lutfullah, to have a Soviet Union consulate general in Hijaz, like all other states. In return, Hijaz will have a commissioned delegate in Moscow. Later, Comrade Jordanski informed someone, 'I do not know who, of our appointment of Comrade Kareem Hakeemov as a Consul General in Hijaz.'[2]

Describing the King of Hijaz, the People's Commissioner for Foreign Affairs said, 'His reputation is the highest and best among the independent Arab princes, and he enjoys the right to inherit authority.' Al-Sharīf Husein is described as an enemy of Turkey, but 'our relations with Turkey do not force us at all to avoid relations with its rival states'. At the same time, it is clear that while the Soviet leaders worked towards the development of relations with Hijaz, at the same time they evaded the deterioration of relations with Turkey.

The attitude of al-Sharīf Husain towards England, according to Checherin, was twofold: 'Hijaz and its neighbour too are somewhat in need of that country, yet Hijaz tries to follow an independent policy in order to avoid disturbing consequences as far as possible.'[3] That was another influential factor in the type of mutual relations between Russia and Hijaz. At the same time, the People's Commissioner shows reservations by saying that entering into relations with the King of Hijaz 'does not mean readiness to recognize the sharīf as a caliph at all'. This was due to the fact that the idea of the caliphate, propagated by the British with the aim of aborting the rise of a unified Arab state, appeared to the Soviet leadership to be contrary to the interests of Russia and its possible allies in the East. Checherin wrote, 'Our government has nothing to do with religious organizations, and does not recognize the existence of institutions like the caliphate. As for Islamic institutions in the lands of the Soviet Union, our government will most probably insist on the complete abolition of the caliphate institution. In that context, we shall try to pressurize the Muslims of other countries. This, in fact, is the best for us.'[4]

On the initiative of Vatslav Vovorsky, Kareem Hakeemov – of a Muslim background, and a former commander in the Red Army – was appointed Consul General in Hijaz. Georgi Checherin wrote to Constantin Joreniev that 'Kareem Hakeemov is familiar with policy as he has assumed positions in Russia for many years.'

In July 1924, Kareem Hakeemov travelled to Rome to meet the Hijazi representatives. Prince Habeeb Lutfullah explained the situation in Hijaz to Kareem Hakeemov, and added that,

> according to the agreement between the Arabs and the British in 1915, an Arab state was to be formed, covering the entire Arabian peninsula, Syria and Mesopotamia. Nevertheless, the end result was the Hijaz states, limited to the area of Makkah and Madinah. Thus, the Arabs were deceived and disappointed. Prince Habeeb asserted that notwithstanding, Hijaz then enjoyed a great importance, as it was frequented by major powers from the Islamic world: Indians, Persians, and Turks. Those powers considered al-Ḥusayn the head of Hijaz state, and the ideological leader of the extensive Arab movement. The representatives of the Islamic world supporting al-Ḥusayn were of two parties: the Islamists,

> who called for the unity of all Muslims, and the nationalistics who called for the unity of all the Arabs.
>
> Therefore, a violent dispute rose up among the various tendencies around al-Ḥusayn. This was aggravated by the policy of the British who bribed some of the personalities and officials around him. Some of those officials belong to the old Turkish regime. We notice that Prince Habeeb Lutfullah branded the Foreign Minister Husain Fuad al-Khateeb as a British spy.[5]

Prince Habeeb Lutfullah suggested to Kareem Hakeemov 'to present himself to al-Ḥusayn as a believer and enlightened Muslim. He should start direct personal relations with al-Ḥusayn, definitely, to avoid middlemen whoever they may be, including the Foreign Minister. Moreover, he should not talk except with al-Ḥusayn himself about the Arab nationalistic movement. It seems that this subject was the most important issue before the Russian diplomat, especially when 'I have to spend the hot summer season in Taʾif, which is considered the summer seat of the king, and where it is necessary to establish relations between my family and that of al-Ḥusayn.'

Out of his early meetings, Kareem Hakeemov came to the following conclusions:

1. There are two political bodies among the Hijazi Arabs: (a) supporters of the caliphate, who try hard to get the title of caliph for al-Ḥusayn; (b) supporters of Arab nationalism who endeavour to establish an independent Arab state.
2. The possibility of choosing Makkah 'for my headquarters, if the present situation helps to start normal relations with al-Hussain'.[6]

On 2 October 1924, Prince Habeeb Lutfullah arrived in Moscow. His reception indicated the serious intentions of the Soviet leadership concerning the development of relations with the Hijazi Sharīf. The Prince was received by the head of the central executive committee Michael Calinin, and was taken to the Savoy Hotel in Central Moscow. On account of the hospitality with which the Russian delegation was received in Hijaz, Prince Habeeb Lutfullah not only did not pay his hotel bill, but also delayed the payment of his restaurant bills. Later on, a decision was taken to pay the cost of the Hijazi delegate's sojourn in Moscow.

In his talks with the official representative in Moscow the Prince explained his theory of the political triangle. He believed that international politics should be based on three points of reference: Moscow, Peking and Baghdad. If those three bases could be brought together, Moscow would be a bastion of struggle against international imperialism.

Sergei Pastokhov spoke of a form of cooperation between Russia and the Arabs as seen by Prince Habeeb Lutfullah. He said 'it is most fanciful, as the Prince wants to form a united state with us, to have our military support for an army of volunteers he wants to form in Caucasia, to use it in liberating either Syria or Mesopotamia from the yoke of imperialism'. In addition to that, the Prince tried to convince the young Soviets to take charge of the caliphate movement, and use the religious factor in the Soviet policy in the East.[7]

Sergei Pastokhov explained to the Prince that Moscow could not, on principle, exploit the religious factor in politics, and that its policy in the East was based on sympathy with the national liberation movements, and supporting them with whatever means were available in this respect.

Pastokhov wrote, 'We are looking with interest at the rise of Arab national unity in the Arabian peninsula and the formation of a strong and united Arab State.'[8]

The representatives of the People's Commissariat for Foreign Affairs agreed with the Prince that 'The more civilized areas to the north, like Syria and Palestine' were the principal source of the Arab movement, and not Hijaz.

In 1924 the Sharīf Husain declared his assumption of the Islamic caliphate, which was abolished in Turkey. He sent a telegram to Checherin to inform the Soviet Russian government of this decision. The Saudi writer Fahd al-Semmari says that Moscow responded by establishing diplomatic relations with Hijaz, encouraged by the worsening relations between Hijaz and Britain at that time.[9]

It seems that al-Ḥusayn's attitude was related to his displeasure with the British, and his intention to show them that he was able to find other allies who could threaten the British interests.

Remembering his negative attitude towards the October Revolution, it is not possible to suppose that al-Ḥusayn was serious about starting a long-term alliance with Moscow. And, considering the dimensions of the war waged by Ibn Saʿūd against al-Sharīf Husain, the Soviet diplomats realized the latter's critical situation, and started to think of alternative measures. But Sergei Pastokhov informed the Consul General of the necessity of keeping friendly relations with the Prince, saying that 'even if the Hijaz state would vanish from existence, and the Prince's commission came to an end, he may remain a useful man for us in Hijaz, as a person connected with the Arab liberation movement'.[10]

In addition to that, it became obvious that Soviet diplomacy was afraid of finding itself supporting the failing party, so it prepared for the possibility of dealing with the other party as well.

In the summer of 1924, Ibn Saʿūd advanced towards Hijaz and was enthusiastically received by his forces there. The victories of Ibn Saʿūd forced al-Ḥusayn to hand the throne over to his son Ali in October 1924. But this measure did not stop the war between Hijaz and Najd. With reference to a letter from Checherin, Moscow considered Ibn Saʿūd's movement constantly antagonistic to Britain, even though Moscow had hoped that al-Ḥusayn could confront Britain, despite a letter sent by Georgi Checherin to Hakeemov on 1 November 1924. 'Ibn Saʿūd's attack on Hijaz was fabricated by Britain, which wants to use it as a means to subdue al-Ḥusayn, who was beginning to break away and try to gain from Britain what he was promised in 1915. Owing to the continuation of the anti-British movement in Egypt, the hopes of forming an Arab government in Palestine, in addition to its affiliation with Hijaz, was raising fears in Britain. If Zionism in Palestine should fail, it would ultimately make the Arab nationalists in Egypt and Palestine come together. This political bridge could have put Britain in an extremely critical situation.'[11]

It seems from the correspondence during this period that the staff in the People's Commissariat for Foreign Affairs either did not fully realize who among the Arab rulers was really displeased with the British, or they did not pay enough attention to the degree of antagonism to Britain harboured by possible allies. A realization of the antagonistic feelings to Britain, noted by several politicians, was of prime importance in convincing the Kremlin of the soundness of its approach, based on pragmatic estimates. In addition, Kremlin diplomats were certain that the fall of imperialism was inevitable.

It is equally easy to observe the absence of any ideological concepts or coordination in the correspondence of Checherin, which aimed at inciting revolution in Palestine and Egypt, and the serious concern of the Comintern to achieve that aim. In those years, principles of Soviet foreign policy were laid down, wherein the pragmatic interests of the state were linked with the purely ideological demands of the Bolshevik movement. It was clear that the Soviet leadership was under no illusions about the breakout of a revolution in the Arab peninsula, though it fully realized the use of a plan to support a movement of Arab coordination, capable of breaking down British control in the Middle East.

Confronting Britain was one of the main factors behind Soviet foreign policy in the Arab peninsula.

Pragmatism was a salient characteristic of Checherin's attitude towards the developments. He also held romantic fancies about the capability of Islamic integration, once saying, 'Our interests in the Arab issue requires the unification of the Arab lands in one whole.' Checherin also talked about the possibility of Turkish–Saudi rapprochement 'in a so-called Islamic movement directed against Western imperialism'. The People's Commissariat for Foreign Affairs comes to the conclusion that,

> in this manner, we find that the temporary balance effected by Britain in the Arabian peninsula has lost its power, as it seems that the concept of Arab nationalism is surging in the middle of Najd. This brings more problems to the British, becoming more complicated as the Mowsil issue is not settled as yet. A situation like this not only suits our own interests, but the Turkish interests as well. Our policy in the Arabian peninsula should be based, as always, on the national factor, and the aspiration of the Arabs towards a unified state.[12]

Considering the antagonistic tendency of the Saudi Islamic movement towards Britain and imperialism – as claimed – the Comintern received with enthusiasm news of the military achievements of Ibn Saʿūd. In one of its sessions in 1924, the Comintern executive committee discussed the situation in the Arabian peninsula. The participants in that session described King Abdul Aziz as 'the leader of a major national movement'. They considered that his victory in Najd will encourage the Muslims to wage a revolutionary struggle against British imperialism. The Comintern supported King Abdul Aziz and Imām Yahia, describing them as 'two leaders working hard to resist British influence, hence they should be helped'.[13]

In September 1924, the brothers and the regular army of Abdul Aziz ibn Saʿūd seized al-Taʾif. They then entered the holy city of Makkah.

To secure Soviet–Hijazi relations the leadership of the People's Commissariat for Foreign Affairs endeavoured not only to form relations with Ibn Saʿūd and ensure his support in the case of his seizure of Hijaz, but also to remain neutral and play the role of mediator at a certain stage. This was in addition to securing a 'link' between Russia and Hijaz through vowing protection of the interests of Soviet Russian citizens residing in Hijaz or going there for the pilgrimage season. The British representatives did their best to raise the fears of the local authorities that the Russian representatives would carry on subversive activities in Hijaz through registering their citizens there. But the Russians succeeded in carrying on with their plans.

In his letter of 5 November 1924 to Checherin, Hakeemov gave an extremely negative report about the results of al-Ḥusayn's rule in the Arabian peninsula. It is noteworthy that the report starts from the premise that the crystallization of the 'Arab unity movement' is among the most important priorities of the Soviet diplomats. He wrote, 'The dire poverty of the country which cannot promise anything in the future either, and the cultural and political backwardness there, despite the presence of the holy cities and their custodians, descendants of the Prophet (saaws) do not qualify Hijaz successfully to lead the Arab unity movement'. Based on this evaluation, the Consul General came to this conclusion:

> Based on these facts, it seems to me that our basic tactics – i.e. considering the Arab unity movement as the issue that justifies our presence in Hijaz – seems to be losing its significance now, or in the near future . . .

> Al-Sharīf Husain is now in a rather awkward position. We may use him or someone else may use him in the same situation, certainly. Or, he may be used to stir a conflict with the British or the Italians, or even to start a campaign against Aseer, which is under British protection, and he may be paid for his efforts . . . in order to achieve temporary and cheap results, especially while no interest is shown about his home situation . . . provided none of the above be connected to our basic policy in the Arabian peninsula.[14]

Most probably, the Consul General was still not certain that Ibn Saʿūd could defeat al-Hussain.

When Checherin became convinced that Ibn Saʿūd had a great chance of success, he asked Hakeemov to make contacts with him. In a letter dated 4 November 1924 Kareem Hakeemov wrote, 'This question came up before me in the days when the Saudis had just captured al-Taʾif, when it was not clear whether they had serious intentions to continue their advance or whether they had enough means. I thought that the issue of our relations with them may come up irrespective of their victory or defeat . . .'

Under the circumstances, it was not possible to make contacts except by writing, and it was not possible to make immediate contacts. The Consul General wrote, '. . . I did not succeed in sending a letter, copy of which included, to Khalid ibn Lou'ay, the commander of the Saudi forces, until after his seizure of Makkah.'[15]

In 1925 the Saudis beseiged Jeddah for almost a whole year. Checherin sent instructions to Hakeemov saying, 'The current events in the Arabian peninsula are passing through a critically important stage. You should stay in Jeddah whatever the cost may be. It is inevitable to establish friendly relations with Ibn Saʿūd. It is also mandatory to follow up the development of the Anglo-French and Anglo-Italian conflict in the Arabian peninsula.'[16]

Kareem Hakeemov continued the development of contacts with the Saudis. In a letter sent to him by Checherin, dated 18 June 1925, there is a positive appreciation of the relations between the Consul General and Ibn Saʿūd. The instructions make a special reference to developing relations of Soviet diplomats in the Arabian peninsula. The People's Commissar for Foreign Affairs wrote, 'Since we do not put our trust in one or the other of the conflicting Arab princes, but are mainly interested in developing our relations with the Arabian life, through the existing centres of that life only, it is necessary for us to have contacts running parallel at the same time with both Hijaz and Najd.' Checherin considered contact with the committee on the caliphate issue an important matter too, not because Moscow favoured the idea of the caliphate, but because the caliphate movement played an important role 'in the struggle of the Islamic nations for the complete liberation'. He also said, 'If one of the Muslim princes were strong enough to unite the Arabian peninsula, we would have, naturally, considered the unification of all the Arabian tribes in one state a large step forward. But there is no one to play that role, and we cannot but take a totally negative attitude towards the endless disputes stirred by Britain among the Arabian princes.'[17]

Based upon these interpretations, Checherin supported Hakeemov's position on helping to achieve reconciliation among the antagonistic parties, but only after King Ali had taken a congenial attitude towards such a reconciliation.

Checherin warned Hakeemov to be careful in expressing his opinion about Britain during the talks with Ibn Saʿūd, for fear he may be a 'British puppet'.

> In fact, we cannot evaluate any details about these talks beforehand, as the real situation is not known to us. But it can generally be said that, on the one hand, we should stress in every way our friendship, with the people of the East in general, as well as our support of the principle of self-determination which lies at the core of our policy. On the other hand, it is necessary to be extremely wary in connection with anything concerning Britain. There should be no pretext for the British to issue a new ultimatum. Ibn Saʿūd is receiving support from the British, so if he is in conflict with Britain today, there is no guarantee they will be reconciled tomorrow. Extreme candour cannot be permitted in such circumstances. It could be said, in general terms, that our sympathy with self-determining nations, struggling for their independence, means that we are against any

> raids, aggression, attacks or oppression of nations by the great powers. But such talk should not be allowed to be overcritical of Britain in order to avoid any diplomatic scandal or dispute. Our friendly relations with the peoples of the east should be made clear through our talk about our friendly relations with Turkey, Iran, Afghanistan, etc. But, in this case we should deal with Britain in the highest degree of caution. Any effort made by the eastern peoples towards independence can rely on our sympathy. Establishing relations with Hijaz means that we are willing to start such relations with the other nations of the Arabian peninsula, and to maintain those relations in the future too. The military achievements of Ibn Saʿūd do not mean that he has really achieved independence. Far from it, as he still has to face bitter struggle against the states that do not want to see the Arabian peninsula a strong, independent state, unifying the Arabs in their struggle against foreign intervention, but rather a European colony or a number of small emirates conflicting with each other.[18]

The instructions of the People's Commissar for Foreign Affairs left the Consul General in no doubt about the way he should carry out his mission. Checherin wrote to Hakeemov saying, 'It should be taken into consideration that the main enemy of the Arabs in the past, Ottoman Turkey, exists no more. But now, Britain is the main enemy of the Arabs.'[19]

At this stage the Soviet Consul in Jeddah tried to bring about a reconciliation between the two rivals, aiming most probably, and above anything else, at raising the reputation of his country, and his own, and to raise the level of contacts with the parties and show neutrality. That activity could have realized some benefits, irrespective of the outcome of the conflict. Yet, it is doubtful whether the Soviet diplomats were seriously thinking they could achieve reconciliation between Ibn Saʿūd and the dignitaries (Sharīfs). According to the Saudi writer al-Semmari, Kareem Hakeemov contacted King Abdul Aziz personally and asked permission for himself and a number of accredited consuls from the Islamic states to go from Jeddah to Makkah to perform *Umra*, without interference in the political affairs of the disputing parties.

In Ramadan 1343 (April 1925, but the report about the trip was not sent to Moscow until 17 June 1925) Hakeemov performed the *Umra* with the deputy consuls of Holland and Iran during the siege of Jeddah. That gave Hakeemov the chance to look at the military situation outside the walls of Jeddah. Hakeemov met with King Abdul Aziz and discussed with him the possibility of granting permission for Fuad al-Khateeb, the Foreign Minister of Hijaz, to come to Makkah for talks with King Abdul Aziz.[20] On 26 Ramadan, Fuad al-Khateeb sent a letter to the king asking for permission to have an audience with him. As a result of the mediation by Hakeemov, correspondence began between the king and Fuad al-Khateeb, leading to their meeting on the last day of Ramadan.[21]

During the talks conducted by Hakeemov in Makkah, he skilfully exploited the king's interest in the visit of Soviet Muslims to the holy Islamic places and their performance of the pilgrimage. The Consul General declared before the king that, 'it is not possible for our organized Muslim masses to achieve cooperation without establishing relations between the Soviet Union and Najd, which will enable the Soviet officials to perform their duties concerning the protection of our citizens' interests'.[22]

According to Samari, Hakeemov wrote to the king asking him to disclaim a report published in *Um al-Qura* daily newspaper about Hakeemov's mediation. In his answer, the king expressed his surprise about Hakeemov's demand, emphasizing that the report was truthful. The king refused to disclaim the report, adding, 'I did not expect accredited officials to say something then deny it. I find nothing harmful in the report, which you did not describe as confidential and I let it be published nevertheless.'[23]

Fahd al-Samari is of the opinion that Hakeemov feared that the news of his mediation might stir unfavourable reactions from the foreign representatives in Hijaz, as they had agreed to observe a neutral stand about the conflict between the two parties. In fact, Mr Jordan, the British representative in Jeddah, informed Mr Chamberlain, the British Foreign Minister, on 29 December 1925, that Hakeemov had promised King Abdul Aziz, during his contacts with him, Russian assistance if he could move away from the British.[24] Al-Samari is certain that there was no evidence to support these claims, as the king was in no need of help, while Jeddah was about to fall at any moment. Moreover, there is no reference to such information in the Russian archives.

It should be mentioned here that the bases of managing the situations that stirred up conflict in the countries concerned were established as a result of Soviet diplomacy during this period. At the same time, the tactic of changing the normal course, followed when handling relations with the conflicting parties, along with the use of secret mediation, crystallized and developed in the region under discussion, came to be regular features of Soviet foreign policy.

In the autumn of 1925, a final Saudi victory seemed inevitable. The Soviet diplomats began to look for ways to strengthen relations with Ibn Saʿūd.[25] Checherin decided to help Ibn Saʿūd in order to show Moscow's friendly attitude towards him. So, he wrote to the Soviet ambassador in Tehran, saying: 'the campaign now led by Britain in the Islamic countries against the Saudis, because of alleged destruction and subversive activities, is one way of imposing pressure on Ibn Saʿūd. In order to isolate Ibn Saʿūd from any support for him in India, Egypt and the countries under their mandate, the British agents incite hatred against the Saudis among the Islamic communities, in order to weaken Ibn Saʿūd and force him as well to come to terms with Hijaz, on the bases of the British conditions.'[26]

In December 1925, Jeddah fell and Ibn Saʿūd was installed King of Hijaz and Sultan of Najd and the annexed areas. On 16 February 1926, Hakeemov sent a letter to the king purporting the full recognition of the Saudi state: 'On behalf of my government, I have the honour of informing your majesty that, out of its consideration for the principle of self-determination of the peoples, and its supreme respect for the will of the Hijazi people, manifested in their pledge of allegiance to your majesty as their king, the government of the Union of the Soviet Socialist Republic, recognizes your majesty king over Hijaz and Sultan over Najd and annexes. Accordingly, the USSR government considers itself in a state of normal diplomatic relations with the government of your majesty.'[27]

So, we find that the Kingdom of Saudi Arabia became the first Arab state with whom the Soviet Union established diplomatic relations.

According to Russian diplomatic archives, the pragmatic policy exercised by the Soviet Union in the Arabian peninsula was at variance with the attitude of the Bolshevik leadership, characterized by an idealistic ideology much more visible in the case of Egypt, Palestine and other eastern countries. There, the leaders of the Bolshevik Party thought there was a possibility of laying the basis for a Proletariat revolutionary movement. Therefore, they adopted an approach that could lead to establishing communist parties in those countries.

We have already seen that the 'Comintern line' was not in fact observed in the Arabian peninsula, not only because the Arabian peninsula community was not prepared to accept or support such a movement, but also because the liberating power of the anti-British activities of the peninsular princes was more important to Soviet Russia. The contradiction between the pragmatic approach towards the interests of the state in the applications of the foreign policy programme, on the one hand, and, on the other, an ideologically justified attitude was retained almost throughout the entire Soviet period This contradiction was later reflected even on the theoretical level, such as in the theories of the national democratic revolution, and of the non-capitalistic development which allowed for a possible bypassing of the local communist factor, or subjecting it to the pure pragmatic support of the 'national democrats', who had anti-communist tendencies in many cases, yet they rose to fight against the West.

After that stage, there were many ebbs and flows in the relations between the Soviet Union and the Kingdom of Saudi Arabia. But the sources of success and failure of Soviet diplomacy in the Arabian peninsula, though not always following a clear path, can be traced to the initial stage of Moscow's interest in the region.

Notes:

1. Checherin to Stalin, 18 December 1923. Archives of the Foreign Policy of the Russian Union (AFPRU), no. 127, list 1, file 1, dossier 2, pp. 6–7.
2. Checherin to Borniev, 4 April 1924. AFPRU, No. 127, list 1, file 1, dossier 5, p. 6.
3. AFPRU, p. 7.
4. Hakeemov to Checherin, 15 July 1924, AFPRU, p. 2.
5. AFPRU, p. 37.

6. Pastokhov to Hakeemov, AFPRU.
7. Fahd ibn Abdullah al-Semmari, 'Saudi-Russian Relations in the Reign of King Abdul Aziz', ms. p. 32.
8. Pastokhov to Hakeemov, 1 November 1924, AFPRU, p. 38.
9. Checherin to Hakeemov, 1 November 1924, AFPRU, p. 31.
10. AFPRU.
11. D. Boersner, *The Bolsheviks and the National and Colonial Question, 1917–1928* (Paris, 1975), p. 190.
12. Hakeemov to Checherin, 5 November 1924, AFPRU, pp. 28–9.
13. Hakeemov to Checherin, 4 November 1924, AFPRU, p. 20.
14. Checherin to Hakeemov, 22 January 1925, AFPRU, 1,2, dossier 14, p. 6.
15. Checherin to Hakeemov, 18 June 1925, AFPRU, p. 49.
16. AFPRU.
17. Checherin to Hakeemov, 27 March 1925, Archives, *op. cit.*, pp. 35–6.
18. Checherin to Hakeemov, AFPRU, p. 30.
19. Al-Semmari, 'Saudi-Russian Relations', p. 36.
20. *Umm al-Qura* (15 Shawwal 1343 H., No. 20), pp. 1–4.
21. Memorandum by Hakeemov to the People's Commissariat for Foreign Affairs, about the trip to Makkah, 17 June 1925, AFPRU, p. 48.
22. *Um al-Qura* (No. 24), pp. 4, 31.
23. Al-Semmari, 'Saudi-Russian Relations', p. 37.
24. Jordan to Chamberlain, 29 December 1925. FO 371/11437–E364–180–91.
25. G. L. Bondarevsky, *Russia and the Gulf in the Twentieth Century: 'The Politics of Oil'* (ed. Paul Tempest; London, Graham & Trotman, 1993), p. 90.
26. AFPRU, Vol. u (Moscow, 1963), p. 548.
27. *Soviet Union and the Arab Countries, 1917–1960* (Moscow, 1961), p. 61.

Chapter 16

History of Architecture in the City of Riyadh

Zāhir ibn ʿAbd al-Raḥmān ʿUthmān

History is regarded as one of the most significant means of discovering facts about earlier peoples in all aspects of life. It is characterized by its wide reach, including its observation of the emergence, development and decline of any aspect of life or branch of learning, including the history of architecture, literature and the arts.

From a linguistic standpoint, history (*taʾrīkh*) is a definition of time. We talk, for example, about the 'history' of something, meaning the time when something happens. It is a discipline that includes statements about events and their causes. History as a discipline appears late, compared with other branches of learning. 'The ancient historical texts that we have at our disposal now were only collected during the Islamic period; and those texts compiled in the Islamic period were found by the early pioneers in the books of the Israelites (*Banū Isrāʾīl*), in Greek books, and in the Persian, Syriac and Latin heritage.'[1]

It took some time for the beginnings of civilization to be converted into what is known as 'history', when the events of past years were recorded in documents written when they occurred, and were not intended to be a reliable documentation of the historiography of the period in which they were written. For example, what is now being written about the city of Riyadh, the achievements of the state, economic and social development, demographical statistics and job opportunities will form part of the documents of the city's history in the near future.

Despite the importance of history in investigating the various stages and aspects of the growth and development of peoples, different circumstances occur along its presumed course which lead to the omission of some periods while placing others within a framework where reason is not a crucial factor. It is always pointed out that history is written by the victorious party and, therefore, depends on the victor's honesty and truthfulness. But this is not always the rule, because of the passage of time and the differences among writers, not to mention the effect of numerous other factors on the pattern of written history. Within this context, the history of a certain state or city is assumed to cover all the political, architectural, social, literary, economic and other aspects; but this is often not realized, so that one aspect of life comes to overshadow all the others.

This chapter deals with the position of the history of architecture – without addressing the history of architecture in detail – in the city of Riyadh in particular and the central Arabian peninsula in general, an aspect of history which sometimes disappears from the annals of Arabia, while at others is a strong and assertive presence, although at different levels of comprehensiveness. This chapter also attempts to present some of the reasons why certain periods are overlooked and the characteristics that affect this, especially in later centuries, and to explain some of the reasons for this. It then turns in particular to discuss, by way of example, the situation of the history of architecture in the city of Riyadh, by investigating the history of some buildings in the area of the Government Palace, which is viewed as the nucleus and throbbing heart of the city, especially during the thirteenth/nineteenth and the beginning of the fourteenth/twentieth centuries, up to the beginning of the rise of the Kingdom of Saudi Arabia.

1. *Characteristics and Stages of the History of Riyadh*

The history of the city of Riyadh may be divided into the following stages:

a. *Ancient History*

This stage appears in cursory references in historical and geographical works dealing with civilizations that rose to prominence and then vanished among the peoples known to historians as the 'bygone Arabs' (*al-ʿArab al-bāʾida*), such as the peoples of ʿĀd, Thamūd, Jurhum, ʿAbīl, Ṭasm and Jadīs.[2] Some accounts tell of a town which used to exist on the site of the city of Riyadh called Ḥajr (or Ḥajar) al-Yamāma, which was the metropolis of Ṭasm and Jadīs. In that town stood their ruins and forts, from one of which Zarqāʾ al-Yamāma looked out in the well-known story.

The remains of those forts survived until the fourth/tenth century; al-Hamadhānī states that he saw one, which was 200 cubits in height.[3] The city was strongly fortified. Its invaders, 'having failed to capture it because of its impregnability and the forts surrounding it, used to ravage and burn down the orchards around it'.[4]

There is no mention of the tribes of Ṭasm and Jadīs in the Qurʾan. Moreover, it is rare to find signs pointing to the rise of civilizations in the area of Riyadh other than to Ṭasm and Jadīs. Most of the sources for this period of history deal at length with civilizations that arose in other parts of the Arabian peninsula, and particularly those mentioned in the Qurʾan, such as ʿĀd, Thamūd and Sabāʾ. This may be because some of those civilizations came after Ṭasm and Jadīs, or left traces that were visible at that time, which made them known to people.

Historians rely almost totally on ancient Greek sources in their accounts of this period. It is also believed that most Arabic writings about it are largely fabulous accounts. Thus, archaeological antiquities and inscriptions are considered a basic source for the elucidation of important aspects of ancient history. This is a field in which researchers, especially Europeans, have, since the latter part of the nineteenth century, striven to discover historical material from the evidence found in ancient Arabic inscriptions.[5] Although this activity was centred on other parts of Arabia, it may also be said that the absence of visible traces of the civilizations of Ṭasm and Jadīs has contributed to the lack of detailed discussion of them, as well as the account that the Himyarites destroyed Yamama, which remained in ruins until the Banū Ḥanīfa came and settled there.[6] No proper history of Ṭasm and Jadīs has been recorded; yet there are signs that they existed between 130 and 250 CE,[7] which indicates that there was a long period of civilization. The Himyarites, on the other hand, existed from 115 BCE until 525 CE.[8]

b. *The Jāhiliyya (Pre-Islamic) and Early Islamic Periods*

There are more references to the history of the area of Riyadh during the Jāhiliyya (pre-Islamic) period; these are more frequent than those about ancient history. Both the Qurʾan and the Sunna refer to the conditions of the Arabs during that period, and to their beliefs and ways of life. Arabic poetry also played a prominent and documented role in noting many events of that period; in fact, it was through poetry that important battles and market-fairs became known. Among the latter was Ḥajr al-Yamāma, which flourished during the period of the Banū Ḥanīfa, who settled there about two centuries before the rise of Islam.[9] Poetry made another contribution by giving details about beliefs and institutions. The gradual conversion of the Arabs to Islam also helped to provide further knowledge about various parts of the Arabian peninsula.

During the early stages of Islam there were allusions to the relations between Makkah and Yamama and the conversion of the people of Yamama to Islam, although most references to Yamama that occurred within the framework of the primary concerns of historians of the early Muslim era were on military campaigns and biographies. Thus the claim of prophethood by Musaylama al-Khadhdhāb ('the liar') and the Wars of Apostasy (*ridda*) were discussed in detail, while other events received little mention. Arab-Islamic history was mainly concerned with the Prophet Muḥammad's *sīra* (biography) and *ghazawāt* (military campaigns), and then with the annals of the early 'Rightly Guided' caliphs.[10]

The location of Najd at the centre of the Arabian peninsula, amid its deserts, is viewed as a factor that helped to protect it from invaders in both ancient and modern times. At the same time, however, it was one of the reasons why it has received little attention, at least from the historical standpoint. Attention was focused instead on the coastal cities and the main trade routes, especially between the two important centres of Arab civilization, Yemen and Bilād al-Shām (greater Syria); also, the two holy cities of Makkah and Madinah enjoyed the attention of Arab and other historians.[11]

The relevant accounts refer to diverse events that, on the whole, do not provide a clear picture of the area's history during any particular period. In fact, it is often difficult to trace the political situation in the region in detail, because it is difficult to arrive at a detailed sequence of events. At the time of the caliph ʿUmar ibn al-Khaṭṭāb (11–23/634–44) Yamama was attached to Bahrain;[12] thus the governors of Bahrain were also the governors of Yamama. Under ʿUthmān ibn ʿAffān (23–35/644–56) Yamama was attached to Basra; but under ʿAlī ibn Abī Ṭālib (35–40/656–61) it was once more attached to Bahrain.

c. *From the Umayyad Period until the Salafiyya Movement*

During the Umayyad period Yamama was officially attached to Bahrain, but from the standpoint of learning it was connected with Madinah. When ʿAbd Allāh ibn al-Zubayr rebelled against the Umayyads, Yamama sided with him. In 64/684 the Kharijites captured Yamama, which remained under their control until about 69/688, when it was restored to Umayyad rule; it remained in this position until the rise of the Abbasids, when it was mainly attached to Bahrain or placed in the same status with it.[13]

There are passing references to some buildings constructed in Yamama. Among the remains of the early days of Islam was a mosque at Ḥajr built by Khālid ibn al-Walīd, and the prison of Dawwār.[14] A palace is mentioned in the account of a revolt in Yamama in 126/743–4, after the death of the Umayyad caliph al-Walīd ibn Yazīd. The rising was led by al-Muhayr ibn Sulamī, who went to ʿAlī ibn al-Muhājir, the governor of Yamama, and gave him the choice of either resigning from his post as governor, leaving the country, or confining himself to his palace in Ḥajr. He (ʿAlī) then found an opportunity for escape, and fled after many of his troops had been killed; and al-Muhayr then seized Yamama.[15]

From the later years of the Abbasid period, obscurity began to veil the history of many parts of the Arab regions, and especially the central Arabian peninsula, while the attention of historians became restricted to 'what was related to the caliphs' care, such as Makkah, Madinah, pilgrimage routes, and information about tribes that might reject the government's authority or do harm to pilgrims, in addition to scattered bits of information about poets who used to come from these regions to pay visits to the caliphs in Baghdad . . . Thus Ḥajr almost fell into oblivion.'[16]

The Ukhayḍirids[17] seized Yamama in 253/867 and kept it under their control until 350/961, when the Carmathians (Qarmaṭīs) arose and put an end to Ukhayḍirids' practical rule.[18] The latter, however, remained a tool in Carmathian hands until after the middle of the fifth/eleventh century. During the Ukhayḍirid period Yamama tax-collectors also collected taxes from Bahrain, while preachers in al-Aḥsāʾ proclaimed the ruler of Yamama and the governor of al-Aḥsāʾ was appointed by the Yamama governor. With the end of Ukhayḍirid rule, after the Carmathians lost power, the region was split into a number of emirates, some of which received help from Bahrain.[19] 'Yamama was not ruled by a strong government nor did it have a state to be reckoned with in order to make historians pay due attention to it. The name of Ḥajr survived because of its long-standing fame. It continued to be known as the seat of government of Yamama among all the historians who wrote about Yamama, not because it was a seat of government in the real sense of the word but as a continuance of its former fame.'[20]

Some sources enjoy a special value because they unravel obscure or misrepresented details about the region at a certain period. A case in point is Nāṣir-i Khusraw's journey to Yamama in around 443/1051, in the account of which he wrote about some trading and manufacturing activities in Yamama. Although he made this journey during the Ukhayḍirid period, he also gives a brief but interesting account of Yamama at the time: 'It has a massive strong wall which displays signs of antiquity. Outside the wall I saw a city and a market where there are all types of manufacturers. The city also has a great mosque . . . Water in Yamama is plentiful where irrigation canals are spread, and palm groves are abundant.'[21]

Ḥajr remained the seat of government of Yamama in the eighth/fourteenth century. It was visited by the traveller Ibn Baṭṭāṭa, who stated, 'It is a beautiful and fertile town with rivers and trees.'[22] It was inhabited by Arab groups, most of them from Banū Ḥanīfa. In the middle of the ninth/fifteenth century it was settled by 'Rabīʿa ibn Mānīʿ, the twelfth forefather of the late king Abdul Aziz ibn ʿAbd al-Raḥmān [ibn] Fayṣal' [r. 1319–73/1902–55], in the area of ad-Dirʿīyah.[23] In the tenth/sixteenth century Ḥajr was split into small villages, among them Muqrin, Miʿkāl and al-ʿAwd. The name of Ḥajr gradually disappeared, until the name 'al-Riyāḍ' (Riyadh) was given to its surviving sites during the twelfth/eighteenth century.[24]

d. *From the Salafiyya Movement until the Formation of the Kingdom of Saudi Arabia*

The Salafiyya movement, supported by Muḥammad ibn Suʿūd (d. 1179/1765), is often considered the torch that ignited the region of Najd, so that, despite various ups and downs, the region's voice reached the ears of the world, making this part of the Arabian peninsula a focus of global attention and, with the formation of the Kingdom of Saudi Arabia, the apogee of its history. The sources for the history of this period can be divided into three categories, as follows:

(i) *Writings of Contemporary Historians*. It was believed in this period that 'shining events' should be recorded by historians who had witnessed them. Among the most famous works written about that period were the histories of al-Manqūr (*Taʾrīkh al-Manqūr*) and Ibn Rabīʿa (*Taʾrīkh Ibn Rabīʿa)*. The most famous of all, however, was *Taʾrīkh Najd*, by Ḥusayn ibn Ghannām (d. 1225/1810–11), for the period between the second half of the twelfth/eighteenth century and the first decade of the thirteenth/nineteenth. He was a contemporary of Muḥammad ibn ʿAbd al-Wahhāb (1115–1206/1703–92);[25] the work was written at the latter's request, and its second part included the Sheikh's letters and answers to religious questions. Another famous book about that period, written around the same time, was *ʿUnwān al-majd fī taʾrīkh Najd* by ʿUthmān ibn Bishr (d. 1290/1877), for the period 1158–1268/1745–1852. Ibrāhīm ibn ʿĪsā completed Ibn Bishr's history with his *ʿIqd al-durar fī mā waqaʿa fī Najd min al-ḥawādith fī awākhir al-qarn al-thālith ʿashar wa-awāʾil al-rābiʿ ʿashar*, on events in Najd in the late thirteenth/nineteenth and early fourteenth/twentieth centuries.

The predominant characteristic of most history written during this period was its concentration on limited aspects while ignoring many other important aspects of life. Ibn Bishr has critically alluded to this point (although he himself is not exempt from the things he criticizes), saying,

> Know that the people of Najd, and their ancient and modern scholars, were little concerned with recording the history of their events and of their home towns, those who established them, what happened in them, who left them or who came to them, except for rare incidents which they recorded and which could be done without. When those writers mentioned the year, they would say, 'So and So the Son of So and So was killed', without giving his name or the reason why he was killed. If they mentioned a fight or an incident they would say, 'In this year such and such an incident took place.' We know that since the days of Adam up to the present there has always been fighting. But we would like to know the facts, and the cause, and the strange and extraordinary things that happened. Yet all this is lacking in their histories.[26]

Writing about raids or military campaigns was the focus of most historians even during relatively peaceful periods, during various phases of the history of the Saudi state. This makes those campaigns seem as if they were the main cause of writing the region's history. Thus Ibn Ghannām says: 'I wanted to record those things whose light has risen and spread, and became widely circulated and well known in most countries: military campaigns that are the brightest highlights of the time, and the Islamic conquests that began in the sixth decade of the twelfth century. I have learned about those campaigns from sources that are foremost in reliability and veracity. Yet I have mentioned only the well-known and recorded campaigns, and only the well-known and previously recorded biographies.'[27] Ibn Bishr states: 'I continuously long for knowledge about their (the Suʿūdī family's) feats and conditions, their huge armies and their battles; for they are kings who possessed the best of virtues and objects of pride, and subdued with their awe-inspiring feats all recalcitrant enemies, whether desert nomads or settled urban and rural dwellers. They filled this peninsula with their conquering swords and their justice and beneficence.'[28] It seems that the reason for interest in raids and military campaigns was that they were the most distinctive aspects of the period. It is related that there were thirty-five raids launched by Muḥammad ibn Suʿūd (r. 1159–79/1746–65) and his son ʿAbd al-ʿAzīz (r. 1179–1218/1765–1803) against the city of Riyadh alone during the period 1159–87/1746–73.[29]

Similarly, historians have generally focused on those aspects of architecture and buildings that related to military campaigns and raids, such as the order 'given by Imām Muḥammad ibn Suʿūd to the Muslims to build at that place (al-Ghadhwāna) a palace which would be a stronghold for them and from which they could harass the people of Riyadh. They spent seven days building it until it was finished.' It was also narrated that 'in 1172 [1758] Sheikh Muḥammad ibn ʿAbd al-Wahhāb and Prince Muḥammad ibn Suʿūd learned that ʿUrayʿir ibn Dujayn, the chieftain of al- Ahsāʾ, was preparing to advance upon Najd. Whereupon they ordered all the Muslim territories to get ready and secure themselves, and ʿAbd al-ʿAzīz built two walls around ad-Dirʿīyah surmounted with towers, for fear of attempts to climb over the walls.'[30]

It appears that one reason why accounts of architectural constructions were neglected was the excessive caution against encroachment on the religious stamp of the Saudi princes, who assumed the title of imām, beginning with Muḥammad ibn Suʿūd, who claimed the imamate 'after twenty years of rule, after having colored his policy and wars with a purely religious hue . . . The first time that Ibn Bishr referred to him as "Imam" was during the events of the year 1166 [1753]. Ibn Ghannām referred to him as "emir" throughout his life, and bestowed on his son and successor ʿAbd al-ʿAzīz the title of "Imam".'[31] Therefore mentions of erecting buildings are rare, except for mosques and constructions related to war. The historical sources are careful to note the religious aspect and the attention devoted to it by the imāms. An example is Ibn Bishr's account of Turkī ibn ʿAbd Allāh (d. 1249/1834): 'Orphans from every village or town frequented his palace. Every widow and destitute person received and enjoyed his beneficence. He clothed them with his own hand out of modesty and humility . . . He never failed to attend the study gatherings and meetings of the Muslims. Every Thursday and Monday he would leave his palace and gather people together for meetings.'[32] He adds:

> No one was killed in cold blood. When he (Turkī) did not attack an enemy, he would camp somewhere amongst the Muslims and stay there according to his plans for settling issues and serving the Muslims' interests. Mosques were founded everywhere. Each congregation had an imām who would gather the people behind him for prayer. Another imām would lead the prayer for those who stayed behind with the equipment and baggage. Thus no one would perform the prayer alone.[33]

He also states: 'We entered with the Imam into his tent and sat with him. Sheikh ʿAbd Allāh ibn Jabr began to read before him the book entitled *Sirāj al-mulūk*, while Sheikh ʿAbd al-Laṭīf was listening; but it was the Imam who made the commentary and ascertained its meaning.'[34]

Deductions from allusions that occur in the narration of events and military campaigns are considered to be the only way to discern architectural features. An example is the story of the martyrdom of Turkī ibn ʿAbd Allāh at the hands of Mushārī ibn ʿAbd al-Raḥmān ibn Ḥasan ibn Mushārī ibn Suʿūd:

> When he performed the Friday midday prayer and the *sunna* (ritual) following it, he went out as usual from the door south of the *miḥrāb* (prayer niche).[35] This door had been prepared for his entry and exit and to enable the Imam to avoid passing through the numerous rows of worshippers assembled in the mosque. The criminal assassins lay in wait for him near the shops between the palace and the mosque. He was holding a letter in his hand and reading it while a man was standing on his left. One of their domestic slaves, called Ibrāhīm ibn Ḥamza, intercepted him, inserted the pistol into his sleeve while he was unaware, and fired it, and he (Turkī) fell dead on the spot as the shot hit his heart. Then Mushārī rushed out of the mosque. He drew his sword and threatened the people, while others also drew their swords in support of him. Those who were there were stunned and realized that the gang of assassins had plotted against (Turkī) in the dark. When Zuwayd, Turkī's well-known slave, saw his master slain, he unsheathed his sword and chased and wounded one of Mushārī's men. But when he found no one to help him he fled to the palace, and Mushārī also swiftly entered the palace with his followers.[36]

Mention is also made of some architectural features in the story of Fayṣal ibn Turkī's (d. 1282/1865) return to Riyadh after that event: '(Imam Fayṣal) ordered those people of Riyadh who were with him to enter the city at night and hold the towers and houses opposite the palace. He ordered other men whom he trusted to march with them. When they reached the city they found its towers and walls fully manned by Mushārī. When the men holding the towers saw and recognized them, they maintained silence and joyfully admitted them.'[37]

(ii) *Writings of Foreign Travellers Who Visited the Region*. The English traveller William Palgrave is regarded as one of the most famous travellers to have visited the region during this period. His visit took place during the reign of Fayṣal ibn Turkī, in 1279/1862. Palgrave began his journey from Ḥāʾil, going to Burayda and then to Riyadh; he recorded it in a book entitled *Personal Narrative of a Year's Journey through Central and Eastern Arabia (1862–1863)* (London, 1865). In this work he wrote a description of Riyadh which remains a uniquely detailed account of that city. He also drew a sketch plan of the city at that time. What he recorded during his journey may be regarded as a model of what is missing in the history of the region. He gave an account of the city's wall, gates, roads, quarters, mosques, markets and most famous dwellings. He also gave precise details about the palace of Fayṣal ibn Turkī and his son ʿAbd Allāh, and discussed nearby areas lying outside the wall and the activities carried out there.[38]

The map Palgrave drew of the city of Riyadh during his visit there is believed to be the first of its kind for that city. He stated:

There is a wall surrounding the city on all sides, with heights varying from one place to another and ranging between twenty to thirty feet. The wall is protected by a trench and barriers extending all along the wall . . . The city of Riyadh has twelve gates, five of which lead eastward; they include Riyadh's main gate, which leads to the al-Aḥsāʾ road. There are three gates on the northern side, three on the western side, and two on the southern side. The main gate leads directly to the main street, which extends on a

> straight line to the city markets and the palace area. On the north of this large street lies the palace of Emir Jalawī ibn Turkī; the palace of Emir ʿAbd Allāh ibn Fayṣal lies on the opposite side and is nearer than the first palace to the royal quarter. Higher than all of these, there is a huge block of buildings which, put together, constitute Imam Fayṣal's citadel.[39]

Palgrave's journey was followed by that of the British High Commissioner in the Gulf, Sir Lewis Pelly, who visited the region in 1281/1865. He recorded his journey in a report that was later published as a book entitled *Report on a Journey to Riyadh in Central Arabia, 1865* (Bombay, 1866). This report differs from Palgrave's account in that Pelly's details about the city of Riyadh were limited, although he elaborated somewhat on certain areas, for example when he described the architectural form of Sadūs. The political character of his journey seems more evident. Like Palgrave, in the appendix to his report he gave data about the numbers of the inhabitants and fighters in some villages of Najd, in addition to demographic data about the tribes. It would not seem reasonable to expect information that differs substantially from that included in Palgrave's journey, even though Pelly expanded on some details of his own journey, because his came only two years later than that of Palgrave.

These journeys are considered an important source of the region's history during this period because of their historiographical format, which differs from other historical sources; this despite the fact that they occasionally contained misrepresentation of some facts, although this, more often than not, touched on political and social aspects.

e. *Recent Works about the History of This Period*

These are exemplified by works specifically related to the purpose of writing about the role of the modern Saudi state: for example, ʿAbd Allāh ibn Khamīs's *Muʿjam al-Yamāma*, Ḥamad al-Jāsir's writings on Riyadh during various historical phases, Aḥmad ʿAṭṭār in the first part of his *Ṣaqr al-jazīra*, Amīn al-Rīḥānī's *Taʾrīkh Najd al-ḥadīth*, or ʿAbd Allāh H. St John Philby's books on Arabia. These works basically drew on the sources referred to above, which were contemporaneous with the period under discussion, but tried to reformulate the contents in a more modern style and form of presentation. A case in point is *Taʾrīkh al-Mamlaka al-ʿArabiyya al-Suʿūdiyya*, by ʿAbd Allāh al-ʿUthaymīn, who drew also from some western sources. He wrote in a highly accessible, simple style, although sometimes to the detriment of neglecting the dates of events, which makes it difficult for the reader to know when some events took place. However, the book remains a useful reference source for the history of this period.

f. *The Formation of the Kingdom of Saudi Arabia*

This phase coincides with the development witnessed by the world and the improvement in the level of knowledge about the Arabian peninsula, including world interest in King Abdul Aziz, his recapture of Riyadh and his embarking on the unification of some parts of the Arabian peninsula. This made Riyadh a goal for both Arabs and non-Arabs, either out of admiration or because of curiosity. This phase can be divided into two parts

> (i) *1309–19/1891–1902*. This period begins with the departure of ʿAbd al-Raḥmān ibn Fayṣal (in 1309/1891) from Riyadh and ends with the triumphant recapture of the city by ʿAbd al-ʿAzīz (in 1319/1902) and the beginning of the unification of some parts of the Arabian peninsula. Much has been written about this period, but it is marked overwhelmingly by accounts of the wars that paved the way to the establishment of the kingdom. For this reason, the history of this period lacks any detailed account of architectural, economic and social features, with a few exceptions here and there, which are usually connected to accounts of wars. This is despite the fact that the invention of photography has contributed to our knowledge of some aspects of this period. What Philby wrote in his many books can be regarded as a systematic documentation of the kingdom's rise, in addition to the writings of some of those who worked with the late King Abdul Aziz, such as Ḥāfiẓ Wahba, Khayr al-Dīn al-Ziriklī and Fuʾād Ḥamza.

The Westerners' journeys represent an important source because of differences in styles and fields of interest. One of these travellers was

Captain Shakespear, who made a journey to Riyadh in 1333/1914. In his diary he incorporated a description of Riyadh and its environs, as well as its general architectural outline. He may have drawn on the photographs he took in presenting an image of the architectural shape of the city. He was the first person ever to take photographs of the city and of King Abdul Aziz and his military campaigns and raids.[40] In the years 1337, 1341 and 1350 (1917, 1922, 1931) Philby gave a general description of Riyadh and the aspects of life there. He also drew rough sketch maps in which he showed some major architectural monuments, such as the mosque, the ruler's palace, the market, and the city wall and gates. He also noted the approximate dimensions of the city and estimated its area, in 1337/1917 and 1341/1922, at nearly 400,000 square metres.[41]

Muḥammad al-Mānīᶜ's *Unification of the Kingdom of Saudi Arabia* covers various aspects of the social and economic developments at the time, since he made the unification of the Arabian peninsula his main theme. In a number of chapters he relates as an eyewitness the story of King Abdul Aziz from the recapture of Riyadh in 1319/1891 up to the first stages of the period of oil discoveries. Although he wrote his book because of the need for 'an Arab citizen to write a book in English to explain the Arab viewpoint on the modern history of his country',[42] the need for such a book in Arabic may be considered more urgent. This need was met when ᶜAbd Allāh al-ᶜUthaymīn translated the book into Arabic, although there are some gaps that call for further investigation.

In its description of Riyadh the book refers to certain architectural features, and states that it is very likely that

> in 1901/1319, just as in 1926/1345, when I commenced my service under His Majesty the King, it (Riyadh) was surrounded with an outer wall built of mortar about 20 feet high. On each of its four sides there was a huge gate. But the city itself was so small that its maximum breadth did not exceed 1500 metres. Inside the city there were winding lanes which were so narrow that it was difficult for two men to walk together side by side. The only open space was the central market that was overlooked by the Great Mosque on one side and by the palace that was usurped by Ibn al-Rashīd from the other side. Adjacent to it was a small market especially

> catering for women. All the buildings were made of mud brick. About half were two-storey buildings, while the rest were a single storey. Many of Riyadh's houses were so close to the city wall that the wall itself constituted the back side of these houses.[43]

He also noted the building works ordered by King Abdul Aziz after his recapture of Riyadh, which included the repair of its fortifications and the rebuilding of the wall.[44]

> (ii) *Beginning with the Year 1351/1932*. This phase begins with the declaration of the establishment of the Kingdom of Saudi Arabia. This period was characterized by the prevalence of security throughout the Arabian peninsula and the beginning of a new stage of looking forward to enjoying a bright future, especially after the discovery of valuable economic resources. Another distinctive feature of this phase was improved documentation of the various aspects of development. The beginnings of this stage, and especially their economic aspects, have been duly documented, particularly by some of those who took part in prospecting for oil, for example K. S. Twitchell.

It is difficult to refer to what has been written about this period because of the steady flow of works which still continue to appear. Yet it may be noted that, with the fast and constant pace of development, this period continues to be viewed as a part of the present; this situation requires caution in dealing with the subject. Another factor that calls for caution is the lack of concordance between the works about this period, as each addresses different topics. It is thus necessary to follow the documentation of all aspects of life, with a comprehensive outlook and within the framework of historical necessity.

g. *Building of the Great (Friday) Mosque and the Government Palace*
The Friday Mosque and the Government Palace represent the most important architectural legacies in the city of Riyadh, and affirm, through their close historical linkage, the fundamental basis of government throughout

the phases of the development of the Saudi state, as represented by the interconnection between religion and state. Despite this importance, however, references to the mosque and the Government Palace were cursory, made in passing in accounts of events or military campaigns. There were no references in earlier works to the builders of the mosque or the palace. And if, more recently, historians have made suggestions as to who built the mosque and the palace, these speculations rely on interpretations of some allusions, or from recurrent and unverified oral accounts. It is difficult to explain such verbal accounts. For example, historians disagree as to who built the palace of al-Muṣmak, which was constructed more recently than the mosque and the Government Palace.

In his history, which agrees with that of Ibn Ghannām, Ibn Bishr notes, in his first reference to a palace in Riyadh, the palace of Dahhām: 'Dahhām sent his brother Mishlib on horseback to Muḥammad ibn Suᶜūd, the Emir of ad-Dirᶜīyah, asking for support. Muḥammad responded by sending his brother, Mushārī ibn Suᶜūd, with several men from ad-Dirᶜīyah. When Dahhām learned about them he went out of his palace and fought the people of Riyadh.'[45] In addition to the reference to Dahhām's palace, or to other palaces that are named, the narrative takes a different turn in referring to the main palace in Riyadh, beginning in 1236/1821. Here are some examples: 'Turkī and the palace men with him were besieged; the Turks threw firebrands at him and fought him. He fled alone from the palace at night' (events of the year 1236/1821);[46] 'Then Imam Fayṣal ordered those people from Riyadh who were with him to enter the city at night and hold the towers and houses opposite the palace. He then ordered other men whom he trusted to go with them. When they arrived at the city, they found its towers and wall fully manned by those whom Mushārī had stationed there. When the men in the towers saw them and recognized them, they maintained silence and joyfully let them in' (events of the year 1249 [1834]).[47]

Frequent accounts state that the Government Palace was built by Ibn Nāṣir, the Turkish Emir of Riyadh. But it is not stated whether this was Nāṣir ibn Ḥamad ibn Nāṣir al-ᶜĀyidhī, who was Emir of Riyadh in 1233/1818, or ᶜAbd Allāh ibn Ḥamad ibn Nāṣir al-ᶜĀyidhi, who was emir when Turkī ibn ᶜAbd Allāh entered the city in 1240/1824. Ḥamad al-Jāsir refers to the palace of Nāṣir ibn Ḥamad al-'Āyidhī, Emir of Riyadh in 1236/1821, and states that it was situated 'to the west of the present Government Palace near the eastern side of al-Muqaybara'.[48] It is also thought that the Government Palace was built as an extension to, or on the ruins of, Dahhām's palace, and that Turkī ibn ʿAbd Allāh lived in it (i.e. in Ibn Nāṣir's palace).[49]

Ḥamad al-Jāsir states that Dahhām ibn Dawwās 'built the palace which later became the seat of the emirate and government, until it was demolished in Ṣafar 1309 [September 1891]. The forts were erected and the wall was built in approximately 1160 [1747].'[50] Then ʿAbd Allāh ibn Fayṣal ordered 'that the palace now known as al-Muṣmak be built. The new palace replaced the palace of Dahhām, which had been the seat of government for nearly 80 years.'[51] When ʿAbd al-Raḥmān (ibn Fayṣal) decided to recapture Riyadh, 'the emir Ibn al-Rashīd surprised him by attacking the city in Ṣafar 1309. He occupied Riyadh and ordered that its walls and both the old and new palaces be demolished.'[52] It appears that only the palaces of Dahhām and al-Muṣmak were not torn down; that is, what is meant here are the palaces of Dahhām and of ʿAbd Allāh.

Al-Jāsir does not mention the source upon which he drew with regard to Dahhām's building of the palace. Assuming that Dahhām remained alive until 1287/1870, and taking into account the eighty-year period, this takes us back to 1267/1851, fifteen years prior to the beginning of ʿAbd Allāh ibn Fayṣal's rule in 1282/1865. But if the eighty-year period is computed as being the date which al-Jāsir puts for the building of Dahhām's palace, it will end in 1240/1824, the year when the rule of Turkī ibn ʿAbd Allāh began. This may be more acceptable, for it tallies with Palgrave's statement that Imām Fayṣal's palace, which is the Government Palace according to the plan he drew and which agrees with Ibn Bishr's description, was built by Turkī ibn ʿAbd Allāh, after he had made Riyadh the capital of his government, completed the construction of the fortifications and the city wall, and then embarked on building the mosque and the Government Palace. Palgrave gave precise details of the palace's components and its functions, and drew a detailed plan of it.

Philby states that Turkī ibn ʿAbd Allāh re-established the Saudi state from Riyadh, which was better situated and easier to organize than ad-

Dirᶜīyah, rather than rebuilding over its ruins. He built a fortified wall around it, in addition to a palace and a mosque.[53] Amīn al-Rīḥānī also says that the palace in which Mushārī ibn ᶜAbd al-Rahmān ibn Suᶜūd was entrenched, and which is also Imam Turkī's palace, was the palace of Dahhām ibn Dawwās.[54]

It is also likely that the palace referred to in Riyadh as a government palace is that of Dahhām ibn Dawwās and of Turkī ibn ᶜAbd Allāh. Ibrāhīm ibn ᶜĪsā refers to the palace as 'the palace of Riyadh', while ᶜAbd Allāh al-ᶜUthaymīn always refers to the palace as the 'government palace', even if the account is quoted on the authority of earlier historians such as Ibn Bishr, who only mentions 'the palace'. It is also possible that the palace underwent gradual stages of rebuilding from the time of Dahhām until that of Turkī ibn ᶜAbd Allāh. King Abdul Aziz is quoted as saying about the recapture of Riyadh, 'Ibn Rashīd had pulled down the city wall. The place of the emir appointed by him was in a palace belonging to Imam ᶜAbd Allāh. It was demolished by Ibn al-Rashīd, who spared in it the fort called al-Muṣmak. We also had houses for the family opposite al-Muṣmak, which were also destroyed by the Rashīdī'.[55]

In the middle of the fourteenth/twentieth century King Abdul Aziz built the palace of al-Mirbaᶜ, on the northern side of the city and outside its walls; 'he used it as a residence for himself and his harem, while the old palace which he had built was reserved for receiving envoys and guests'.[56] This shows that ᶜAbd al-ᶜAzīz built a new palace for government at the beginning of his rule. 'The king's palace was the largest building in Riyadh. Its area was around 8,000 square metres and, like other houses in the city, it was built of unbaked bricks and mortar. Although it was demolished a long time ago, one can still see the old castle of Riyadh, which has been carefully preserved. It resembles the old palace in terms of design and general appearance. The palace comprised two storeys and four wings extending from its centre to the four directions.'[57] The Government Palace built by King Abdul Aziz was demolished and replaced by a new one, to which were added the emirate of Riyadh's functional offices, during the 1970s, using modern building materials.

The city plan drawn by Palgrave shows the site of the Government Palace, which he referred to as Imam Fayṣal's palace, situated south of the Friday Mosque at the site of the Government Palace built in the reign of King Abdul Aziz (as shown by Philby's maps), near the site of the new Government Palace.

h. *The Friday Mosque*

The historical sources are more sparing in their reference to the Great (Friday) Mosque in Riyadh than they are with those to the Government Palace. Yet it seems that the mosque's reputation went beyond the borders of the Arabian peninsula. The Finnish traveller George Wallin states that Riyadh, and the lectures held in its mosque, were the main reason for his first journey to the Arabian peninsula in 1261/1845, and that before beginning his second journey in 1264–5/1848 he was eager to hear the lectures held at Riyadh's mosque.[58]

The most significant references to the mosque appear in accounts of the martyrdom of Turkī ibn ʿAbd Allāh after his exit from the door south of the *miḥrāb* near the shops between the palace and the mosque.[59] It has already been noted that Palgrave says that the building was completed during Turkī's rule. But it seems that the door was replaced, because of this event, with a bridge linking both buildings, during the reign of Fayṣal ibn Turkī. Palgrave described the Friday Mosque as large enough to accommodate more than 2,000 worshippers, with an outer courtyard that could accommodate over 2,000 more. It was devoid of decoration, indeed of any aesthetic features whatsoever. It had no minaret; but there was a small enclosure directly above the *miḥrāb* to be used by Imam Fayṣal in the Friday midday prayer.[60]

Many accounts state that Fayṣal ibn Turkī built the mosque, when he noticed the central location on which it was erected between the palace in which he resided and 'several residential quarters such as Dakhna, al-Ẓahīra, and al-Murayqib'.[61] But what seems more certain is that it was Turkī who built it; had Fayṣal been the builder, Ibn Bishr and Palgrave would have mentioned this. It is possible that Fayṣal built an extension to it. The mosque was demolished in the early 1970s and then rebuilt; it was one of the earliest buildings for which modern building materials were used.

The mosque and the Government Palace were demolished in 1408/1988 and were rebuilt within the framework of a developmental programme for the city centre, under the sponsorship of the High Commission for Development of the City of Riyadh, with a view to reactivating the area of the Government Palace in appreciation and confirmation of its historical importance and its unique legacy. The building was completed in deference to the wish of His Royal Highness Prince Salmān ibn ʿAbd al-ʿAzīz Āl Saʿūd, Emir of Riyadh Province and President of the High Commission for Development of the City of Riyadh; the name of Turkī ibn ʿAbd Allah, the founder of the second Saudi state, was attached to the mosque to symbolize his historical role and to commemorate his establishment of the mosque and building of the Government Palace.

2. *Conclusion*

The history of Najd in general, and of Riyadh in particular, is characterized by obscurity, especially in the period extending from ancient times until the rise of the Salafiyya movement, and its failure to include the varied aspects of history throughout the phases of the Saudi state until the beginning of the modern era. This chapter may be regarded as an attempt to offer specialist insights in order to give a picture of the architectural history of the central Arabian peninsula in general and of Riyadh in particular. It is almost inconceivable that Najd, which has been famed throughout history, did not figure prominently until the rise of the Salafiyya movement and the establishment of the Saudi state; it continued to be an arena of conflict until King Abdul Aziz recaptured Riyadh and founded the Kingdom of Saudi Arabia.

Archaeological antiquities and sites are important clues in delineating an area's architecture throughout its various periods of history. But the view that archaeological antiquities were 'useless burdens' in some periods has often led to the destruction of valuable monuments and sites. The neglect of archaeological monuments and antiquities by the local inhabitants and their wariness towards foreign excavators have contributed to the loss of important landmarks of the history of the region.[62] In Sadūs, for example, 'the antiquities and the palace said to have belonged to Solomon, son of David, and his metropolis were destroyed'.[63] Lewis Pelly speaks of a round column in Sadūs which was nearly 20 feet high (approximately six metres), which no one knew about at that time (1281/1865), although it was thought to pre-date the time of the Prophet Muḥammad.[64] That column had disappeared when Philby visited the area in 1337/1918.[65] In Yamama, ancient archaeological remains also disappeared, although they had existed until the early fourth/tenth century. Conservation of and care for antiquities was confronted later on with attitudes that sometimes led to the loss of antiquities which had survived for hundreds of years, especially those that represented animate beings.

The obscurity of the region's ancient history continues, along with the need for more care for its antiquities and the excavation of them. No example is more striking than the fact that the project for revival of the old city of ad-Dirʿīyah, despite the relative recentness of the city's history, the existence of clearly visible monuments, and the city's historical and political importance, has failed to bring to light what was in 1395/1975 one of the most significant programmes for the conservation of antiquities.

This huge project included 'the establishment of a large cultural centre equipped with all facilities, such as libraries and exhibition halls, which would present the aspects of the spread of Wahhābī preaching and its effect today on various parts of the world'.[66] This is in addition to the absence of a suitable comprehensive museum demonstrating what the Kingdom of Saudi Arabia represents as a country occupying the largest portion of the Arabian peninsula, as a meeting point of ancient civilizations, and as the source, and witness to the development, of Islamic civilization.

Obscurity veils the region's history in the pre-Islamic period too, except for the powerful voice of poetry, which then flourished. Obscurity also surrounds the period from the beginning of Islam until the emergence of the Salafiyya movement and the rise of the first Saudi state, except for fleeting glimpses that slipped through the veil of neglect from which the central Arabian peninsula suffered. With the indifference to the region's history in general, it could not be expected that its architectural aspects would receive any real attention.

The Salafiyya movement was a period of renewal and self-assertion, and it was when the documentation of the region's history began. It was started by Husayn ibn Ghannām, who was a contemporary of Muḥammad ibn ʿAbd al-Wahhāb and wrote his *Taʾrīkh Najd* on the Sheikh's directive, which makes it possible to consider him as the founder of the modern historiography of the Arabian peninsula.[67] He was followed by a number of historians who documented the region's history until the beginning of the rule of ʿAbd al-ʿAzīz. But Ibn ʿAbd al-Wahhāb's preaching and the rise of the Saudi state were accompanied by writing on the history of that state.[68] Thus knowledge of numerous aspects of history, such as architecture, has been absent. Some of this neglect can be rectified through the writings of travellers who visited central Arabia; yet many aspects of history, from the formation of the first Saudi state until the rise of the Kingdom of Saudi Arabia, remain unrecorded, but have been handed down (orally) from one generation to another. To this we may add the Nabaṭī (colloquial) poetry from which we can benefit by discovering events, and accounts of buildings and sites, that have been embedded in this type of poetry for many centuries.[69]

A clear vision of the region and of the comprehensive character of its history began when the affairs of the Arabian peninsula became stabilized during the rule of King Abdul Aziz. However, most books on the history of this period do not deal with architecture. Ziriklī states: 'Most of the books written about King Abdul Aziz, or those which were largely filled with information about him, would constitute a library on their own, while chapters and articles are only too many.' He cited the titles of fifty-six books in Arabic and twenty-three in other languages.[70] The early stages of ʿAbd al-ʿ Azīz's rule, and the wars for consolidation of the state that accompanied them until 1344/1925, lacked documentation of other aspects of history, in particular architecture.

ʿAbd al-ʿAzīz restored to the Arabian peninsula its position in the world. He was the first member of the Saudi dynasty to transform the traditional system of government into an institutional one with a clear-cut methodology. Yet most of what was written about him does not discuss his personality and achievements. Writings varied from mere colourless narration to insincere flattery, and distortion of the facts, including the fabrication of unrealistic roles by some foreign writers, particularly about their varied contributions in laying down some of the principles of government there. One may add that non-Arabs who wrote about the kingdom's history, regardless of the aims of their visits and writings, could not, owing to differences in culture and traditions, conceive of or appreciate some characteristic local attitudes and values. It is therefore necessary for specialists to write a true picture of King Abdul Aziz and his endeavours in the establishment of the Kingdom of Saudi Arabia in a manner that will cover various aspects of history, especially architecture.

Appendices

The following pages comprise two appendices. The first includes a brief outline of the journeys of Europeans to the Arabian peninsula, other than those already referred to in this chapter. The second includes sketchy notes of the majority of references in the histories of Ibn Ghannām and Ibn Bishr to architectural aspects of Najd, as a means of providing further elucidation of the extent to which this side of history is covered.

Appendix 1. *European Journeys to the Arabian Peninsula*[71]

The journeys made by Europeans to the Arabian peninsula represent an important source of its history, as these accounts are usually concerned with what Arab historians neglected, such as documentation of architectural and social features. Regardless of the motives that lay behind these journeys, they had, in addition to the results discussed in this chapter, other aspects such as unearthing the antiquities of ancient Arab civilizations,[72] as well as occasional purely academic observations, absent in the accounts of many of their contemporaries, on some events in Arabia, such as the Salafiyya movement in the central Arabian peninsula. It is not only fair, but indeed a recognition of merit, to say that everyone concerned with the history and geography of the Arabian peninsula is dependent on the older works which those orientalists edited and published.[73]

Reinaud, the British Vice-Consul in Basra, is considered the first political envoy to have been sent to Najd; he arrived at ad-Dirʿīyah in 1214/1799, as the first European to visit the capital of the first Saudi state.[74] The English Resident in Basra sent him as an envoy to Emir Suʿūd, seeking a truce; he stayed in ad-Dirʿīyah for one week. The report he compiled about his journey and his impressions included a letter written in 1220/1805, in which he states that 'he was stunned at seeing that the city was so small, although it had a pleasant location'.[75] Napoleon also sent a political envoy, M. de Lascaris, to ad-Dirʿīyah in 1226/1811.[76] The documents he wrote have not been found. This journey was followed by numerous others. Among the most well-known journeys to Riyadh were those of Palgrave in 1279/1862 and Lewis Pelly in 1281/1865; both have been discussed above.

It seems that the documentation of the history of Riyadh suffered from bad luck. More than once the arrival of travellers to the city was disrupted during occasional periods that required filling some gaps of history. For example, the English traveller Sadleir visited the Arabian peninsula in 1233/1819, after the destruction of ad-Dirʿīyah. The real purpose of his journey was political. He arrived at Manfūḥa but was told that Ibrāhīm Pasha had left ad-Dirʿīyah, which forced Sadleir to change his route.[77] The Finnish traveller George Wallin visited the Arabian peninsula in 1261/1845 and 1264–5/1848. He stayed in Ḥāʾil for a short period, hoping that he would be able to reach Riyadh, the basic goal of his journey, via al-Qaṣīm. But one of the brothers of Ibn al-Rashīd, the Emir of Ḥāʾil, who had just returned from a bloody battle there (in Riyadh), warned him against the dangers of travel at that time.[78]

The Danish Barclay Raunkiaer also journeyed to the heart of the Arabian peninsula in 1331/1912, but fell ill in Kuwait. Upon his arrival in Riyadh he could walk only with difficulty. It seems that his condition was clearly known to ʿAbd al-Rahmān ibn Fayṣal, who, according to Raunkiaer, treated him so well that he felt better, although his illness adversely affected his undertaking of the discoveries he had hoped to make. Therefore, he accepted the help offered to him to continue his journey to the eastern shore without delay, while his hopes for his journey to Riyadh were not fulfilled.[79] He also believed that taking photographs in the region might be dangerous, and so he depended on sketches. He notes that when he arrived at the outskirts of Riyadh he learned that King Abdul Aziz had left it two days before, moving westward in a raid against the tribe of ᶜUtayba.[80]

European journeys to other parts of the Arabian peninsula may be regarded a supplementary source for the history of its central region; for in many such journeys there were references to the conditions of the region. Carsten Niebuhr travelled to the periphery of the Arabian peninsula in 1176/1762. In Basra he heard about the rise of the reformist movement in Najd. 'Through him Europeans knew of this movement for the first time.' This traveller considered the reformist movement 'an attempt to unite Najd and put an end to the prevailing state of tribal fragmentation. He expected that it would play a significant part in the future of the entire Arabian peninsula.'[81] His mission was essentially a geographical one, but he could not draw a complete map of the Arabian peninsula because he could not travel everywhere. Among the cities, Niebuhr mentions ad-Dirᶜīyah and al-ᶜUyayna; the latter was the birthplace of Ibn ᶜAbd al-Wahhāb, who was still alive when Niebuhr was visiting the Arabian Gulf area.[82]

In 1225/1810 the German Zetsin travelled to the Hijaz under the name of Ḥājmūsā, and met Imām Suᶜūd in Makkah.[83] In 1229/1813 Napoleon sent one of his Spanish agents, Domingo Badia y Leblich (who was known as ᶜAlī Bey al-'Abbāsī), to explore conditions in Najd. He never reached Najd,[84] although 'he referred to the virtues of the Wahhābīs in Makkah'.[85] Burckhardt travelled to Arabia in 1230/1814, but he too failed to reach Najd. Nevertheless, he made contacts with some tribes, traders and officials during his stay in the Hejaz. He referred to the scholarly situation in Najd, saying that 'every manuscript on history and religious studies that was found in Makkah, Madinah or the Yemeni cities was quickly bought by the Saudi state and taken to ad-Dirᶜīyah. He also says that the library of Imām Suᶜūd was regarded at that time to be the richest of its kind beyond dispute in Arabic manuscripts dealing with historical subjects.[86]

2. *Architectural Features of Najd*

a. Ibn Ghannām's History

Source: Husayn ibn Ghannām, *Rawdat al-afkār wa-al-afhām li-murtād ḥāl al-Imām wa-taʿdād ghazawāt dhawī al-Islām* (ed. Naṣir al-Dīn al-Asad, collated with the original by ʿAbd al-ʿAzīz ibn Muḥammad ibn Ibrāhīm Āl al-Sheikh; Riyadh, 3rd edn, 1403/1982–3), I.

Page 89: 'They rallied against him, surrounded his palace and besieged him therein, whereupon Dahhām sent his brother Mishlib on horseback to Muḥammad ibn Suʿūd.'

Page 91: 'Muḥammad ibn Suʿūd was ordered to fight him; he sent a detachment to Riyadh at night. They entered the city, came to the door of the castle, and cut off the door with a saw.'

Page 92: 'Dahhām went out with the people of Riyadh; they engaged (in battle) at a place called al-Wishām, outside the wall.'

Page 93: 'They met in battle at the centre of the city; thus it was called the battle of Dalqa. They fought fiercely, and the fighting was hottest at the palace gate.'

Page 95: 'The other detachment marched to Muqrin and entered the town, whose people had fought near the palace of Dahhām ibn Dawwās.'

Page 96: 'When the ambush went out (of hiding), the people of Tharmadā fled and took refuge at a palace outside the town called Qaṣr al-Ḥarīṣ.'

Page 107: 'Then ʿAbd al-ʿAzīz, with his Muslim followers, made for Riyadh; they reached the southern gate at night.'

Page 110: 'On their way back they halted with their mounts for rest at al-Ghadhwāna. ʿAbd al-ʿAzīz ordered the Muslims to build a palace at that place, to function as a stronghold for them and to be used for harassing the people of Riyadh. They spent seven days in building it until it was finished.'

Page 111: 'In 1172/1758–9 Muḥammad ibn ʿAbd al-Wahhāb and Muḥammad ibn Suʿūd learned that 'Uray'ir ibn Dujayn, the military leader of al-Ahsāʾ, intended to attack Najd. They ordered all the Muslim territories there to prepare and to fortify themselves. ʿAbd al-ʿAzīz built two walls around ad-Dirʿīyah, with towers, in fear of attempts to climb the walls.'

Page 116: 'Then ʿAbd al-ʿAzīz marched on until he halted between al-Far'a and Ushayqir; he built a palace there to function as stronghold and an outpost.'

Page 124: 'Then ʿAbd al-ʿAzīz marched from Manfūḥa to Qasr al-Ghadhwāna, where he stayed for some days carrying out repairs, and then returned to ad-Dirʿīyah.'

Page 150: 'He built a palace near that place, Qaṣr al-Bidaʿ, to be used as a fort and an outpost.'

Page 183: 'Many inhabitants of the country (al-Aḥsāʾ) advised Suʿūd to build a fort for himself.'

Page 194: 'Then he built a strong palace wherein he stored the food and weapons required by the fighters stationed there.'

Page 125: 'He captured Burūj Hisān [or: fortified towers].'

Page 128: 'ʿAbd al-ʿAzīz stayed at Qaṣr al-Ghadhwāna for some days; he launched raids against Riyadh from there, and then returned to his position.'

Page 134: 'In 1187 [1773] ʿAbd al-ʿAzīz and the Muslims marched towards Riyadh, where he clashed with its people for some time. He fought them daily, until the Muslims seized some of the towers of the town and destroyed them, along with its lofty observation post.'

Page 150: 'Then he built a palace near that place, Qaṣr al-Bidaʿ, to be a stronghold and an outpost for the Muslims.'

b. Architectural Features in Ibn Bishr's History

Source: ʿUthmān ibn ʿAbd Allāh ibn Bishr, *ʿUnwān al-majdfī taʾrīkh Najd* (Riyadh, 4th edn, 1402/1982), I–II.

Events of the Year 1159 [1746]

Whereupon Dahhām sent his brother Mishlib on horseback to Muḥammad ibn Suʿūd, Emir of ad-Dirʿīyah, asking him for support. Muḥammad responded by sending his brother Mushārī ibn Suʿūd, together with some men from ad-Dirʿīyah. When Dahhām learned about them he went out of his palace and fought the people of Riyadh.

When news of this reached Muḥammad ibn Suʿūd and his brothers, they pledged that the first assault they would make against him would be in his palace. Then they marched against him, reached the gate of the fortress in his palace, and cut down its door with a saw. Dahhām and his men came out; they fought at a place called al-Wishām, outside the wall.

Events of the Year 1161 [1748]
The people of Ḥuraymilā and ʿAraqa made for Muqrin, which they entered at noon. All the people of the town had already gathered there at the palace of Dahhām.

Events of the Year 1170 [1756–7]
ʿAbd al-ʿAzīz marched with his Muslim followers and halted at the southern gate of Riyadh.

On his return from that raid (the second battle of al-Baniyya), ʿAbd al-ʿAzīz ordered the building of the palace at al-Ghadhwāna, a well-known place west of Riyadh at the bottom of the valley, from which he wanted to harass the people of Riyadh and to make it function as a stronghold for the Muslims. They spent seven days building it.

Events of the Year 1179 [1765–6]
In this year ʿAbd al-ʿAzīz marched with the Muslim troops, made for Riyadh, and seized some of its towers. When Dahhām learned of this he sent a rider to the tribe of Subayʾ, who were close to him, and called on the Muslims to fight, to preoccupy them until the arrival of Subayʿ. When the Muslims saw the horses, ʿAbd al-ʿAzīz ordered his men to leave the towers and come down from them.

Events of the Year 1181 [1776–7]
Then there took place a battle called the battle of Bāb al-Thumayrī. Men were killed on both sides, and ʿAbd al-ʿAzīz halted at al-Ghadhwāna palace and stayed for some days, raiding Riyadh.

Events of the Year 1187 [1773–4]
In that year ʿAbd al-ʿAzīz, along with the Muslim troops, made for Riyadh. He fought with its people for many days, beleaguered them, seized some of their towers, destroyed most of them and demolished the watchtower.

(Dahhām) became alarmed and afraid. He and his followers mounted up. When he emerged from the palace, he said: 'O people of Riyadh, I have been fighting Ibn Suᶜūd for years.'

Events of the Year 1234 [1818–19]

(The Egyptian ruler Muḥammad ᶜAlī) ordered his son Ibrāhīm to destroy ad-Dirᶜīyah and raze it completely. Accordingly, (Ibrāhīm) ordered the inhabitants to leave (the city). Then he ordered his troops to pull down its houses and palaces, to cut down its palms and other trees, and to show no mercy to either young or old.

At the end of this year Muḥammad ibn Musharī ibn Muᶜammar left al-ᶜUyayna for ad-Dirᶜīyah. When he settled there he embarked on the rebuilding of the town and the resumption of (Wahhābī) preaching.

Events of the Year 1235 [1819–20]

Ibn Muᶜammar regretted his withdrawal from this affair and intended to recover power for himself . . . They made for ad-Dirᶜīyah and entered the city suddenly. Ibn Muᶜammar and his followers broke into the quarters of Musharī ibn Suᶜūd in his palace, captured and imprisoned him; then Ibn Muᶜammar established his son Musharī in the palace.

Turkī stayed in Ḍarmāʾ. Some people from the south, Subayᶜ and others, came to him. He marched from Ḍarmāʾ and headed to attack Ibn Muᶜammar and ad-Dirᶜīyah in Rabīᶜ I of this year [December 1819]. He and his men entered the city and made for Ibn Muᶜammar in his palace. (The latter) decided to resist; but the people of ad-Dirᶜīyah betrayed him and his companions. Turkī seized him and put him in prison.

Events of the Year 1236 [1820–1]

Everyone came to Riyadh, which was then controlled by Turkī ibn ᶜAbd Allāh ibn Muḥammad ibn Suᶜūd. He prepared to fight the Turks, gathered men around him, and thought that the people of the city would fight alongside him. But when those crowds arrived they entered the city without resistance, and besieged Turkī and the men of the palace who were with him.

Events of the Year 1238 [1822–3]

Suwayd and men from Jalājil, Sudayr, al-Mahmal, and Munayyikh rode to Turkī at the town of ʿAraqa. When they arrived he raised the banner of war, mobilized his troops, and fought against Riyadh and Manfūḥa.

Events of the Year 1240 [1824–5]

Turkī ibn ʿAbd Allāh, and his troops from Manfūḥa, made for Riyadh, halted there and fought its people; Egyptian troops were there too. Numerous engagements took place between them and many people were killed on both sides. Then Turkī ordered his troops to cut down its fruit trees; they cut down the palm trees after the fruits had gone red and yellow. They destroyed its plantations, except those defended by shots fired from the castle; and they remained besieged in the city's fortress for over one month.

Events of the Year 1249 [1833–4]

When (Imam Turkī) performed the Friday ritual midday prayer and the *sunna* (customary procedure) which followed, he went out, as was his habit, from the door south of the *miḥrāb*. This door had been prepared for his entry and exit, and to enable the Imam to avoid passing through the worshippers' numerous rows in the mosque. The criminals lay in wait for him near the shops between the palace and the mosque. He was holding a letter in his hand and reading it; there was a man standing on his left. One of their domestic slaves, called Ibrāhīm ibn Hamza, intercepted him, inserted a pistol into his sleeve while he was unaware, and fired it; Imam Turkī fell dead, as the shot did not miss his heart. Then Mushārī rushed out of the mosque. He drew his sword and threatened the people, while other men also drew their swords in support of him. The people there were stunned, and realized that the gang of assassins had plotted against him. When Zuwayd, Turkī's well-known slave, saw his master slain, he drew his sword and chased and wounded one of Mushārī's men. But when he found no one to help him, he fled to the palace; Mushārī in turn immediately rushed into the palace with his supporters.

Then Imam Fayṣal ordered the people of Riyadh who were with him to enter the city at night and seize the towers and the houses opposite the palace. He ordered other men whom he trusted to march with them. When they arrived at the city they found its towers and walls fully manned by Mushārī. When the men holding the towers saw them and recognized them, they kept silent and joyfully admitted them.

He (Mushārī) was terrified and realized that this was a severe disaster and a terrible event. They locked the doors and climbed their towers, preparing to fight.

After the morning prayer Fayṣal and the Muslims rode out from his position and entered Riyadh. He stayed at the house of Zuwayd, deployed the Muslims in the houses and towers of the city, and attacked those entrenched in the palace (about 140 men, including Mushārī). Orphans from every town were with him in his palace; every widow and destitute person had enjoyed his beneficence. He used to clothe them with his own hand out of modesty and humility . . . He never failed to attend study gatherings and meetings of Muslims. Every Thursday and Monday he would go out of his palace and call people together for meetings.

He killed no one in cold blood. When he was not attacking an enemy, he would camp at a particular place along with the rest of the Muslims, and stay there according to his plans for settling issues and serving the interests of Muslims. He founded mosques everywhere. Each group of worshippers had a regular imām to lead the prayer. Another imām would lead the prayer of those who stayed behind guarding the equipment and baggage. Thus no one would perform the prayer alone.

Events of the Year 1250 [1834–5]

When Mushārī and his followers were killed or dispersed, by God's decree, Imam Fayṣal entered the palace.

Events of the Year 1253 [1837–8]

Fayṣal and his troops halted at Riyadh and kept close to its wall, while his men surrounded the city and erected their sheltered fortifications opposite the square towers and the wall.

Then Khālid and his men entrenched themselves in the public meeting hall of the city, blocked its gates with mortar and deployed the inhabitants of Riyadh and the combatants at the city centre. They stationed thirty-five men in each square tower, and between every two towers they positioned five men armed with rifles. At each of Riyadh's gates they placed one of the Turkish aghas.

Events of the Year 1259 [1843]
When he entered Riyadh, Ibn Thunayyān distributed arms and money, demolished the houses around the palace, brought into it all types of military and siege equipment, and organized the city and its square towers.

On Thursday night, five days before the end of Rabi' II [24 May 1843], Fayṣal mobilized some of his brave men under his brother Jalawī, and ordered them to enter the city; this was done in collusion with collaborating local chiefs.

Jalawī and his men entered through Bāb Dakhna, which was opened for him. Ibn Thunayyān also used to go out of the palace with some of his men to make rounds in the city and inspect the square towers and their garrisons.

Fayṣal settled in the palace and took full control of affairs there. Ibn Yaḥyā and his followers were defeated and made for the palace (in al-Qaṣīm).

Events of the Year 1265 [1848–9]
He left ʿAbd Allāh as his deputy in Riyadh and told him not to leave the palace.

Their chief, ʿAbd al-ʿAzīz, fled, carried by one of his people's horsemen, and along with the expelled notables went to the well-known Ṭu'miyya palace ... When ʿAbd al-ʿAzīz saw them leave he left the palace and passed by Burayda. He headed towards Ibn Rashīd, the chief of the mountain, who was staying at Qaṣr al-Quwwāra, the well-known town in al-Qaṣīm.

Notes:

1. Amīn Madanī, *al-Taʾrīkh al-ʿArabī wa-maṣādiruh* (Cairo, 1971), p. 28.
2. *Ibid.*, p. 32.

3. See ʿAbd Allāh ibn Khamīs, *Muʿjam al-Yamāma* (Riyadh, 2nd edn, 1400/1980), I, p. 293, quoting from al-Hamadhānī, *Ṣifat Jazīrat al-ʿArab*. There may be some exaggeration in height here, meant to show the building's status and high level of architecture; or perhaps the only building that al-Hamadhānī saw was erected for a special purpose.
4. Ḥamad al-Jāsir, *Madīnat al-Riyāḍ ʿabr aṭwār al-taʾrīkh* (Riyadh, 1386/1966), p. 43.
5. Al-Sayyid ʿAbd al-ʿAzīz Sālim, *Taʾrīkh al-ʿArab qabl al-Islām* (Alexandria, 1967), p. 14.
6. *Ibid*., p. 60.
7. Madanī, *al-Taʾrīkh al-ʿArabī*, p. 34.
8. Sālim, *Taʾrīkh al-ʿArab*, p. 83.
9. al-Jāsir, *Madīnat al-Riyāḍ*, p. 40.
10. Madanī, *al-Taʾrīkh al-ʿArabī*, pp. 39, 40.
11. *Ibid*., p. 35.
12. The name 'Bahrain' included an area larger than the island known today. Historically, it encompassed a large part of the eastern province, the northern extremities of Oman, Qatar and Kuwait. See Ḥamad al-Jāsir, *al-Muʿjam al-jughrāfī lil-bilād al-Suʿūdiyya, al-manṭiqa al-Sharqiyya, al-Baḥrayn qadīman* (Riyadh, 1399/1979), I, pp. 7, 13.
13. Maḥmūd Shākir, *Shibh Jazīrat al-ʿArab: Najd* (Beirut, 1396/1976), pp. 139–43.
14. ʿAbd Allāh ibn Khamīs, *Taʾrīkh al-Yamāma* (Riyadh, 1407/1987–8), II, p. 51.
15. *Ibid*., II, p. 236.
16. Al-Jāsir, *Madīnat Riyāḍ*, p. 13.
17. The Ukhayḍirids descend from Muḥammad ibn Yusuf ibn al-Ukhayḍir, a descendant of ʿAlī ibn Abī Ṭālib (d. 40/660). He revolted in Yamama in 253/867 (his brother Ismāʿīl had seized Makkah in 251/865), exploiting the weakness of the Abbasids. In his journey to Yamama in 443/1051, the Persian poet Nāṣir-i Khusraw indicates the Shīʿī faith of its rulers: 'These rulers enjoy great power; for they have between three and four hundred horsemen. They belong to the Zaydī sect. They say in the *ādhān* (call to prayer): "Muḥammad and ʿAlī are the best of mankind", and "Come ye believers to perform the most righteous work". They claim to be *sharīfs* (descendants of the Prophet Muḥammad).' See Ṣāliḥ al-Washmī, *Wilāyat al-Yamāma* (Riyadh, 1412/1991–2), pp. 171–4; Nāṣir-i Khusraw, *Safarnāma* (trans. Aḥmad al-Badlī, Riyadh, 1403/1982–3), p. 167. (See also *Nāṣir-i Khusraw's Book of Travels* [trans. Wheeler M. Thackston; Costa Mesa, CA, 2002], pp. 110–11.)

18. The Carmathians (Qarmaṭīs, Qarāmiṭa) were a Bāṭinī (esoteric) movement which was considered heretical. Their name is taken from Ḥamdān ibn Qarmaṭ (d. 293/906). The movement is believed to have started in Kufa, and then moved to parts of greater Syria, Bahrain and al-Aḥsāʾ. A prominent Qarmaṭī was Abū Ṭāhir al-Qarmaṭī, who ravaged and pillaged Makkah in 317/930, and carried the Black Stone of the Kaʿba away to al-Aḥsāʾ. (See *Encyclopedia of Arabic Literature* [ed. J. S. Meisami and P. Starkey; London, 1998], art. 'Carmathians'.)
19. Shākir, *Shibh Jazīrat al-ʿArab*, pp. 135–251.
20. Al-Jāsir, *Madīnat al-Riyāḍ*, p. 79.
21. Nāṣir-i Khusraw, *Safarnāma*, p. 167.
22. Al-Jāsir, *Madīnat al-Riyāḍ*, p. 80.
23. *Ibid.*, pp. 85–6. It appears from the context of al-Jāsir's account as if Rabīʿa ibn Māniʿ were the twelfth ancestor of King Abdul Aziz, although Māniʿ himself is the twelfth ancestor.
24. *Ibid.*, pp. 87–94.
25. The enemies of this reformist movement called it 'al-Wahhābiyya' ('the Wahhābīs'), a nomenclature that has been widely circulated, particularly in the West. This name, however, was never accepted by the supporters of the movement because it might suggest a new trend deviating from the path of the *ahl al-sunna wa-al-jamāʿa* (the Sunnī mainstream of the Muslim community). They preferred to be called 'al-Muslimān' ('the Muslims') or 'Ahl al-daʿwa' ('the people of the preaching, or movement'), or 'Ahl al-tawḥīd' ('the monotheists'). Moreover, giving the name 'Wahhābiyya' to the reformist movement contradicts the reality, for this movement arose as an outcome of the efforts of both Muḥammad ibn Suʿūd and Muḥammad ibn ʿAbd al-Wahhāb. I have left the term 'Wahhābīs' as it occurs when referring to foreign sources, although the name has become more widely circulated and acceptable even in the Arabian peninsula.
26. ʿUthman ibn Bishr, *ʿUnwān al-majd fī taʾrīkh Najd* (Riyadh, 4th edn, 1402/1982), I, p. 29.
27. Ḥusayn ibn Ghannām, *Rawḍat al-afkār* (ed. Nāṣir al-Dīn al-Asad, Riyadh, 3rd edn, 1403/1983), I, pp. 5–6.
28. Ibn Bishr, *ʿUnwān*, I, p. 27.
29. Al-Jāsir, *Madīnat al-Riyāḍ*, pp. 95–6.
30. Ibn Ghannām, *Rawḍat al-afkār*, pp. 110–11.
31. Khayr al-Dīn al-Ziriklī, *Shibh al-Jazīrath fī ʿahd al-Malik ʿAbd al-ʿAzīz* (Beirut, 3rd edn, 1405/1984–5), I, p. 35.
32. Ibn Bishr, *ʿUnwān*, II, p. 111.

33. *Ibid.*, II, p. 112.
34. *Ibid.*, II, p. 257.
35. Perhaps this door, which was not previously a general characteristic of mosques, may have been invented by Turkī ibn ʿAbd Allāh, and became a new element in mosque architecture.
36. Ibn Bishr, ʿUnwān, II, p. 99.
37. *Ibid.*, II, pp. 92–102.
38. A number of writers questioned the veracity of Palgrave's journey to central Arabia. While some assumed that he reached the eastern province only, and from there relied on oral accounts in his writings about other regions, others, like Philby, denied that Palgrave had ever made the journey. Lewis Pelly points out that Fayṣal ibn Turkī told him that he (Pelly) was the first European who was allowed entry to Riyadh. This is rejected by R. Bidwell in his introduction to Pelly's book; Bidwell suggests that envy was the reason for that denial, although Pelly's narration on the authority of Imām Fayṣal may be true, as in his visits to Riyadh Palgrave was disguised as an Arab trader. It is perhaps illogical to assume that the minute details given by Palgrave about Riyadh were conflicting or dependent on oral accounts, as some of them cannot be conceived of except as the result of precise observation. Captain Shakespear pointed out that Palgrave's map of Riyadh was excellent; D. Houghart stated that the veracity of Palgrave's journey is not debatable. See Abū ʿAbd al-Raḥmān ibn ʿAqīl al-Ẓāhirī, 'Riḥlat Palgrave ilā al-Jazīra al-ʿArabiyya', in his *Masāʾil min Taʾrīkh al-Jazīra al-ʿArabiyya* (Riyadh, 1413/1993), pp. 6–212.
39. Muḥammad Āl Zalāfa, 'al-Riyāḍ fī ʿahd al-Imām Fayṣal', *al-Tawbād* 4 (1408/1988), pp. 21–2.
40. H. V. F. Winstone, *Captain Shakespear: A Portrait* (London, 1976), p. 161.
41. Environment Consultative Group. Research presented by the High Commission for Development of the City of Riyadh on 'Revival of Riyadh's Wall and Gates'.
42. Muḥammad al-Mānīʿ, *Unification of the Kingdom of Saudi Arabia* (trans. ʿAbd Allāh al-ʿUthaymīn [as *Tawḥīdal-Mamlaka al-Arabiyya al-Su'ūdiyya*] Dammam, 1402/1982, p. 18).
43. *Ibid.*, p. 42.
44. *Ibid.*, p. 5.
45. Ibn Bishr, *ʿUnwān*, I, p. 52.
46. *Ibid.*, I, p. 452.
47. *Ibid.*, II, p. 102.
48. Al-Jāsir, *Madīnat al-Riyāḍ*, p. 179.
49. Khālid ʿAlī al-Sulaymān, *Muʿjam madīnat al-Riyāḍ* (Riyadh, 1404/1984),

p. 197, quoting from Ḍārī ibn Fuhayd al-Rashīd, *Nubdha Taʾrīkhiyya ʿan Najd* (Riyadh, 1966?), p. 35.

50. al-Jāsir, *Madīnat al-Riyāḍ*, p. 95.
51. *Ibid.*, p. 108.
52. *Ibid.*, p. 114.
53. H. St. John B. Philby, *Arabia* (London, 1930), p. 107.
54. Amīn al-Rīḥanī, *Taʾrīkh Najd al-ḥadīth* (Beirut, 6th edn, 1408/1987–8), p. 93.
55. Fuʿād Ḥamza, *al-Bilād al-ʿArabiyya al-Suʿūdiyya* (Riyadh, 2nd edn, 1388/1968), p. 20. Opinions differ as to who built al-Muṣmak. The most likely person seems to be, according to research prepared by the Projects and Planning Centre of the High Commission for Development of the City of Riyadh, Muḥammad ibn ʿAbd Allāh ibn Rashīd, perhaps on the ruins of the palaces of Āl Saʿūd. Ḥamza's account points out that the palace of Imam ʿAbd Allāh was demolished by Ibn al-Rashīd, who left the castle called al-Muṣmak intact. Captain Shakespear also says that Ibn al-Rashīd destroyed all the palaces of Āl Saʿūd except for a castle in the palace of Imam ʿAbd Allāh, which he made a seat for his viceroy until King Abdul Aziz recaptured it (see Winstone, *Captain Shakespear*, p. 161).
56. al-Jāsir, *Madīnat al-Riyāḍ*, pp. 121–2.
57. al-Māniʿ, *Tawhid*, p. 220.
58. M. Trautz, 'A Forgotten Explorer of Arabia', in G. A. Wallin, *Travels in Arabia (1845 and 1848)* (Cambridge, 1979), pp. 33–4.
59. Ibn Bishr, *ʿUnwān*, p. 99.
60. W. G. Palgrave, *Personal Narrative of a Year's Journey through Central and Eastern Arabia (1862–1863)* (London, 1985), p. 266.
61. al-Sulaymān, *Muʿjam*, p. 265.
62. Ibn Khamis, *Taʾrīkh al-Yamāma*, II, p. 129.
63. Ibn Khamis, *Muʿjam al-Yamāma*, II, p. 18.
64. Lewis Pelly, *Report on a Journey to Riyadh in Central Arabia* (Cambridge, 1978), p. 40.
65. H. St John B. Philby, *Arabia of the Wahhābis* (London, 1977), p. 77.
66. *Ibid.*, p. 13.
67. See Philby, *Arabia*, Introduction.
68. Abū ʿAbd al-Raḥmān ibn ʿAqīl al-Ẓāhirī, *Dīwān al-shiʿr al-ʿāmmī bi-lahjat ahl Najd* (Riyadh, 1402/1982), I, p. 38.
69. ʿAbd Allāh al-ʿUthaymīn, 'al-Shiʿr al-Nabaṭī maṣdaran li-taʾrīkh Najd', in *Maṣadir taʾrīkh al-Jazīra al-ʿArabiyyah* (ed. ʿAbd al-Qādir Maḥmūd ʿAbd Allāh *et al.*, Riyadh, 1399/1979), I, p. 380.

70. Al-Ziriklī, *Shibh jazīrat al-ʿArab*, III, p. 901.
71. For further information see Robin Bidwell, *Travellers in Arabia* (London, 1976 [trans. ʿAbd Allāh Naṣīf as *al-Raḥḥāla al-gharbiyya fī al-Jazīra al-ʿArabiyya*, Riyadh, 1409/1998–9]); Lee David Cooper, *Writings of Foreign Travellers as a Source for the Study of the Wahhābi Movement* (trans. ʿAbd Allāh al-Walīʿī as *Kitābāt al-raḥḥāla al-ajānib ka-marja' lidirāsāt al-ḥaraka al-Wahhābiyya* [Riyadh, 1412/1991–2]); and Richard Trench, *Arabian Travellers* (London, 1986). This last is considered more comprehensive than the first two, particularly with respect to architectural references in these travels.
72. Ḥamad al-Jāsir, introduction to Jaqueline Pirenne, *Iktishāf Jazīrat al-ʿArab* (trans. of *À la découverte de l'Arabie* [Paris, 1958] [trans. Qadrī Qal'ajī (Riyadh, [n.d.]), p. 8]).
73. *Ibid.*, pp. 5–6.
74. Jamāl Qāsim, 'al-Dawāfiʾ al-siyāsiyya li-riḥlāt al-U- rūbiyyīn ilā Najd wa-al-Ḥijāz', in *Maṣādir*, II, p. 10.
75. Pirenne, *Iktishāf*, pp. 182–3.
76. Qāsim, 'Dawāfiʿ', p. 12.
77. R. Bayly Winder, *Saudi Arabia in the Nineteenth Century* (New York, 1965), p. 43.
78. Trautz, 'Forgotten Explorer', p. xxxiii. This may agree with Ibn Bishr's statement, under the events of 1261/1845: 'In this year, on the fourth day of Ramaḍān [6 September 1845], took place the battle between Ibn Rashīd, the Chief of the Mountain, with the tribe of 'Unayza [or: ʿAnaza?]. This happened because ʿAbd Allāh ibn Salmān ibn Zāmil, the Emir of ʿUnayza, had captured camels belonging to Ibn al-Rashīd, who claimed damages from him. ʿAbd Allāh refused. He was cautioned and warned. Ibn Rashīd sent his brother ʿUbayd against him, with a force of 250 mounts (camels) and 50 horses' (Ibn Bishr, *ʿUnwān*, II, p. 234).
79. Gerald de Gaury, 'Introduction', in Barclay Raunkiaer, *Through Wahhabiland on Camelback* (trans G. de Gaury, London, 1969), p. 5.
80. Raunkiaer, *Through Wahhabiland* (London, 1969), p. 120. This agrees with the account that King Abdul Aziz sent his brother Saʿd to the ʿUtayba tribe, who were camping between al-cĀriḍ and al-Washm on one side, and al-Washm and the Hejaz on the other side, trying to rouse them to support him. In Rajab 1912 he encountered horsemen from ʿUtayba whom he thought had come to welcome him. But soon he realized the truth of the matter, and rode with ten of his companions, heading for Riyadh. A number of the 'Utaybīs overtook him, reassuring him of his safety, so that he was duped. They seized him and handed him over to Sharīf Ḥusayn; whereupon ʿAbd

al-ʿAzīz hastened to rescue him. (Ibrāhīm Jumʿa, *al-Atlas al-taʾrīkhī lil-dawla al-Suʿūdiyya* [Cairo/Beirut, 1398/1979], p. 154.)

81. Ṣalāḥ al-ʿAqqād, 'Riḥlat Carsten Niebuhr fī shibh jazīrat al-ʿArab', in *Maṣādir*, II, p. 449.
82. Pirenne, *Iktishāf*, p. 174.
83. Al-Rīḥānī, *Taʾrīkh Najd*, p. 79.
84. Qāsim, 'Dawāfiʿ', p. 11.
85. Al-Rīḥānī, *Taʾrīkh Najd*, p. 79.
86. Muḥammad Saʿīd al-Shaʿfī, 'Kitāb Burckhardt ka-maṣdar taʾrīkhī wa-iqtiṣādī lil-dawla al-Suʿūdiyya al-ālā', in *Maṣādir*, II, p. 455.

Index